DECISIONS OF INTERNATIONAL INSTITUTIONS BEFORE DOMESTIC COURTS

by
CHRISTOPH SCHREUER

OCEANA PUBLICATIONS, INC.
LONDON • ROME • NEW YORK

Library of Congress Cataloging in Publication Data

Schreuer, Christoph.
    Decisions of international institutions before
domestic courts.

    "Substantially revised and updated version of
a book first published ... in 1977 under the title
'Die Behandlung internationaler Organakte durch
staatliche Gerichte.'"
    Bibliography: p.
    Includes index.
    1. International and municipal law. 2. Treaties
—Interpretation and construction.   I. Title.
JX1248.S343   1980   341'.04   80-27503
ISBN 0-379-20709-5

Manufactured in the United States of America

TABLE OF CONTENTS

IV. THE LEGALITY OF INTERNATIONAL DECISIONS

V. INTERNATIONAL DECISIONS IN THE COURTS OF THIRD STATES

VI. INTERNATIONAL DECISIONS AND DOMESTIC LAW

VII. IMPLEMENTING MEASURES IN THE PRACTICE OF COURTS

VIII. THE PUBLICATION OF INTERNATIONAL DECISIONS

IX. SUBSTANTIVE PRESCRIPTIONS OF DOMESTIC LAW AND INTERNATIONAL DECISIONS

XIV. CONCURRENT JURISDICTION OF DOMESTIC COURTS AND INTERNATIONAL ORGANS

PREFACE

This study is a substantially revised and updated version of
a book first pulished in German in 1977 under the title
"Die Behandlung internationaler Organakte durch staatliche
Gerichte". I am grateful to Professor Dr. J.Broermann of
Duncker & Humblot, Berlin for giving his permission to
publish this book in English. It was approved by Yale Law
School in March 1979 for the J.S.D. degree. A number of
preparatory studies have appeared in the International and
Comparative Law Quarterly, The Israel Yearbook on Human
Rights, the German Yearbook of International Law and the
Houston Law Review. (For precise references see the biblio-
graphy at p.384seq.)

Ms Susanne Klozenbücher has borne the heavy burden of not
only preparing the original manuscript but also the camera
ready copy for this book. Her sense of commitment and her
unceasing cheerfulness in pursuing this difficult task are
very much appreciated.

Salzburg, October 1980.   C.S.

LIST OF ABBREVIATIONS

A.C.	Appeal Cases
AD	Annual Digest of Public International Law Cases
AFDI	Annuaire Français de Droit International
AJCompL	American Journal of Comparative Law
AJIL	American Journal of International Law
Annuaire	Annuaire de l'Institut de droit international
AöR	Archiv des öffentlichen Rechts
ASIL Proc	Proceedings of the American Society of International Law
AVR	Archiv des Völkerrechts
AWB	Außenwirtschaftsdienst des Betriebsberaters
BGBl.	Bundesgesetzblatt (Federal Gazette, Germany or Austria)
BGE	Entscheidungen des Schweizerischen Bundesgerichtes (Decisions of the Swiss Federal Court)
BGH	Bundesgerichtshof (German Federal Court)
BGHZ	Entscheidungen des Bundesgerichtshofes in Zivilsachen (Decisions of the German Federal Court in Civil Matters)
BLG NR	Beilagen zu den stenographischen Protokollen des Nationalrats (Austrian Parliamentary Materials)
BVerfGE	Entscheidungen des Bundesverfassungsgerichts (Decisions of the German Constitutional Court)
BVerwGE	Entscheidungen des Bundesverwaltungsgerichts (Decisions of the German Administrative Court)
BYIL	British Yearbook of International Law
CalLR	California Law Review
CambLJ	Cambridge Law Journal
CanYIL	Canadian Yearbook of International Law
Clunet	Journal du Droit International
CMLRep.	Common Market Law Reports
CMLRev.	Common Market Law Review
D.C.	District of Columbia
D.L.R.	Dominion Law Reports
DVerwBl	Deutsches Verwaltungsblatt
ECSC	European Coal and Steel Community
EEC	European Economic Community
ETS	European Treaty Series
EuGRZ	Europäische Grundrechte-Zeitschrift
F.2d	Federal Reporter, Second Series

Fontes	Fontes Iuris Gentium
F.Supp.	Federal Supplement
GP	Gesetzgebungsperiode (Legislative Period)
HarvILJ	Harvard International Law Journal
H.L.C.	House of Lords Reports (Clark)
ICJ Rep	International Court of Justice, Reports of Judgments, Advisory Opinions and Orders
ICLQ	International and Comparative Law Quarterly
ICSID	International Centre for the Settlement of Investment Disputes
IJIL	Indian Journal of International Law
ILC	International Law Commission
ILM	International Legal Materials
ILR	International Law Reports
Int.Org.	Internaional Organization
IRO	International Refugee Organization
Israel YBHR	Israel Yearbook on Human Rights
Italian YBIL	Italian Yearbook of International Law
Jahrb.IR	Jahrbuch für internationales Recht
JapAIL	Japanese Annual of International Law
JBl	Juristische Blätter
JZ	Juristenzeitung
K.B.	King's Bench Division
Kiss	Répertoire de la pratique française en matière de droit international public
LNTS	League of Nations Treaty Series
LQR	Law Quarterly Review
Martens, N.R.G.	Nouveau Recueil Général des Traités
Modern LR	Modern Law Review
NewLR	New Law Review
NILR	Netherlands International Law Review
NJW	Neue Juristische Wochenschrift
NTIR	Nederlands Tijdschrift voor Internationaal Recht
NYIL	Netherlands Yearbook of International Law
N.Y.S.	New York Supplement
OGH	Oberster Gerichtshof (Austrian Supreme Court)
ÖJZ	Österreichische Juristenzeitung
OLG	Oberlandesgericht (Court of Appeals, Germany)
ÖZöR	Österreichische Zeitschrift für öffentliches Recht
PCIJ	Permanent Court of International Justice
Q.B.	Queen's Bench Division
RabelsZ	Rabels Zeitschrift für ausländisches und internationales Privatrecht
RBDI	Revue Belge de Droit International
RC	Recueil des Cours. Académie de Droit international

RCDIP	Revue Critique de Droit International Privé
RDI	Revue de Droit International de Sciences Diplomatiques et Politiques
RDILC	Revue de Droit International et de Legislation Comparé
Rec.	Recueil des décisions du Conseil d' Etat (France)
Revista Esp.DI	Revista Espanola de Derecho Internacional
Rev.Trim.Dr.Eur.	Revue Trimestrielle de Droit Européen
RGBl	Reichsgesetzblatt(Official Gazette,Germany)
RGDIP	Revue Générale de Droit International Public
RGSt	Entscheidungen des Reichsgerichts in Strafsachen(Decisions of the German Reichsgericht in Criminal Matters)
RGZ	Entscheidungen des Reichsgerichts in Zivilsachen(Decisions of the German Reichsgericht in Civil Matters)
RIAA	Reports of International Arbitral Awards
Rivista DI	Rivista di Diritto Internazionale
RIW	Recht der internationalen Wirtschaft
SchwJIR	Schweizerisches Jahrbuch für internationales Recht
Sirey	Recueil général des Lois et des Arrêts
Slg.	Sammlung(Collection of Decisions)
SZ	Sammlung Zivilsachen(Decisions of the Austrian Supreme Court in Civil Matters)
UNCIO	United Nations Conference on International Organization
UNJYB	United Nations Juridical Yearbook
UNTS	United Nations Treaty Series
U.S.	United States Reports
VaJIL	Virginia Journal of International Law
VerfGH	Verfassungsgerichtshof(Austrian Constitutional Court)
VRÜ	Verfassung und Recht in Übersee
VwGH	Verwaltungsgerichtshof(Austrian Administrative Court)
Whiteman	Digest of International Law
WLR	Weekly Law Reports
YaleLJ	Yale Law Journal
YBEur.Conv.HR	Yearbook of the European Convention on Human Rights
YILC	Yearbook of the International Law Commission
ZaöRV	Zeitschrift für ausländisches öffentliches Recht und Völkerrecht
ZSR	Zeitschrift für schweizerisches Recht

I. INTRODUCTION

A. THE FRAMEWORK OF ENQUIRY

Traditional investigation into the treatment of international
prescriptions, including decisions of international institutions, by domestic decision-makers has been almost entirely
concerned with perspectives to the exclusion of operations.
The problem was perceived as being one of the relationship
of sets of rules international and national. Once the basic
problem of "incorporation", "internal validity", and "rank"
had been solved, little attention was paid to the actual
behavior of decision-makers. An empirical evaluation of
decisions rendered by domestic courts on questions of international law reveals that they can adequately be explained
neither in terms of rules determining the validity of international prescription in domestic law nor in terms of all-
embracing simplistic theories on the relationship of international law to municipal law. A meaningful investigation
must adopt a realistic contextual approach examining also
actual decisions and all factors affecting them.

In a similar vein, there is frequently no clear perception
of the interrelationship of authority and control and of the
dynamic nature of law as a decision-making process. Excessive
focus on "binding rules" has prevented a clear perception of
the diverse procedures and manifestations of authority in
the international decision-making process. A decision has
authority if it is in conformity with community expectations
as to who renders the decision, in what procedure, and by
what criteria. Since these expectations are largely
shaped by the flow of previous decisions, a decision-maker
wishing to act "lawfully" will choose a decision which is in
conformity with past authoritative decisions. In some cases
this choice may be relatively simple. Treaty provisions may
be clearly applicable and easy to interpret or a uniform
practice may indicate a clear custom. In such cases it is
tempting to try to formulate a "rule" by way of an analytical
abstraction from previous decisions.

Formulations and formulas such as these may be useful and legitimate as long as they are clearly perceived as mere
abstractions. Where the law is, however, exclusively perceived in terms of binding rules there is the distinct
danger of a misleading narrowing of perception. The formula
once abstracted from real authoritative decisions is miscon-
ceived as the true substance of the law; it is then simply
accepted at the expense of a fresh evaluation of the entire
decision-making process. In place of a critical examination

of all the contemporary relevant authoritative material for
decision, a ceremonious derivation from formalized rules is
undertaken.

The model of a rule as a prescription in the form of a clear
imperative sentence or of an unequivocal conditional statement is only applicable to a limited number of situations.
This is particularly so in a horizontal system of public
order, characterized by the co-equal interaction of its
members based on reciprocities and retaliations. In some
cases, the policies apparent in the available authoritative
material militating in favor of a particular decision may be
overwhelming, but are of such heterogeneous nature (treaty
provisions, practice, judicial precedents, recommendations
etc.) that it is extremely difficult to integrate them into
"rules". In other cases, these policies may be persuasive,
but by no means so overwhelming as to permit the formulation
of a "binding norm". In all these situations it is futile to
try to proceed from a simplistic dichotomy between "binding
rules" and "no law". A jurisprudential framework not based
on derivation from abstracted rules but on a problem-oriented examination of the flow of authoritative decisions is
more likely to lead to meaningful results.

This study subscribes to a framework of inquiry which is
both contextual and policy-oriented. A contextual approach
takes into account a wide range of factors affecting decisions. They include the participants in the decision-making
process, the perspectives affecting their behavior, the
arenas in which they interact, the bases of power at their
disposal, the strategies utilized by them to achieve goals,
as well as the outcomes and effects engendered by their
interactions. A policy-oriented approach is based on the
realization that the law is neither a static crystal nor a
mechanical procedure, but an ongoing process involving
choices. An investigation attempting to make a constructive
contribution to the solution of specific problems must go
beyond the contemplation of logical or grammatically possible
derivations from alleged rules and spell out preferred
policies in the light of a systematic empirical investigation
of past decisions.

This study is therefore directed at the following five
intellectual tasks:
1.   The clarification of basic community goals: To attempt
      a value-free exmination of legal problems independently
      of any policy preferences would be not only dishonest
      but also sterile. All participants in the social pro-
      cess, whether parties, decision-makers, or scholarly

observers, entertain value preferences which influence
their behavior consciously or unconsciously. Irrational
or arbitrary attitudes cannot be eliminated by a sup-
pression of preferences, but only through an open and
critical examination of the policies involved. Those
who reject the discussion of policies as not belonging
to the tasks of the lawyer, in reality proceed from the
tacit policy that it is the function of the law to
maintain the *status quo*. A retreat into derivational
logic does not further the course of objectivity but
merely obfuscates the preferences of the author.

Before entering into the presentation of any of the
empirical material, it is therefore necessary to clarify the basic community goals governing the field of
this study.

2. The description of past trends in decision: A thorough
    examination of the problems raised by the invocation of
    decisions originating from organized international
    arenas in domestic courts necessitates a detailed
    empirical study of the past behavior of courts. This
    empirical examination quickly reveals that the variety
    and complexity of problems is by far greater than any
    speculative reflection would suggest.

The collection, processing and presentation of this
voluminous and heterogeneous practice of domestic
courts on a broad comparative basis, not restricted to
any particular group of countries, involves a number of
difficulties. The first such difficulty lies in the
discovery and collection of the case material. In this
study a large number of national and international
collections is utilized, and no available source of
information is excluded. The obvious regional gaps
(e.g., communist countries) are entirely due to the
fact that the relevant material is not accessible. On
the other hand, completeness in such a vast and only
partly accessible field as decisions of domestic courts
can naturally never be achieved. Nevertheless, there is
some justification for the hope that the evaluated
material of over 4oo cases yields a fairly representative sample.

Processing is, of course, made difficult by the variety
of languages in which this material is published. Most
of the material published in English, German, French,
Italian, and Spanish was examined in the original. In
addition, an increasing portion of other materials of

international relevance is nowadays translated into
English and French and published in international
periodicals. In a few cases outside advice was sought
for translations from other languages (Hebrew, Dutch).

In presenting the material the possibility of organizing
it by countries was discarded. Instead, a systematic
organization was chosen which puts emphasis on different
questions of substance or policies and not on geography.
This systematic presentation sometimes involves repeated
references to individual cases in different contexts.
Many of the more important cases raise a whole number
of different questions which must be examined separately.
This means that the presentation is not case by case, a
method which could easily degenerate into an anecdotal
case-book style and would make it extremely difficult
to keep a clear focus on the questions discussed. For
comprehensive information on specific cases, the reader
will therefore have to consult the cited sources.

3.   The analysis of conditioning factors: In comparison to
     other decisions, court judgments have the advantage of
     usually explaining their motives. An analysis of fac-
     tors leading to a court decision will certainly first
     have to carefully scrutinize the reasons presented in
     the judgment. However, a comparative survey of court
     decisions in different countries quickly reveals the
     diverse styles of reasoning and the varying extent to
     which judges are prepared to divulge their true motives.
     This fact alone is an important indication of the
     limited value of the reasons given in judgments for an
     elucidation of the conditioning factors. Domestic
     courts have a tendency - although to varying degrees -
     to emphasize certain aspects in their reasons and to
     mention others only in passing or not at all. Frequent-
     ly only a formalistic legal reasoning is considered
     acceptable, which does by no means represent the entire
     spectrum of motives underlying a judgment. In many
     cultures courts are expected not to mention considera-
     tions which are not deemed "legal" in a strict sense,
     even if all participants involved are perfectly aware
     of the fact that the judgment does not present all the
     relevant reasons for the decisions. Frequently the
     presence of dominant "political" aspects in a case only
     strengthens the tendency to base a judgment on narrow
     formalistic criteria. In addition, many judges tend not
     to balance the policies speaking in favor of or against
     the decision reached by them, but to emphasize the

arguments which support their verdict only.

A meaningful analysis of conditioning factors for court practice therefore has to investigate possible motives for decisions also beyond the reasons given by the court. For this purpose it is necessary to take into account all ascertainable relevant circumstances of the cases. The identity of the parties, their value demands, possible identifications - especially with the forum State - and prominent basic policy considerations are some such factors which have to be ascertained.

The formal rules adduced by judges to support their decisions are not infrequently interchangeable and convey a deceptive picture of a clear and "correct" solution:
> Scholarship which would be creative, must look behind technical formulas and authoritative procedures to the conditions that importantly determine which formulas and procedures are in fact employed.(1)

4. Projection of possible future developments: A study only directed at a retrospective investigation of past judicial behavior would not present a complete and meaningful picture of the decision-making process. Wherever possible an attempt must be made to draw conclusions concerning probable future decisions in the light of all the available information. This projective task is not the same as deriving rules which can be extrapolated in the form of customary norms from past practice and from which future behavior is calculated. Often it is only possible to point out certain trends in decisions which are likely to continue in the future. But even in the absence of clear statements about positive law, the predictability of court behavior is an important goal.

5. The invention of policy alternatives: As mentioned before, this study is not directed at mere description without an attempt to outline preferred solutions. Wherever possible, an explicit choice will therefore be made between different policies. This will not be done by postulating alleged "rules", but by pointing out the reasons why certain policies appear more in accordance with basic community goals than others.

B. DOMESTIC COURTS AS INTERNATIONAL DECISION-MAKERS

Courts of law as impartial and relatively independent decision-makers for legal disputes are probably known to practically all contemporary legal systems. Of course, there are considerable national and regional differences in organization, jurisdiction and procedure, and certain marginal institutions may be difficult to categorize. But the essential features of the judicial settlement of disputes, as an authoritative and controlling third-party decision based on objective criteria and usually supported by reasons, seem to be universally recognized.

The involvement of domestic courts with questions of international law has so far found relatively little general attention in scholarly writing.(2) One of the reasons for this neglect may be the fact that until relatively recently domestic courts were only rarely seized of disputes showing important international aspects. The increasing number of interactions across state boundaries as well as a clear tendency of the international community to widen the areas of international regulation have more recently made international aspects a common feature in legal disputes before domestic judiciaries.

The failure to focus on this question may also be due to certain preconceived dogmatic conceptions concerning the relationship of national and international law. The application of international law by State organs, not specialized in the conduct of international relations, was usually seen only in terms of the incorporation of international legal rules into the State's legal order. Once this basic question had been answered, the actual behavior of internal decision-makers appeared relatively unimportant.

A conceptual framework which regards international law as a system of rules merely regulating the conduct of effective elites, that is, State governments in their mutual relations, is blind to important procedural aspects of transnational interaction. In particular, the fiction of the State as a self-contained and uniform subject of international law seems in urgent need of revision. A realistic inquiry has to examine the rôle of different State organs in the international decision-making process in a systematic and differentiated manner.

In view of the structural peculiarities of international law as a loose horizontal order, the existence and actual conduct of implementing organs are especially important. Not infrequently, questions of substantive law are overshadowed by problems of enforcement through controlling procedures. In contemporary international law the considerable extension of subject-matters of inclusive concern is, in most cases,

not marked by a concomitant extension of international
procedures of implementation. This scarcity of procedures
for implementation and enforcement means that a substantial
section of the international decision-making process takes
place before State organs including courts. The forum of
domestic courts is open not only to the participants in the
international arena but also to the actors who are affected
by international decisions without having access to international fora.(3) Collections of municipal cases dealing
with questions of international law(4) clearly show that
almost any important international legal question can come
before municipal courts in one way or another.(5)

This has led to a peculiar dual function of domestic courts,
which on one hand are organs of nation states, that is, of
participants in the international legal process pursuing
their own interests, but on the other hand find themselves
in the rôle of functional international decision-makers.
George Scelle has termed this phenomenon "dédoublement
fonctionnel"(6): organs use the jurisdiction conferrred upon
them by the legal order instituting them to act as decision-
makers also for another legal order which lacks appropriate
organs.(7)

C. DECISIONS OF INTERNATIONAL INSTITUTIONS

1. The Concept of International Institutions

In the loose structure of the international society of
previous centuries the main emphasis of transnational interaction was on bilateral contacts between sovereigns. The
increasing exchange of goods, information, persons, and
diseases across state boundaries has more recently required
closer structures of co-operation than traditional diplomatic
channels. This closer cooperation led to the establishment
of international institutions for the settlement of disputes,
first *ad hoc*, later also on a permanent basis. In addition,
a number of permanent institutions were created to help
solve common problems of the States involved. This inclusive
jurisdiction of international institutions today covers
numerous areas which under traditional international law
were regarded as falling within the exclusive jurisdiction
of States. There is an obvious continuing trend towards a
further shifting of competences in favor of international
institutions.

In addition to this increasing cooperation between nation
States, the twentieth century has also seen a rapid growth
of private contacts and transactions across State boundaries.

Individuals, corporations and interest groups organize
transnationally in order to pursue common goals with the
help of temporary or permanent institutions. The close
interaction of states and other participants in the international arena, especially in the field of commercial transactions, has led to a situation in which it would be unrealistic to distinguish between inter-State relations and
private transactions in the international social process.
Especially in the field of the international settlement of
disputes, there is an increasing trend to establish fora
which admit both States and non-State participants.

This study is therefore not restricted to the activities of
inter-State institutions in the strict sense, but also covers
activities of mixed participation. For practical reasons,
international institutions which are exclusively based on
private initiatives, that is to say, which have neither been
established by treaties nor have States as participants in
their activities, are excluded.

International instituions as defined in this context, of
course, also include the so-called supranational European
institutions. The relationship between the activities of the
European Communities and the domestic organs of the Member
States is already the subject of extensive scholarly attention. The large volume of writings on European Community
Law, and the often specialized nature of the problems involved make a fresh comprehensive review of European law in
this study dispensable. Nevertheless, whenever policies
adopted in European Community Law appear interesting for the
problems discussed here, reference will be made to them.

2. Decisions of International Institutions and the Traditional Sources of International Law

One of the fundamental problems of the traditional treatment
of decisions of international organs is their compatibility
with the established sources of international law as enumera-
ted in Article 38 of the Statute of the International Court
of Justice. Some would, no doubt, be inclined to dismiss
these efforts to classify and delimit sources of law as
futile playing with theoretical concepts without much practical value. However, even the most theoretical conceptualism
can assume considerable practical significance, if effective
decision-makers are influenced by it and behave accordingly.
As long as courts see fit to operate with the traditional
sources of international law a reference to the purely
theoretical aspect of this question will not suffice. Especially in connection with the courts' notions on the relation-

ship of international law and domestic law, the classification of an international decision as belonging to a particular source of law can be important. The constitutions of most States refer to international prescriptions in terms of the traditional sources. The treatment of a decision of an international institution in domestic proceedings may therefore not least depend on whether the court treats it as a treaty obligation, as part of customary law, or whether it is unable to accomodate it within any of the "recognized sources".

The insecurity of domestic courts when confronted with new and unusual types of international prescriptions emanating from international institutions is best exemplified by the frequent endeavor to categorize them among the established sources of law. This assimilation to the traditional sources is undertaken for the solution of various problems, such as, the already mentioned question of "incorporation" into domestic law (Chapters VI.B. and VII. below) or the authority of recommendations (Chapter III.B. below).

Since the decision-making functions of international institutions are usually based on treaty provisions, it seemed obvious to regard these decisions as a new form of treaty law.(8) This is exemplified by the attempts of domestic courts to characterize Security Council resolutions,(9) decisions of international Conciliation Commissions,(1o) the Annexes to the Paris Convention on Aerial Navigation passed by CINA,(11) the Code of Liberalization of the Organization for European Economic Cooperation(12) and European Economic Community regulations(13) as treaty obligations.

The difficulties caused by a strict adherence to the rigid pattern of sources, as represented by Article 38/1 of the Statute, have repeatedly given rise to doubts whether this provision can be taken as a complete list of the procedures whereby international prescriptions are created.(14) At the beginning of our century, this catalogue could possibly still claim to be an exhaustive description of the sources of international law. Today such a restrictive view of the sources of law can hardly cope with the new realities of organized international cooperation and communication.

Even as an account of legal sources to be applied by the International Court of Justice, Article 38/1 does not appear to be complete. The International Court of Justice, especially when giving advisory opinions, has relied on decisions of international organs, including recommendations, to an extent and in a way which would make any attempt to explain

this practice by reference to Article 38/1 implausible. The
United Nations General Assembly has not been oblivious of
this development. In Resolution 3232 (XXIX) of 22 November
1974 it found that:

> ...the development of international law may be reflec-
> ted *inter alia*, by declarations and resolutions of the
> General Assembly which may to that extent be taken into
> consideration by the International Court of Justice,...

A closer look at the realities of international decision-
making shows that an attempt to divide the law neatly into
separate rules which can be allocated to official types of
sources is not satisfactory. Very often it is impossible to
base a decision or even a general prescription on any one
type of source. The process of communication leading to
legal expectations, and to a conduct corresponding to them,
can take place in a variety of forms which are interrelated
and often not clearly distinguishable. Even a relatively
clear-cut prescription like a treaty provision is in constant
interaction with other types of international law, from its
drafting up to its application, and can lead a decision-
maker through the whole maze of sources of international
law, including the resolutions of international institutions.

Each of several relevant elements for a particular decision
may not, on its own, be authoritative enough to qualify as a
binding rule or to present a sufficient basis for the decision.
Their combined effect, however, can be conclusive. For
example, the old principle whereby reservations to a multilateral treaty are only admissible if they are accepted by
all other parties has lost its validity today. An advisory
opinion of the International Court of Justice,(15) a resolution of the United Nations General Assembly(16) containing instructions to the Secretary General and a recommendation to Members, the work of the International Law Commission,(17) and provisions of a treaty,(18) only recently
in force, have all contributed to this change.

Rather than searching for abstract rules classified by types
of sources, it seems more appropriate to examine the entire
body of legally significant authority for a particular
decision. The traditional procedures of concluding treaties
by explicit submission or of creating customary patterns of
behavior by implicit conduct are two very important and
typical ways to secure an orderly and predictable conduct of
international relations. Since the establishment of organized
new machinery for cooperation and intercourse in the international community, the law-creating process of communication
has been expanded and diversified. Therefore, it does not

seem useful *a priori* to reject the results reached in these
new procedures just because they do not fit the traditional
pattern of sources of law. It would, however, be equally
mistaken to try and see these organized community acts
entirely detached from the traditional sources.

Just as the material prescriptions of international law are
subject to development and change, so are the procedures
whereby the law is created. In other words, not only the
public order process but also the world constitutive process
continuously adapts to new circumstances. Article 38/1
should not therefore be seen as a petrified constitutional
rule of international law which determines definitively in
what way the law is created and changed and from which the
authority of international rules is derived. It is probably
no more than a descriptive catalogue with a reasonable
degree of historical accuracy.

Some authors have drawn consequences from these difficulties
by suggesting that decisions of international institutions
constitute a new formal source of international law.(19) This
suggestion is supported by the importance of international
institutions for contemporary international law. Furthermore,
the social process governing decision-making in international
organs is quite different from the process of explicit
submission to treaty obligations or from the often haphazard
and slow evolution of State practice. On the other hand, the
heterogeneous legal nature of various acts of international
institutions, ranging from U.N.General Assembly recommendations to E.E.C. regulations and from specific court decisions to general declarations of principle, makes the useful-
ness of such a new category in the sources of international
law doubtful, unless it is accepted for the sake of classification itself.

It seems hardly helpful to divide international law rigidly
into individual sections by allocating it to different types
of sources. As has been pointed out before, the sources of
law can never be stated exhaustively and, still less, laid
down by a legal norm.(2o)

The alternative would be a flexible extension and adjustment
of the concept of the sources of international law.(21) This
new approach should not be based on any notion of mutually
exclusive types of sources, but on the awareness that the
evolution of the law is a process of communication which can
take place in a variety of forms. This does not imply that
certain typical forms of this process should not be characterized and described, as long as such a system remains

sufficiently flexible and adaptable to accommodate new phenomena. A classification of sources of law is questionable only where it becomes rigid and exclusive and attempts to measure new methods for the creation of legal expectations by the standards of a past period of international relations.

A meaningful alternative would be a classification of activities of international institutions not by types of sources of law but by decision functions. The following decision functions appear relevant for the subject-matter of this study:

1.   Intelligence, that is, the collection, processing, and dissemination of information important for decisions. International institutions pursue this function in a variety of manners. International courts and tribunals have to establish the facts of the case before reaching a verdict. Preparatory work in international organs leading to the passing of formal decisions, the formulation of treaty drafts, and other prescriptions embrace a host of intelligence gathering.

2.   Recommendation, that is, the promotion and advocacy of certain policies. A large portion of the activities of contemporary international organisations is directed at this function. Recommendations by international organs are a common feature in the international decision-making process. Resolutions of the General Assembly of the United Nations and the Parliamentary Assembly of the Council of Europe are typical examples. Their invocation and application raise a number of problems, especially concerning their authority.

3.   Prescription, that is the projection of authoritative policy for future conduct. A number of international organs are specifically authorized to formulate authoritative general prescriptions. Typical examples are EEC regulations, enactments passed by certain United Nations specialized agencies, such as, ICAO and WHO, and decisions passed by OECD and EFTA.

4.   Invocation, that is, the provisional characterization of facts in terms of prescriptions in order to institute the process of application. Invocation is a constant feature in the work of international institutions. Parties invoke prescriptions before international courts and tribunals, but also before so-called political international organs.

5. Application, that is, the authoritative evaluation of
    specific facts in the light of general prescriptions.
    Where it is coupled with implementation, it is the
    transformation of authoritative prescriptions into
    controlling events. Typical cases are international
    judgments and arbitral awards or operative decisions by
    the United Nations Security Council.

6. Termination, that is, the abrogation of existing pre-
    scriptions and situations, often coupled with an attempt
    at the amelioration of unjustified value deprivations
    caused by it. The terminating function of international
    institutions is most prominent in areas of highly
    political interests. Examples are the steps towards
    decolonization taken in the United Nations and the
    territorial changes connected with it or the efforts to
    enlist international organizations for the creation of
    a new international economic order.

D. INTERACTIONS BETWEEN INTERNATIONAL INSTITUTIONS AND
    DOMESTIC COURTS

Domestic courts and international institutions are two types
of arenas which seem to have little in common at first
sight. They differ in participants, perspectives, bases of
power, strategies, outcomes, and effects. Nevertheless,
there are important points of contact. Traditional investigation into contacts between state judiciaries and organized
international decision-makers,(22) mostly international
courts and arbitral tribunals, are strongly influenced by
the procedural notions of appeal or cassation.(23) The
international organ is usually seen as a kind of higher
court, whose task is to review the domestic judgment. Attention is first focussed on the requirement of the exhaustion
of local remedies and then at the usually very limited
possibilities for review of the domestic decision by the
international organ. The final conclusion is usually that a
formal annulment of the domestic decision by the international organ is not possible.(24)

But the relations between domestic and international decision-makers show reciprocal effects. The consequences of the
activities of domestic courts for international decisions
are matched by a largely unobserved field consisting of the
effects of organized international decisions on domestic
courts.

As a consequence of the rapidly growing jurisdiction of
international institutions and their advance into numerous

areas of inclusive concern, domestic courts are more and more often called upon to rely on their decisions. This is not only true for traditional fields of international law, in which decision-making by international courts and organizations is to be expected, but also for numerous other fields like individual liberties, civil aviation, commercial transactions, and public health.

However, the strong increase of inclusive jurisdiction in favor of international institutions is one-sided. Although an increasing number of tasks and competences was assigned to them for authoritative decision-making, they were in most cases not also endowed with the capacity to make these decisions controlling through effective enforcement procedures. The implementation of the measures decided by them is nearly always dependent on the cooperation of State organs. In some situations domestic courts play a decisive rôle. Although the treatment of international decisions in domestic arenas is often also dependent on internal legislative enactments and the attitude of the executive, the far-reaching functions of courts in the authoritative and controlling settlement of disputes are often of crucial importance for their effective implementation.

In view of the difficulty and novelty of this situation, a certain degree of insecurity and uneasiness on the part of domestic courts when confronted with such questions is not surprising. Not infrequently attempts are made to escape these difficulties by ambiguous language or by relying on analogies from better-known legal situations and concepts.

In approaching the legal questions arising from the invocation of decisions of international institutions before domestic courts, it is advisable to avoid ill-considered analogies to prescriptions regulating the relationship of different state organs. The principles, procedures, and myths governing the cooperation of organs within relatively homogeneous structures, such as, domestic legal systems, are not transferable to the interaction of organs established by different constitutive processes. A rejection of radical dualist conceptions must not turn into a monist procedural euphoria in which international institutions are simply regarded as organs of super-States. Concepts like "binding force", "valid rules", "binding precedent", "appeal", and *"res judicata"* may have some value as symbols of communication in domestic legal systems to designate complicated but largely clarified structures and processes. In the context of this study they would only contribute to confusion.

Even the somewhat more related parallels from the conflict
of laws have to be treated with great caution. The policies
governing the interplay of legal prescriptions emanating
from different States are not necessarily applicable to the
relationship between decision-makers and prescriptions from
international and domestic arenas.

E. BASIC POLICY CONSIDERATIONS

The formulation of basic policy considerations for the
subject-matter of the present study raises certain difficulties. At first sight, the primarily procedural aspects do
not appear to have any direct influence on the distribution
of values permitting a clear evaluation in terms of basic
community goals. However, it must always be remembered that
in specific decision-situations procedural questions can be
of decisive material importance. For a claimant grave procedural difficulties can lead to a complete loss of his
rights. For instance, solemn assurances of individual liberties by international organs are of little use for individuals if there are no appropriate procedures for their
implementation.

In considering which interests deserve protection, community
interests as well as individual interests must be taken into
account. The work of international institutions is largely
directed at the protection of common interests, although individual interests may be the subject-matter of certain
international procedures for the settlement of disputes. In
proceedings before domestic courts claims are usually directed at the implementation of individual interests, although
public or common interests may have a certain rôle to play.

At the present early stage of international integration, increased organized international cooperation can be expected
to be helpful in the solution of most common problems. A
call for the effective implementation of decisions of international institutions, therefore, seems an acceptable starting point for the formulation of basic policies. Nevertheless, this demand for an effective support for the activities of international institutions by domestic courts must
be understood subject to certain qualifications. Firstly,
the goals and tasks of the international institution in
question have to be taken into account. For instance, the
activities of an international organization striving for the
maintenance of international peace will have to be regarded
higher than those of an international organisation concerned
with the fixing of prices for certain commodities. In the
vast majority of cases the activities of contemporary inter-

national organisations are directed at the solution of
problems whose importance for the entire international
community is beyond doubt, such as, human rights, civil
aviation, public health, and international commerce.

Secondly, the contents of specific decisions must also be
examined. Not all decisions of an international organ serve
its purposes to the same degree. Where groups of members
succeed in using international organisations for the pursuance of their special interests, a demand for maximum effectiveness of international decisions does not always appear
appropriate.

In addition to an improvement of procedures for the solution
of common problems, the activities of international institutions may lead to an increased uniformity of prescriptions
to be applied by internal decision-makers in the countries
concerned. This uniformity of legal provisions in areas of
intensive transnational interaction, such as, commercial
law, foreign exchange, civil aviation, and public health,
can be an important advantage in predicting authoritative
decisions. The effective and uniform enforcement of decisions
of international institutions can therefore also be beneficial in terms of calculating future events.

In certain situations the basically justified demand for an
effective implementation of international decisions may
collide with other legitimate interests. Unlike most developed domestic legal systems, international institutions
usually lack satisfactory procedures of supervision and
guarantees for the protection of individual rights. The main
reason for these shortcomings is probably the prevailing
contemporary tendency to widen the scope of activities of
international institutions and not to subject them to checks
and limitations. In the course of a further growth of competences for international organisations the creation of
appropriate procedures of supervision for the protection of
individual rights will become necessary.

The protection of human rights is a particularly important
field in the activities of a number of international organizations. Pertinent decisions of international organs therefore often fully accord with the demand for a maximum protection of individual liberties. In other cases, the tendency
of international decisions can be contrary to policies
directed at the furtherance of human rights. For instance,
an interest in the solution of common economic problems can
be pursued at the expense of individual liberties. Since
most international institutions either have no or only

rudimentary procedures for the protection of individual rights vis-à-vis the organisation or its decisions, a domestic court called upon to implement these decisions may have important functions in the protection of human rights. The call for an effective implementation of decisions of international institutions by domestic courts must therefore also be subjected to the reservation of sufficient safeguards for human rights.

Sometimes the activities of international institutions give rise to important consequences in terms of wealth allocations. Transnational commercial transactions often depend on decisions of international organs for the settlement of disputes. In the area of the protection of foreign investments, international institutions can play important rôles both as decision-makers in specific disputes and as organs for the elaboration of general prescriptions. Respect for these international decisions in matters of wealth allocation is an important factor for the reduction of risks in international business transactions. The advancement of stability in international commerce promotes not only the interests of the corporations directly involved but also the economic welfare of broad sectors of the international community.

Finally, certain basic procedural interests of individuals and corporations give rise to important policy considerations. Inspite of an increasing significance of non-State actors in the international arena, individuals and corporations are still not admitted to a large number of international fora. This fact is aggravated by a tendency of domestic courts to avoid a decision on the merits in cases with prominent international elements either by adopting a restrictive interpretation of the parties' *locus standi* or by relying on the doctrine of political questions and on other arguments. The procedural gaps caused by this attitude can cause grave difficulties to non-State participants and may in some cases completely frustrate their legitimate claims. From a policy-oriented perspective it is therefore important not to foreclose proceedings before domestic courts merely because of the presence of international elements, such as, decisions of international institutions. In the majority of cases the exclusion of claimants from proceedings for purely formal or technical reasons and without an examination of the merits will lead to arbitrary results. Unless the invocation of an international decision before domestic courts evidently serves improper purposes, a procedure is therefore to be preferred in which the claims based on the international decision are examined on the merits.

From the viewpoint of a maximization of values for all
participants, the most important policy considerations for
the subject-matter of this study can be summarized as follows:

1. In principle, decisions of domestic decision-makers,
    including courts, are to be preferred which contribute
    to the <u>effectiveness</u> of authoritative decisions of
    international institutions. Due consideration should be
    given to the material contents of the international
    decision as well as to aspects of uniformity and pre-
    dictability.

2. In making decisions, the protection of <u>human rights</u> as
    formulated in the pertinent national and international
    documents is of paramount importance. In cases of
    conflict with the effectiveness of international deci-
    sions a policy sustaining human rights is to be pre-
    ferred.

3. Final dispositions concerning <u>wealth allocations</u> made
    by authoritative international decision-makers should
    be respected and should be turned into effective con-
    trol over the resources in question.

4. Claimants relying on decisions of international insti-
    tutions should not be denied <u>access to domestic pro-
    ceedings</u> for formal reasons.

(1) McDougal and Lasswell, The Identification and Appraisal of Diverse Systems of Public Order, 53 AJIL 1, 14(1959).

(2) For the most important recent writings see Falk, The Role of Domestic Courts in the International Legal Order (1964); Wengler, Réflexions sur l'application du droit international public par les tribunaux internes, 72 RGDIP 921(1968); Lillich, The Proper Role of Domestic Courts in the International Legal Order, 11 VaJIL 9(197o/71); Reuter et al.(Ed.), L'application du droit international par le juge français (1972).

(3) Schermers, International Institutional Law Vol.II, p.6o6(1972).

(4) Of these collections the International Law Reports (edited by E. Lauterpacht), formerly Annual Digest, is, no doubt, the most important one. It is supplemented by a number of national collections, either as independent publications, as parts of comprehensive "digests" or in periodicals. See esp. Mosler, Repertorien der nationalen Praxis in Völkerrechtsfragen - Eine Quelle zur Erschließung des allgemeinen Völkerrechts?, En Hommage à Paul Guggenheim, p.46o(1968); Cf. also the somewhat outdated survey in Ways and Means of Making the Evidence of Customary International Law more Readily Available, Memorandum submitted by the Secretary General, p.58seq.(1949).

(5) H.Lauterpacht, Decisions of Municipal Courts as a Source of International Law, 1o BYIL 65,67seq.(1929); Hyde, The Supreme Court of the United States as an Expositor of International Law, 18 BYIL 1(1937); McDougal, The Impact of International Law upon National Law: A Policy-oriented Perspective, 4 South Dakota LRev 25,74(1959).

(6) Le phénomène de dédoublement fonctionnel, Rechtsfragen der Internationalen Organisation: Festschrift für Hans Wehberg, p.324(1956); ibid., Précis de droit des gens Vol.I 42seq.,54seq.esp.56(1932); ibid., Droit international public, p.53oseq.(1944); ibid., Manuel de droit international public, p.21seq.(1948); Wiebringhaus, Das Gesetz der funktionellen Verdoppelung (1955).

(7) Similar ideas concerning the function of domestic courts are already expressed by Kaufmann, Die Rechtskraft des Internationalen Rechts und das Verhältnis der Staatsgesetzgebungen und der Staatsorgane zu demselben,

p.1o3seq.(1899); cf. also Tammes, Decisions of International Organs as a Source of International Law, 94 RC 265,344seq.(1958,II); van Panhuys, Relations and Interactions between International and National Scenes of Law, 112 RC 7,8seq.(1964,II); Friedmann, National Courts and the International Legal Order: Projections on the Implications of the Sabbatino Case, 34 George Washington LRev 443seq.(1968); Falk, The Interplay of Westphalia and Charter Conceptions of International Legal Order, in Falk and Black (Eds.), The Future of the International Legal Order Vol.I, p.32,69(1969), Lillich, The Proper Role, p.12; Reisman, Nullity and Revision, p.8o2(1971).

(8)   See especially Skubiszewski, A new Source of the Law of Nations: Resolutions of International Organisations, En Hommage à Paul Guggenheim p.508,517seq.(1968); ibid., Enactment of Law by International Organizations, 41 BYIL 198,22oseq.,242seq.(196566); ibid., Legal Nature and Domestic Effect of Acts of International Organizations, in Rapports polonais presenté au VIIIe Congrès international de droit comparê, p.195(1970); ibid., Resolutions of International Organizations and Municipal Law, 2 The Polish Yearbook of International Law 8o,83seq.(1968/69); Dubouis, Le juge administratif, p.23; Tammes, Decisions of International Organs, p.269; Bianchi, Security Council Resolutions in United States Courts, 5o Indiana LJ 83,85(1974/75).

(9)   Diggs v. Shultz, 31 Oct.1972, 47o F.2d 461.

(1o) Compagnie des Wagons-Réservoirs v. Ministry of Industry and Commerce and Italian Railways, Tribunal Civil de la Seine, 7 Oct.1950, 18 ILR 394(1951).

(11) Staatsanwaltschaft des Kantons Thurgau v. Lang u. Legler, Swiss Federal Court, 27 Jan.1950, BGE 76 IV 43, 17 ILR 3o6(1950); cf.also Dominicê, La nature juridique, p.257.

(12) Hurwits v. State of the Netherlands, Dist.Ct.The Hague, 12 June 1958, 6 NTIR 195(1959).

(13) Administration des Contributions Indirectes et Comitê Interprofessionnel des Vins Doux Naturels v. Ramel, Cour de cass.(Fr.), 22 Oct.1970,1o CMLRep. 315(1971).

(14) Ross, Lehrbuch des Völkerrechts, p.81seq.(1951); Jaenicke, Völkerrechtsquellen, in Wörterbuch des Völkerrechts

Vol.III,p.767,772(1962); Parry, The Sources, p.21seq.,
109seq.; Falk, On the Quasi-Legislative Competence of
the General Assembly, 6o AJIL 782(1966); Friedmann,
General Course in Public International Law, 127 RC 39,
142seq.(1969,II); Falk, The Status of Law in International Society, p.141seq.(1970); Castaneda, Legal
Effects of United Nations Resolutions, p.2seq.(1969);
Ermacora, Das Problem der Rechtsetzung durch internationale Organisationen (insbesondere im Rahmen der UN),
1O Berichte der Deutschen Gesellschaft für Völkerrecht
51,73seq.(1971); Simma, Völkerrecht und Friedensforschung, 57 Die Friedenswarte 65,75(1974); Verzijl,
International Law in Historical Perspective Vol.I,
p.74(1968).

(15) Reservation to the Convention on the Prevention and
Punishment of the Crime of Genocide, ICJ Reports
p.15(1951).

(16) 598(VI) of 12 Jan.1952.

(17) For references see Rosenne, The Law of Treaties,
p.182seq.(197o).

(18) Art.19-23 of the Vienna Convention on the Law Treaties.

(19) Dahm, Völkerrecht Vol.I,p.19,25(1958); Hexner, Die
Rechtsnatur der interpretativen Entscheidungen des
Internationalen Währungsfonds, 2o ZaöRV 73,81(1959);
Kelsen, Principles of International Law, p.5o6seq.
(1967); Economides, Nature juridique des actes des
organisations internationales et leurs effets en droit
interne, 23 Revue Hellenique de Droit International
225,228(197o); Tammes, Decisions of International
Organs, p.269seq.; Skubiszewski, A new Source, p.52o;
ibid., Enactment, p.245 with further references.

(2o) Fitzmaurice, Some Problems Regarding the Formal Sources
of International Law, in Symbolae Verzijl, p.153,
161(1958). Ross, Lehrbuch p.81; See also Thirlway,
International Customary Law and Codification, p.36seq.
(1972).

(21) Falk, The Status, p.141seq.; Simma, Völkerrecht und
Friedensforschung, p.75seq.; Hambro, Some Notes on the
Development of the Sources of International Law, 17
Scandinavian Studies in Law 77,83seq.(1973).

(22) For an early study see Root, The Relations between
     International Tribunals of Arbitration and the Juris-
     diction of National Courts, 3 AJIL 529(19o9).

(23) Simons, Verhältnis der Nationalen Gerichtsbarkeit;
     Hallier, Völkerrechtliche Schiedsinstanzen für Einzel-
     personen und ihr Verhältnis zur innerstaatlichen Ge-
     richtsbarkeit (1962); Heise, Internationale Rechts-
     pflege.

(24) Simons, Verhältnis der nationalen Gerichtsbarkeit,
     p.41; Hallier, Völkerrechtliche Schiedsinstanzen, p.99;
     Heise, Internationale Rechtspflege, p.127seq.,145; Cf.
     also Partsch, Die Anwendung des Völkerrechts im inner-
     staatlichen Recht, 6 Berichte der Deutschen Gesellschaft
     für Völkerrecht 114seq.(1964); Vogler, Spruchpraxis der
     Europäischen Kommission und des Europäischen Gerichts-
     hofs für Menschenrechte und ihre Bedeutung für das
     deutsche Straf- und Verfahrensrecht, 82 Zeitschrift für
     die gesamte Strafrechtswissenschaft 743,779(197o).

II. TYPES OF CLAIMS BASED ON INTERNATIONAL DECISIONS

Before entering into any of the detailed questions concerning the behavior of domestic courts when confronted with decisions of international institutions, we first have to ask ourselves in what ways parties try to invoke these decisions in domestic judicial proceedings. The invocation of international decisions and the claims based on them can be directed at totally different goals. It would therefore make little sense to turn directly to questions like the "binding force" of international decisions for the domestic courts without first asking ourselves in what way the international decision is connected to the claim raised in domestic proceedings. A closer look at the practice of courts reveals that the treatment of international decisions is decisively influenced by the purpose for which they are invoked. In looking at the types of claims based on decisions of international institutions, it is also necessary to consider the decision alternatives open to the court. The true significance of a decision ostensibly based on certain grounds often becomes much clearer if one looks at the alternatives open to the decision-maker and the outcomes of the decision. Such a functional perspective will not infrequently add a new dimension to an examination of the grounds given for the verdict.

The available case material yields three typical types of claims based on decisions of international institutions before domestic courts:

1. The goal of the party may be the <u>implementation</u> of an international decision favorable to it or the <u>review and frustration</u> of an unfavorable decision. In this context it is particularly important to take a functional view and not to restrict one's focus to the formal solution of legal problems. Not infrequently a judgment based on narrow procedural grounds can have far-reaching consequences for the implementation or frustration of the international decision involved. This is particularly so in cases in which courts refuse to make any decision on the merits.

2. In other cases the claim before the domestic court is not directed at the enforcement of the international decision. Rather, the invocation is aimed at the domestic court's recognition of a determination of facts or of specific rights made by the international organ in a decision between third parties. Here the claim to deference by the domestic court is not based on the

material identity of the legal relationships before the
international and national fora, but on the assertion
that certain determinations must on account of their
declaratory nature be considered authoritative *erga
omnes*. The decision of the international institution is
then put forward to help answer a <u>preliminary question</u>.

3.   In a third group of cases the international decision
and the case before the domestic court concern different
sets of facts, but involve similar questions of law or
policy. The demand is then to treat the international
decision as a "<u>precedent</u>", that is, to accept the
policies applied there also for the case before the
domestic court.

A. IMPLEMENTATION OR REVIEW OF INTERNATIONAL DECISIONS

1. Modes of Implementation

The modalities of implementation can be relatively simple if
the international decision involved determines an obligation
of one party to make specific payments to the other. In
such cases the domestic court is called upon to transform
the wealth allocation made by the international organ,
usually a court or arbitral tribunal, into effective control
over the assets in question. In a number of cases, the
courts have actually performed this function. Thus pecuniary
obligations arising from international government contracts,
which had been adjudicated upon by international arbitral
tribunals, were repeatedly enforced by domestic courts.(1)

The international decision whose enforcement or implementation is sought can, however, also concern values other than
wealth. Cases dealing with human rights or nationality often
have a decisive impact on the well-being of the individuals
involved.(2)

In some cases attempts are made to enlist the help of domestic courts for the implementation of international decisions concerning power. Typical examples are efforts to
force the executive branch of the forum State to comply with
sanctions imposed by the United Nations Security Council.
In most situations it is, however, clearly beyond a domestic
court's jurisdiction and effective power to enforce such
an international decision directly. In these situations
a domestic court can play an indirect rôle in the implementation of international decisions concerned with power.
Since disputes concerning wealth are a typical and frequent subject-matter of domestic litigation, the efforts

to have the international decision concerning power implemented can be presented as ostensible claims directed at
wealth. In fact, economic sanctions imposed by international
organs have drawn suggestions to utilize domestic courts for
their execution: Proposals were made to enforce the United
Nations decisions on Namibia and Rhodesia(Zimbabwe) through
a seizure of the goods exported from these areas.(3) In
both cases, the bodies entitled to exercise authority over
these areas - the United Nations in the case of Namibia and
the United Kingdom Government in the case of Rhodesia - were
to claim rights of property to the exported goods. The
pertinent decisions by the United Nations would furnish the
legal basis for these claims before domestic courts. The
effects of the seizures on the economy of the "rebelling"
territories were designed to make the United Nations decisions in question effective.

Another indirect mode of implementation is the non-recogni-
tion and refusal to enforce commercial and other transac-
tions(4) or foreign legal prescriptions(5) which are in
contravention of decisions of international institutions.

In a wider sense, not only the enforcement of operative
international decisions but also any application of a general
prescription emanating from an international organ can be
regarded as the implementation of an international decision.
Any observance of such an international policy, whether it
be regarded as binding or not, ultimately contributes to the
international decision's implementation and, hence, to its
effectiveness.

In actual practice domestic courts have in a multitude of
cases applied prescriptions, such as resolutions of the
United Nations General Assembly,(6) the Staff Rules issued
by the U.N.Secretary General,(7) regulations of the International Civil Aviation Organization(8) and the World Health
Organization,(9) the Code of Liberalization enacted by the
Organization for European Economic Cooperation,(1o) decisions by the Council of the European Free Trade Association,(11) official interpretations by the International
Monetary Fund,(12) regulations, directives, and decisions of
the European Communities,(13) and other prescriptions enacted
by international institutions. In all these cases domestic
courts were instrumental in ultimately putting the international decisions into effect.

2. Modes of Review

In another group of cases the claims of parties directed at

international decisions are not aimed at their implementation
but at the very opposite, namely their revision and frustration. In examining the modalities of review of international
decisions by domestic courts, it is particularly important
not to be trapped by formal concepts of domestic procedure.
Obviously there can be no question of appeal, cassation,
abrogation, or annulment in the technical sense. (14) Domestic
courts only rarely deal openly with the validity or nullity
of international judgments and awards or the legality of
decisions of political international organs. (15)

A functional view of the possibilities open to domestic
courts, when dealing with decisions of international institutions, quickly reveals that the question of the courts'
formal competence to review and to annul the international
decision is only of secondary importance. The statement of
the Permanent Court of International Justice in the Chorzow
Factory Case (16) to the effect that judgments of domestic
courts cannot invalidate the judgment of an international
court (17) is hardly open to dispute. However, from the
viewpoint of the actual potentialities open to domestic
courts to frustrate the consequences of an international
decision, this question is only of very limited relevance.

The opportunities to oppose and review decisions are considerably wider than a formalistic view of the jurisdiction of
domestic courts would suggest. A domestic court has a wide
range of possibilities at its disposal which can lead to the
same outcome in terms of value distribution as a material
revision of the international decision.

One strategy, which is still relatively easy to recognize as
an attempt at indirect revision, is a claim directed against
a State, which participated in the establishment of the
international institution (18) or against an individual who
acted in such an organ, to obtain redress for any value
deprivations suffered through the international decision. In
most cases of this kind the claim will fail due to procedural
immunities of the defendants. In exceptional cases it may,
however, be successful. In the case of X.v.Y. and the Greek
State (19) before the Athens Court of Appeal, the plaintiff
felt aggrieved by a decision of the Greek-Bulgarian Emigration Commission. His action for compensation was directed
both against a member of the Commission and against the
Greek State. The action was dismissed as far as it was
directed against the Greek State, but was upheld against the
member of the Commission. The Court found that, although the
Commission's decisions were final and not subject to review,
this did not preclude an action for damages against members

in respect of wrongs committed in the course of their activities in the Commission. Since the treaty establishing the Commission did not provide for any immunity of its members, a claim to immunity was dismissed.

In <u>Zoernsch v. Waldock and Another</u>,(2o) a similar attempt was made to review a decision of the European Commission of Human Rights. In this case the English Court of Appeal had no difficulty in dismissing the action for damages instituted against the Commmission's Chairman and Secretary based on allegations of "negligence and corruption". The Court found that the procedural immunities in favor of the members of the Commission, and of the employees of the Council of Europe, were a clear bar to this action. In the case of the first defendant, the Court added that his immunity continued to have effect even after the expiry of his term of office.

Another indirect way to oppose an international decision is to claim that it is in conflict with the domestic law of the forum State and hence cannot be applied. In this case too, the formal authority of the international decision remains intact but its effectiveness can be completely frustrated. A typical example would be the contention that the international decision cannot be implemented because of its unconstitutionality.(21)

The problem of review of an international decision before a domestic court need not arise in the context of procedures instituted primarily for the purpose of its revision. In the majority of cases questions of review arise incidental to claims for implementation, often upon the instigation of the party against whom the international decision is to be enforced. A domestic court called upon to implement the verdict of an international organ, like any decision-maker confronted with the task of carrying out a previous decision, is in a sense always exercising a function of review.(22) It has to examine whether the decision can or should be implemented at all and whether the factual conditions for carrying it into effect are met. Thus it has to make sure that what is presented to it is a valid decision and that the party relying on it is entitled to its benefits vis-à-vis the other party. It has to examine whether the decision should be implemented at this time by this organ and in the way demanded. More delicately, the reviewing organ may have to make up its mind whether the intrinsic value of the international decision is such that it should be given effect to within the court's sphere of effective power. The outcome of this process of review may be a decision to implement, to refuse implementation, or to implement in a modified form.

Municipal law has developed detailed and sophisticated procedures for the process of review. The occasions and organs for review are minutely circumscribed and there is a strong tendency to separate review procedures for the re-evaluation of the merits of the original decision from those at the stage of implementation or execution. Not so in international law. The near absence of so-called appeals procedures and the scarcity of organized processes of execution means in most cases that the organ or party charged with the implementation is expected to perform both or all functions of review at the same time.

A look at judicial practice reveals that domestic courts have a multitude of grounds at their disposal to refuse the implementation of international decisions. Apart from the usual impediments known to domestic law for the execution of decisions, like lack of material or local jurisdiction, the international nature of a decision to be applied presents numerous further hazards for its effective implementation: Doubts concerning the authority or "binding force" of the international decision can persuade the court to reject it (Chapter III.). The absence of a formal incorporation into the domestic law of the forum State can lead to a refusal to take notice of it (Chapter VII.). A conflict with the law of the forum State can lead to a non-application of the international decision (Chapter IX.). The absence of an international connecting point establishing the jurisdiction of the domestic court can lead to a refusal to implement it (Chapter V.). Procedural immunities of defendants, like the forum State, a foreign State, an international institution, or its officials, can ostensibly make enforcement impossible (Chapter XII.). Claims based on an international decision can be rejected because the claimant cannot establish a privity to it, for example because he is not admitted to the international arena from which it originates (Chapter XII.D.). A lack of precision and specification of the international provisions can prompt the court to refuse its application (Chapter VI.B.3.).

In all these cases there can be no question of review or revision of the merits in the strict sense. On the contrary, the various grounds for the rejection of the claim to implementation would seem to preclude any treatment of the question of the international decision's validity, legality, or wisdom. A closer look at the outcome of such a refusal to implement for formal or procedural reasons, however, shows that it can be tantamount to a material invalidation of the international decision unless other procedures are available for its implementation. The continuing formal authority of the international decision is of little consequence in the absence of any procedure to obtain effective control. The loss of respect suffered by the international institution through an abortive decision may, moreover, under certain circumstances, have adverse effects beyond the specific instance.

An examination of these forms of international review is handicapped by the fact that the grounds given by a court for the non-application of an international decision need not represent its true motives. Thus, a refusal to implement an international decision based on procedural grounds can have its true reasons in the disapproval of its material contents. The withdrawal into procedural niceties is often the only possibility to resist a disagreeable decision and to avoid its consequences. On the other hand, the endeavour to eliminate the international decision as quickly as possible from the proceedings can also result from an insecurity and aversion on the part of the judge due to the international character of the decision involved.

The formulation of appropriate limits for the review function of domestic courts when implementing decisions of international institutions is by no means easy. On one hand, it is impossible to exclude elements of review entirely. The domestic court has to examine whether the basic requirements of the international decision's validity and its applicability to the dispute before it are met and cannot merely rely on the assertion of the party invoking it. On the other hand, a generous and unrestrained exercise of review functions by the national judge is liable to introduce a strong element of instability into the activities of international institutions. An international decision which is subject to an examination on the merits by a domestic court, possibly of an interested party, before it is put into effect, will lose much of its value. The question where to draw the line between the necessary ascertainment of the conditions for implementation and a re-examination going to the merits of the decision is often extremely difficult.

In examining individual cases it is, therefore, not sufficient merely to test the conclusiveness of the legal grounds given for the refusal to implement. It is necessary also to look at the consequences of such a refusal in order to discover possible covert motivations for the courts' behavior. In later chapters dealing with specific circumstances of refusals by domestic courts to give deference to international decisions, this aspect will always be borne in mind. The often far-reaching impacts, intended or incidental,

of these impediments to the implementation of international
decisions require the rigorous examination of such refusals.

3. Nondecisions

As mentioned before, the reasons given for decisions frequently do not reflect their actual consequences. This is particularly so in the case of nondecisions, that is, a refusal by
the decision-maker to accede to the claim without entering
into the merits of the case. Functionally speaking, a nondecision is of course an operative decision. As soon as a
forum is seized of a claim there will also be a reaction to
it even if it is clothed in the form of a rejection of a
claim *a limine*. The claim has then failed before that particular decision-maker. This is not the same as if no decision
had been made. A restitution of the dispute into the *status
quo ante* is not possible. Reisman describes this phenomenon
in the following words:

> From the standpoint of scholarly appraisal and evalua-
> tion of authoritative decision, it is crucial to assimi-
> late non-decisions to the general category of positive
> decisions and to examine the real social and political
> consequences which they precipitate. Nondecisions
> cannot be dismissed as cases in which courts simply
> refused to exercise their mandate and which, hence, are
> not part of the legal order...In the final analysis,
> nondecision is simply a variant form of judgment
> redaction, a form which generates some problems, but
> which, in appropriate circumstances, is legitimate. (23)

Decisions refusing to decide are by no means limited to
international questions. They are, however, conspicuously
frequent in cases where domestic courts have to deal with
questions of international law. The reluctance of domestic
courts to enter into matters touching upon questions of
foreign affairs has frequently led to the development of
myths and formulas, such as, the "doctrine of political
questions", which are invoked whenever courts choose to
decline a decision on the merits (Chapter XIII.). In other
cases courts also rely on procedural provisions of their
municipal law to avoid entering into the substance of a
delicate case.

Where decisions of international institutions are invoked, a
mere reference to their international character is sometimes
considered sufficient to justify the domestic court's refusal to deal with the claim. A group of judgments by United
States courts after the Second World War is characteristic
for this decision technique: Appeals against sentences

imposed by United States Military Tribunals in occupied
enemy territory were rejected on the ground that these
courts had been established in the name of the Allied Powers
and had thus to be regarded as international tribunals.(24)
In a similar vein the German Bundesverfassungsgericht
refused to review decisions of the Supreme Restitution Court
in Germany since this court had been set up by a treaty.(25)

In a large number of cases courts refused to review decisions
of international organizations vis-à-vis their employees,(26)
even if the claims were not directed against the organizations
themselves.(27)

In other cases the refusal to enter into the substance of
claims was not based on a general lack of jurisdiction for
domestic judiciaries, but on a lack of competence of the
particular court. A special competence of the Supreme Court
of Uruguay for disputes involving diplomats was interpreted
narrowly in order to reject an action brought by an international official.(28) The French Conseil d'Etat refused to
exercise any function of supervision not only over the
activities of the International Commission of the Danube(29)
but also over the administration of the New Hebrides jointly
exercised as a condominium by France and Great Britain(3o)
and also over an organ of the French Mandates administration,(31) since all these activities were not "actes d'une
autorité administrative française". In proceedings concerning construction work on behalf of the Organization for
Economic Cooperation and Development (OECD) the lack of
competence of the ordinary French courts was based on the
argument that the activities in question had to be regarded
as "travaux publics" in the sense of the French law.(32) The
Belgian Conseil d'Etat refused to review decisions of the
delegate of the United Nations High Commission for Refugees,
which he had made in the exercise of authority conferred
upon him by the Belgian Foreign Ministry. The court found
that the delegate was not an "administrative organ" in the
sense of the statute on the Conseil d'Etat.(33) American
courts, on the other hand, tend to withdraw behind the
"doctrine of political questions" when questions concerning
international decisions are raised before them.(34)

Although the formal reasons given for these decisions differ
widely and are strongly influenced by the peculiarities of
the law of the forum, the decision technique is basically
always the same. As soon as an international decision plays
a dominant rôle in the proceedings, the action is rejected
and the claim fails. Where the action is aimed at the review
of the international decision in order to have it revised on

the merits or to have its implementation frustrated, a nondecision will usually lead to results which are in accordance
with community policies supporting the effectiveness of
international decisions and are consequently to be welcomed
in most cases. As a conscious strategy to uphold the international decision this decision technique may be acceptable
even though the grounds given obscure the true policies
underlying it. On the other hand, it must be borne in mind
that a different claim also changes the outcome of a nondecision. If the reliance on the international decision is not
directed at its frustration but at its implementation, the
consequences of a nondecision will be exactly the opposite.
The value outcome of nondecisions therefore entirely depends
on the demands in question. A claim is always doomed to
failure whatever its contents.

This is best demonstrated with the help of two French cases:
Both concerned awards by Mixed Arbitral Tribunals established
by the Peace Treaties after World War I. In the first case
the plaintiff before the domestic court had been found
liable by the international tribunal and, therefore, tried
to challenge the international award before the ordinary
French courts and before the Conseil d'Etat.(35) In the
second case the plaintiff tried to enforce the terms of an
international award favorable to him with the help of the
courts.(36) In both cases the claims were turned down by
reference to the international nature of the awards. The
claim to enforcement failed in the same way as the claim to
revision.

An undifferentiated refusal to decide on claims connected
with decisions of international institutions would therefore
lead to random results not governed by rational considerations. The effects of a general policy of nondecision by
domestic courts on the enhancement or reduction of the
effectiveness of international institutions would entirely
depend on whether claims are directed at their frustration
or their implementation. A consistent application of this
purely negative decision technique would therefore eliminate
domestic courts not only to the extent that they could
threaten the effective application of international decisions
but also in situations where they are instrumental for their
effective implementation.

B. INTERNATIONAL DECISIONS AND PRELIMINARY QUESTIONS

Consequences of decisions are not exhausted in the value
allocation between the immediate participants. They often
show additional subsequent effects. A later dispute can be

concerned with the existence or legal evaluation of the same facts albeit in the context of a different claim or between different parties. If a decision maker has to deal with incidental questions of law or fact, which have already been the subject-matter of an authoritative decision, he is often inclined to rely on the previous findings in determining the preliminary question before him. The first decision then determines further decisions relating to the same facts even if the claims and the parties are different. Two types of preliminary questions arise before domestic courts to which decisions of international organs can offer answers. In one set of cases the international decision offers an authoritative determination of a legal question which is relevant to the domestic proceedings. In other cases the international organs may have established certain facts which are important to the domestic court's decision.

1. Preliminary Questions of International Law

The most common and typical situations in which international decisions offer guidance on preliminary points are territorial questions. Territorial decisions of international organs can be relevant to a host of legal questions arising before domestic courts. They include the venue of the State organs, including the adjudicating court itself,(37) the citizenship of the inhabitants of a particular area,(38) the law applicable to disputes which have a connecting point to the territory,(39) and other questions.(4o) In all these cases the domestic court has to deal with the international decision on the status of the territory in question.

A case before the Supreme Court of Norway, Rex v. Cooper,(41) offers an instructive example. In proceedings for the prosecution of a British fisherman who had been caught fishing off the Norwegian coast, the legality of Norway's fishery zone was disputed by counsel for the defense. The Supreme Court of Norway dismissed an appeal based on that argument and relied on the judgment of the International Court of Justice, which had shortly before confirmed the legality of the Norwegian fishery limits.

The situation is not very different if the international decision does not concern territorial questions, strictly speaking, but specific rights to jurisdiction. Moroccan court decisions delivered in the wake of the judgment of the International Court of Justice concerning the Rights of Nationals of the United States of America in Morocco(42) are obvious examples. In its judgment the International Court of Justice had found that the American consular jurisdiction in

Morocco was essentially restricted to disputes between
American citizens and that the jurisdiction of the ordinary
Moroccan courts was consequently only limited to that
extent. Moroccan courts in determining questions of their
jurisdiction subsequently relied on this judgment of the
International Court and rejected objections to their competence beyond the limit drawn by the International Court for
the jurisdiction of the consular courts.(43)

These cases also vividly illustrate the interaction of
decisions on preliminary questions and implementation. From
the domestic courts' perspective the International Court's
judgment only offered an answer to the preliminary question
of jurisdiction. At the same time the exercise of this
jurisdiction, in effect, also constituted an act of implementation for the international decision.

Questions concerning the permissible extent of state jurisdiction are by no means the only preliminary questions which
can be resolved by reference to international decisions.
Other examples offered by the practice of domestic courts
include the legality of measures of expropriation,(44) the
right of a state-owned enterprise to immunity before foreign
courts,(45) the status of a non-recognized revolutionary
government,(46) or the right of a domestic court to try a
defendant whose arrest had been contrary to international
law.(47)

2. Preliminary Questions of Fact

Sometimes international decisions can offer answers to
factual questions arising in domestic proceedings. Intelligence activities exercised by international organs can be of
particular significance in this context. In a wider sense,
factual determinations are also accepted whenever domestic
courts rely on decisions of international organs on preliminary questions of a legal nature, since these decisions are
always based on an ascertainment of facts. On the other
hand, a domestic court can also simply rely only on a factual determination by an international organ.

The practice of courts on this point is still somewhat
scarce. One example is offered by the judgment of a United
States Military Tribunal after the Second World War.(48) In
this case the defendants were acquitted of crimes against
peace, since the court followed the determination of the
International Military Tribunal at Nuremberg on a point of
fact. The tribunal considered itself bound by the finding of
the International Military Tribunal that the criminal con-

spiracy to wage an aggressive war was formulated in 1937 by Hitler and disclosed by him only to a few of his top leaders in four secret conferences from which the accused were absent.

A determination of facts can also take place without any specific decision being taken upon it by the international organ. The ascertainment of factual circumstances is often a difficult task in international disputes. For this reason, international institutions sometimes employ fact-finding organs or observers. These activities can be of relevance also to proceedings before domestic courts, provided their modalities ensure the necessary impartiality and objectivity.

3. Preliminary Questions and Effectiveness

From the viewpoint of an international decision's effective-ness, its utilization for the determination of preliminary questions before domestic courts is usually only of secon-dary importance. While proceedings for their implementation or revision are often decisive to make them controlling, a reliance on them for the solution of preliminary points before domestic courts is normally not of immediate impor-tance to make them operative. Nevertheless, the effects shown by international decisions in marginal areas of their application should not be underestimated. In the long run, a large number of domestic judgments, which take account of, say, a determination of an international territorial question, can have an influence on the operative effect of the inter-national decision.

In addition, any manifestation of an international decision's effect, even if only indirect, will be taken as a sign of its effectiveness and can thus influence its further signi-ficance. At the present precarious stage of organized inter-national cooperation, the realization that decisions of international institutions do, in fact, obtain controlling effect in certain contexts can be significant. Disregard for the activities of international institutions by other deci-sion makers, including domestic courts, will in the end only further a pessimistic attitude concerning their relevance.

C. INTERNATIONAL DECISIONS AS "PRECEDENTS" FOR ANALOGOUS
   LEGAL QUESTIONS

Another type of claim based on international decisions is the invocation of policies formulated in them, coupled with a demand to have them applied to the case before the do-mestic court. In the same manner as with the utilization of

international decisions for the clarification of preliminary
points, the claims and the parties are usually different in
the international decision and in the domestic case. In
addition, there is also no identity of facts before the
national and international decision makers. The common
factor lies only in the similarity of material facts and,
hence, in the policies to be considered.

The reliance on past decisions is a ubiquitous feature in
almost any orderly decision-making process. Whether this is
done overtly or without reference to previous determinations
of like or similar kind, a decision-maker will invariably
find it useful to ascertain what others before him have
thought and decided. Obviously, the thoroughness of such an
examination of past practice will, apart from purely subjective elements, vary greatly with the significance of the
decision to be made and the availability of information.
There can be little doubt that the utilization of past
experience and its meaningful application to new circumstances is a key element of any stability or progress. Drawing
on the experience of previous decisions plays an important
rôle in securing the necessary uniformity and stability of
the law as well as contributing to its flexibility where
past solutions are considered unsatisfactory or new circumstances call for new remedies.

The great importance attributed to judicial proceedings as a
means for conflict settlement coupled with the high degree
of publicity that usually goes with them makes courts of law
particularly susceptible to this pressure for examining the
past. In addition, judicial decisions have the advantage of
normally offering explanations for the policies underlying
the verdict. The orderly exposition of reasons, which is
generally considered an essential element of judicial decision-making, as well as the accessibility of previous decisions are important prerequisites for their examination in
subsequent cases dealing with analogous facts.

This preference for judicial "precedents" also manifests
itself in the treatment of decisions of international institutions by domestic courts. In many cases international
judgments and arbitral awards can offer useful guidance to
domestic courts on questions of international law. This is
not to say that decisions of non-judicial international
organs cannot have any value as "precedents" for domestic
decision-makers.(49) The relatively free availability of
international judgments and awards and the ostensible or
real distinction between legal and other aspects of disputes
maintained in international adjudication, however, has in

most cases prompted parties and courts to look for guidance in the activities of international courts and tribunals.

The reference of domestic courts to international decisions on similar matters, of course, raises the question of whether they should follow the example of common law or of civil law judges in the treatment of past judicial decision. Taken at their face value, the doctrine of binding precedent and the civil law principle of the judge's subjection only to the letter of the code seem to stand in marked contrast. As soon as one leaves the realm of abstract theorizing and descends to the level of everyday practice, the situation, however, quickly assumes quite a different shape. Even a novice in the common law will, after reading a few series of cases on a couple of legal questions, be struck by the high degree of discretion left to the judge by past authority and by the considerable flexibility displayed by him in applying it. It would be an overreaction to this realization to deny the effect of judicial authority altogether and to claim that the true key to a verdict ought to be found primarily in the particular judge's idiosyncrasies. The application of the technique of distinguishing, overruling and interpreting the *ratio decidendi* of a past case, have nearly always allowed judges to draw upon the wisdom of past decisions without being tied to past mistakes or obsolete circumstances.(5o)

This is not to deny that there has been a certain amount of variation in the application of *stare decisis* in different countries and at different times. Thus precedents seem to have been treated with more flexibility in the United States than in England, and it is probably not wrong to say that the doctrine as interpreted by the United States Supreme Court is more designed to achieve a consistency of decision at a particular time than continuous uniformity. There is, however, evidence that the rather rigid attitude towards changes of policy adopted by English courts in the course of the last century(51) is giving way to an approach that is more responsive to change.(52)

The ostensible freedom of the judge in the civil law coun- tries to apply legislation and only legislation unfettered by previous judicial practice, is disproved by a constant pattern of reference and deference to past decisions both of superior tribunals or the same court. The theoretically non- binding character of this practice is often all that remains of the doctrine in the face of almost constant adherence to precedents. Although legal education is largely oriented towards learning, interpreting, and understanding the code, no responsible practitioner will be foolish enough to give

legal advice to a client without first consulting court
practice. Moreover, editions of statutory enactments illustrated by detailed surveys of decisions are an indispensible
tool for every lawyer. Here too, changes in policy do occur,
sometimes working their way up through the judicial hierarchy
rather than being imposed from above.

Upon closer examination, the alleged fundamental difference
in the treatment of past decisions in the common law and
civil law countries, therefore looses much of its plausibility.
Both doctrines in their unmitigated form are victims of the
conception that the correct solution to a legal question can
be logically derived on the one side from previous cases or
on the other from the code. Concepts like "precedent",
"binding", or *res judicata* merely serve as shorthand terms
for a highly complicated process of evaluation. Their uncri-
tical or doctrinaire use is likely to do little more than to
confuse the real issues. The judge's function in this context is not to discover a formal criterion rendering a
previous decision or rule binding on him, but to make
optimum use of past experience with similar problems.
The traditional concepts therefore describe the outcome
rather than the starting-point in this evaluating process.
By examining the rationality of past decisions and then
deciding whether to apply their policies to the cases before
them, the courts under both systems of law have, despite
dogmatic impediments, developed reasonably effective methods
to satisfy both the need for legal stability and for social
change.

Against this background, any debate as to which model should
be more closely followed by domestic courts in the treatment
of international judicial decisions becomes rather meaningless. Neither the concept of international judgments and
awards as binding precedents nor the view of their complete
legal irrelevance would do justice to their real significance in domestic litigation.

In international law with its scarcity of organized procedures for prescription and application, judicial pronouncements are of particular significance for subsequent cases.
In the words of Sir Hersch Lauterpacht:

> It is to be expected that in a society of States in
> which the opportunities for authoritative and impartial
> statements of the law are rare, there should be a
> tendency to regard judicial determination as evidence
> or, what is in fact the same, as a source of inter-
> national law. (53)

In analyzing the relevance of international judicial pronouncements for domestic adjudication, it is futile to try
to make a clear conceptual distinction between their function as a "source of law" and an "evidence of law". The
statement by Sir Hersch Lauterpacht that "...the distinction
between the evidence and the source of many a rule of law is
more specualtive and less rigid than is commonly supposed"
applies with particular pertinence to this area. The once
widely held conception of courts as pure law applying agencies without any function in the prescribing and development
of the law has been largely discarded also in the field of
municipal law. The idea of a mere "discovery" of the law by
the courts was given up and has given way to the recognition
that every application of the law partakes of an element of
its development. The United States Supreme Court has described this interaction of intelligence, applying and prescribing functions of the courts in the following manner:

> International law, or the law that governs between
> States, has at times, like the common law within States,
> a twilight existence during which it is hardly distin-
> guishable from morality or justice, till at length the
> imprimatur of a court attests its jural quality.(55)

(1)   See e.g. <u>Myrtoon Steamship Co. c/ Agent judiciaire du</u>
       <u>Trésor</u>, Cour d'appel de Paris, 1o Apr.1957, 85 Clunet
       1oo3(1958), 24 ILR 2o5(1957); <u>Galakis c/ Trésor public</u>,
       Cour de cassation (Fr.), 2 May 1966 confirming a judg-
       ment of the Cour d'appel de Paris of 21 Feb. 1961, 9o
       Clunet 156(1963), 93 Clunet 648 (1966), 41 ILR 452;
       <u>N.V.Cabolent v. National Iranian Oil Co.</u>, Court of
       Appeal of The Hague, 28 Nov. 1968, 9 ILM 152(197o);
       <u>Ministre de l'Economie et des Finances c/ Sieur Canino</u>
       Conseil.d'Etat (Fr.), 29 Nov.1974, 1o2 Clunet 294(1975).

(2)   <u>Musulman c/ Banque Nationale de Grèce</u>, President of the
       Civil Court of Saloniki, 1937, 65 Clunet 9o8(1938).
       This case concerned the recognition by the forum State
       of the applicant's nationality, which had been deter-
       mined by an international commission.

3)   E.Lauterpacht, Implementation of Decisions of Interna-
       tional Organizations through National Courts, in Schwe-
       bel (Ed.), The Effectiveness of International Decisions
       57(1971); Sagay, The Right of the United Nations to
       bring Actions in Municipal Courts in Order to Claim
       Title to Namibian (South West African) Products Exported
       Abroad, 66 AJIL 6oo(1972).

(4)   Cf. the decision of the German Bundesgerichtshof of 22
       June 1972, BGHZ 59,83, and the note by Bleckmann in 34
       ZaöRV 112(1974).

(5)   See below XI.B.2.

(6)   See below III.B.

(7)   <u>Keeney v. U.S.</u>, Court of Appeals Dist. of Columbia, 26
       Aug. 1954, 218 F. 2d 843, 2o ILR 382(1953).

(8)   See below III.C.3.

(9)   <u>Dame Maury et Pivert c/ Ministère public</u>, Cour d'appel
       de Paris, 18 Nov. 1967, 95 Clunet 728(1968).

(1o)   <u>Hurwits v. State of the Netherlands</u>, District Court of
       The Hague, 12 June 1958, 6 NTIR 195(1959).

(11)   Austrian Constitutional Court, 6 June 1969, Slg.5935.

(12)   See below III.C.2.

(13)   See below VII.E.1.b)

(14) See however isolated cases, in which domestic courts purported to act like courts of appeal or courts of cassation towards international arbitral awards: Republic
of Colombia v. Cauca Co., 190 U.S. 524(1903); National
Iranian Oil Co. v. Sapphire International Petroleums Ltd.,
District Court of Teheran, 1 Dec. 1963, 9 ILM 1118(1970).

(15) See below IV.

(16) PCIJ Ser.A, No.17

(17) On p.33.

(18) See Comptoir Agricole du Pays Bas Normand, Tribunal
administratif Caen, 4 Feb.1969, 16 AFDI 919(197o),
Conseil d'Etat, 5 Nov.1971, 17 AFDI 25(1971). This was
an unsuccessful attempt to oppose an EEC regulation
through an action against the French government. See
also Excursus IV below.

(19) 1934, 7 AD 387(1933-34).

(20) Court of Appeal, 24 March 1964, /1964/2 All E.R. 256,
/1964/ 1 WLR 675, 8 BILC 837, 41 ILR 438, 4o BYIL
372(1964), 93 Clunet 9o5(1966).

(21) Maghanbhai Ishwarbhai Patel and Others v. Union of India,
9 IJIL 234(1969); Lake Ontario Land Development and
Beach Protection Association Inc. v. Federal Power Commission, Court of Appeals, Dist.of Columbia, 29 Jan.1954,
48 AJIL 498(1954); See also below IX.B.1.

(22) Reisman, Nullity and Revision, p.163.

(23) Reisman, Nullity and Revision, p.634.

(24) Flick v. Johnson, Court of Appeals, D.C., 11 May 1949,
174 F. 2d 983, 44 AJIL 187(195o), 73-76 Clunet 145
(1946-49); Hirota v. MacArthur, Supreme Court, 2o
Dec.1948, 338 U.S.197, 15 AD 485(1948); See also the
list of cases in 15 AD 49o(1948); See however Eisentra-
ger et al. v. Forrestal, Court of Appeals, D.C.,
15 Apr.1949, 174 F.2d 961, 44 AJIL 185(195o) reversed
by the Supreme Court on 5 June 195o, 339 U.S. 763, 44
AJIL 773(195o).

(25) 6 Nov.1956, BVerfGE 6,15, 12 JZ 55(1957), 52 AJIL
354(1958).

(26) E.g.: Dame Klarsfeld c/ Office franco-allemand pour
     la jeunesse, Cour de Paris, 18 June 1968, 15 AFDI
     865(1969).

(27) E.g.: Sieur Weiss, Conseil d'Etat (Fr.), 2o Feb.1953,
     81 Clunet 745(1954).

(28) J.C.Meira Coelho c. Asociacion latinoamericana de libre
     comercio, 29 Dec.1965, 94 Clunet 972(1967).

(29) Cosmetto, 19 Jan.1927, Rec. p.54 quoted from Ruzié, Le
     juge français, p.1o4.

(3o) Syndicat indépendant des fonctionnaires du condominium
     des Nouvelles Hébrides, 2 Dec.197o, 75 RGDIP 56o(1971).
     Cf. also two decisions of the French Conseil constitu-
     tionnel of 3o Dec.1976 and of 5 Dec.1978 refusing to
     review decisions of the European communities: 1o4
     Clunet 66(1977) and 1o6 Clunet 79(1979).

(31) Baladi, 8 Jan.1959, Rec.17. Cf. also Netherlands and
     German decisions refusing to subject route charges by
     Eurocontrol to review: Trans-Mediterranean Airways v.
     Eurocontrol, Administrative decision of the Crown, 16
     Jan1974, 8 NYIL 258(1977); Bundesverwaltungsgericht,
     16 Sept.1977, NJW 1759(1978).

(32) Sté Dumont et Besson et Sté Dumez c/ Association de la
     Muette et autres, Cour de cassation, 22 July 1968, 15
     AFDI 864(1969). Cf. also Procureur Général of the Court
     of Cassation v. Syndicate of Co-Owners of the Alfred
     Dehodencq Property Company, Cour de cassation, 6 July
     1954, 21 ILR 279(1954).

(33) Kare-Merat et Kabozo c. Etat belge, min.de la Justice
     et délégué du Haut Commissariat pour les réfugiés, 25
     Sept.197o, 8 RBDI 675,687(1972). Cf. also Trans-
     Mediterranean Airways v. Eurocontrol, administrative
     decision of the Crown, 16 Jan.1974, 8 NYIL 258(1977).

(34) The Brig "General Armstrong", Court of Claims, 17 March
     1856 and 1 Feb.1858, Moore, International Arbitration
     Digest Vol.II, p.11o2; Z&F Assets Realization Corpora-
     tion et al. v. Hull et al., Supreme Court, 6 Jan.1941,
     311 U.S. 47o; Diggs v. Dent, Dist.Ct.D.C., 13 May 1975,
     14 ILM 797(1975), affirmed sub nom. Diggs v.Richardson,
     Court of Appeals D.C., 17 Dec.1976, 555 F.2d 848;
     Kangai v. Vance, Court of Appeals D.C., 6 Oct.1978, 73
     AJIL 297(1979).

(35) Sté Bouvraie-Anjou c/ Office des biens et intérêts privés, Cour d'appel d'Angers, 17 May 1938, 66 Clunet 64o(1939); Conseil d'Etat, 26 Oct.1938, Rec.795, Kiss Vol.5, No.75.

(36) Re Reitlinger, Conseil d'Etat, 1o March 1933, Sirey 1933, III, 93, 7 AD 489(1933-34).

(37) Y. v. Public Prosecutor, District Court of Breda, 11 Feb. and 2O March 1957, 7 NTIR 282(1960); Attorney-General of Israel v. El-Turani, District Court of Haifa, 21 Aug.1951, confirmed by the Supreme Court of Israel on 31 Dec.1952, 18 ILR 164(1951), see also below XI.A.

(38) In re Krüger, Netherlands Council for the Restoration of Legal Rights (Judicial Division), 13 Sept.1951, 18 ILR 258(1951).

(39) Willis v. First Real Estate and Investment Co. et al., U.S.Cir.Ct. of App. 5th Cir., 24 Jan.1934, 68 F.2d 671, 11 AD 94(1919-42), see also below XI.B; Re Bartholomeus T., District Court of Cracow, 21 Dec.197o, 1o1 Clunet 359 (1974), 52 ILR 28(1979).

(4o) U.S. v. Vargas, 29 Jan.1974. US Dist.Ct.D.Puerto Rico, 37o F.Supp.9o8. In this case, which concerned a prosecution under the Selective Service Act, the court had to determine whether Puerto Rico was an "occupied territory" for the purposes of the Geneva Convention relative to the protection of civilian persons in time of war. In doing so it relied on several resolutions of the U.N. General Assembly.

(41) 24 Oct.1953, 2o ILR 166(1953), 82 Clunet 451(1955); See also Rex v. Martin before the Norwegian Supreme Court, 12 Feb.1953, 2o ILR 167(1953). In this case an appeal alleging the illegality of Norway's fisheries limits under international law was withdrawn as soon as the ICJ had given its judgment in favor of Norway.

(42) ICJ Reports 1952, p.176.

(43) Ministère public c/ Mohamed Ben Djilalli Ben Abdelkader, "Teignor", Tribunal criminel de Casablanca, 6 Nov.1952, 8o Clunet 666(1953); Administration des Habous c/ Deal, Cour d'appel de Rabat, 12 Nov.1952, 19 ILR 342(1952), 42 RCDIP 154(1953); see also the judgment of the French Cour de cassation in Re Bendayan, 4 March 1954, 49 AJIL 267(1955).

(44) Anglo-Iranian Oil Co. v. S.U.P.O.R., Civil Court of
     Rome, 13 Sept.1954, 22 ILR 23(1955); Anglo-Iranian Oil
     Co. v. Idemitsu Kosan Kabushiki Kaisha, District Court
     of Tokyo, 27 May 1953, 2o ILR 3o5,3o9(1953), 1 JapAIL
     55(1957).

(45) In re Investigation of World Arrangements with Relation
     to ... Petroleum, US Dist.Ct.D.C., 15 Dec.1952, 19 ILR
     197,2oo(1952).

(46) U.S.S.R. v. Luxembourg and Saar Company, 2 March 1935,
     32 RCDIP 489(1937), 8 AD 114(1935-37).

(47) Eichmann, District Court of Jerusalem, 12 Dec.1961, 36
     ILR 5,57seq.

(48) In re Krupp and Others, 3o June 1948, 15 AD 62o(1948).
     See also In re Dame Pêcheral, Cour de Paris, 17 July
     1948, 15 AD 289(1948). In this case the authentication
     of personal data by the IRO was accepted as authorita-
     tive.

(49) Cf. Schachter, The Quasi-Judicial Rôle of the Security
     Council and the General Assembly, 58 AJIL 96o,964(1964).

(5o) For a penetrating analysis of these 'precedent techni-
     ques' see esp. Llewellyn, The Common Law Tradition,
     Deciding Appeals, p.77seq.(196o). See also Allen, Law
     in the Making, p.275seq.(1958).

(51) In Beamish v. Beamish (1861), 9 H.L.C. 274 and in
     London Street Tramways v. London County Council /1898/
     A.C. 375 the House of Lords laid down a policy of
     strict adherence to its own previous decisions. See
     also Allen, Law in the Making, p.228.

(52) In a 'Practice Statement' of 1966 the House of Lords
     made it known that it would henceforth "depart from a
     previous decision when it appears rights to do so."

(53) The Development of International Law by the Interna-
     tional Court, p.14(1958).

(54) Op.cit., p.21.

(55) New Jersey v. Delaware (1933), 291 U.S.383; See also the
     dissenting opinion of Judge Alvarez in ICJ Reports 1951,
     p.5o.

III. THE AUTHORITY OF INTERNATIONAL DECISIONS

A principal question for the domestic court before which an
international decision is invoked is its international legal
relevance or authority. Authority is the expression of
community expectations with respect to decision-makers,
decision-procedures, and the material contents of decisions.
Unlike the traditional term "binding force", the notion of
authority, as used here, is not to be understood as an
absolute concept in the sense of a strict dichotomy between
binding rules and no law. A flexible framework which investi-
gates and evaluates all factors contributing to community
expectations concerning decisions is more in accord with the
realities of contemporary international law.

International institutions are endowed with jurisdiction or
decision-making functions for certain areas of inclusive
concern. The authority of decisions made in the exercise of
these functions is determined primarily by the treaty establishing the international institution, subsequent practice,
and a number of additional factors. The assignment of decision-making functions to international institutions as such,
does not indicate the extent of their authority. Thus the
fact that an international organ has jurisdiction to deal
with certain questions does not necessarily mean that its
decisions are mandatory for other participants and deprive
them of any latitude in choosing their conduct. Limitations
of authority are a characteristic feature of the decision-
making functions of international institutions. The functions
assigned to international organs are typically a careful
compromise between the necessity for more efficient international cooperation and the endeavor to retain some measure
of exclusive jurisdiction. The result of this compromise is
often a complex arrangement delimiting inclusive and exclusive competences. The typical difficulties in interpreting
treaty provisions expressing compromise solutions are a
common feature also with the prescriptions regulating the
constitutive setup of international institutions. This often
leads to considerable uncertainty concerning the degree of
authority that their decisions were meant to enjoy. This is
not to deny that there are also areas of general agreement
on a very large extent of authority for certain decisions to
which other decision-makers are expected to give unequivocal
deference. Decision-making functions of international institutions which fit the traditional concept of law-making
through binding rules or decisions, however, are the exception rather than the rule.

A domestic court, therefore, cannot simply restrict itself
to ascertaining whether the international organ, whose
decision is invoked, is authorized to enact mandatory rules
or to make binding decisions, in order to disregard the
international decision in the case of a negative finding.
Decisions of international institutions can have a wide
variety of legal effects for domestic litigation. An investigation into these effects is made even more difficult by the
fact that the international decisions normally only represent
part of the authoritative material before the domestic
courts determining the outcome of the particular litigation.

From the viewpoint of decision-techniques, that is, the
presentation of grounds for particular verdicts, the examination of the international decision's authority is one of
several available strategies to refuse deference to it and
to reject the claim based upon it. Pronouncements of international institutions enjoying only a low degree of authority
for the questions to be decided by the domestic court are
easily discarded. Further arguments to support the disregard
shown for the international decision, like lack of incorporation into the law of the forum, the absence of a connecting
point to the parties, or the immunity of the defendant, are
then dispensible.

International institutions exercise their functions in a
large variety of forms and procedures. This diversity of
activities makes a systematic investigation somewhat difficult. It is therefore hardly surprising that scholarly
writings on the subject show almost as many different attempts
to categorize them as there are authors.(1)

A classification of international decisions that will seem
obvious to a constitutional lawyer would follow the separation of powers underlying most modern constitutions. We need
not here discuss the question to what extent the tripartite
concept of State activities that distinguishes legislative,
executive, and judicial functions, corresponds to the complex realities of contemporary nation States. A transfer of
this classification of State functions to international
institutions, however, would certainly be highly misleading.(2)

This is not to deny that a cursory glance at the activities
of international institutions reveals certain superficial
similarities of behavior between international organs and
certain State organs. The activities of international courts
and tribunals, especially when passing their judgments or
awards, bear a strong resemblance to the functions of domestic courts. Unlike domestic courts, however, they do not

provide a comprehensive system for the protection and implementation of claims, which is open to all or nearly all
participants in the social process. The intervention of
international courts and tribunals is usually conditional on
a multitude of factors, especially the consent of all parties
concerned. Only in exceptional cases do they exercise functions of review over the activities of other organs.

The work of the General Assembly of the United Nations and
of similar international organs is characterized by procedures strongly reminiscent of the activities of legislative
bodies of States.(3) Nevertheless, there is general agreement that their pronouncements do not carry the same effects.
There can be no question of "international legislation" in
the traditional sense through their activities. Some specialized or regional organizations enjoy functions of prescription, which could be described as legislative. Nevertheless,
these functions are so limited and rudimentary, that they
can hardly be compared with the comprehensive powers of
national parliaments.(4) The prescribing function in international law is still largely characterized by an unorganized
process of communication on the basis of reciprocities and
retaliations. Organized procedures of prescription still
only represent a small portion of this process, although its
significance is increasing.

The work done in secretariats of international organizations
has certain ostensible similarities to that of State execu-
tives or administrations. But these activities are usually
fundamentally different from the complex and comprehensive
system of public administration exercised by modern States.
Even where competences comparable to individual functions of
State administration have been conferred upon international
institutions, their extent and controlling effect is conspicuously different.(5)

As pointed out before, the classification of organized
international decisions adopted in this study for the purpose of examining the behavior of domestic courts is not
modelled on structural but on functional considerations.
This means that certain types of organs are not necessarily
linked to specific functions in the decision-making process.
Obviously, the task assigned to particular organs of international institutions creates certain points of emphasis in
the decision-functions exercised by them. Courts and tribunals are primarily specialized in application, although
intelligence, promotion, prescription, invocation, and
termination may also play a rôle. The General Assembly's
emphasis is on promotion, nevertheless, it also participates

in other decision-functions. The Council of Ministers of the
European Communities has wide functions of prescription but
also exercises promotion, application, and other functions.

In addition to decision-functions, the different types of
claims, as outlined in the preceding chapter, also have to
be kept in mind. A decision never has authority as such, but
only in relation to claims concerning the conduct of participants in the social process. The purpose for which an
international decision is invoked, is therefore of decisive
relevance in determining its authority for the particular
case before the domestic court. A distinction of decision-
functions in terms of outcomes (intelligence, promotion,
prescription, invocation, application, and termination) is
important, but gives no necessary indication of effects in
relation to subsequent claims based on decisions. Not infrequently the real phases of the decision-making process
partake of several of these functions simultaneously. Thus,
any application in a particular case can create community
expectations for the future and, thus, be an element in the
process of prescription.(6) For the purpose of this study
this means that we always have to ask ourselves for what
purpose the authority of a decision is invoked. In other
words: What course of action is demanded of domestic courts,
and in what way is this demand linked to the international
decision? The question of authority can take completely
different shapes depending on whether a particular decision
is invoked for the purpose of its implementation or review,
for the purpose of resolving a preliminary point, or for the
purpose of providing a "precedent".

The types of claims based on particular international decisions are, nevertheless, to a large extent conditioned by
the nature of these decisions. The gathering of information
(intelligence) by international organs invariably serves to
answer preliminary questions in domestic litigation. Reliance on recommendations of international institutions before
domestic courts is usually directed at their implementation.
This is also the case with prescriptions. Reference to
invocation before international organs is rare in domestic
proceedings. Where it occurs it is usually concerned with
preliminary points. The applying function of international
organs can give rise to all three types of claims considered
here: The implementation or revision of operative decisions
of international organs can be sought with the help of
domestic courts. They are used for the clarification of
preliminary questions or are put forward as "precedents" to
guide the court in the solution of similar legal problems.

A. INTELLIGENCE

The gathering of factual information is an ubiquitous feature
in the activities of international institutions. It is
undertaken as a necessary prerequisite for the exercise of
all other decision functions. In some circumstances fact-
finding itself can also be the primary purpose of intelligence operations.

The practice of courts shows relatively few examples of a
reliance on intelligence activities of international organs.
In many situations this is, at least partly, due to the
lack of renown of this activity and to the unfamiliarity of
domestic judges with the pertinent documents. Nevertheless,
even the limited case material available shows a considerable
variety of international decisions relied upon by domestic
courts in the context of the intelligence function.

An example in which an establishment of facts by an international tribunal was considered conclusive by a domestic
court has already been given above.(7) It concerned the
finding of the International Military Court in Nuremberg
that the defendants had not participated in crimes against
peace. More informal decisions of international organs
containing relevant information for domestic courts concerned
the authentication of personal data by the delegate of the
United Nations High Commissioner for Refugees(8) or the
confirmation of the refugee status of parties in domestic
proceedings.(9)

The work of expert bodies in international organizations,
like the International Law Commission, can sometimes yield
valuable information. Although these documents enjoy no
formal authority and are only preparatory to conventions or
formal decisions by other organs, domestic courts occasionally rely upon them. Already, material assembled within the
League of Nations on questions like piracy(1o) or State
immunity(11) was utilized by domestic courts. Since the
International Law Commission has taken up its activities,
courts have repeatedly also made use of its work on such
questions as State immunity,(12) diplomatic relations,(13)
the law of the sea,(14) and the law of treaties.(15)

In some cases the information provided by international
institutions is in response to specific enquiries by the
domestic courts concerned. It can deal with the question of
the status of a dependant of a United Nations employee in
immigration disputes,(16) or the status of persons otherwise
associated to international organizations for the purposes
of determining questions of immunity.(17)

Not surprisingly, domestic courts have not displayed any
hesitation in acting upon the information received from the
international institutions. The directions offered by the
international institutions in question were not perceived as
decisions in a formal sense but simply as an item of factual
evidence. The question of their authority was never discussed.

B. RECOMMENDATION

The formulation of general standards of international conduct in the form of recommendations is a common feature of
the work of contemporary international organizations. The
conflicting interests in cooperation and in freedom of
action have led to a compromise in which the limited authority of the prescriptions involved is designed to encourage
maximum participation in their adoption and implementation.

The range of subject-matters for recommendations of international organs is extremely wide. It is therefore not
surprising that parties to domestic litigation have in a
considerable number of cases tried to rely on them. Nevertheless, a survey of the available case-material shows that
certain recommendations are much more frequently invoked
before domestic courts than others. Especially the Universal
Declaration of Human Rights adopted by the General Assembly
of the United Nations on 1o December 1948 is very popular
in domestic proceedings.(18) This is probably due to several
factors. The rights covered by the Universal Declaration are
the subject-matter of frequent decisions by domestic courts.
Consequently, there are ample occasions to rely on it. In
addition, few international documents have obtained a comparable degree of fame and popularity. Even persons with
little or no knowledge of international law are aware of its
existence and have often considered it beneficial to rely on
it, in spite of the existence of other guarantees of human
rights in treaties and constitutions.

Im most cases of a reliance on the Universal Declaration of
Human Rights and on other international recommendations
before domestic courts, their invocation is only auxiliary
or subsidiary, that is, to support claims which are primarily based on other prescriptions. Consequently, recommendations only rarely represent the primary motive supporting
a court's decision. In most cases courts only refer to them
in passing or hand in hand with other policies to be applied.
It is then extremely difficult to ascertain if and to what
extent the recommendation was instrumental to the particular
judgment. Nevertheless, even these short references can give
certain clues as to the authority attributed to recommenda-

tions. In some cases the courts even specifically enter into the question of the legal consequences of recommendations.

The legal status of recommendations emanating from organs such as the United Nations General Assembly has also been the subject of much scholarly discussion. Viewpoints have varied not only according to the theoretical standpoint of the observer, but also according to the sympathy for the contents of a particular recommendation or the political inclinations of the majority controlling the organ.

1. Are Recommendations Legally Irrelevant ?

First it is appropriate to warn against a superficial lite- ral interpretation of the term "recommendation". It would be misleading necessarily to understand it as non-binding or even legally irrelevant. There are provisions in which the term "recommendation" is clearly used to denote an obligation of compliance,(19) to indicate an obligation to take certain actions,(2o) to describe situations in which non-compliance can draw certain adverse consequences,(21) or to represent cases in which the recommendation constitutes an authorization to act only within the confines of its clauses.(22) There is no obvious or necessary meaning attached to its use.

Nevertheless, there is general consensus that, in the absence of evidence to the contrary, a recommendation does not carry the same legal consequences as a treaty. It does not normally contain "binding rules".(23) For some authors this recog- nition is the crux of the matter;(24) a legal relevance short of binding rules is either not contemplated or categori- cally rejected.

The practice of domestic courts shows a comparatively small but by no means negligible group of cases in which the lack of a binding force has led to the conclusion that the recom- mendation was of no relevance to the domestic court's deci- sion. Thus, the courts simply either stated that the Univer- sal Declaration of Human Rights was not part of positive law(25) or refused applications based on the Universal Declaration to have convictions reviewed.(26) In other cases, they rejected attempts to oppose retroactive penal law relying on Article 11/2 of the Universal Declaration(27) or refused to interpet treaty provisions in conformity with recommending resolutions.(28) The Supreme Court of Ireland was particularly clear on this point in a case concerning extradition proceedings,(29) in which the accused had relied on his right to asylum as laid down in Article 14 of the Human Rights Declaration:

> This Declaration does not ...purport to be a statement
> of the existing law of nations. Far from it. The Decla-
> ration itself states that it proclaims a 'common stan-
> dard of achievement...'. The Declaration therefore,
> though of great importance and significance in many
> ways, is not a guide to discover the existing principles
> of international law.(3o)

It is, however, not without interest that even in cases in
which any "binding force" of the Universal Declaration of
Human Rights was specifically denied, the courts, nevertheless, attempted to show that the terms of their judgments
were in accordance with its provisions.(31) Egon Schwelb has
aptly commented on an Italian decision,(32) in which Article
15 of the Universal Declaration of Human Rights was not
relied upon as a legal norm but as a "direttiva di massimo
di alto valore morale":

> The theoretical difference between a rule of law and a
> rule of morality becomes of little practical importance
> when the court accepts the latter as a guide for its
> decision.(33)

A look at international practice reveals a constant reliance
on the recommendations-type of decision of international
organizations.(34) States, international decision-makers,(35)
including the adopting organs themselves,(36) frequently
rely upon them and apply them to specific situations. Furthermore, there is an evident reluctance openly to contravene
recommendations such as resolutions of the United Nations
General Assembly.(37) Whenever possible, States confronted
with recommendations will not attempt to rely on an assertion
of their legal irrelevance, but will either deny violations,
assert the inapplicability of a recommendation to the specific case, or claim that the particular recommendation was
irregular or *ultra vires*. Comparison with other types of
international law sometimes suggests that the effectiveness
of some recommendations does not fall short of certain
treaty provisions or customary rules.

Practice thus supports the view that recommendations, though
not binding in the sense of a municipal statute, exercise a
considerable influence on the international decision-making
process. Their dismissal as extra-legal phenomena is therefore probably just the result of a too limited conception of
the law, which does not offer appropriate categories for
this type of international prescription. Recommendations are
difficult to reconcile with the typology of the law that we
know from contemporary municipal legal systems, but the
fundamentally different structure of the present international

community makes such an analogy with municipal law of doubtful validity. In a horizontal system characterized by reciprocities and retaliations, such as, contemporary international law, the authoritative enactment of generally binding rules is only of minor importance. The emphasis of the decision-making process is on the joint development of common standards of conduct by the members of the community themselves. From this perspective, a recommendation worked out within the organized framework of an international institution appears to be a particularly apt device with which to influence international behavior.

Apart from the actual exercise of a certain degree of control by recommendations of international institutions, the constitutive setup of the adopting organs lends additional support to an argument in favor of their authority. These organs are specifically authorized by their constitutive instruments to issue recommendations. The solemn bestowal of formal authority to make recommendations is a strong indication that these decisions are not devoid of legal significance. It seems hardly convincing to regard decisions of institutions, specifically entrusted by the international community with the task of drawing up formal statements of international tenets of behavior, in the same manner as "recommendations" of a group of persons without any formal jurisdiction.

Most of the more recent writings on this question(38) support the view that the discovery of the non-binding nature of recommendations is a truism which misses the core of the problem. On the other hand, the explanations offered for their legal significance differ widely. Not infrequently a choice of solutions is offered, sometimes distinguishing between different types of recommendations.(39)

The radical alternative to a dismissal of recommendations would be their acceptance as mandatory prescriptions based on legislative powers of the respective international organs. This view is rarely put forward in international practice and scholarly writings.(4o) Even that part of court practice which shows a positive attitude towards international recommendations does not contain any examples of courts subscribing to this extreme attitude.

2. Recommendations and Art.38 of the ICJ-Statute

In assessing the legal significance of recommendations, many authors display a strong tendency to try to explain this relatively new phenomenon in terms of the established sources of international law as laid down in Article 38/1 of the

Statute of the International Court of Justice. For the
opponents of their legal relevance the absence of recommendations from the list of sources contained in Article 38
serves as an additional argument.(41) The supporters of
their legal significance rely on Article 38 in the opposite
sense. Almost every heading of Article 38/1 is offered as an
explanation for the legal character of recommendations.

a) Recommendations as Part of Treaty Law

One view sees recommendations as a modern supplement to the
law of treaties.(42) Especially in the case of unanimous
resolutions, the concurrent casting of votes is sometimes
seen as a new and simplified procedure for the conclusion of
agreements.(43) Understandably enough, this construction is
usually accepted only subject to the condition that there
are unmistakable indications that the States concerned
intended to enter into obligations in the nature of treaties.
(44) Although there are some odd examples which might support
this view,(45) they are limited to a few cases and can by no
means offer a satisfactory general explanation for the legal
nature of recommendations. The few cases in which courts
treated recommending resolutions of international organizations like treaties(46) are probably due to thoughtlessness
or ignorance rather than to profound reflections concerning
their legal nature.

A somewhat different opinion of the rôle of recommendations
in the law of treaties sees them as authoritative interpretations or guidelines for the interpretation of existing
treaties. In particular, resolutions of the United Nations
General Assembly are regarded as nothing more than specifi-
cations of the provisions of the Charter.(47) Thus the
Universal Declaration of Human Rights has repeatedly been
conceived as a detailed statement of the obligation to
respect human rights as already contained in the Charter.(48)
Domestic courts have, in fact, repeatedly relied on the
Universal Declaration of Human Rights to interpret treaties,
though not in connection with the United Nations Charter.
The European Convention on Human Rights(49) and other treaties
based on the Universal Declaration,(5o) as well as an extradition treaty,(51) were interpreted by reference to the
provisions of the Human Rights Declaration.

The value of recommendatory resolutions of international
institutions for the interpretation of treaties is indisputable. Nevertheless, this theory also does not offer an
adequate general explanation of their legal nature. Not all
recommendations can reasonably be regarded as deriving their

material contents from treaty provisions. Even in those
cases where they could be taken as just a detailed exposition
of the obligations assumed by the Members in the constitutive
agreement of the organization, it is difficult to see why
they should fundamentally differ in their authority from
other recommendations which also lie within the functions of
the organization.

b) Recommendations as Part of Custom

The most widely accepted theory about the legal nature of
recommendations sees them within the framework of international customary law. A casting of votes by State representatives is regarded either as a form of the practice of Sta-
tes(52) or as an expression of an *opinio iuris*.(53) The
evolution of a general practice of States which used to be
unorganized and often spread over a long period of time is
thus coordinated and channeled into certain directions.
Sometimes the result can be the sudden emergence of a new
customary rule, an "instant custom".(54)

It is, however, usually admitted that the subsequent conduct
of the States concerned is also of material importance. Not
infrequently, the aspirations nursed in the hot-house atmos-
phere(55) of an organ, like the United Nations General
Assembly, do not withstand the rough climate of international
everyday life. For this reason, a recommendation is often
seen only as a step towards the formation of customary law
or as a starting-point for such an evolution.(56)

A strong emphasis on the subsequent State practice to a
recommendation, however, runs the danger of seriously under-
rating its significance. Under this conception it is not the
recommendation which serves as a standard for the conduct of
States, but the conduct which serves as the standard for the
evaluation of the recommendation. This applies particularly
to areas like the rights of individuals, minorities, or
ethnic groups which are usually not the object of traditional international intercourse and are therefore not subject
to the process of reciprocities and retaliations between
States. In assessing the situation at law, a heavy reliance
on examples of practice deviating from the principles of a
recommendation would largely deprive it of its value.

References to recurrent violations of human rights in various parts of the world can hardly serve as proof that
States are entitled to disregard recommendations of international organizations on human rights questions. An attempt
to quantify the State practice in favor or against the

material provisions of, for example, the Universal Declaration
of Human Rights is hardly possible and would not make much
sense.

The practice of domestic courts only rarely permits the
reliable conclusion that recommendations of international
organs were applied as part of customary international law.
A Belgian Military Court(57) referred to it in the following
terms:

> In searching for principles of international law arising
> out of the usages established by civilized nations, the
> laws of humanity, and the requirement of the public
> conscience, the Military Court is today guided by the
> Universal Declaration of Human Rights, adopted without
> opposition by the General Assembly of the United Nations
> on 1o December 1948.

A number of Italian judgments in which provisions of the
Human Rights Declaration were recognized as "norme del
diritto internazionale generalmente riconosciute", in the
sense of Article 1o of the Italian constitution,(58) could
possibly serve as evidence that recommendations were regarded as part of customary law. However, these cases, too, do
not contain any indication that the courts were motivated by
any profound reflections on the nature of the sources of
international law.

The seemingly plausible view of recommendations of international organs as an element in the creation of customary
rules, in particular as part of State practice, is therefore
not without doubts and difficulties. To regard the international organ as nothing more than a trading center for the
statements and votes of individual States would not do
justice to its express authority to pass resolutions in its
capacity as an international body. The international organ
would thus be seen purely as a permanent conference of
States; its resolutions would be nothing more than the
aggregate of the communications of States represented in it.

This question becomes particularly acute in cases where the
persons acting in the organ are not State representatives in
the traditional sense. The General Conference of the International Labor Organization and the Parliamentary Assembly of
the Council of Europe are pertinent examples. To regard the
voting behavior of representatives of employers and of
workpeople in the Labor Conference and of parliamentarians
in the Consultative Assembly as State practice is unorthodox,
to say the least, and would give a somewhat novel interpretation to this concept.

Even the acceptance of recommendations within the framework
of customary law, not as State practice but as practice of
the organization itself, is not wholly satisfactory. There
can be no doubt that every international organization deve-
lops its practice in making decisions on problems that arise
from day to day. To equate formal recommendations or solemn
declarations of a general character concerning the future
conduct of members of the international community with this
everyday practice is hardly convincing.

c) Recommendations as Expression of General Principles of Law

Another explanation for the place of recommendations in
international law is their classification with the "general
principles of law recognized by civilized nations."(59) They
are thus considered as a convenient expression of the legal
ideas and concepts common to the States represented in the
respective international organs.

This view is sometimes reflected in decisions of domestic
courts utilizing formulas describing the provisions of the
Human Rights Declaration as "the heritage of all enlightened
peoples",(60) as "indicative of the spirit of our times",(61)
as "eternal law of nature",(62) or as "rights of the individual intrinsic to any legal order."(63)

The persuasive force of an acceptance of recommendations as
an expression of general principles of law will largely
depend on the observer's view about this enigmatic concept.
The subject-matter of most recommendations makes it difficult
to regard them as statements of corresponding principles of
domestic law. This would leave the possibility of accepting
them as pronouncements of universal legal principles or of
general principles of international law. A survey of recommendations passed by international organs, however, creates
the impression that a large number of their material provisions are of a rather specific character, which makes their
characterization as general principles unconvincing.

d) Recommendations as Means for the Determination of Rules
    of Law

Finally, another commonly held theory sees recommendations,
or at least part of them, as declaratory statements of
existing law or as evidence of international law.(64) The
authentication of certain prescriptions by representatives
of a large number of States is, on this view, to be accepted
as a common authoritative confirmation of the existence and
contents of rules of international law.

Thus the Supreme Court of Israel found in the <u>Eichmann</u> case
that the United Nations General Assembly Resolutions affirming
the Nuremberg principles and the resolution affirming that
genocide is a crime under international law were proof that
these principles had formed part of the customary law of
nations "since time immemorial".(65)

It is beyond doubt that part of the resolutions of, for
example, the General Assembly of the United Nations are
declaratory in nature and are based on already existing law.
However, it seems questionable whether this fact is really
of much help in determining their legal character. Any
attempt to draw a sharp line between an official statement
of the law and the creation of new law is of doubtful value.
Every authoritative determination or application of the law
partakes of a certain degree of its development. Even if it
were possible to make a clean theoretical distinction between application and formation of the law, we would be left
with the problem of discovering whether a particular recommendation restricted itself to a statement of the *lex
lata* or attempted to formulate new policies. The necessity
of such an investigation would largely offset the cognitive
value of the recommendation itself.

Sometimes resolutions contain specific indications that they
are based on existing law. They themselves assert to be only
declaratory and might therefore readily be applied as positive law.(66) Nevertheless, it seems doubtful whether even
such a self-professed restriction to existing law can always
be relied upon. Only part of the resolutions purporting to
contain statements on legal questions are drafted by expert
bodies like the International Law Commission. In some cases
the expert knowledge of the drafters of such "authoritative
restatements" is, to say the least, subject to doubt. Spontaneous announcements of political organs are not necessarily
a good guide to discovering the state of the law. There is,
moreover, a distinct danger that, in preparing an allegedly
declaratory resolution, Members will be strongly influenced
by their political preferences.(67) If so-called declaratory
resolutions really become accepted as an authoritative
expression of existing international law, there will be a
strong temptation to establish legislative desiderata by way
of declarations. A majority strongly committed to a particular
policy in a legal controversy would find it only too easy to
improve its position decisively by declaring its opinion as
a statement of the existing law.

All these various attempts to classify recommendations of
international institutions in terms of the traditional sources

of international law are somewhat artificial. They are meant
to explain why and how these non-binding decisions ultimately
obtain some legal significance after all. The different
theories either use general models or distinguish between
different types of recommendations in order to prove that
they are elements in the creation of rules of law. Although
these theories may give some satisfaction from a purely
analytical viewpoint, they are of little or no help to
decision-makers having to deal with these resolutions. A
normative outlook perceiving the law as a static system of
rules can see these resolutions as constitutive elements of
rules only, but it cannot offer an explanation as to how
recommendations influence decisions or should influence
decisions. All the parts of the decision-making process
falling short of the emergence of a clear-cut rule cannot be
described in this way. The recommendation is identified as
an element of the legal edifice, but no description is
offered of the process leading to its construction.

Apart from the theoretical difficulties engendered by these
attempts to fit recommendations into the accepted compartments
of legal sources, these explanations are also of doubtful
practical value. A decision-maker such as a court can find
little help in the proposition that a recommendation, invoked
by a party, may possibly and under certain circumstances
play a rôle in the formation of a legal rule or may be
declaratory of an existing rule. The detailed examination
required to establish whether the provisions of the recommendation are really supported by a general practice accepted
as law or are really an expression of already existing rules
of law would deprive the recommendation of its practical
significance for a particular decision.

In the vast majority of cases domestic courts do not enter
into any fundamental discussion concerning legal sources
when dealing with recommendations of international institutions. In most cases the problem of sources is not even
mentioned. The courts merely indicate that in making decisions
they are guided or at least influenced by the Universal
Declaration of Human Rights(68) or other resolutions.(69)

3. The Authority of Recommendations

An approach not excusively directed at the discovery of rules,
but at a critical exmination of the decision-making process and
all factors legitimately affecting it will lead to the
realization that recommendations of international organizations can exercise an important influence on this process.
Richard Falk(7o) has persuasively argued that the function

of certain tenets of behavior as law is by no means restricted to binding rules. In a community whose law-creating process is not dominated by a central legislator but by the co-
equal interaction of its members, the expectations of authority attached to policies can be of differing intensity. Neither the insistence on an explicit consent by every participant to every new prescription nor the call for legislation
through an omnipotent central legislator is in accordance
with the requirements and realities of the contemporary international social process. Organized procedures for the
elaboration of standards of conduct with limited authority
are important factors in the international decision-making
process.

Recommendations of international organs, as a new form of
communicating desired policies by the international community,
are often the most effective method to create legal expectations where the establishment of obligations in the traditional sense appears unrealistic. Conduct which is in accordance
with recommendations need not be carried by a sense of unqualified obligation or "binding force" but may be prompted
by other considerations, such as, an interest in stable relations with other members of the international community, a
sense of rectitude, or the desire to gain respect. An individual member is left a large amount of discretion, and a
contravention is not automatically an "illegal act". A consistent disregard of the standards set by the international
community in the form of recommendations may, however, ultimately expose a State to legitimate counter-measures. As
Judge Lauterpacht has pointed out:
> /It/ may find that it has overstepped the imperceptible
> line between propriety and illegality, between discre-
> tion and arbitrariness, between the exercise of the
> legal right to disregard the recommendation and the
> abuse of that right, and that it has exposed itself to
> consequences legitimately following as a legal sanc-
> tion. (71)

In examining the legal significance of recommendations, it
is appropriate to make careful distinctions concerning their
authority and the legal consequences flowing from them. Not
every formally adopted resolution has the same significance.
Its value as a basis for decision depends on a number of
circumstances, all influencing the extent of its authority. (72)

Part of these circumstances are the objectives of its spon-
sors and the sentiments underlying its adoption, which can
often be ascertained from preparatory work, the wording of
the text, especially the preamble, and attendant statements.

In this context, attention should be directed not so much at
the intentions of individual Members but at the discovery of
a broad consensus. The motives of individual delegations
supporting a recommendation may be more influenced by special
interests than by its spirit and are hence of secondary
importance. In international relations conduct having certain
effects is by no means always carried by the intention to
attain that effect. This is well exemplified by processes
leading to customary law.

The frequency of re-citations and of reliance on a recommendation in later decisions of the adopting organ may offer
additional clues to the significance attributed to it by the
organ beyond the moment of its adoption.(73)

The degree of consensus underlying a recommendation cannot
be ascertained by a simple counting of votes, although a
unanimous or near-unanimous vote will certainly endow a
resolution with considerable added authority. The support by
the politically most important Members is, no doubt, of
special relevance.(74) A recommendation showing a broad
consensus between Members of the different "blocs" or of
groupings with divergent interests will carry a high degree
of authority.

In this context the subject-matter of a recommendation may be
of particular importance. Recommendations involving questions
of highly developed technology, like outer space or the use
of nuclear energy, will not carry much weight unless endorsed
also by the Members who have that technology at their disposal.

A recommendation involving strongly controversial subjects,
such as, certain economic questions, will not enjoy much
authority if it does not represent the interests of both or
all sides but has been forced through by a purely numerical
majority. A recommendation carried by a majority of Members
with corresponding interests against the will of a determined
sizeable minority may be no more than the assertion of a
claim by that group of States.

The degree of a resolution's realism is not infrequently
reflected in the division of Members voting for or against
it. Extreme and intransigent language is often a sign of
impotence rather than of determination. Indeterminate and
vague wording may just be the expression of an agreement to
disagree between the States voting for a recommendation.

Sometimes the weight to be attributed to a recommendation
may be gathered from the attitude of the adopting organ

towards questions of its implementation. The institution of
formal procedures for the supervision of its implementation
can be taken as the sign of determination to pursue the
recommendation's objectives.

A recommendation's significance will not least depend on the
moral authority of the adopting organ. Only the maintenance
of high and impartial standards of decision-making in the
international organ will endow its recommendations with
persuasive force for all sectors of the international community. The application of politically motivated double-
standards or the use of general resolutions to champion
positions in political quarrels are liable to undermine the
credibility of the international organ even in areas of
relative agreement.

Of course, the long term effects of a recommendation are ultimately dependent on the actual conduct of its addressees.(75)
If a decision-maker confronted with a recommendation has
knowledge of subsequent practice, he will, no doubt, have to
take it into consideration. Individual cases of non-observance,
which are not expressive of a general rejection of its
principles, should not, however, be credited with too much
importance and should not be taken to override a Member's
otherwise positive attitude. There can be no doubt that the
provisions of the Universal Declaration of Human Rights have
repeatedly been violated since its adoption in 1948. These
violations, as far as they have become known, have generally
been regarded as unlawful and have prompted a variety of
reactions.(76) The States responsible have usually not
maintained that these violations were legal but have either
denied them or justified them by reference to special circumstances.

A decision-maker like a domestic court will not always find
it easy to examine all these complicated and sometimes
elusive factors contributing to the authority of a recommendation. The thoroughness of such an examination will partly
depend on its importance for the decision to be made and
partly on the difficulties involved. But even a recommendation whose precise authority is not known to a decision-
maker may be of assistance in a decision which also rests on
other prescriptions.

4. The Legal Consequences of Recommendations

The limited and qualified authority of recommendations also
requires a view of their legal consequences which is different from those of mandatory rules. By virtue of their

non-binding character, they do not absolutely require a
decision in conformity with their provisions. On the other
hand, this does not mean that it is open to decision-makers
to ignore them arbitrarily. The addressees, usually State-
organs including domestic courts, are at least under a duty
to consider them in good faith.(77)

A recommendation is only in rare cases the sole basis for a
claim in domestic litigation. Domestic courts normally only
rely on this type of international decision in conjunction
with other authoritative material. A recommendation can,
however, usually serve as a presumption of legality in favor
of conduct which is in accordance with its tenets. A State
acting in accordance with the recommendations of the United
Nations General Assembly will enjoy the benefit of doubt
should the legality of its conduct be called into question.(78)
This was evidently the meaning attributed to the Resolution
on the Exploitation of Natural Resources by Japanese courts
when they relied upon it in order to determine the legality
of Iranian expropriation measures concerning the petroleum
industry.(79) On the other hand, action contrary to the
provisions of a recommendation can result in a shifting of
the burden of proof against the person violating it. A State
or an individual charged with war crimes may well be put in
the position of having to try and prove the legality of
conduct which is contrary to the Universal Declaration of
Human Rights.

As a general policy proposition, decisions by domestic
courts are to be preferred which are in accordance with
generally held expectations of the international community
as expressed in widely accepted recommendations of representative international institutions. Especially in the interpretation of legal prescriptions like treaty provisions and
domestic statutes, recommendations can be an important help.
In such a situation a decision which is in accordance with
the policies expressed by an authoritative recommendation
should be given preference. A look at the practice of courts
shows that reliance on the Universal Declaration of Human
Rights for the interpretation of domestic law, primarily the
law of the forum, is, in fact, the most frequent form of its
application.(80) Recommendations are also of particular
value where authoritative prescriptions in the traditional
sense are lacking or where the cumbersome process of creating
legal expectations through reciprocities and retaliations
has not yet led to the establishment of a clear practice.

On the other hand, situations can arise where recommendations
are in contradiction to indisputable legal obligations,

arising, for instance, from treaties. In such a case, the
recommendation will usually have to yield to the conflicting
prescription. In the case of Manderlier v. UN & Belgium(81)
the court found that the United Nations had evidently acted
contrary to a provision of the Universal Declaration of
Human Rights. Nevertheless, it refused to grant a remedy in
view of clear treaty provisions establishing the organization's
jurisdictional immunity.

A further promising field for recommendations of international
organizations is the application of the policies enunciated
by them as a kind of international *ordre public* for the non-
recognition of foreign law, foreign decisions, and private
transactions. This suggestion, made in scholarly writings,(82)
has already found entry into court practice in several
instances.(83)

A survey of the behavior of domestic courts when dealing
with general recommendations of international institutions
reveals that this type of international decision is invoked
in a large number of domestic litigations and is explicitly
relied upon by domestic courts. In the relatively small
group of cases in which the application of recommendations
was refused, there are only a few cases in which the lack of
"binding force" was given as the reason for their rejection.
Other reasons given for their non-application were the
absence of their incorporation into the domestic law of the
forum(84) or contrary provisions of the local law.(85) In some
cases domestic courts simply ignored the invocation of
recommendations without offering reasons.(86) It must be
assumed that in addition to these cases, there is a considerable number in which courts consciously or unconsciously
simply passed over pertinent international recommendations.

C. PRESCRIPTION

The prescribing function in international relations remains
largely unorganized. Typical procedures are the evolution of
patterns of behavior in conjunction with expectations of
authority and control or the explicit formal acceptance of
written prescriptions by all participants concerned. Thus
the drawing up of written international prescriptions is
still largely restricted to agreements. There is no "international legislation" in the technical sense of the word.

Organized international cooperation in international organizations has led to certain prescribing techniques deviating
from traditional treaty procedures, but similar or identical
in outcome. In most instances the treaty origins of these

procedures are still clearly perceptible. Roughly these techniques can be categorized into amendments to treaties, official interpretations of treaties, and regulations issued in addition to treaties. To a greater or lesser degree all three types of procedures show a departure from the principle of explicit submission by all participants involved or from the traditional formalities attendant on treaties.

The rapid growth of the international community has dramatically complicated the process by which explicit consent to multilateral prescriptions or to their alteration is obtained from all participants. This has led to certain decision-techniques in which simplified procedures are applied within international organizations. One of the main directions in attempting to achieve economy and simplification is a deviation from the requirement of universal consent. Amendments to treaties, their authoritative interpretation, or the creation of "secondary law" are entrusted to decision processes which do not require the assent of all Parties to the treaty. Even where unanimity is maintained in the international organ, the initiative in the decision process can be decisively shifted. An undecided or reluctant partner is usually subject to considerably more pressure in an international organ than in the course of the traditional process of ratification. Procedural provisions permitting the adoption of decisions in spite of an abstention can be a further limitation of the principle of consent. However, in some instances these deviations from the principle of consent are coupled with "escape clauses" permitting a recalcitrant State to withdraw from the amended prescrition.

Parallel to these developments, the need for more expedient and economic procedures has also led to the modification of the formalities leading to the entry into force of general prescriptions. Particularly in highly specialized and technical fields, States are prepared to waive the requirement of an express and formal submission to treaty provisions and to yield certain prescriptive functions to international organs. The evident advantages of an efficient treatment of common problems by international expert bodies are seen to outweigh the partial surrender of direct influence and absolute control over the terms of obligations assumed by individual States. The exclusion of procedures to obtain the consent of the constitutionally competent organs of the participating States - mostly legislative assemblies - considerably facilitates and expedites the creation of international prescriptions.

The two trends towards prescription through majority voting and towards simplified procedures of acceptance within the

framework of international organizations are often utilized
in conjunction and have led to a number of prescriptive
procedures in international institutions.

Domestic courts before which these novel and unorthodox prescriptions emanating from international organizations are
invoked tend to show insecurity and perplexity. These prescriptions cannot be dismissed as easily as recommendations,
yet their hybrid status between treaties and "international
legislation" defies any attempt to classify them comfortably
in terms of the traditional sources. Court practice expressly
dealing with them is not particularly prolific. Sometimes
these prescriptions are simply treated like treaty law and
their origin as decisions of international institutions is
ignored. Their designation as "amendment to the treaty" or
"annex to the treaty" obviously supports this tendency. In
most instances judgments contain no discussion of their
legal nature whatsoever.

A second factor obscuring the question of the international
authority of these kinds of prescriptions from the viewpoint
of domestic courts is the practice of formally incorporating
them into domestic law by legislative enactments of the
forum State. In most instances these international prescriptions are, in fact, specifically designed with a view to
further prescriptions in the States concerned. The European
Communities are an important exception. These measures of
transformation usually preclude any direct reliance on the
international prescription. Domestic courts applying them
may not even be aware of their international origin.

In view of these facts, it seems hardly surprising that
questions concerning the authority of prescriptions emanating
from international organizations have played very little
rôle in the practice of domestic courts. The existence of a
specific incorporation either in the form of a reference in
domestic law to the international prescription or by way of
a domestic statute reflecting its material contents make the
question of its international authority seem irrelevant from
the domestic courts' viewpoint. In cases in which courts
treated these international prescriptions simply as treaties,
problems concerning their authority also did not arise.

1. Amendments to Treaties

Amendment procedures to multilateral conventions, especially
constitutive instruments of international institutions,
deviating from the traditional procedures of treaty-making
are a common phenomenon. These amendments often take effect

without the consent of all Members. A constitutional amendment adopted by an organ of the institution by majority vote
can take effect also for Members which have neither voted
for nor ratified it.(87) Where an amendment affects prescriptions to be applied in domestic litigation, a court may find
itself in the position of having to apply "treaty law" which
has been enacted by an international institution in conjunction with the majority of its Members but without the active
cooperation of the forum State. The treaty nature of these
prescriptions can only be upheld by way of a fiction based
on the original acceptance of the treaty provision concerning amendments.

The treaty establishing the European Free Trade Association
affords an instructive example. The EFTA Council, a plenary
organ, is authorized to adopt unanimous mandatory decisions.(88)
Abstentions are no bar to such decisions. Even though the
implementation of decisions is largely left to the legislative and executive departments of Members, they can nevertheless be of direct significance for domestic courts. A large
part of the Treaty's material provisions, to be applied also
by the courts, are subject to amendments by the Council. The
Council has made extensive use of this authority. Once
amended, only the revised version of the treaty is to be
applied.

Court practice touching upon the authority of these prescriptions is almost impossible to trace, since courts will
normally apply the treaty without even realizing that an
international organ has intervened in its amendment. One
instance is a decision of the Austrian Constitutional Court(89)
applying Article 7 of the EFTA Treaty. The Court not only
applied this provision as amended by the Council, but, in
addition, relied on a further decision by the EFTA Council
containing directions for its interpretation.

2. Official Interpretations

The interpretation of treaties is a ubiquitous feature of
decision-making by international organizations. Interpretation is a necessary concommitant to any application of
prescriptions. It is undertaken by judicial as well as
"political" organs and plays a decisive rôle in the creation
of legal expectations and, hence, in the development of the
law. The effects of these interpretations as "precedents"
for the behavior of domestic courts are dealt with in chapters II.C. and III.E.3.

In some international institutions certain organs are specifically endowed with the power to adopt official authoritative
interpretations of the constitutive treaty or of other
conventions falling within the institution's scope of activities. Apart from the competence of judicial international
organs to give advisory opinions, (See chapter III.E.1.a))
or to give preliminary rulings upon the application of
domestic courts, (See excursus II and chapter XIV.D.2) non-
judicial organs too have been endowed with this task in some
instances.(9o) This function is particularly prominent with
the Financial Organizations among the United Nations Specialized Agencies. Article XXIX (formerly Article XVIII) of the
Articles of Agreement of the International Monetary Fund,
Article IX of the Articles of Agreement of the International
Bank for Reconstruction and Development, Article VIII of the
Articles of Agreement of the International Finance Corporation,
and Article X of the Articles of the Agreement of the International Development Agency provide for official interpretations of the respective treaty by the Executive Directors.(91)
Article XXIX (a) of the Fund Agreement runs in part:

> Any question of interpretation of the provisions of
> this Agreement arising between any member and the Fund
> or between any members of the Fund shall be submitted
> to the Executive Board for its decision.

There is a possibility of appeal against such an interpretation to the Board of Governors, whose decision is final.

An official interpretation is admissible both in the context
of a specific dispute to assist in its resolution and by way
of a general statement to guide the future conduct of the
Organizations and its Members. In actual practice, general
interpretations *pro futuro* are much more frequent. The
outcome of these official interpretations is generally
regarded as final and mandatory. Apart from these formal
statements of interpretation on the basis of specific authorizations, there is naturally a multitude of cases in which
the organs of these international organizations informally
interpret and apply their constitutive instruments in the
course of their everyday practice.

It would be artificial to deny the prescriptive function of
these interpretations by pretending that they are purely
declaratory and that, hence, the rights and obligations
clarified by them all derive from the treaty itself. Any
authoritative interpretation, whether it is undertaken in
the context of application or not, contains an element of
choice and is therefore creative. To the extent that it
determines the behavior of future decision-makers it partakes
of the prescribing function.

The official interpretation most significant for the practice
of domestic courts is, certainly, the one adopted by the
Executive Directors of the International Monetary Fund on 1o
June 1949 on the interpretation of Article VIII/2(b) of the
Fund Agreement.(92) Article VIII/2(b), first sentence, pro-
vides:

> Exchange contracts which involve the currency of any
> member and which are contrary to the exchange control
> regulations of that member maintained or imposed con-
> sistently with this Agreement shall be unenforceable in
> the territories of any member.

In its official interpretation the Executive Directors
specifically deal with the duties of the judicial and administrative authorities of Member States not to lend their assistance in the implementation of contracts contrary to exchange
control regulations as described in Article VIII/2(b). The
interpretation goes into considerable detail in explaining
that certain pleas purporting to exclude the application of
the foreign exchange control regulations, such as, *ordre public* or non-applicability under the forum's conflict of laws,
shall not be allowed by domestic courts.(93)

The frequency of domestic cases touching upon questions which
involve Article VIII/2(b) of the Fund Agreement provides a
relatively extensive and reliable picture of judicial behavior towards its official interpretation.(94)

In a number of cases domestic courts explicitly refer to the
Monetary Fund's official interpretation and follow its instructions.(95) Questions concerning its authority are not
discussed. Its final and manadatory character is apparently
accepted as a matter of course.(96)

The accessibility of court practice on Article VIII/2(b) of
the IMF, however, permits an examination not just of cases
which mention this international decision. A complete picture of its currency can only be obtained through the examination also of those cases in which the international interpretation could or should have been applied but was, in fact,
ignored. A survey of court practice reveals that the latter
category of cases is by far the larger one. However, this
recognition should not lead to the rash conclusion that the
courts wilfully disregarded the Executive Directors' interpretation because they considered it devoid of authority and
legal significance. In a number of cases Article VIII/2(b)
was applied by the courts in a way which is in evident accord
with the official interpretation but without any mention of
its existence.(97) It seems futile to speculate whether a
tacit deference to the terms of the interpretation is an

argument in favor of or against its authority. In other
cases the non-application of Article VIII/2(b) of the Fund
Agreement is substantiated by the courts in a way which
suggests that the decision would not have come out different-
ly had there been recourse to the official interpretation.(98)
One group of cases, however, creates the strong impression
that the courts were only able not to apply Article VIII/2(b)
by either wilfully ignoring or overlooking the official
interpretation.(99) Sometimes these decisions do not even
specifically deal with Article VIII/2(b), but simply reject
the application of the Fund Agreement in general terms.(1oo)

A good part of these decisions may simply be attributable to
the fact that the official interpretation had not been
invoked by the parties and was unknown to the court. However,
in those cases in which the lower courts explicitly relied
on the official interpretation, its neglect by the appellate
courts(1o1) cannot be explained away by mere ignorance.

A critical general evaluation of cases touching upon the
subject-matter of the official interpretation by the International Monetary Fund of 1o June 1949, thus yields quite a
different picture than an examination of only those cases
which expressly mention the interpretation. It is true that
there is not a single known case in which doubts were cast
upon the authority of the official interpretation. The
considerable number of judgments in which courts simply
ignored it, especially those cases in which the outcome is
in clear contradiction to its terms, however, must be taken
as an indication of the limited degree of authority attributed to it by domestic courts. It should, nevertheless, be
noted that the only evident strategy employed by domestic
courts who refuse the official interpretation's application
is to ignore it. There is no known case in which a court
based its rejection on its lack of authority or "binding
force", the lack of its incorporation into the law of the
forum, its non-self executing character, or a collision with
contrary domestic law.

3. Regulations

Of the various prescribing techniques employed by contemporary
international institutions, the adoption of regulations is
the one most divested of the traditional formalities of
treaty-making. Certain international organizations are
authorized to adopt general prescriptions which are designed
to supplement and specify treaties for the solution of
common problems. In some cases, the treaty origin of these
techniques is still indicated by the designation of the
prescriptions as "annexes to the treaty".

The oldest type of prescribing functions of this kind exercised by international organs is the authority of international river commissions to adopt regulations. Thus under the
Revised Convention of Mannheim(1o2) the Central Commission
for the Navigation of the Rhine is authorized to enact
certain regulations in cooperation with the Member States.
The Supreme Court of the Netherlands has in two recent cases
applied the Rhine Police Regulations, enacted by the Central
Commission, in conjunction with Article 32 of the Mannheim
Convention providing for criminal sanctions.(1o3) The European Danube Commission(1o4) enjoyed even more far-reaching
prescriptive powers concerning the navigation on the
Danube.(1o5)

In the early administrative unions and the later specialized
agencies of the United Nations, prescriptive activities have
assumed an important rôle. Especially the predecessor of the
International Civil Aviation Organization (ICAO), CINA,
established by Treaty of 13 October 1919,(1o6) had far-
reaching jurisdictions. It had the authority to amend the
technical annexes to the treaty by majority decisions.(1o7)
In 195o the Swiss Federal Court(1o8) had to deal with such
an amended annex. It found that, in principle, the prescription enacted by CINA was applicable as part of treaty law.
In the particular case, it, nevertheless, dismissed the
claim based upon it since Swiss membership had terminated
shortly before.

Within the United Nations specialized agencies, organs are
sometimes vested with prescriptive functions subject to so-
called "contracting out" procedures. The basic idea is a
reversion of traditional treaty procedures: A regulation
adopted by a majority decision of the international organ
becomes effective for all Members except for those who
specifically reject it.

The need for an expeditious adaptation of the international
provisions governing civil aviation was decisive for the
adoption of this procedure in ICAO. The Council, an organ
composed of 27 Members, is empowered to enact and amend by
majority vote "international standards" and "recommended
practices" which can be attached as annexes to the Convention.
These annexes enter into force if they are not rejected by a
majority of Members. In addition, it is open to individual
Members to deviate from an "international standard" thus
adopted if they find it "impracticable" to comply with it.
Only in respect of flights over the high seas are the regulations mandatory as adopted by the organization.(1o9) With
respect to other annexes the only unqualified obligation is

to notify the organization of any deviation. Apart from
that, the contracting States only undertake to secure "the
highest practicable degree of uniformity".

These provisions of the Chicago Convention that leave a
large amount of discretion to Members have repeatedly led to
reflections in scholarly writings concerning the differentiated
and qualified obligations arising from ICAO regulations.(11o)
In addition, an examination of State practice reveals that a
large number of Members have not complied with their obligations to notify deviations from regulations,(111) and that,
hence, the absence of a notification cannot be regarded as a
basis for justified expectations of compliance. A practice
of reciprocity in the application of these annexes further
increases the effects of this non-compliance.(112)

All these complex and interesting questions concerning the
authority of the annexes to the ICAO Agreement are not
discussed by domestic courts. In the absence of specific
measures of incorporation into domestic law, an invocation
of the annexes is usually rejected.(113) In the few cases in
which courts nevertheless relied upon them, they simply
treated them as part of the Treaty.(114) This creates the
impression that the annexes were confounded with the Convention itself, and that their character as regulations emanating from international organs was not recognized.

The World Health Organization exercises similar powers of
prescription.(115) The Health Assembly has the authority to
adopt regulations by majority vote which enter into force
for the Members unless they notify their rejection or reservation to the Organization. Here too, implementing legislation is considered a prerequisite for the application of the
international prescriptions. This requirement forecloses any
discussion of the international decision's authority by
domestic courts.(116)

The enactment of regulations in regional organizations, that
is, institutions with a limited and rather more uniform
membership, is not so much aimed at avoiding the difficulties
in obtaining the express consent of all members but at
expeditious procedures of adoption. Thus in OECD the Council,
a plenary organ, adopts decisions and recommendations,
usually by unanimous vote. An abstention is no bar to a
decision. Here too, the practice of domestic courts, however,
provides little or no indication concerning the legal status
attributed to these prescriptions. The requirement of measures
of implementation into the law of the forum precludes any
discussion of their authority.(117)

The most far-reaching and comprehensive prescriptive powers
of contemporary international organizations are, no doubt,
those provided for by the Treaties establishing the European
Communities. These Treaties contain numerous authorizations
for the Council of Ministers and the Commission to adopt
prescriptions specifying and developing the provisions of
the Treaties. In the terminology of the EEC Treaty the most
important types of prescriptions are "regulations", "directives", and "decisions" (Art.189). Regulations are to apply
generally and directly in all Member States. Directives are
to be binding on Member States only in respect of the result
to be achieved, leaving to individual Members the choice of
form and methods. Decisions are to be binding only in
respect of their immediate addressees. The authority of EEC
regulations has never been subject to any doubt in principle.
There is extensive practice to demonstrate that they are
applied unquestioningly by domestic courts. The relatively
few cases in which difficulties concerning their application
have arisen in domestic litigation involve questions either
of their self-executing nature or of conflicting domestic
provisions. Courts have even accepted the authority of
directives and decisions directed at States and have applied
them to cases before them, irregardless of implementing
prescriptions of the local law. (See also chapters VII.F.
and XII.D.2.)

By way summary, we can say that domestic courts have paid
little or no conscious attention to the question of the
authority of general prescriptions emanating from international institutions. In cases in which they were actually
applied, they were apparently accepted without any further
reflections upon their legal significance. In other cases
courts avoided the question of their authority by pointing
to the absence of implementing measures into the law of the
forum. In a third group of cases they were simply ignored.

D. INVOCATION

The invoking function is omnipresent in the activities of
international institutions. Whenever participants wish to
influence decisions, they invoke prescriptions ostensibly
supporting their claims. Occasionally international institutions themselves exercise this function when making claims
before other decision-makers. In spite of their frequency,
instances of invocation exercised in or by international
institutions only rarely influence decisions of domestic
courts. Normally this function cannot be sufficiently
isolated in the decision-making process to constitute an
independent feature in domestic litigation.

The most frequent occasions for an invocation of prescriptions
by international institutions affecting domestic proceedings
arise from a direct participation of international organs in
litigation before domestic courts. In nearly all these cases
the prescriptions invoked touch upon questions of the international organization's procedural status, that is, its right
to sue or its jurisdictional immunity. These problems will be
discussed below in the section devoted to participants.
(XII.C.)

A rare example of an authoritative invocation of policy on
the merits by an international institution in domestic litigation arose in a dispute between the World Bank and the International Monetary Fund on one side and a number of telegraph companies on the other.(118) It concerned the rates for
telecommunication messages to be paid by the two international organizations. The two conventions setting up the Bank
and the Fund contain a most favored nation clause for the
treatment of their official communications. The two organizations utilized their authority to give official interpretations of their constitutive instruments in order to support
their claims to the more favorable rates. The Federal Communications Commission, before which the dispute was pending, entertained no doubts as to the authoritativeness of this official interpretation by the two organizations in their own
cause:

> We believe that the question as to the application of
> the term 'treatment' in the Bank and Fund articles to
> rates has been conclusively determined by the Bank and
> Fund Executive Directors' interpretation... Under the
> terms of the Bank and the Fund Articles of Agreement,
> this interpretation, in effect, is final. This procedure
> for issuing interpretations binding on member govern-
> ments does indeed appear novel; but it also appears to
> point the way toward speedy, uniform and final interpre-
> tations.(119)

In other cases invocations before an international institution, namely, the International Court of Justice, were given
decisive importance by domestic courts. In Anglo-Iranian Oil
Co. v. Jaffrate (The Rose Mary) the Supreme Court of Aden(12o)
had to deal with the legality of Iranian measures of expropriation. It found that the mere fact that the International
Court of Justice had been seized of this question, albeit
unsuccessfully, was sufficient evidence that a purchaser of
expropriated oil could not have acquired it *bona fide*.

Yet another case(121) in which a mere invocation before the
International Court of Justice was found relevant by a

domestic court concerned the status of the defendant as a
department of a foreign government:

> This Court notes that one of Great Britain's contentions
> before the International Court of Justice in 1951, with
> regard to the Iranian Oil disputes, was that the agree-
> ment of 1933 between the Iran and the Anglo-Iranian Oil
> Company was in effect a treaty or convention between
> *two sovereign States* and therefore the International
> Court of Justice did have jurisdiction over the contro-
> versy.(122)

This meek acceptance of the contention made before the
International Court is difficult to understand. It seems to
have escaped the domestic court's attention that the International Court of Justice had unequivocally rejected this
contention.(123)

These isolated examples of invocations by or before international institutions playing important rôles in domestic
cases permit of no general conclusion. The only really
significant group of cases in which the invoking function
plays an important part in connection with international
institutions concerns the invocation of jurisdictional
immunities by the organizations themselves. (See below chapter XII.C.2.)

E. APPLICATION

Operative decisions of international institutions are relatively often relied upon in proceedings before domestic
courts. This holds true both for international judgments and
arbitral awards and for decisions of non-judicial organs.
The applying function of international institutions also
gives rise to the greatest variety of claims. All three
types of claims, as explained above, (implementation or
review, clarification of preliminary questions, and "precedents") are based on them.

1. Implementation or Review

a) Of Judicial International Decisions

Decisions of international judicial organs, including arbitral awards, enjoy a large measure of authority with respect
to the participants in the proceedings. In general, judicial
proceedings give rise to a high degree of expectations for
compliance by the parties. In other words the "binding
character" of the decision is usually beyond doubt. The
constitutive instruments setting up international judicial
organs frequently emphasize the mandatory nature of their

verdicts.(124) It is therefore not surprising that domestic
courts have hardly ever cast any doubt upon the final character of decisions of international courts and tribunals
unless there was reason to suspect procedural irregularities.

A rather perplexing exception to this rule is a judgment in
which the United States Supreme Court assumed a jurisdiction
to review an international award between a foreign State and
a national of the United States on the merits. In Republic of
Colombia v. Cauca Co. 19o U.S. 524(193o) a dispute had
arisen between the United States Corporation and Colombia
under a concession agreement to build a railroad. Pursuant
to a diplomatic exchange between the United States and
Colombian Governments, a "Special Commission" was set up to
decide upon the dispute between Colombia and the Company.
The Commission gave a decision awarding a certain sum to the
Company, despite the withdrawal of the Colombian commissioner
immediately before the completion of the proceedings. Colombia
claimed that the award was void and brought a suit in the
U.S. courts to have it set aside. The Supreme Court rejected
the plea of nullity since "neither party could defeat the
operation of the submission...by withdrawing or adopting the
withdrawal of its nominee when the discussions were closed."
Without expressing the slightest misgivings as to its jurisdiction over the award, it continued by going into the
merits of the international decision, upholding most of the
items but finding that it could not allow certain sums
awarded by the Commissioners.

This bold assumption of review jurisdiction by the Supreme
Court is certainly extraordinary. The only conceivable
connecting point for the competence of the United States
courts was the nationality of the defendant. The Supreme
Court simply acted as a court of appeal rehearing the merits
of the international proceedings.

Two recent French cases present similar problems. In both
cases the Cour d'appel de Paris subjected arbitral awards in
disputes between individuals and an international organization or a foreign State respectively to the review procedures
provided by the code of civil procedure for French awards.
The court of cassation has rejected this kind of review
holding it inapplicable to international awards.(125)

In the vast majority of cases domestic courts entertain no
doubts concerning the authority and final character of
international judgments and awards. Their acceptance is
based either on explicit prescriptions providing for their
finality(126) or simply on their origin from an international

judicial organ.(127) Even in cases in which the domestic
courts frustrated the outcome of international decisions,
their authority remained unquestioned. The rejection of
applications for their implementation was based on other
reasons. In most cases the authority of international judicial decisions seemed so evident to domestic courts that
they did not even enter into this question.

Advisory opinions are international judicial decisions
displaying rather special features. Proceedings leading to
advisory opinions have no parties in the strict sense, and
their outcome is not an operative decision but merely the
authoritative expression of a legal opinion. It could therefore be subject to doubt whether this type of judicial
pronouncement is actually an exercise of the application
function capable of being implemented by other decision-
makers. However, a view of actual practice reveals that an
advisory opinion is invariably triggered off by a specific
dispute, that the international judicial organ is conscious
of the contentious character of the request,(128) that
claims and counterclaims are raised before it by interested
parties, and that the opinion eventually handed down is
normally a decisive factor in the dispute's settlement. A
functional view of advisory opinions therefore justifies
their treatment in this context.

So far, no case has become known in which the advisory
opinion of an international judicial organ has played a
direct and prominent rôle in the enforcement of a claim by a
domestic court.(129) This should not lead to the rash conclusion that this type of decision will not exercise an influence
in litigation before domestic courts. An important question
for a domestic judge would, no doubt, be the fact that an
advisory opinion, by its terms, does not constitute a final
disposition in a dispute between clearly identifiable litigants and is not a "binding decision".(13o) Its function is
often to guide a requesting organ in its activities or to
endow its decisions with an additional degree of authority.
The advisory opinion by itself has only limited authority
and much depends on its acceptance by the requesting organ
and on whether it is put into effective control. But in
conjunction with the decision of another international organ
it can attain considerable significance. A decision of an
international institution prescribing a certain line of
conduct, which is subject to doubts concerning its authority
or legality, may acquire such a high degree of authority
with the help of an advisory opinion confirming it that
subsequent decision-makers entertain no doubt concerning its
legal significance.

A typical example would be a call by the Security Council to follow a certain line of conduct. Such a decision can raise the question whether it is to be considered mandatory in the sense of Article 25 of the United Nations Charter, whether it was taken within the Security Council's framework of jurisdiction, or whether it was adopted with the necessary number of affirmative votes. All these question can be clarified by an advisory opinion to such a degree that any doubts of a decision-maker in a subsequent dispute concerning the authority and legality of the original international decision are removed. It seems futile to argue which of the two international decisions is decisive. The original decision in conjunction with the advisory opinion confirming it are of such overwhelming authority that subsequent decisions are determined by them.

This is roughly the situation after the Advisory Opinion of the International Court of Justice concerning Namibia of 1971,(131) which confirms the decision of the General Assembly terminating the Mandate for South West Africa and several decisions of the Security Council on this question, especially concerning the duties of Member States arising from the termination of the Mandate. Obviously the Advisory Opinion did not in any way alter the legal nature of the controversial General Assembly and Security Council Resolutions. Nevertheless, their authority was considerably enhanced in spite of the strong dissenting opinions.

Other situations are feasible in which an advisory opinion of the International Court of Justice could support a claim based on another decision of an international institution. Possible examples would be a confirmation of the judgment of an administrative tribunal or of a request for payment of membership fees by the competent organ of an international institution. The enforcement of claims of this kind does not as yet seem to have been attempted with the help of domestic courts. It seems uncertain whether it would succeed.

b) Of Non-Judicial International Decisions

Operative decisions of so-called political organs of international institutions show a large measure of diversity, ranging from procedural questions or relatively insignificant organizational problems to far-reaching financial, political, and territorial decisions.

The form in which decisions of political organs are normally couched gives no reliable indication of their significance or legal character. Thus the General Assembly of the United

Nations adopts resolutions which are normally recommendations. Nevertheless, its resolutions can, under certain circumstances, have an immediate operative effect.(132)

The practice of domestic courts shows relatively few cases involving the implementation or review(133) of decisions of this kind. The main reason for this scarcity of case-material is, no doubt, the fact that the enforcement of specific operative decisions of political international organs is normally outside the scope of a domestic court's effective power. An attempt to implement them in this way would not normally be promising. The question of the international decisions' authority therefore only arises in few exceptional cases before domestic courts.

The proposals to enlist the help of domestic courts for the enforcement of certain Security Council decisions imposing sanctions, (see above II.A.1.) have so far met with little practical consequence. But a short look at the question of the authority of the international decisions concerned is still justified. Decisions directed by the League of Nations against Italy seem to have been regarded by domestic courts rather like facts or *force majeure* which did not raise questions of their authority.(134)

In the cases, so far known, in which attempts were made to enforce Security Council Resolutions in domestic courts, the courts expressed no doubts concerning the authority of the international decisions but refused their implementation for other reasons. In Diggs v. Shultz(135) the Security Council Resolution's application was rejected because of a contrary Act of Congress, although the Court of Appeals for the District of Columbia specifically pointed out that this was in "blatant disregard of our treaty undertakings" and that it made the United States a "certain treaty violator".(136)

In Diggs v. Dent(137) the District Court specifically emphasized the binding character of the sanction decisions concerning Namibia under Article 25 of the United Nations Charter, but rejected the claim to have it implemented for other reasons.

In a similar manner, the High Court of Australia(138) recognized the sanction decisions against Rhodesia(Zimbabwe) as binding under Article 25 of the Charter, but frustrated their implementation since they had not been incorporated into the domestic law.

In spite of the docile verbal acceptance of the international authority of Security Council resolutions displayed in these

cases, the question of their legal significance for domestic
courts should not be underestimated. The debate surrounding
the International Court's Advisory Opinion on <u>Namibia</u> already
outlines the spectrum of possible objections and problems
which could confront a domestic court.(139) In view of the
uncertainties and contradictions on this question,(14o) a
court's task in such a situation will not be easy. There is
general consensus in scholarly writing that decisions of the
Security Council can be mandatory under Article 25 of the
Charter, but not to which decisions this should apply.
Neither the preparatory works nor subsequent practice give
a clear answer to this question. The view that the effects
of Article 25 are restricted to measures under Chapter VII
is usually rejected in contemporary literature.(141) One of
the main difficulties in assessing the authority of a particular decision of the Security Council is the fact that resolutions very often give no clue under what Charter provisions the Security Council purported to act in the particular case. The solution outlined by the International Court
of Justice in its Advisory Opinion on <u>Namibia</u>,(142) which
is also advocated by Higgins,(143) does not envisage a link
between the authority of Security Council resolutions and
specific provisions of the Charter. The outer limits of its
jurisdiction are seen in Article 24 and in the purposes and
principles of the Charter.(144) Whether or not a particular
resolution enjoys the effect of Article 25 is to be ascertained with the help of a number of contextual criteria: The
terms of the resolution, the dicussions leading to it, any
Charter provisions invoked by it and, in general, all circumstances that might assist in determining the legal consequences of the resolution are to be taken into account.(145)

The difficulties in assessing the authority of operative decisions of so-called political international organs cannot
be resolved but can, at least, be put into their right
perspective if it is remembered that the problem is not one
of choosing between "binding effect" and "total irrelevance".
Recommendatory decisions of the Security Council, too, can
be an important basis for decisions of domestic courts. The
court can implement or apply them unless other authoritative
aspects militate against such an implementation.

2. Preliminary Questions

The question of an international decision's authority arises
in a similar way in cases in which it is not the object of
an attempt at its enforcement but is otherwise decisive for
a decision. If a decision on the main claim depends on a
preliminary question on which an international institution

has made a specific determination, the domestic court is
faced with the question to what extent the international
decision is authoritative for the litigation before it and
thus determines the outcome of the proceedings.

The primary problem in resolving a preliminary question of
an international character arising before a domestic court
with the help of an international decision, is to determine
the applicability of the international decision to the
particular case. The possibilities to reject the international decision's invocation are, thus, decisively extended by
the convenient argument that the international decision is
without significance to the particular case, since its
consequences do not embrace the dispute. This kind of reasoning is often more attractive and convincing than a "frontal
attack" against the international decision. Nevertheless, a
survey of the available case-material yields instructive
indications as to the authority attributed by domestic
courts to decisions of international organs in these situations.

In assessing this case-material one important reservation
should be made at the outset. A considerable number of the
cases concern territorial questions or other problems touching upon essential interests of the forum State. The difficulties for domestic courts arising from a strong identification with the forum State's special interests will be
dealt with below in chapter XIII.B.1.

The obligatory nature of international judicial decisions
was never drawn into doubt in cases in which they were
invoked for the resolution of preliminary questions. Where
the courts endorsed the reliance on international judgments
or advisory opinions their authority was accepted as a
matter of course.(146) If the court adopted another solution,
the international decision's authority was not questioned
but its applicability to the case before the domestic court
was denied.(147)

Compared to the relatively small number of cases in which
decisions of non-judicial international organs were the
object of enforcement proceedings in domestic courts, the
number of cases in which such international decisions were
adduced to help answer preliminary questions before domestic
courts is large. Here too, domestic judges indicated that
they accepted the authority of certain international decisions as decisive for preliminary points pending before them.
In particular, certain operative decisions were accepted as

conclusive which had been adopted by international organs
which are normally only vested with the authority to issue
recommendations.(148)

Thus the Commercial Court of Luxemburg(149) in 1935 had to
decide on the *locus standi* of the plaintiff, the Soviet
Trade Delegation, at a time when the Soviet Union had not
yet been recognized by Luxemburg. The court relied on the
joint membership of both countries in the League of Nations,
and pointed out that the decision to admit the Soviet Union
was binding on all Members. The court found that, as a
consequence of this indirect form of recognition, the Soviet
Trade Delegation had the right to sue. Although the Court's
evaluation of the admission to the League as having effects
erga omnes is beyond criticism, the conclusions drawn for
the question of the right to sue are not entirely convincing.

The largest group of cases in this context concern territorial
decisions, in particular by the General Assembly of the
United Nations in the exercise of powers conferred upon it
by Chapter XII of the Charter or by particular treaties.

In general, domestic courts unquestioningly accepted the
authority of these territorial decisions. Thus the French
Conseil d'Etat(15o) squarely based the termination of its
jurisdiction over Cameroon on the General Assembly Resolution
which had declared the French Trusteeship over that territory
terminated. In a similar way the Italian Court of Cassation
gave deference to General Assembly Resolutions concerning
the former Italian colonies(151) without questioning their
authority. It declined jurisdiction to sit in appeal over
judgments of courts in Ethiopia-Eritrea(152) or to hear the
case of a Libyan enterprise,(153) since these two territories
had been declared independent by the General Assembly.(154)
In the latter case the court specifically mentioned that the
new legal situation had been brought about by the international decision and independently of a bilateral treaty concluded to carry out the Resolution.

In a constitutional dispute in 1964 the Supreme Court of
Cyprus(155) had to decide on the existence of Cyprus as an
independent State. One of the judges, in giving an affirmative reply, relied on Security Council Resolutions concerning the legal status of Cyprus.

The practice of domestic courts, however, shows a realistic
attitude towards the effectiveness of international territorial decisions. Resolutions not supported by effective
control over the territory in question were not given deci-

sive relevance. In an Italian case touching upon the United
Nations Partition Plan for Palestine,(156) the Consiglio di
Stato(157) found that it had to apply Israeli law to property
situated in Jerusalem although there was a "convenzione"
concerning Jerusalem(158) and Members of the U.N. were under
an obligation to abide by it. Similarly, the Supreme Court
of Spain(159) in a case dealing with the Spanish enclaves of
Ceuta and Melilla made reference to the decolonization
campaign in the United Nations without finding it decisive
for the particular question.

South African(16o) and Rhodesian(161) courts circumvented
the question of the authority of resolutions by the General
Assembly and the Security Council by either quietly ignoring
them or by turning their meaning into the opposite.

Only in exceptional circumstances are courts prepared to
question the authority or obligatory nature of U.N. decisions.
In a case before an Israeli Military Court sitting in Ra-
mallah(162) on the occupied West Bank, counsel for the
defence, *inter alia* invoked Security Council Resolution 242
of November 22, 1967, which in her opinion "points to withdrawal and therefore no jurisdiction exists". The contention
was brushed aside by denying the Resolution's authority for
Israel. After pointing at the lack of its incorporation into
Israeli law, the court continued:

> It is well known that the Declaration of Human Rights
> and the Security Council Resolution have therefore
> declaratory value only and that they assist the General
> Assembly, the Security Council and the other organs of
> the United Nations in their work, but that is all.

This extreme formulation is undoubtedly a misinterpretation
of the Resolution's authority. The evaluation of the authority of Security Council resolutions is certainly not easy,
and there is no simple yardstick for their legal significance. To limit their effects only to the organs from which
they originate is, however, clearly a gross misjudgment of
the expectations of compliance attached to them by the
international community. The court would have been better
advised to probe the question of whether the terms of the
resolution calling for withdrawal really implied a lack of
jurisdiction until such withdrawal was effected.

The authority of international decisions becomes particularly
acute and critical in cases in which opposing claims and
arguments are based on different decisions of international
organs which ostensibly contradict each other in their terms
or at any rate in their consequences. The treatment accorded

to these international decisions can then give important
clues as to the relative authority attributed to them.

In the Eichmann case before the Israeli courts, the defence
relied on a Security Council Resolution which was censorious
of the defendant's abduction, in order to dispute the jurisdiction Israeli courts. (163) Neither the District Court of
Jerusalem(164) nor the Supreme Court(165) attempted to
question the authority of the Resolution, but simply found
that it did not affect their jurisdiction to try the defendant. (166) In addition, the District Court relied on earlier
General Assembly Resolutions to prove the legality of the
arrest:

> Moreover, the United Nations Assembly has in recurrent
> Resolutions (Resolutions of February 12-13, 1946, and
> October 31, 1947) enjoined all States, whether or not
> Member States of the United Nations, to arrest war
> criminals and the perpetrators of crimes against humani-
> ty wherever they may hide and to surrender them, even
> without resort to extradition, with a view to expedi-
> tious prosecution. (167)

In addition, the Supreme Court referred to further General
Assembly Resolutions, that had accepted the principles of
Nuremberg and had declared genocide an international cri-
me. (168)

A case before the United States District Court of Puerto
Rico, U.S. v. Vargas, (169) is particularly instructive for
the question of competing United Nations decisions. In the
course of a prosecution under the Selective Service Act,
counsel for the defence contended that under the Geneva
Convention relative to the protection of civilian persons in
time of war(17o) a conscription of persons from occupied
territories was prohibited. The Court rejected the classification of Puerto Rico as an occupied territory, *inter alia*,
by pointing to a General Assembly Resolution which had
recognized that Puerto Rico had attained an autonomous
status and that the people of Puerto Rico had effectively
exercised their right of self-determination. More recently,
the U.N. Special Committee on Colonialism had, however,
passed a resolution indicating that it did not consider the
question of self-determination for Puerto Rico as settled.
In view of these conflicting declarations by U.N. organs,
the Court held:

> To this date the special committee on colonialism has
> not made any formal declaration and the General Assembly
> Resolution of 1953 is in all force and effect and is
> the last pronouncement of the highest body of the

> United Nations in relation to the political status of
> Puerto Rico.(171)

In addition the court also relied on Article 21/3 of the
Universal Declaration of Human Rights and concluded that the
United Nations could not impose independence on Puerto Rico
without violating the principle of self-determination.

This judgment presents a clear attempt to introduce a classification of different decisions of international organs
according to their authority. The implication appears to be
that the latitude of a United Nations organ in adopting
decisions can be limited by decisions of another higher
United Nations organ or by certain previous decisions of
principle.

By way of summary, we can say that problems of authority
have not played a dominant part in cases in which decisions
of international organs were adduced to help resolve preliminary questions before domestic courts. The courts were
nearly always content to accept the obligatory nature of the
international decisions even in cases where there was place
for doubt. In cases in which deference to United Nations
decision was refused, courts usually preferred to rely on
other grounds for disregarding the international decisions.
In some cases, courts were prepared to make a choice between
ostensibly conflicting United Nations decisions. The circumstances of these cases, however, suggest that problems of
identification with special interests of the forum State
have played an important rôle in the courts' verdicts.

3. "Precedents" for Analogous Legal Questions

The authority of international decisions invoked for the
purpose of elucidating analogous questions of law or policy
pending in proceedings before domestic courts differs from
the authority of international decisions relied upon for the
purpose of their implementation or the resolution of preliminary questions. The only link between the original decision
and the case to be decided is an alleged similarity of
circumstances coupled with the claim to adopt the same
policies.

The international decision-makers in question, usually
international courts or arbitral tribunals, have no formal
competence to adopt general prescriptions. Nevertheless,
their impact on the creation of legal expectations and hence
on the international decision-making process is undeniable.
While the international decisions in question are regularly

"binding" in the classical sense in settling the particular
dispute, their undeniable authority for subsequent decisions
before other decision-makers and between different parties
is elusive and difficult to determine. Their authority as
"precedents" depends on a variety of contextual factors
which are difficult to pinpoint in abstract terms, but can
only be weighed in the circumstances of a particular decision
situation.

a) The Rejection of International "Precedents"

The difficulties in grasping and substantiating the legal
significance of international decisions for subsequent cases
involving similar questions have sometimes led to a tendency
to deny the cognitive value of international "precendents"
altogether. This rejection is sometimes based on the assertion that the international judgment or award must, by
necessity, be restricted in its effects to the specific case
before the tribunal. It cannot, runs the argument, affect
the legal situation of third parties or of future disputes
and can consequently not bind the judge in another case.(172)

In its simplest form, this theory presents nothing more than
a confusion between *res iudicata* and the doctrine of binding
precedent and does not really deserve serious treatment. The
dispositive outcome of a judgment naturally only has an
immediate impact on the parties to the case. The long term
effects of the policies expressed in the decision and their
influence on subsequent decision-makers is, however, an
entirely different question.

The Permanent Court of International Justice in its earlier
interpretations of Article 59 of its Statute(173) has itself
contributed to a tendency to underrate the significance of
its own practice for later cases.(174) On the other hand,
the Court itself later ignored these *dicta* and regularly
refers to its own practice.(175) In the case of the Temple
of Preah Vihear,(176) the International Court tried to
specify its position in this respect. After pointing out
that one of its previous decisions was "by reason of Article
59 of the Statute, only binding, *qua* decision, as between
parties to that case", it immediately continued to probe its
earlier decisions "as a statement of what the Court regarded
as the correct legal position".(177)

One reason for the reserved attitude towards judicial practice may be the rather unhappy and ambiguous wording of
Article 59 of the Statute. Its drafting was severely criticized in the Arbitral Award in the Lighthouses Case:

On pourrait soutenir ensuite - autre argument juridique -
que le texte de l'article 59 du Statut de la Cour
internationale de Justice et de la disposition qui l'a
précédé est mal rédigé et qu'on doit nécessairement
l'interpréter dans un sens plus libéral que ses termes
ne semblent le justifier. Il y a beaucoup à dire en
faveur de cette thèse, d'autant plus que ce texte n'a
pas été emprunté au projet du Comité de juristes qui a
élaboré le Statut de 1920, mais a été déformé par
l'amendement mal venu d'un corps politique. S'il était
vrai qu'un arrêt de la Cour n'est revêtu de l'autorité
de la chose jugée que dans le seul cas qui a été
décidé, cela signifierait que, si le "cas" concerne
l'interprétation d'une clause de traité, l'interprétation donnée pourrait être remise en discussion dans
des "cas" futurs ayant trait à la même clause de traité.
Un tel résultat ne serait pas seulement absurde, mais
mettrait l'article 59 en contradiction inconciliable
avec la phrase finale de l'article 63 du même Statut
déclarant que, lorsqu'un Etat tiers intervient à un
procès dans lequel il s'agit de l'interprétation d'une
convention multilatérale à laquelle il est partie ensem-
ble avec les Etats litigants, *l'interprétation* contenue
dans la sentence est également obligatoire à son égard.
La *res judicata* s'étend, par conséquent, hors des
limites strictes du cas décidé.(178)

Even the basically legitimate insistence on the inapplicability of a doctrine of *stare decisis* to international law tends
to lead to the other extreme of underestimating the value of
international judicial decisions in subsequent lawsuits.(179)
A compromise solution is sometimes seen in the suggestion to
relegate international "precedents" into the realm of *autorité scientifique*(180) and to declare a reliance on them to be
a matter of common sense and practicability.(181)

The practice of domestic courts only rarely shows examples
of an outright rejection of the authority of international
practice on grounds of principle. One example of such an a-
prioristic rejection of international judicial authority by
a domestic court is furnished by an Italian case. In Pavia c.
Amministrazione Finanze(182) the Court of Appeal of Genoa
had to interpret Article 78 of the Treaty of Peace with
Italy of 1947,(183) exempting United Nations nationals from
taxes levied for the purpose of meeting charges arising out
of the war. The Article included persons who during the war
had been treated as enemies among "U.N. nationals". The
Court found that persons of the "Hebrew race" who were of
Italian nationality could not benefit from this provision,

notwithstanding decisions to the contrary given by the Conciliation Commission established in accordance with Article 83
of the Treaty:

> ...The references to these decisions which can be found
> in scholarly writings demonstrate that they had concerned
> controversies relating to individual cases affecting
> private persons and that... the Contracting States had
> thus not entrusted the Commissions themselves with the
> task of ascertaining the meaning of Art.78, 9 of the
> Treaty with respect to all possible cases to which the
> said rule refers. It would thus be a question of judgments
> with an effect limited to the individual case decided
> and not of judgments containing a determination of the
> interpretation to be given to the Treaty-rule valid for
> all the cases regulated by this rule in abstracto: A
> determination which, had it really been requested by
> the Contracting States and given by the deciding Com-
> mission, should then, in order to be received in the
> internal Italian order, have been rendered effective in
> Italy by a legislative measure: This did not happen
> precisely because these decisions only purported to
> resolve the individual controversies and to have effect
> only in respect to them.(184)

This wholesale denial of any cognitive value of past decisions, as a necessary consequence of the non-application of
a doctrine of binding precedent, seems an unnecessarily
radical substantiation for the Court's decision to depart
from the policy of the international decisions. The refusal
to follow an international decision may be justifiable and
appropriate in certain cases. To substantiate such a deviation with an assertion that international judicial practice
is generally irrelevant is misleading and at variance with a
proper understanding of the judicial process.

In other cases it is rather obvious that the refusal to
apply the policies of an international decision to an analogous case was not so much based on dogmatic considerations
of principle but on the endeavor to justify a different
outcome. In <u>Mackay Radio & Telegraph Co. v. Lal-la Fatma &
Others</u> the Court of Appeal of the International Tribunal of
Tangier (a domestic court) refused to follow a judgment of
the International Court of Justice, which had decided the
practically identical question for Morocco. It held, *inter
alia*:

> /T/he judgment of the International Court of Justice of
> 1952 is not applicable to the Tangier Zone because,
> first, it does not create precedent, the Judgment
> itself declaring that its applicability is limited to

the French Zone of Morocco; secondly, because, even if
this were not so, such decision might at best provide
inspiration and guidance, although not because its
judgments have any binding force in municipal courts;(185)

In spite of all this the Court, only shortly afterwards,
refers to the parallel situation in Morocco relying on the
dissenting opinions to the International Court of Justice's
very judgment the relevance of which it had just before
emphatically denied.

In a similar vein, the Supreme Court of Czechoslovakia in a
case dealing with expropriation rejected references to the
practice of the Permanent Court of International Justice.(186)
It first declared that these judgments had no import beyond
the specific case, but shortly later itself interpreted a
judgment of the PCIJ and drew conclusions from it.

In other cases domestic courts found international decisions
invoked before them "inapplicable"(187) or refrained from
making any reference to them.(188)

The practice of international judicial organs exercizes an
important influence on the continuity, uniformity, and predictability of the international decision-making process,
and is, hence, an important element in the creation of
stable legal expectations. A dogmatic *a priori* rejection of
international practice as an aid for decision in domestic
courts must necessarily have a negative impact on the coordi-
nation of the activities in domestic and international fora.
The ultimate consequence of a consistent disregard for
international practice by domestic courts could be decisions
contrary to international law involving the danger of the
forum State's responsibility.

A much larger group of cases show reference and deference by
domestic courts to international practice. This should not
tempt us to undertake a superficial quantitative analysis.
The cases mentioned above in which courts refuse to follow
international practice but explicitly refer to it are surely
exceptional. There is good reason to believe that in most
cases, in which courts decide to deviate from international
practice, they will pass over conflicting international
"precedents" with silence.

On the other hand, a court may not overtly refer to international practice even where it relies on it.(189) Theoretical uncertainties concerning the status of this unorthodox
"source of law" in the court's legal frame of reference may

persuade it not to mention international practice. A subsequent attempt to find out whether it has, in fact, sought guidance in international judgments or awards is usually not promising.

In an English case, <u>Attorney-General v. Nissan</u>,(19o) however, the paraphrasing of a well-known passage from an advisory opinion of the International Court(191) of Justice is so obvious, that even without a reference it is clear from where the judge drew his inspiration.

Probably one of the most important factors for an absence of references to international judicial practice is not so much to be found in theoretical misgivings about the propriety of such a procedure or in a lack of clear prescriptions determining its exact relevance to the domestic court, but simply in a lack of information available to the domestic judge. Despite increasing efforts to publicize decisions of international courts and tribunals, these materials remain for the most part strange and foreign to domestic courts as well as to legal practitioners while language difficulties also constitute an added impediment in many countries.

b) The Authority of International Practice

Neither the assumption of a "binding force" of pertinent international decisions on analogous questions of law nor the outright rejection of their relevance do justice to their significance for domestic courts. The dismissal of these extreme propositions, of course, does not offer a satisfactory answer to the question to what extent deference should be given to international practice in a particular case. A meaningful alternative to efforts trying to determine the binding or non-binding force of a particular international precedent for a domestic court has to see it in the perspective of its place in the flow of communications which determines the continuous change and development of international law.

International judicial decisions, just like other internationally relevant acts, unilateral or multilateral, organized or spontaneous, formal or informal, leave their mark in the minds of all interested participants, whether they have taken part in the particular proceedings or not, and are liable to create expectations of authority for future occasions. This phenomenon of authority cannot be adequately perceived in terms of a dichotomy of binding and non-binding. Although such a concept of legal obligations is tempting in its apparent logical simplicity, it is often misleading and

does not reflect social realities. More realistically, it
has to be understood as the result of a process affected by
a whole series of elements the outcome of which is a higher
or lower degree of authority. Such a view of authority not
as an absolute qualitiy but as a continuum cannot derive
legal obligations from one particular clear-cut connecting-
point like consent or participation, but has to consider a
number of factors all contributing to the normative weight
of an invoked policy or prescription.

In order to determine the degree of deference due to an
international judicial decision, the domestic decision-maker
first has to examine these elements of authority before
deciding whether to adopt the same or a similar policy,
whether to reject the solution adopted by the international
decision-maker as unsound or to find it inapplicable to the
case before him. This method does not supply the judge with
a simple yardstick which tells him whether to apply a previous decision mechanically or to ignore it, but is designed
to provide a framework of enquiry enabling him to make
optimum use of past experience and wisdom to reach a solution
in accordance with contemporary international law.

1. THE SIMILARITY OF FACTUAL CIRCUMSTANCES: This is, as might
be expected, an important element in the persuasive power of
previous practice. To state that the authority of an international "precedent" does not least depend on the degree to
which the relevant facts of the two cases are alike may seem
rather obvious, and is certainly not a speciality of international judicial decisions. In domestic law the judge when
confronted with judicial authority the subject-matter of
which is too remote to be reasonably relevant to his case
will proceed to "distinguish" it. It would, however, not be
helpful to see this procedure of distinguishing as a simple
mechanical operation determining whether the facts of the
previous case make the decision either totally irrelevant or
"binding". Rather, it is the outcome of a subtle evaluating
process in which the judge decides whether the similarity of
the two cases and the wisdom of the earlier decision are
such that the policy applied in the earlier one could be
usefully employed in the one before him.

Although this intellectual process is essentially the same,
reliance on international judicial precedents is, nevertheless, likely to present its own peculiar problems. The
relative scarcity of international adjudications does normally create far greater difficulties for the domestic judge
looking for international judicial authority on a specific
point of international law than a search for domestic prece-

dents on municipal law would usually cause. The consequence
is a need to work by way of a relatively high degree of
generalization and somewhat remote analogy in order to find
guidance in the sparse network of international precedent.

An illustrative example of the loose manner in which courts
sometimes attempt to draw on international authority is
offered by a judgment of the Tribunale di Roma.(192) This
case involved an action against the Yugoslav State and the
question of the sovereign immunity of the defendant. In
resolving this problem, the Court saw fit to rely on the
principle of *bona fides*, which it derived not only from the
Covenant of the League of Nations and the Charter of the
United Nations, but also from an award of the Permanent
Court of Arbitration of 19o4.(193) A look at the international
decision(194) reveals that it has not the slightest connection with the question of immunity of foreign States in
domestic courts.

The tendency to draw far-fetched conclusions from international practice is sometimes encouraged by generalizing statements and *dicta* of the international decision-maker. This
point is well illustrated by the extent to which inferences
have been drawn from the International Court's Advisory
Opinion on Reparation for injuries suffered in the service
of the United Nations.(195) In this opinion the International
Court found it appropriate to support its finding that the
Organization was capable of exercizing a certain amount of
protection over its employees by making some very broad
statements on the United Nations' international personality.
(196) Domestic courts subsequently seized upon these statements and drew far-reaching conclusions from them.

The attempt of an American court(197) to base the United
Nations' right to sue for breach of a contract on this part
of the Advisory Opinion may still have some persuasive
power. In other cases the inferences drawn from this part of
the International Court of Justice's decision appear somewhat strained. In U.S. v. Melekh the U.S. District Court for
the Southern District of New York(198) had to deal with
criminal proceedings against a U.N. employee for espionage.
The Court denied diplomatic immunity, distinguishing between
foreign diplomats and U.N. employees. In doing so it relied
on and quoted the passage from the International Court's
Opinion to support the proposition that the Organization had
separate personality and was distinct from its Member States.
(199)

In the English case of Nissan v. Attorney-General the Court

of Appeal(2oo) was referred to the same Advisory Opinion in
support of the assertion that only the United Nations and
not a Member providing contingents for U.N. forces was
responsible for the actions of such troops.(2o1) The argument
was accepted by the Court although no reference was made to
the International Court in the judgment.

It is true that the International Court itself contributed
to the broad conclusions that were drawn in these cases from
its verdict on what was substantially a very limited point.
Nevertheless, the cases show well how, by a combination of
inductive and deductive reasoning, decisions can be made
authority for points that were not at all decided by them.
From a confirmation of specific rights of the United Nations,
generalizations as to its legal personality led to deductions
about certain obligations of the organization and its employees.

This is not to deny that the International Court's opinion,
by virtue of the prominence it has received, has had an
important impact on doctrine and practice concerning the
legal personality of international organizations. However,
to attempt a derivation of specific rights and duties from a
general confirmation of legal personality seems especially
unconvincing in the case of international organizations.

In drawing upon a past decision, it is advisable to distinguish between the actual determination made on the merits
and the court's vocal behavior accompanying it. While broad
general statements or *obiter dicta* may not be devoid of any
cognitive value, a prudent decision-maker in a subsequent
case will approach them with a far higher degree of caution.

Only by trying to identify the relevant legal problems
raised by the factual situation, notably the various possible
alternatives for their solution and the motives and policy-
considerations leading to the solution eventually adopted,
will a decision-maker be able to draw on the authority and
experience of past decisions.

Most importantly, the quest for authority in the form of
precedents should not induce the judge to make it up, where
it does not exist, by logical derivation in order somehow to
cover a question which may be quite a novel one. The nature
of law as a social science only admits of a very limited
measure of purely logical operations by way of syllogisms or
analogies. New problems require new solutions. The policy
considerations governing a *prima facie* similar case may,
upon closer examination, be quite different. In such a

situation an original and bold decision will be of far
higher value than a spurious reliance on past authority.

On the other hand, there are fields in which a specific and
detailed international practice is available. In these
areas, meaningful decisions without reference to this practice
are hardly possible. Thus the extensive judgments of the
International Military Tribunal in Nuremberg have decisively
contributed to the shaping of the contemporary law of war.
Domestic cases dealing with questions of the law of war have
quite rightly extensively relied upon them in numerous
cases.(2o2)

The question of an international decision's authority becomes
particularly evident and interesting in cases in which the
international organ has interpreted a treaty provision which
subsequently plays a rôle in domestic litigation. The provision interpreted by the international organ may not even be
contained in the same treaty, but may just be similar or
identical. The Court of Appeal of The Hague,(2o3) in a case
in which it had to interpret and apply a provision of the
Convention on the Privileges and Immunities of the United
Nations, came across a judgment of the Court of Justice of
the European Communities dealing with an analogous dispute
concerning the Protocol on the Privileges and Immunities of
the European Coal and Steel Community. The Netherlands court
rejected the contention of the Commissioner of Internal
Revenue that the judgment of the Court of Justice of the
European Commmunities was irrelevant since it concernend
another treaty:
> Naturally, one must grant the Commissioner that the
> answer to the present problem is not necessarily the
> same in relation to the European Communities as in
> relation to the United Nations and also that the Court
> of Justice of the European Communities has not given
> a decision, nor indeed could it have done so, on the
> interpretation of the Convention on the Privileges and
> immunities of the United Nations.
>
> Nevertheless, the great similarity of the relevant pro-
> visions of that Convention and those of the Protocols
> of the European Communities is remarkable...
>
> In view of this similarity between Art.V, section 18
> of the Cnvention on the Privileges and Immunities of
> the United Nations and the Provisions of the European
> Communities on the same subject, everything in the
> Court's view points to the first-mentioned provision
> being interpreted in the same way as the Court of
> Justice of the European Communities interpreted the
> last-mentioned provision of the aforementioned case.(2o4)

The question of harmonized interpretations of treaties by
national and international decision-makers becomes particularly acute where a treaty is constantly interpreted and
applied by specialized international organs and by domestic
courts.(2o5) Especially in situations in which international
organs are authorized to supervise the application of treaty
provisions by domestic decision-makers or where an intervention of international organs in litigation still pending
before domestic courts is possible, the uniformity of interpretations becomes a central question. The experiences made
in this respect with the European Convention on Human Rights
and with European Community law appear important enough to
warrant treatment in two separate short chapters (see EX-
CURSUS I and II below).

2. THE INTERNATIONAL OR DOMESTIC CHARACTER OF THE PRESCRIP-
TION INVOKED: This important element also determines the
authority of international practice. It would be wrong to
assume that every question decided by an international
judicial organ must by necessity be considered a determination of a point of international law. International courts
and tribunals have often had to settle disputes by applying
domestic prescriptions,(2o6) and the sole reason for the
submission of the case to the international judiciary may
have been an international element which in the actual litigation either did not play a dominating rôle or was merely
one of several aspects of the case. Complicated international
judicial proceedings invariably involve questions of domestic
law apart from international legal problems.

Interpretations of domestic law by international courts or
tribunals may be of relatively limited weight in the face of
other authority. A consistent and effective practice of the
local domestic tribunals is likely to represent the internal
law far more truthfully than any international judicial
decision.(2o7)

The Permanent Court was evidently quite aware of this in the
Serbian Loans Case(2o8) in which it had to construe a gold-
clause in a contract under French law:
> For the Court itself to undertake its own construction
> of municipal law, leaving on one side existing judicial
> decisions, with the ensuing danger of contradicting the
> construction which has been placed on such law by the
> highest national tribunal and which, in its result,
> seems to the Court reasonable, would not be in conformi-
> ty with the task for which the Court has been estab-
> lished and would not be compatible with the principles
> governing the selection of its members...It is French

legislation, as applied in France, which really constitutes French law.(2o9)

This is not to say that domestic courts will invariably find
international judicial decisions worthless where they concern
questions of internal or foreign municipal law. In Bank voor
Handel en Scheepvaart v. Slatford(21o) Devlin J. sitting in
the King's Bench Division had to interpret the Treaty of
Peace (Hungary) Order 1948. In distinguishing between a
company as a legal entity on one side and the shareholders
and their rights on the other, he found it convenient to
quote an international arbitral award(211) as authority on a
point of comparative law. By erroneously attributing the
award to the Permanent Court of International Justice, he
may, however, have done somewhat too much honor to it:

> It is worth noting, when a document of an international
> character is being indirectly construed, that these
> principles are not peculiar to English law. The point
> was considered by an international tribunal, the Perma-
> nent Court of International Justice, in Standard Oil
> Company's Claim, where it declares that "the decisions
> of principle of the highest courts of most countries
> continue to hold that neither the shareholders nor
> their creditors have any right to the corporate assets
> other than to receive, during the existence of the
> company, a share of the profits, the distribution of
> which has been decided by a majority of the shareholders,
> and, after its winding up, the proportional share of
> the assets".(212)

International judicial decisions on points of municipal law
may thus represent a valuable analysis of the law just as
domestic decisions may constitute an important contribution
to international legal practice. Their relative weight will
however be considerably greater if the question at stake is
one of public international law.

3. THE IMPACT OF THE INTERNATIONAL DECISION ON THE INTERNA-
TIONAL DECISION-MAKING PROCESS: This important element also
determines its authority in a particular case before a domestic court. It would be quite insufficient for the domestic
judge to restrict his enquiry to the actual text of the
international judicial decision. In order properly to eva-
luate its weight as a means for the clarification and shaping
of international law, it is always necessary to see the
decision not in isolation but as an element in a much wider
process of communication of which it merely forms a part.
This process of communication takes place in a multitude of
forms. This broader context includes previous and subsequent

judicial decisions, national and international, statements
and practice of other state organs, especially the executive,
activities of international institutions and transactions by
private companies, scholarly writings and the like. All
these activities leave their marks in the minds of participants, create expectations and influence subsequent decisions. They can therefore only be understood if they are not
analysed in isolation but are seen in conjunction.(213)

In determining the significance of a "precedent" in the
international decision-making process, the question of
whether the disposition between the parties to the original
decision was "binding" in the technical sense should not be
given much weight. It would not be appropriate to see the
question of an international decision's value as a precedent
in necessary conjunction with its legal significance in
settling the original dispute.(214) The authority of a
decision for the clarification and development of the law
has a completely different basis from its operative effect
for the particular case. An advisory opinion though not
"binding" can have far-reaching impacts on the legal expectations of the international community, and can thus exercise a momentuous influence on the subsequent flow of decisions concerning legal questions which were discussed in it.
It would, therefore, be quite erroneous to attribute a generally lower cognitive value to advisory opinions or other
recommendations for subsequent decisions. In actual fact,
domestic courts have repeatedly referred to advisory opinions
of the Permanent Court of International Justice and the
International Court of Justice;(215) there is no known case
in which doubt was cast upon the authority of an international
"precedent" just because it had only been a recommendation.

On the other hand, much of the value of an international
judicial decision as an authoritative statement of the law
depends on the effectiveness it was able to achieve in the
post-adjudicative phase. A decision, whether it was formally
"binding" or merely advisory, which was ignored by many or
all of the parties or rejected by the requesting organ, is
not likely to exercise a significant influence on future
conduct. A judicial organ deciding in a later dispute will
not be able to find that such an opinion has given rise to
significant expectations of authority.

The measure of effect accomplished by a judicial decision
will, however, not only depend on the behavior of its immediate addressees, but to a large extent also on its influence on subsequent practice, judicial and non-judicial. It
is this ensuing practice which eventually discloses whether

the decision was just an isolated episode or a momentuous
factor in international legal development.

The significance of a particular precedent may thus be
supported, reduced, or even outweighed by other legally
relevant elements. On the other hand, international judicial
decisions of otherwise limited import can become decisive in
situations where other pertinent factors do not yield any
conclusive result. This is well illustrated by a case before
the United States Court of Claims.(216) In this case, the
Court had to decide on the amount of interest to be paid for
a wrongful detention and requisition of a neutral ship. It
found that:

> There does not appear to be any uniform rule, of
> universal application, governing either the rate of in-
> terest or the period for which it is allowable. ...In
> the absence of a universal rule upon the subject, we hold
> that the rate adopted by the /US-German/ Mixed Claims
> Commission, and by that commission made applicable to a
> great number of claims, varying widely in their nature,
> that is five per centum per annum...should be allowed, and
> also in accordance with the rule adopted by that commis-
> sion, that the interest should begin to run from the
> date of the enquiry...(217)

Much of an international precedent's authority in subsequent
judicial proceedings also depends on factors not so much
connected with the objective factual or legal circumstances
surrounding the cases but with the particular international
decisions-maker itself and its performance. There can be
little doubt that a decision handed down by the International
Court of Justice will usually have considerably more impact
than the award of a Mixed Claims Commission or an *ad hoc*
arbitral tribunal. The general reputation of an international
judicial organ based on the quality of its past decisions,
its composition, the extent of its jurisdiction, or its
affiliation to an important international organization will
therefore endow its pronouncements with a weight that may
otherwise be lacking.

Perhaps, more importantly, its general effectiveness in
settling disputes and its ability to secure compliance with
its verdicts is likely to affect any expectations of authority created by a particular decision. An international
judicial organ like the Court of Justice of the European
Communities, whose decisions are supported by effective
enforcement procedures, is liable to command considerably
more respect than a tribunal unable to have its verdicts
carried out. This measure of effective power is not only

reflected by enforcement procedures but also by the extent
to which the court or tribunal is able to assert its jurisdiction.

Other important aspects of the international judicial organ's
authority are its permanency and the degree of continuity
displayed by it. A court which, by virtue of continuity in
its composition, succeeds in developing a *jurisprudence
constante*, permitting reasonably safe predictions about its
future judicial behavior, is likely to exercise considerably
more influence than an *ad hoc* tribunal even though its
members may have been selected from a permanent list.

Ultimately, much of a precedent's persuasive power simply
depends on its intrinsic quality. A decision, even if perfectly reasonable in its outcome, will fail to impress a subsequent decision-maker if it is badly argued or supported by
inconclusive reasoning. The orderly exposition of all relevant legal arguments and policy considerations, therefore,
plays an important rôle in securing its influence on future
decisions. Part of this persuasiveness is, naturally, also
indicated by the degree of consensus a decision was able to
secure in a composite judicial organ and the cogency of any
dissenting opinions.(218)

c)   Specific Prescriptions

The difficulties in evaluating the authority of international
"precedents" have repeatedly led to suggestions to regulate
the question of an international judicial decision's effect
on subsequent litigation. This seems to have been first
mooted by the *Institut de Droit International* at its Copenhagen session in 1897 in the context of its discussions on
the constitutions of international tribunals to be established
for the interpetation of multilateral conventions.(219) Suggestions to make arbitral awards binding also for future
disputes between parties to the treaties who had not participated in the proceedings, were, however, rejected by the
majority.(22o)

The question came up again at the Hague Peace Conferences in
the debates on a Convention for the Pacific Settlement of
International Disputes and was discussed at great length by
the First Commission of the 19o7 Conference. Several suggestions to render arbitral decisions operative also for
subsequent disputes and to recognize their legal force for
future cases in domestic courts(221) were made, but did not
prevail in the face of severe criticism directed at them.(222)
The solution eventually adopted by Article 84 of the Convention

closely followed the example of Article 56 of the 1899
Convention in merely providing for a right of intervention
in cases concerning the interpretation of multilateral
conventions, with the result that a verdict was also binding
on the intervening party.(223)

A desire to ensure the uniform interpretation of conventions
for the unification of private law led to the revival of
similar proposals on several occasions.(224) At the 1928
Hague Conference for Private International Law, a suggestion
was made by the Netherlands delgate,(225) which was subsequently amended by French and Norwegian drafts,(226) to
insert a clause into Private Law Conventions recognizing the
competence of the Permanent Court of International Justice
to decide on differences concerning their interpretation. A
decision would then have to be implemented by legislation or
similar measures by the Contracting Parties. But the subsequent discussion at the Conference showed a strong dislike
for the idea that an international decision should direct
domestic courts in subsequent cases on matters of private
law.(227)

When the same question was raised at the *Institut de Droit
International* in the following year, a resolution was adopted
under which a declaratory judgment of the PCIJ on a Private
Law Convention was to be effective for all Contracting
States which would then be under an obligation to take the
necessary measures to make this interpretation binding on
their organs.(228)

A similar proposal was endorsed by the *Institut* in 1956
in the course of its deliberations on a model clause conferring compulsory jurisdiction on the International Court for
inclusion in conventions.(229) Practical success in the form
of concrete treaty drafts was, however, not achieved.(23o)

EXCURSUS I: Impact of the Supervisory Organs of the European
             Human Rights Convention on Domestic Courts

The constant application and interpretation of a multilateral
treaty like the European Convention on Human Rights by the
international organs specifically created for this task as
well as by the courts of Member States should afford a model
example for an investigation into the influence of international decision-making on the practice of domestic courts.
The activity of the Commission, the Committee of Ministers
and the Human Rights Court as supervisors of the Convention's
application makes a harmonizing effect of their practice
seem obvious and desirable.

Scholarly opinion is generally agreed on the relevance of
the international practice for the Convention's subsequent
interpretation by State-organs, although the theoretical
foundation for this effect is not entirely undisputed. Assertions of a "binding force" of the practice of the Convention-
organs for domestic decision-makers,(231) on the one hand,
and denials of their relevance for lack of "binding force",
on the other,(232) are the exception. The weight of the
findings of the Strasbourg organs for subsequent domestic
decisions is usually rated somewhere between these two
extremes.(233)

The influence of the practice of the international organs
supervising the Convention's Implementation is often taken
for granted.(234) A detailed examination of the influence of
the Commission and the Human Rights Court on the practice of
domestic courts of all Member States to the European Human
Rights Convention would go far beyond the confines of this
short chapter. Two detailed recent studies(235) which examine
this problem in some depth indicate that domestic courts
were relatively slow in grasping the significance of the
international practice but that there is now a rapidly
increasing awareness that the decisions of the Strasbourg
organs are of the highest importance as guides to the interpretation of the Convention.

A comparison between the behavior of English and Continental
courts in their treatment of the international practice as
"precedents" would, of course, be highly interesting. Such
an inquiry is seriously hampered by the British constitutional practice requiring specific implementing legislation
before prescriptions emanating from treaties can be applied
in the domestic sphere.(236) No such implementing measures
have been taken with respect to the European Convention on
Human Rights. This has severely restricted the development
of a practice with regard to the Human Rights Convention by
the English courts.(237) Although a number of cases have
been reported since 1974, in which English judges have
referred to the European Human Rights Convention,(238) these
references were chiefly in the context of interpreting
English statutes. There is consequently not sufficient case-
material available that would permit an empirical examination
of any differences in the treatment of the international
practice to the Convention in the two legal traditions of
common law and continental law. Whether a common law court
would actually defy an international pronouncement in favor
of a domestic precedent,(239) or would, as has been suggested,(24o) treat the international case-law like foreign
law, thus feeling free to depart from a previous domestic

decision, is hard to predict. But it is certainly an encouraging sign that Lord Scarman, expressing the opinion of the entire House of Lords, in a recent decision found that a certain unconvincing interpretation of the Convention would not be adopted "unless and until the European Court of Human Rights declares that it is correct".(241)

The incorporation of the European Convention on Human Rights in Austria as part of constitutional law has led to unusually frequent invocations of its provisions before the Austrian Constitutional Court. This justifies a closer look at the practice of this Court to highlight the problems encountered by domestic courts when confronted with invokations of the international practice. For quite a long time, the Austrian Constitutional Court paid relatively little attention to the practice of the Strasbourg organs to the Convention. Only rarely did the Court find it necessary to analyze the international practice carefully. This disregard for the international decisions on the Convention does not seem to have led to any major difficulties or dramatic discrepancies. Two examples show, nevertheless, that the loose manner in which the Court initially treated the international decisions can very easily lead to divergent results.

In one case(242) the Constitutional Court, in interpreting Austria's reservation to Article 5, found it unnecessary to analyse the Commission's relevant practice, but restricted itself to a cursory reference to a scholarly publication dealing with a decision of the Commission.(243) In doing so it misinterpreted a somewhat equivocal translation used in that publication which led the Constitutional Court to conclusions which were evidently at variance with the policies advocated by the Commission.

In another case(244) the same Court was confronted with the admittedly difficult task of interpreting the phrase "civil rights and obligations" contained in Article 6 of the Convention. The Constitutional Court found it appropriate to define this expression in the sense of the concept of "civil law matters" *(Zivilrechtswesen)* as contained in Article 1o/1(6) of the Austrian Constitution. It ignored a long standing practice of the Commission which had repeatedly declared that:

> /Civil rights and obligations/...cannot be construed as
> a mere reference to the domestic law of the High Contrac-
> ting Party concerned, but on the contrary, relates to
> an autonomous concept which must be interpreted inde-
> pendently of the rights existing in the law of the High
> Contracting Parties, even though the general principles

of the domestic law of the High Contracting Parties
must necessarily be taken into consideration in any
such interpretation;(245)

More recently, the attitude of the Austrian Constitutional
Court towards the practice of the international organs of
supervision has undergone a marked change. Careful references
to international decisions are becoming more frequent.(246)
Especially, the Human Right Court's judgment in the Ringeisen
case is often consulted and even quoted in the original.(247)
Remarks regretting the absence of pertinent international
precedents(248) indicate a methodical search in the practice
of the Strasbourg organs. The Constitutional Court does not
seem to entertain any doubts that the interpretations adopted
by the Commission and the Human Rights Court are decisive
for it.(249)

The Austrian Supreme Court even went a step further.(25o) After relying on two judgments of the Human Rights Court, it
refers, evidently approvingly, to an opinion expressed in
scholarly writings to the effect that the practice of the
international organs is binding on State organs in subsequent
cases.

Inspite of these indications of a new trend towards a stronger
observation of and deference to the practice of the Commission
and the Human Rights Court, the basic problems are by no
means resolved. Part of the difficulties may be due to a
theoretical uncertainty about the relevance of decisions of
international organs in the courts' framework of "sources of
law". This may even lead to a tendency to consult the international practice by way of a precaution, but to refrain
from specifically mentioning it, though this is difficult to
prove.

The most important reason for a scarcity of references to
the practice of the supervisory organs of the European
Convention on Human Rights in the practice of domestic
courts is probably a lack of adequate information on the
part of the bench and bar and an unfamiliarity with the
published material. Only if the reports of the practice of
the Convention-organs become a regular part of the reference
libraries of courts and practitioners and are referred to in
the same manner as the law reports of the higher domestic
courts is there justified hope that the activity of the
international organs actually shows the unifying influence
it should exercise, leading to a truly "European standard"
also in the decisions of domestic courts.

A systematic observation of and reliance on not only the
international but also the foreign practice to the Convention
would, moreover, have an additional beneficial effect. A
large part of the difficulties arising from the Convention's
abstract and sometimes unconventional terminology, which has
sometimes led courts to declare it "non-self executing",(251)
could thus be overcome. The rich and detailed practice on
the individual provisions of the Convention should be able
to resolve a great deal of the problems of interpretation
arising from its abstract language.

EXCURSUS II: International Preliminary Rulings as "Precedents"

The establishment of procedures for preliminary rulings to
be given by international decision-makers upon the request
of domestic courts creates very close patterns of interaction
between the two sets of decision-makers. (See also chapter
XIV.D.2.) It is not surprising that international practice
has shown its strongest effects upon the behavior of domestic
courts in this field. Some treaties instituting procedures
for preliminary rulings even specifically declare previous
preliminary rulings binding on domestic courts or at least
waive an obligation to make a fresh submission for a new
ruling.

The German-Polish Agreement on Upper Silesia of 1922(252)
provided for an Arbitral Tribunal competent to give preliminary rulings on questions concerning the Agreement's interpretation by domestic courts. (Article 588). These courts were
in subsequent cases bound by such rulings if they had been
published, unless they were able to secure a new preliminary
ruling departing from the original decision. (Article 592).

The Mixed Court established by the French-German Treaty of
1956 returning the Saar-territory to Germany(253) was designed
to ensure uniformity in the application of French legislation
remaining in force in the territory during the transition
period. (Article 42). Its rulings were always binding in
future cases before the Saar courts.

The provisions in the treaties establishing the European
Communities dealing with the procedure before the Court of
Justice contain no reference to any authority of preliminary
rulings as "precedents" for subsequent cases.(254) Nevertheless, in no other field is the impact of the practice of an
international judicial organ upon domestic courts so evident
and ubiquitous as in European Community law. Reliance on
decisions of the European Court by domestic courts is a
natural part of everyday practice. The influence of the

European Court's practice upon the interpretation and application of Community law by domestic courts can be felt in
all areas of Community law, but is particularly conspicuous
on questions such as "primacy" or "direct applicability" of
Community law.(255)

The European Court itself has recognized this strong effect
of its decisions as precedents. It has held that even a
court of last instance, which normally would be under an
obligation to request a preliminary ruling, can refrain from
submitting a question of Community law if it has already
been answered by the Court in a previous case.(256) This
does not mean that the domestic court is precluded from re-
submitting a question. But if a court of last instance
follows an interpetation given by the European Court in a
previous preliminary ruling, there is no violation of its
obligation to submit questions of Community law.(257)

The supreme courts of Members have repeatedly explicitly
availed themselves of this possibility to simplify their
procedure.(258) They refrain from re-submitting questions
pending before them already answered by the European Court.
The courts found that these previous rulings sufficiently
clarified the questions before them or even held that they
were bound by the previous preliminary rulings.(259) Nevertheless, the right to resubmit is also utilized occasionally.
(26o) Under this practice the alternative for a court of
last instance is thus clear: it either has to follow the
European Court's "precedents" or it can try to achieve a
change in the Court's position by submitting the question
afresh. The course adopted by the French Conseil d'Etat in
Minister of the Interior v. Cohn-Bendit,(261) where the Court
refused to follow the practice of the European Court and dis-
allowed a request for a preliminary ruling, is not only an
inglorious exception to this practice but also a clear violation of Community law.

The situation is not quite so clear for the lower courts.
For them there is no duty but just a right to submit. Does
this imply that they are free to depart from the holdings of
the European Court without making a submission for a preliminary ruling? In the majority of cases the courts do not
discuss this question. Nevertheless, there are a few cases
in which courts, whose decisions are subject to an appeal,
expressed their views on this point. In some cases the
courts made it unequivocally clear that they felt bound by
the previous preliminary rulings.(262) The European Court's
practice was simply perceived as an integral part of Community law, which enjoys precedence over the domestic law of
Members just like the Treaties themselves.(263)

In other cases, however, courts rejected rulings of the
European Court given in previous cases and chose a different
interpretation of Community law.(264) One court of last
instance even dismissed an appeal directed against a judgment,
which was in contradiction to a finding of the European
Court given in a previous case.(265)

It would be difficult to argue in favor of a formally binding
effect of precedents of the European Court for the lower
courts. On the other hand, policy-considerations strongly
militate in favor of a practice whereby lower courts, just
like courts of last instance, should either follow or submit.
Practically all aspects affecting the authority of international "precedents", as set out in detail above, speak in
favor of decisions of the Court of Justice of the European
Communities: The frequent and detailed practice of the
European Court usually offers precise and pertinent guidance
to the domestic courts. There is, consequently, usually no
need to resort to any far-fetched analogies or syllogisms
when relying on the European Court's case law. The jurisdiction of the European Court as an authoritative organ for the
interpretation of Community law is beyond doubt. Its controlling influence on the application of Community law by the
other Community organs and by domestic decision-makers is
evident.

In addition to the very high degree of authority enjoyed by
the European Court's case law, there are also aspects of
procedural economy which militate in favor of a deference to
previous preliminary rulings. It does not make much sense to
permit a lower court to deviate from precedents which are
binding on the courts of last instance. Provided the supreme
courts act in accordance with their obligations towards
Community law, an appeal to a court of last instance must,
by necessity, lead to a reversal of decisions of lower
courts deviating from the European Court's practice. The
answer to the question of a lower court's proper reaction
towards precedents by the European Court is probably best
summarized by a Netherlands District Court:

> A sound administration of justice demands that a judge
> of a national court of a member-State - notwithstanding
> the existence of a right of appeal from his judgment -
> should either respect an earlier decision of the Court
> of Justice of the European Communities or alternatively
> that the judge himself should refer the case to the
> Court of Justice for a preliminary ruling concerning
> the interpretation of the E.E.C. Treaty, even though he
> is not compelled to do so under Art.177(2) of the
> Treaty.(266)

(1) For different attempts to categorize decisions of
     international institutions see Sloan, Implementation
     and Enforcement of Decisions of International Organiza-
     tions, 62 ASIL Proceedings 1,3(1968); Miele, Les organi-
     sations internationales et le domaine constitutionel
     des Etats, 131 RC 319,335seq.(197o, III);Economides,
     Nature juridique, p.225,229; Dominice, La nature juri-
     dique, p.249seq.

(2) Parry, The Sources, p.1oo; van Panhuys, Relations and
     Interactions, p.11; Hexner, Die Rechtsnatur, p.8o;
     Huber, Die internationale Quasilegislative, 27 SchwJIR
     9,22seq.(1971); Thieme, Das Grundgesetz und die öffent-
     liche Gewalt internationaler Staatengemeinschaften, 18
     Veröffentlichungen der Vereinigung der Deutschen Staats-
     rechtslehrer, 5o,59f(196o) with further references.

(3) Cf. Bleicher, The Legal Significance of Re-Citation of
     General Assembly Resolutions, 63 AJIL 444,453(1969).

(4) Cf. also Merle, Le pouvoir réglementaire des institutions
     internationales, 4 AFDI 341seq.(1958).

(5) See also Mosler, Internationale Organisation und Staats-
     verfassung, in Rechtsfragen der Internationalen Organisa-
     tion, Festschrift für Hans Wehberg, p.273,274seq.(1956).

(6) Higgins, United Nations and Lawmaking: The Political
     Organs, 64 ASIL Proceedings 37,44(197o); Huber, Die
     internationale Quasilegislative, p.23seq.

(7) Page 34/35.

(8) In re Dame Pêcheral, Cour de Paris, 17 July 1948, 15
     AD 289(1948).

(9) Kare-Merat et Kabozo c. Etat belge, min. de la Justice
     et délégué du Haut Commissariat pour les réfugiés, Bel-
     gian Conseil d'Etat, 25 Sept.197o, 8 RBDI 675 and 687
     (1972).

(1o) In re Piracy Jure Gentium, Privy Council, 26 July 1934,
     /1934/ A.C.586, 3 BILC 836,842seq.

(11) Dralle case, Austrian Supreme Court, 1o May 195o, SZ
     XXIII/143; German Bundesverfassungsgericht 3o Apr.1963,
     BVerfGE 16,27, 45 ILR 57,76.

(12) See note 11.

(13) German Bundesverfassungsgericht 3o Oct.1962, 11 AVR
     112(1963/64), 38 ILR 162,166.

(14) Re Martinez and Others, Italian Court of Cassation,
     25 Nov.1959, 45 Rivista DI 256(1962), 28 ILR 17o.

(15) Attorney-General of Israel v. Kamiar, Israel Supreme
     Court, 9 June 1968, 44 ILR 197,248,261seq., 267seq.,
     277seq.,285seq.; N.V.Holland-Amerika Lijn (H.A.L.) v.
     Wm. H. Müller & Co. N.V., Hague Court of Appeal,
     28 Feb.1969, 1 NYIL 224(197o).

(16) Cf. Menon v. Esperdy, U.S. Court of Appeals 2d Cir.
     3O June 1969, 413 F.2d 644,650; 64 AJIL 419(1970).

(17) Pappas v. Francisci, New York Supreme Court, 6 Feb.1953,
     119 N.Y.S. 2d 69, 47 AJIL 505(1953); X. v. Y., Hague
     Court of Appeal, 2O Nov.1969, 1 NYIL 210(1970).

(18) See Schreuer, The Impact of International Institutions
     on the Protection of Human Rights in Domestic Courts, 4
     Israel Yearbook on Human Rights 6o,76seq.(1974); Skubi-
     szewski, Recommendations of the United Nations and
     Municipal Courts 46 BYIL 353(1972-73).

(19) Art.14(3) ECSC: "Recommendations shall be binding with
     respect to the objectives which they prescribe,...";
     Art.II of the agreement between the United Nations and
     UNESCO, 1 UNTS 24o: "...such recommendations shall be
     accepted..."

(2o) See especially the duty to submit recommendations to
     legislative organs and to furnish reports under Art.19
     ILO, Art.IV,4 and VIII UNESCO, Art.XI, 1 FAO, and
     Art.15(b) Council of Europe.

(21) Art.31(3),(4) EFTA; Art.33 ILO.

(22) See especially the provisions of the U.N. Charter
     authorizing the General Assembly to decide "upon the
     recommendation of the Security Council". On the legal
     nature of such recommendations under Art.4(2) of the
     Charter see esp. the second Admissions Case, ICJ Reports,
     p.4(1950).

(23) This is also supported by the travaux préparatoires to
     the U.N. Charter. See esp. UNCIO vol.III p.536/7,
     vol.IX p.7o,316, vol.XIII p.7o9/1o. See also Sloan, The
     Binding Force, p.6seq.; Arangio-Ruiz, The Normative
     Role, p.5o4.

(24) Guradze, Zur Rechtsnatur normativer Entschließungen der
     Vollversammlung der Vereinten Nationen, 19 Zeitschrift
     f.Luftrecht u.Weltraumrechtsfragen 49(197o); _ibid._, Are
     Human Rights Resolutions of the United Nations General
     Assembly Law-Making?, 4 Human Rights Journal 453(1971);
     Kelsen, The Law of the United Nations, p.195seq.; Kiss,
     Nature juridique, p.26o, Kunz, The United Nations
     Declaration of Human Rights, 43 AJIL 316(1949); Seidl-
     Hohenveldern, Die Allgemeine Deklaration der Menschen-
     rechte als Rechtsquelle, 74 JBl 558(1952); Smith, The
     Binding Force of League Resolutions, 16 BYIL 157(1935).
     Cf. also the remark in the dissenting opinion by Jessup,
     ICJ Rep.,p.325,432(1966).

(25) Kammergericht Berlin, 14 Sept.1961, 14 NJW 22o9(1961);
     BGH, 1o Jan.1966, 19 NJW 726(1966); Bavarian Constitu-
     tional Court, 3 July 1961, 14 NJW 1619(1961); 12 July
     1962, Fontes A, II, 5 No.71; Austrian Supreme Court,18
     June 1975, 2 EuGRZ 492(1975); A.v.State-Secretary of
     Justice, Netherlands Administrative decision of the
     Crown, 12 Feb.1974, 7 NYIL 3o6(1976); Stichting Communi-
     catie Belangen Nederland v. State-Secretary for Trans-
     port and Waterways, Netherlands administrative decision
     of the Crown, 27 Dec.1976, 9 NYIL 3o9(1978).

(26) De Meyer c. Etat belge, Conseil d'Etat (Belg.), 9
     Feb.1966, 4 RBDI 569(1968); In re Rauter, Netherlands
     special Court of Cassation, 1949, 16 AD 546(1949).

(27) In re Beck, Netherlands, Special Court of Cassation, 11
     Apr.1949, 16 AD 279(1949); In re Best and Others,
     Supreme Court of Denmark, 17 March 195o, 17 ILR 434(195o).

(28) Karadzole et al. v. Artukovic, U.S. Court of Appeals,
     9th Circ., 24 June 1957, 247 F.2d 198, 24 ILR 51o(1957);
     X. v. Minister of Defence, 'Administrative Decision'
     (Neth.), 14 Nov.1968, 1 NYIL 219(197o).

(29) The State (Duggan) v. Tapley, 12 Dec.195o, 7 BILC 1o74,
     18 ILR 336(1951).

(3o) 18 ILR 342(1951).

(31) German Bundesverwaltungsgericht, 22 Feb.1956, BVerwGE
     3,171, DVerw.Bl. 378(1956), Fontes A, II, 4, No.256;
     Bundesverwaltungsgericht, 29 June 1957, Fontes A, II,
     4, No.297; Military Prosecutor v. Halil Muhamad Mahmud
     Halil Bakhis and Others, Israel Military Court in
     Ramallah, 1o June 1968, 47 ILR 484. Miriam Streit v.

Nissim, the Chief Rabbi of Israel, Israel Supreme
Court, 1o July 1964, 18 Piskei Din 598,612(1964).

(32) Re Tovt, Court of Taranto, Giurisprudenza Italiana II,
573,581(1954), UN Yearbook of Human Rights 169,171(1954).

(33) In 53 ASIL Proc 227(1959).

(34) On the practical significance of the Universal Declara-
tion of Human Rights see esp. McDougal & Bebr, Human
Rights in the United Nations, 58 AJIL 6o3,615seq.;
Schwelb, The Influence of the Universal Declaration of
Human Rights on International and National Law, 53 ASIL
Proc 217(1959); Skubiszewski, Legal Nature, p.2o4;
Sohn, Die allgemeine Erklärung der Menschenrechte, 8
Journal d. Internationalen Juristen Kommission 21(1967).

(35) See esp. the numerous references of the I.C.J. to
resolutions of U.N. organs and cf. Engel, "Living"
International Constitutions and the World Court (The
Subsequent Practice of International Organs under their
Constituent Instruments), 16 ICLQ 865(1967); especially
on the Universal Declaration of Human Rights see Schwelb,
The Influence, p.228; ibid., Neue Etappen der Fortent-
wicklung des Völkerrechts durch die Vereinten Nationen,
13 AVR 17(1966); Schreuer, The Impact, p.76; Tammes,
Decision of International Organs, p.268seq.

(36) Cf. the practice on the Universal Declaration of Human
Rights in the General Assembly but also in the Security
Council discussed by Schwelb, Die Menschenrechtsbestimmungen der Charta der Vereinten Nationen und die Allgemeine Erklärung der Menschenrechte, 21 Vereinte Nationen 18o, 182seq.(1973).

(37) Bindschedler, La délimitation des compétences des
Nations Unies, 1o8 RC 3o7,348(1963, I); Virally, La
valeur juridique, p.87.

(38) See the references on the following pages.

(39) See e.g. the generous selection offered by Skubiszewski,
Legal Nature, p.2o2seq.

(4o) But see the dissenting opinion by Judge Alvarez in the
Reservations to the Genocide Convention Case, ICJ Rep.,
p.52(1951); and in the Anglo-Norwegian Fisheries Case,
ICJ Rep., p.152(1951); Lande, The Changing Effectiveness, p.165; Elias, Modern Sources of International

Law, in Transnational Law in a Changing Society, Essays
in Honor of P.C.Jessup (1972) p.34,51.

(41) Verdross, Kann die Generalversammlung, p.692; Guradze,
Zur Rechtsnatur, p.54; ibid., Are Human Rights Resolutions, p.456seq.

(42) See esp. Castaneda, Legal Effects, p.15oseq.

(43) See esp. the references to Soviet authors by Uibopuu,
Die Sovjetische Doktrin, p.122seq.; by Skubiszewski,
Resolutions, p.95 and by Tunkin, Das Völkerrecht,
p.1o3; ibid., Theory of International Law, p.163(1974).

(44) Arangio-Ruiz, The Normative Role, p.486seq.; Asamoah,
The Legal Significance, p.63seq.; Bindschedler, La
délimitation, p.349; Castaneda, Legal Effects, p.154,
Johnson, The Effect of Resolutions of the General
Assembly of the United Nations, 32 BYIL 97,121(1955-
56); Sloan, The Binding Force, p.22; Virally, La valeur
juridique, p.85.

(45) E.g. the Declaration of Legal Principles Governing the
Activities of States in the Exploration and Use of
Outer Space, adopted unanimously on 13 Dec.1963, U.N.G.A.
Res.1962(XVIII). On this point see esp. Castaneda,
Legal Effects, p.162seq.; McWhinney, International Law
and World Revolution, p.8o(1967).

(46) See two cases before the High Court of Mauritius in
which the Universal Declaration of Human Rights and the
European Convention on Human Rights were treated on the
same legal footing: Director of Public Prosecutions v.
Labavarde and Another, 9 March 1965, 44 ILR 1o4;
Roussety v. The Attorney General, 30 March 1967, 44 ILR
1o8.

(47) Asamoah, The Legal Significance, p.6,35seq.,42seq.;
Bleicher, Re-Citation, p.448seq.; Castles, Legal Status,
p.82; Miele, Les organisations internationales, p.366seq.;
Schachter, The Relation of Law, Politics and Action in
the United Nations, 1o9 RC 169, 186(1963, III); Tunkin,
Das Völkerrecht, p.1o7. See also the references by
Uibopuu, Die sovjetische Doktrin, p.125seq.; Tunkin,
Theory of International Law, p.171.

(48) Bleicher, Re-Citation, p.461seq.; Piotrovski, Les
résolutions de l'Assemblée générale des Nations Unies
et la portée du droit conventionnel, 33 Revue de Droit

International, 111, 229(1955); Robinson, The Universal
Declaration of Human Rights, p.36seq.,43seq.(1958);
Sibert, Traitê de droit international public Vol.I,
p.454seq.(1951). See also the references by Sohn,
Protection of Human Rights through International Legis-
lation, in Renê Cassin Amicorum Discipulorumque Liber
Vol.I, p.325,328(1969); and cf. Schwelb, Die Menschen-
rechtsbestimmungen, p.18o.

(49) A.J.K. v. Public Prosecutor, Dist.Ct.Maastricht,
27 Jan.1959, 8 NTIR 73(1961), confirmed by the Supreme
Court loc.cit.; German Bundesverfassungsgericht, 4 May
1971, 24 NJW 15o9(1971).

(5o) German Bundesgerichtshof, 21 Jan.1953, 6 NJW 392(1953);
2o ILR 37o(1953); Mejia v. Regierungsrat des Kantons
Bern, Swiss Bundesgericht, 9 May 1963, 32 ILR 192.

(51) Hackstetter v. State of Israel, Sup.Ct.of Israel, 1972,
2 Israel YBHR 344(1972), 51 ILR 331(1978).

(52) Arangio-Ruiz, The Normative Role, p.471seq.; Asamoah,
The Legal Significance, p.52; Bailey, Making Interna-
tional Law in the United Nations, 61 ASIL Proc 233,
235seq.(1967); Higgins, The Development of International
Law through the Political Organs of the United Nations,
p.2seq.(1963); Stavropoulos, The United Nations and the
Development of International Law, UN Monthly Chronicle
78,8o(197o,6). See also the dissenting opinion by Judge
Tanaka to the judgment in the South-West Africa case,
ICJ Rep., p.25o,291(1966).

(53) Arangio-Ruiz, The Normative Role, p.478; Asamoah, The
Legal Significance, p.55seq.; Bleicher, Re-Citation,
p.45o; Thirlway, International Customary Law and Codification, p.66seq.(1972). Cf. also the German Bundesverfassungsgericht, 4 May 1971, 24 NJW 15o9(1971), which
refers to the Universal Declaration of Human Rights as
an expression of international legal conviction.

(54) Cf. the dissenting opinion of Judge Tanaka to the
judgment in the South-West Africa case, ICJ Rep.,
p.291seq.(1966); Cheng, United Nations Resolutions on
Outer Space: 'Instant' International Customary Law? 5
IJIL 23(1965); cf. also Thirlway, Customary Law,
p.72seq. and D'Amato, On Consensus, 8 CanYIL 1o4,11o
(197o).

(55) Engel, "Living" International Constitutions, p.91o.

(56) Asamoah, The Legal Significance, p.7; Di Qual, Les
effets des rêsolutions des Nations Unies, p.249seq.;
Engel, Procedures for the *de facto* Revision of the
Charter, 59 ASIL Proc 1o8,116(1965); Golsong, Das
Problem, p.32seq.; Hambro, Some Notes on the Development
of the Sources of International Law, 17 Scandinavian
Studies in Law 77seq.(1973); Schlüter, The Domestic
Status of the Human Rights Clauses of the United Nations
Charter, 61 CalLR 11o,145seq.(1973); Tunkin, Völkerrecht,
p.11o; Tunkin, Theory of International Law, p.172seq.
Verdross, Kann die Generalversammlung der Vereinten
Nationen das Völkerrecht weiterbilden?, 26 ZaöRV 69o,
693seq.(1966); Thirlway, Customary Law, p.73; Lachs, Le
rôle des organisations internationales dans la formation
du droit international, in Mélanges offerts à Henri
Rolin, p.157,166(1964); Hambro, The Sixth Commitee in
the Law Creating Function of the General Assembly, 21
Revista Esp.DI 387,389(1968).

(57) Auditeur Militaire v. Krumkamp, Military Court of
Brabant, 8 Feb.195o, 17 ILR 388,39o(195o).

(58) Soc. elettrica della Venezia Giulia c. Presidenza del
Consiglio dei ministeri del tesoro e degli affari esteri,
Tribunale di Roma, 2 July 1958, Il Foro Italiano 1959,
I, 1156; Corte d'appello di Milano, 27 Nov.1964, Il
Foro Italiano, 1965, II, 122,126; Ministry of Home Affairs
v. Kemali, 1 Feb.1962, Corte di cassazione, 4o ILR
191,195; Re Matile, Corte Constituzionale, 23 Nov.1967,
51 Rivista DI 384(1968). See also the decision of the
Supreme Court of the Philippines in Borovski v. Commis-
sioner of Immigration and Director of Prisons, 28
Sept.1951, UN Yearbook on Human Rights 287(1951).

(59) Asamoah, The Legal Significance, p.61seq.; Cassin, La
Déclaration universelle et la mise en oeuvre des droits
de l'homme, 79 RC 237, 294(1951,III); Golsong, Das
Problem, p.34; Hambro, Some Notes, p.92; Tchirkovitch,
La déclaration universelle des droits de l'homme et sa
portée internationale, 53 RGDIP 359,38oseq.(1949);
Verdross, Kann die Generalversammlung, p.694; Zemanek,
The United Nations and the Law of Outer Space, 19
Yearbook of World Affairs 199,2o8seq.(1965).

(6o) American European Beth-El Mission v. Minister of Social
Welfare, Israel Supreme Court, 12 Nov.1967, 47 ILR
2o5,2o8.

(61) Wilson v. Hacker, New York Supreme Court, 195o, 1o1
N.Y.S. 2d 461, quoted from Schwelb in 53 ASIL Proc
226(1959).

(62) OLG Stuttgart, 5 Nov.1962, 1o Zeitschrift für das
     gesamte Familienrecht 39,41(1963).

(63) German Bundesverwaltungsgericht, 16 Jan.1964, 83 DVerwBl
     983(1968).

(64) Asamoah, The Legal Significance, p.47seq.; Castaneda,
     Legal Effects, p.165seq.; Detter, Law Making, p.213; Di
     Qual, Les Effets, p.243seq.; Golsong, Das Problem,
     p.28seq.; Gross, The United Nations and the Role of
     Law, 19 Int.Org. 537,557(1965); Johnson, The Effect,
     p.116; Skubiszewski, The General Assembly of the United
     Nations and its Power to Influence National Action, 58
     ASIL Proc 153,156seq.(1964); Sloan, The Binding Force,
     p.24; Sørensen, Principes, p.98seq.; Tunkin, Theory of
     International Law, p.175seq.; cf. also D'Amato, On
     Consensus, p.1o6.

(65) 36 ILR 296seq.; cf. also Re Liebehenschel and Others
     before the Supreme Court of Poland, 1947, quoted by
     Skubiszewski, Recommendations, p.36o.

(66) Cf. Bleicher, Re-Citation, p.447.

(67) Higgins, United Nations and Lawmaking, p.39seq.

(68) German Bundesverfassungsgericht: 17 Jan.1957, 6 BVerfGE
     55(1957); 3o June 1964, 18 BVerfGE 112,118; 15 Dec.1965,
     19 NJW 243(1966); 3 Oct.1969, 23 NJW 235(197o); German
     Bundesgerichtshof, 12 July 1955, 8 NJW 1365(1955); for
     further decisions of German Courts on the Human Rights
     Declaration see 28 ZaöRV 131(1968). In re Flesche, Ne-
     therlands Special Court of Cassation, 27 June 1949, 16
     AD 266,269(1949); Public Prosecutor v. F.A.v.A. Supreme
     Court of the Netherlands, 1951, UN Yearbook of Human
     Rights 251(1951); I.C. v. Minister of Justice, 4
     March 197o, Administrative decision of the Crown, 2
     NYIL 238(1971); Civil Court of Courtrai (Belgium):
     Re Pietras, 16 Nov.1951, UN Yearbook of Human Rights
     14(1951); In re Jacqueline-Marie Bukowicz, 1o Oct.1952,
     loc.cit. 21(1953); Decision of 1o June 1954, loc.cit.,
     21(1954); Vanderginste v. Vanderginste, 18 Nov.1955,
     loc.cit. 23(1956); Vanderginste v. Sulman, 26 Apr.1956,
     loc.cit.; In re Hauck, Voigt and Others, Cour de
     cass.(Fr.), 3 June 195o, 17 ILR 388(195o); Stê Roy Ex-
     port and Charlie Chaplin c/ Société Les Films Roger
     Richebê, Cour d'Appel de Paris, 29 Apr.1959, 87 Clunet
     128(196o); Fuji v. California, Dist.Ct. of Appeal
     California, 24 Apr.195o, 44 AJIL 59o(195o); US Supreme

Court: <u>American Federation of Labor v. American Sash and Door Company</u>, 3 Jan.1949, 335 U.S. 538,549; <u>Kennedy v. Mendoza-Martinez</u>, 18 Feb.1963, 372 U.S. 144,161; <u>R. v. Romano</u>, Court of Criminal Appeal (Engl.), 15 July 1963, 8 BILC 79o; <u>Re Noble and Wolfe</u>, Ontario Court of Appeal, 9 June 1949, /1949/ 4 D.L.R. 375,399; <u>Choitram Verhomal Jethwani v. A.G. Kazi and Others</u>, India, 1966, 6 IJIL 247,251(1966); <u>Satwant Singh Sawhney v. Assistant Passport Officer, New Delhi</u>, Supreme Court of India, 1967, 7 IJIL 542,55o(1967); Turkish Constitutional Court, 19 June 1968, Council of Europe, Collection of Decisions of National Courts referring to the European Convention on Human Rights, Art.1, First Prot.p.8.

(69) <u>Excess Profits of Nationalized Copper Companies</u>, Chile Special Copper Tribunal, 11 Aug.1972, 11 ILM 1o13,1o46, 1o59(1972); <u>Anglo-Iranian Oil Co. v. Idemitsu Kosan Kabushiki Kaisha</u>, Dist.Court of Tokyo, 27 May 1953, High Court of Tokyo, 1953, 2o ILR 3o5,3o9,313(1953).

(7o) On the Quasi-Legislative Competence of the General Assembly, 6o AJIL 782(1966); <u>ibid.</u>, The Interplay; <u>ibid.</u>, The Status of Law in International Society, p.126seq.(196o).

(71) Dissenting opinion to the <u>South West Africa - Voting Procedure</u> Advisory Opinion, ICJ Rep., p.12o(1955).

(72) See esp. Miehsler, Zur Autorität von Beschlüssen internationaler Institutionen, in Schreuer (Ed.), Autorität und internationale Ordnung (1979) p.35 with references to the extensive literature on this topic.

(73) Cf. esp. Bleicher, Re-Citation, p.453seq. with detailed statistical references; Schwelb, Neue Etappen, p.16seq.; <u>ibid.</u>, An Instance of Enforcing the Universal Declaration of Human Rights - Action by the Security Council, 22 ICLQ 161(1973); Sohn, Protection of Human Rights, p.329; Cf. also the dissenting opinion by Judge Tanaka to the <u>South-West Africa</u> Judgment, ICJ Rep., p.25o, 292(1966).

(74) For the contrary opinion see D'Amato, On Consensus, p.117, who seems to subscribe to a somewhat narrow, purely military concept of big powers.

(75) Cf. Memorandum by the Office of Legal Affairs, U.N.Doc. E/CN.4/L. 61o(1962), where it is pointed out that a 'declaration' creates "a strong expectation that Members

of the international Community will abide by it. Consequently, in so far as the expectation is gradually
justified by State practice, a declaration may by
custom become recognized as laying down rules binding
upon States."

(76) See Buergenthal, The United Nations and the Development
of Rules Relating to Human Rights, 59 ASIL Proc 132(1965).

(77) Cf. Judge Lauterpacht's dissenting opinion to the
South West Africa-Voting Procedure Advisory Opinion,
ICJ Rep., p.118seq.(1955). To the same effects Klaestad,
loc.cit. p.88; Asamoah, The Legal Significance, p.59,227;
Bindschedler, La délimitation, p.346; Dugard, The Legal
Effect of United Nations Resolutions on Apartheid, 83
The South African Law Journal 44,5oseq.(1966); Sørensen,
Principes, p.98.

(78) Vallat, The Competence of the United Nations General
Assembly, 97 RC 2o3,231(1959,II); cf. also Schermers,
International Institutional Law, p.497 on the 'legiti-
mizing effect' of recommendations and the references
cited there.

(79) Anglo-Iranian Oil Co. v. Idemitsu Kosan Kabushiki Kaisha,
District Court of Tokyo, 27 May 1953, Court of Appeal
of Tokyo, 1953, 2o ILR 3o5,3o9,313(1953).

(8o) Cf. below IX.B.1.

(81) Tribunal civil, Brussels, 11 May 1966, 45 ILR 446.

(82) Cassin, La Déclaration, p.295; Lerebours-Pigeonnière,
La Declaration universelle des Droits de l'Homme et le
droit international privé français, in Mélanges Ripert,
p.255,262seq.(195o).

(83) For detailed treatment of this point see below XI.B.2.

(84) Generally on this point see below VII.B.

(85) See below IX.B.2.a).

(86) Shelley v. Kraemer, U.S. Supreme Court, 3 May 1948, 334
U.S. 1; In re O'Laighléis, Supreme Court of Ireland, 3
Dec.1957, 8 BILC 853,864; cf. also The State v. Furlong,
High Court of Ireland, 24 Jan.1966, 9 BILC 369,372. See
also X. v. Public Prosecutor, Court of Justice of the
Netherlands Antilles, 6 Feb.1968, 18 NTIR 81(1971)

where the court held that it would examine an application only on the basis of the European Human Rights Convention and not on the basis of the Universal Declaration, since only the former provided for a right to individual petition; Austrian Constitutional Court, 11 Oct.1974, Slg.74oo.

(87) Art.1o8 UN; Art.36 ILO; Art.73 WHO; Art.XIII UNESCO; Art.3o UPU; Art.XVIII IAEA; Art.XXVIII IMF; Art.VIII BANK; Art.41 Council of Europe; Art.XXXIII OAU.

(88) See esp. Mori, Rechtsetzung und Vollzug in der Europäischen Freihandelsassoziation, p.91seq.(1965); Lambrinidis, The Structure, Function and Law of a Free Trade Area, 31seq.(1965).

(89) Slg. 5935, 6 June 1969.

(9o) Cf. also the function of the 'Nomenclature Committee', under Art.IVc of the Convention on the Nomenclature for the Classification of Goods in Customs Tariffs of 15 Dec.195o, 347 UNTS 129, whose task is "to prepare explanatory notes as a guide to the interpretation and application of the Nomenclature". See the decision of the Swiss Zollrekurskommission, of 22 March 1961, which recognized the binding force of these "explanatory notes" but nevertheless reserved the right to examine their conformity with the Convention. Quoted by Dominicé, La nature juridique, p.256,259. See also the two decisions by the Spanish Tribunal Enonomico-Administrativo Central of 24 Sept.1963 and 14 Jan.1964, 18 Revista Esp.DI 225(1965), 19 Revista Esp.DI 79(1966), in which the decisions adopted by the 'Valuation Committee', established under Art.V of the Convention on the Valuation of Goods for Customs Purposes of 15 Dec.195o, 171 UNTS 3o6, are accepted as having "valor juridico". The 'Valuation Committee' under Art.VI of this Convention has similar functions as the above-mentioned 'Nomenclature Committee'.

(91) Cf. also similar functions of the Councils under Commodity Agreements. E.g.: Art.4o of the International Sugar Agreement of 1 Dec.1958, 385 UNTS 138,19o; Art.XVII of the International Tin Agreement of 1 Sept.196o, 4o3 UNTS 3,6o; Art.5o of the International Wheat Agreement of 19 Apr.1962, 444 UNTS 3,5o; also Art.XVII of the Charter of OAU.

(92) Generally on this provision see esp. Gold, The Fund
      agreement in the courts (1962); Meyer, Recognition of
      Exchange Controls after the International Monetary Fund
      Agreement, 62 YaleLJ 867(1953); Nussbaum, Exchange
      Control and the International Monetary Fund, 59 YaleLJ
      421(195o).

(93) The official interpretation is reproduced by Gold, The
      Fund Agreement in the Courts, p.12, and by Gold, Cer-
      tain Aspects, p.89. For a critique of the official
      interpretation see Seidl-Hohenveldern, Probleme der
      Anerkennung ausländischer Devisenbewirtschaftungsmaß-
      nahmen, 8 ÖZöR 82,9o(1957).

(94) For detailed treatment see esp. Gold, The Fund Agree-
      ment in the Courts, and a number of Articles in Inter-
      national Monetary Fund Staff Papers, under the same
      title.

(95) Société Filature et Tissage X. Jourdain c/ Époux Heynen-
      Bintner, Tribunal d'Arrondissement de Luxembourg, 1
      Feb.1956, 83 Clunet 957(1956), 22 ILR 727(1955); Moojen
      v. Von Reichert, Cour d'Appel Paris, 2o June 1961, 51
      RCDIP 67(1962), 89 Clunet 718(1962), 8 AFDI 974(1962),
      cf. esp. Gold & Lachmann in 89 Clunet 666(1962).
      Southwestern Shipping Corp. v. The National City Bank of
      New York, New York Supreme Court, 17 March 1958, 23 ILR
      581(1956); Banco do Brasil S.A. v. A.C. Israel Commodity
      Co.Inc., Court of Appeals of New York, 4 Apr.1963, 32
      ILR 371; Theye y Ajuria v. Pan American Life Insurance
      Co., Court of Appeal of Louisiana 4th Circ., 14 June
      1963, 58 AJIL 19o(1964), 4 VaJIL 117(1964); BGH, 27
      Apr.197o, JZ 728(197o); Cf. also the decision of the
      U.S. Department of Justice In the Matter of Brecher-
      Wolff, 13 Dec.1955, 22 ILR 718(1955).

(96) Cf. also Kahler v. Midland Bank Ltd., Court of Appeal
      (Engl.), 19 Apr.1948, /1948/ 1 All E.R. 811,819.

(97) White v. Roberts, Hong Kong Supreme Court, 3 Nov.1949,
      16 AD 27(1949); Perutz v. Bohemian Discount Bank in
      Liquidation, Court of Appeals of New York, 9 Jan.1953,
      8o Clunet 797(1953), 22 ILR 715; Confederation Life As-
      sociation v. Ugalde, Supreme Court of Florida, 24
      Feb.1964, 38 ILR 138; Clearing Dollars Case, Landgericht
      Hamburg, 28 Dec.1954, 22 ILR 73o(1955); Lessinger v.
      Mirau, Oberlandesgericht Schleswig-Holstein, 1 Apr
      1954, 5 Jahrb.IR 113(1955), 22 ILR 725(1955); BGH, 9
      Apr.1962, AWB 146(1962), 9o Clunet 1124(1963); BGH, 21

May 1964, AWB 228(1964); BGH, 11 March 197o, JZ 727(197o), NJW 1oo2(197o); BGH, 17 Feb.1971, NJW 983(1971); Frantz-mann v. Ponijen, Dist.Ct. Maastricht (Netherl.), 25 June 1959, 3o ILR 423; Banque nationale de Paris "Inter-continentale" c/ Ets Elkaim et sieurs Elkaim, Cour de cass.(Fr.), 7 May 1974, 1o2 Clunet 66(1975).

(98) Sharif v. Azad, Court of Appeal (Engl.), 4 Oct.1966, /1967/ 1 Q.B. 6o5, 41 ILR 23o; cf. Mann, Bretton Woods Agreement in English Courts, 16 ICLQ 539(1967); Wilson Smithett and Cope Ltd. v. Terruzzi, Court of Appeal, 2o Jan.1976, /1976/ 2 WLR 418; Constant v. Lanata, Cour de cassation (Fr.), 18 June 1969, 59 RCDIP 464(197o); Stephen v. Zivnostenska Banka National Corporation, New York Supreme Court, 25 March 1955, 22 ILR 719(1955); Statni Banka et Banque d'Etat tchêchoslavique c/ Englan-der, Cour d'appel d'Aix-en-Provence, 14 Feb.1966, 93 Clunet 846(1966); Republic of Indonesia et al. v. Brum-mer et al., Court of Appeals of Amsterdam, 9 Apr.1959, 3o ILR 25; Banco Francês e Brasileiro S.A. v. John Doe No.1 et al., New York Court of Appeal, 8 May 1975, 37o N.Y.S. 2d 536, 14 ILM 144o(1975).

(99) Emek v. Bossers & Mouthaan, Commercial Tribunal of Courtrai (Belg.), 9 May 1953, 22 ILR 722(1955); OGH, 2 July 1958, JBl 73(1959), 86 Clunet 868(1959); Pan Ameri-can Life Ins.Co, v. Raij, Florida District Court of Appeal, 1963, 58 AJIL 517(1964).

(1oo) In re Sik's Estate, US Surrogate's Court New York County, 8 March 1954, 22 ILR 721(1955); Indonesian Cor-poration P.T. Escomptobank v. N.V. Assurantie Maat-schappij de Nederlanden van 1845, Netherl. Sup.Court, 17 Apr.1964, 4o ILR 7, 13 NTIR 58(1966).

(1o1) Southwestern Shipping Corp. v. The National City Bank of New York, New York Court of Appeals, 8 July 1959, 28 ILR 539, cert.den. 361 U.S. 895; Theye y Ajuria v. Pan American Life Insurance Co., Supr.Ct.of Louisiana, 24 Feb.1964, 38 ILR 456. For the decisions of the lower courts see note 95 above.

(1o2) Martens, Nouveau Recueil Général Vol.2o, p.355. See also German BGBl 1969 II, p.597.

(1o3) K.F.O. v. Public Prosecutor, 15 June 1971, 3 NYIL 296(1972); Verenigde Tankrederij N.V. v. Willem Geer-vliet, 25 Feb.1972, 4 NYIL 413(1973).

(1o4) See esp. the Conventions of 2 Nov.1865, 4 Recueil des traités et conventions conclus par l'Autriche 3o4(1877), and of 23 July 1921, 26 LNTS 175.

(1o5) Cf. the decision of the French Conseil d'Etat in the Cosmetto case of 19 Jan.1927, Rec. p.54, quoted from Ruziê, Le juge français, p.1o4, in which a decision of the Danube Commission is classified as an 'acte de gouvernement', which is not subject to an examination by the courts.

(1o6) 11 LNTS 173.

(1o7) Art.34(c).

(1o8) Staatsanwaltschaft des Kanton Thurgau v. Lang u. Legler, 27 Jan.1950, BGE 76 IV 43, 17 ILR 3o6(1950).

(1o9) Art.12.

(11o) Riese, Luftrecht, p.125seq.; Erler, ICAO, p.132seq. with further references; Buergenthal, Law-Making, p.81seq.; Bernard, Die Transformation der Normen der ICAO in die österreichische Rechtsordnung, 17 Zeitschrift für Verkehrsrecht, 353(1972).

(111) Erler, ICAO, p.141; Manin, L'OACI, p.125; Buergenthal, Law-Making, p.98seq.

(112) Cf. the note in 19 AFDI 979(1973).

(113) Belgium v. Marquise de Croix de Maillie de la Tour Landry et al., Cour de cassation (Belg.), 3 Oct.1957, 24 ILR 9(1957); Régie des voies aériennes et Etat belge c.Verhoeven et commune de Steenokkerzeel, Cour d'appel, Brussels, 15 June 1965, 5 RBDI 385(1969).

(114) Public Prosecutor and Customs Administration v. Schreiber and Air France, Court of Appeal of Dakar, 15 May 1957, 24 ILR 54(1957), confirmed by the French Cour de cassation, 8 Nov.1963, quoted from Ruziê, Le juge français, p.1o7; Oberlandesgericht Frankfurt/Main, 25 Feb.1965, 16 Zeitschrift f.Luftrecht u.Weltraumrechts-fragen 185,188(1967); Re Males, Cour de cassation (Fr.), 29 June 1972, 1o1 Clunet 142(1974), 19 AFDI 979(1973).

(115) Art.21,22; see also Art.8(d) of the WMO.

(116)Dame Maury et Pivert c/ Ministère public, Cour d'appel
de Paris, 18 Nov.1967, 95 Clunet 728(1968), 14 AFDI
866(1968).

(117)Hurwits v. State of the Netherlands, Dist.Ct.of The
Hague, 12 June 1958, 6 NTIR 195(1959). In a decision of
12 July 1974, 1 EuGRZ 14(1974), the Swiss Federal Court
held that there was no need to answer the question
whether a decision by the OECD Council, which had been
invoked by a party, was binding under international law
and valid under domestic law, since it was not sufficiently specific to be directly applicable.

(118)International Bank for Reconstruction and Development &
International Monetary Fund v. All America Cables and
Radio Inc. et. al., Federal Communications Commission,
23 March 1953, 22 ILR 7o5(1955).

(119)22 ILR 7o7(1955).

(12o)9 Jan.1953,/1953/1 WLR 246,2o ILR 316(1953).

(121)In re Investigation of World Arrangements with Relation
to... Petroleum, U.S.Dist.Ct.D.C., 15 Dec.1952, 19 ILR
197.

(122)19 ILR 2oo.

(123)ICJ Rep. p.111seq.(1952).

(124)Art.94 UN Charter; Art.59,6o Statute of the ICJ; Art.52,
53 European Convention on Human Rights; Art.171,176
EEC. For instances in which domestic courts have been
endowed with a function of review see Reisman, Nullity
and Revision, p.161.

(125)Société Bruynzeel Deurenfabrik N.V. c/République mal-
gache, Cour de cassation, 3o June 1976, 1o4 Clunet
114(1977); Beaudice c/ ASECNA, Cour d'appel de Paris,
25 Nov.1977, 1o6 Clunet 129(1979).

(126)Musulman c/ Banque Nationale de Grèce, Civil Court of
Saloniki, 1937, 65 Clunet 9o8(1938);

(127)See the cases cited above II.A.3., in which the refusal
to review the decisions was simply justified with their
international Character. See also Maghanbhai Ishwarbhai
Patel and Others v. Union of India, Supreme Court,
1969, 9 IJIL 234,258seq.(1969).

(128) See esp. the Advisory Opinion of the ICJ on the <u>Western
Sahara</u>, ICJ Reports, 1975 on p.22seq., with references
to the previous practice of the ICJ and PCIJ.

(129) See, however, the reference <u>In re Krüger</u>, Netherlands
Council for the Restoration of Legal Rights (Judicial
Division), 13 Sept.1951, 18 ILR 258(1951) to an advisory
opinion of the PCIJ for the clarification of the preliminary question of applicant's nationality.

(13o) See, however, the view of the PCIJ: "the view that
advisory opinions are not binding is more theoretical
than real" PCIJ Ser.E, No.4, p.76.

(131) ICJ Reports 1971, p.15. See also the reliance on this
Advisory Opionion in <u>Diggs v. Dent</u>, US Dist.Ct.D.C., 13
May 1975, 14 ILM 797(1975).

(132) "...it would not be correct to assume that, because the
General Assembly is in principle vested with recommendatory powers, it is debarred from adopting, in specific
cases within the framework of its competence, resolutions
which make determinations or have operative design."
ICJ Reports, 1971, p.5o. See, however, the contrary
view in the dissenting opinion of Judge Fitzmaurice
loc.cit. p.28oseq.

(133) See, however, <u>Landesversicherungsanstalt Schlesien v.
Rybnickie Gwarectwo Weglowe and Others</u>, Supreme Court
of Poland 5 Apr.1929, 5 AD 345(1929-3o). In this case
the Court refused to implement a decision of the Council
of the League of Nations because it had not been incorporated into Polish law.

(134) <u>Bertacco v. Bancel and Scholtes</u>, Tribunal de Commerce
de Saint-Etienne, 17 Jan.1936, 8 AD 422(1935-37);
<u>Soc. Anglo Italiana Carboni c. Soc. Kuhlmann</u>, ital.Corte
di cassazione, 1o June 1938, 66 Clunet 185(1939).

(135) U.S. Court of Appeals D.C., 31 Oct.1972, 47o F.2d 461,
cert.den. 411 U.S. 931(1973).

(136) On p. 466.

(137) U.S. Dist.Ct.D.C., 13 May 1975, 14 ILM 797(1975). The
Court of Appeals did not reach the question of the
binding authority of Security Council decisions:
<u>Diggs v.Richardson</u>, 555 F. 2d 848.

(138) Bradley v. The Commonwealth of Australia and the Postmaster-General, 1o Sept.1973, Australian Law Reports
Vol.I, p.241(1973), 1o1 Clunet 865(1974), 52 ILR 1(1979).

(139) See esp. Higgins, The Advisory Opinion on Namibia:
Which UN Resolutions are Binding under Art.25 of the
Charter? 21 ICLQ 27o(1972). For South African objections
against the authority of the Security Council Resolutions,
see especially a study published by the Department of
Foreign Affairs of the Republic of South Africa: South
West Africa Advisory Opinion 1971, p.9oseq.(1972).

(14o) In addition to Higgins op.cit. und Kelsen, The Law of
the United Nations, p.95seq.,293seq., see especially
the following more recent studies and the extensive
literature cited there: Manin, L'organisation des
Nations Unies et le Maintien de la paix, p.13seq.(1971);
Kewenig, Die Problematik der Bindungswirkung von Entschei-
dungen des Sicherheitsrats, in Festschrift für Ulrich
Scheuner, p.259(1973); Castaneda, Legal Effects, p.7oseq.;
Bianchi, Security Council Resolutions in United States
Courts, 5o Indiana Law Journal 83,89seq.(1974/75).

(141) Higgins, The Advisory Opinion, p.277; Kewenig, Die
Problematik, p.274; Manin, Nations Unies, p.48seq.

(142) ICJ Reports, 1971, p.51seq.

(143) Note 139.

(144) For the same view see Castaneda, Legal Effects, p.71seq.,
who bases his conclusions on an examination of Security
Council Practice.

(145) ICJ Reports, 1971, p.53.

(146) Rex v. Cooper above p.33, Anglo-Iranian Oil Co. v.
S.U.P.O.R. above p.44, In re Krüger above p.43.

(147) Willis v. First Real Estate and Investment Co. et al.,
US Ct.of Appeals, 5th Cir., 24 Jan.1934, 68 F.2d 671,
see also below XI.B.1.

(148) Cf. also the decision of the Austrian Constitutional
Court of 1o Oct.1969, Slg.6o52, p.69oseq., in which the
Court, *inter alia* relies on a Regional Air Navigation
Plan by ICAO, a recommendation. Cf. Buergenthal, Law-
Making in the International Civil Aviation Organization,
p.117seq.(1969).

(149) U.S.S.R. v. Luxembourg and Saar Company, 2 March 1935,
      8 AD 114(1935-37), 32 RCDIP 489(1937).

(15o) Mbounya, 3 Nov.1961, Rec.612, 8 AFDI 942(1962); Union
      des Populations du Cameroun, 24 Jan.1962, 9 AFDI 1o1o
      (1963); See also the decision of the Cour de cassation
      of 3 July 1939 in De Bodinat v. Administration de l'En-
      registrement 11 AD 52(1919-42) in which the Court
      relies on the Resolution of the League Assembly on the
      establishment of the Mandate for Cameroon.

(151) Para 3 of Annex XI to the Treaty of Peace with Italy of
      1o Feb.1947 had conferred upon the General Assembly the
      power of disposition over Italy's territorial possessions
      in Africa. 42 AJIL Supp.121(1948).

(152) Passi c. Sonzogno, 5 March 1953, 37 Rivista DI 579(1954).

(153) Cassa di risparmio della Libia c. Dainotto, 18 Aug.1959,
      44 Rivista DI 295(1961); See also the judgment of the
      Court of Appeal of Rome in Ministero degli esteri, Mi-
      nistero del tesoro e Amministrazione fiduciaria italia-
      na in Somalia c. S.A.I.C.E.S., 23 June 1965, 5o Rivista
      DI 694(1967).

(154) GA Res 289(IV) of 21 Nov.1949, 387(V) of 17 Nov.195o
      and 388(V) of 15 Dec.195o.

(155) Attorney-General of the Republic v. Mustafa Ibrahim and
      Others, 1o Nov.1964, 48 ILR 6(1975).

(156) GA Res. 181(II) of 29 Nov.1947. See also Attorney-
      General of Israel v. El-Turani, District Court of
      Haifa, 21 Aug.1951, confirmed by the Supreme Court on
      31 Dec.1952, 18 ILR 164(1951), in which the Court
      relied on the Partition Plan to confirm its jurisdiction
      over a disputed border area.

(157) Opinion upon the request of the Foreign Ministry,
      9 Dec.1958, 43 Rivista DI 321(196o).

(158) The Court evidently meant the Partition Plan providing
      for an international status. Cf. also the English case
      Schtraks v. Government of Israel and Others, House of
      Lords, 6 Sept.1962, /1964/ A.C.556, in which the appli-
      cation of an extradition treaty with Israel was exten-
      ded to the part of Jerusalem under Israeli control
      without any reference to the Partition Plan.

(159) D.Tomás G.M. / Ministerio de la Gobernación, 5 May
1965, 2o Revista Esp.DI 478(1967).

(16o) S. v. Tuhadeleni and Others, Appelate Division, 22
Nov.1968, 18 ICLQ 789(1969), 52 ILR 29(1979). The
Court dealing with a point concerning South-West Africa
and the obligations under the Mandate completely
ignored General Assembly Resoulution 2145(XXI) of
27 Oct.1966, which had terminated the Mandate.

(161) Madzimbamuto, see below chapter XIII.B.1.

(162) Military Prosecutor v. Halil Muhamad Mahmud Halil Bakhis
and Others, 1o June 1968, 47 ILR 484.

(163) 36 ILR 58.

(164) 12 Dec.1961, 36 ILR 18.

(165) 29 May 1962, 36 ILR 277.

(166) 36 ILR 59seq.

(167) 36 ILR 74.

(168) 36 ILR 296.

(169) 29 Jan.1974, 37o F.Supp. 9o8.

(17o) 75 UNTS 287.

(171) 37o F.Supp. 918

(172) Nippold, Die zweite Haager Friedenskonferenz, 1.Teil:
Das Prozeßrecht, p.2o4(19o8); Wehberg, Kommentar zu dem
Haager 'Abkommen betreffend die friedliche Erledigung
internationaler Streitigkeiten vom 18.Okt.19o7', Archiv
des öffentlichen Rechts, 1.Sonderheft 153(1911); Janssen-
Pevtschin, Velu, Vanwelkenhuyzen, La Convention de
sauvegarde des droits de l'homme et des libertés fondamentales et le fonctionnement des juridictions Belges,
15 Chronique de Politique Étrangère 199,24o(1962);
Papacostas, Nature juridique des actes des juridictions
internationales et leurs effets en droit interne, 23
Revue Hellenique de Droit International 3o8,313(197o).

(173) "The decision of the Court has no binding force except
between the parties and in respect of that particular
case".

(174)Cf. PCIJ Ser.A, No.7 on p.19, PCIJ Ser.A, No.13 on
     p.21.

(175)Bernhardt, Homogenität, p.19seq.; Rosenne, The Law and
     Practice, p.62o.

(176)ICJ Reports 1961.

(177)On p.27. Cf. also the statement by Judge Guggenheim in
     the Nottebohm Case in ICJ Reports, 1955, p.61, and the
     ICJ in ICJ Reports, 1963, p.37.

(178)12 RIAA on p.194.

(179)E.g.: Berger, Bindung an Präjudizien im Völkerrecht?, 6
     ÖZöR 3o3(1955); Scheuner, Comparison of the jurisprudence
     of national courts with that of the organs of the
     Convention as regards other rights, in Human Rights in
     National and International Law (Robertson, Ed.) p.214,
     234(1968); Golsong, loc.cit. p.27o.

(18o)Limburg, L'Autoritê de chose jugée des decisions des
     juridictions internationales, 3o RC 523,549(1929,V);
     Hallier, Völkerrechtliche Schiedsinstanzen, p.94seq.

(181)Basdevant, Le Rôle du juge national dans l'interpreta-
     tion des traités diplomatiques, 38 RCDIP 413,428(1949);
     Fawcett, The British Commonwealth in International
     Law, p.55,73(1963); Dominicé La nature juridique,
     p.261seq.

(182)5 Jan.1965, 49 Rivista DI 395(1966).

(183)49 UNTS 126,162.

(184)On p.399.

(185)31 Aug.1954, 21 ILR 136,137(1954).

(186)Czechoslovak Agrarian Reform (Swiss Subjects) Case,
     8 Apr.1927, 4 AD 147(1927-28).

(187)Austrian Supreme Court, 16 Feb.1926, SZ VIII/55 on
     p.155; High Court of Kenya, Kenya v. C.O.Mushiyi and
     Kenya v. D.M.Ombisi, 3 Nov.1969, 9 ILM 556,558(197o).

(188)For examples of cases in which international practice
     was invoked but was not mentioned in the courts' judg-
     ments see: Hoani Te Heuheu Tukino v. Aotea District Maori

Land Board, Privy Council, 3 Apr.1941,/1941/ A.C. 3o8;
Attorney General v. Nissan, House of Lords, 11 Feb.1969,
/197o/ A.C.179; J.A.M. v. Public Prosecutor, Supreme
Court of the Netherlands, 21 Jan.1969, 1 NYIL p.222(197o).

(189)Cf. French cases, in which courts follow the practice
of the EEC Court without referring to its decisions,
quoted by Kiss, Nature juridique des actes des organisations et des juridictions internationales et leurs
effets en droit interne, Etudes de droit contemporain,
8. Congrès international de droit comparê, Pescara
197o, Contributions françaises p.259,267.

(19o)House of Lords, /197o/ A.C.179, Lord Pearce on p.223:
"The United Nations is not a super-state nor even a
sovereign state..."

(191)ICJ Reports, 1949, p.179.

(192)Castiglioni v. Federal People's Republic of Yugoslavia,
28 Jan.1952, 19 ILR 2o3(1952).

(193)On p.2o9.

(194)Award of 22 Feb.19o4, Scott, The Hague Court Reports,
p.56(1916).

(195)ICJ Reports, 1949, p.174.

(196)See esp. p.179.

(197)Balfour, Guthrie & Co.Ltd. v. U.S., U.S. Dist.Ct.
Northern Dist. of Calif., 5 May 195o, 9o F.Supp. 831,
45 AJIL 198(1951), 17 ILR 323(195o).

(198)28 Nov.196o, 19o F.Supp. 67, 55 AJIL 734(1961).

(199)19o F.Supp. 81.

(2oo)/1968/ 1 Q.B. 286.

(2o1)On p.334. The Advisory Opinion of the ICJ does not seem
to have been invoked when the case reached the House of
Lords, /197o/ A.C. 179.

(2o2)See e.g.: In re Garbe, OLG Kiel, 26 March 1947, 15 AD
419,42o(1948); In re Hauck, Voigt and Others, French
Cour de cassation, 3 June 195o, 17 ILR 388(195o);
In re Graff and Others, French Cour de cassation,

3 Aug.195o, 78 Clunet 578(1951), 17 ILR 385(195o);
In re Fröhlich, Netherl. Special Court of Cassation,
17 Oct.1949, 16 ILR 393(1949); See also the following
judgments by U.S. Military Tribunals: In re Milch,
17 Apr.1947, 14 AD 299(1947); In re List and Others,
19 Feb.1948, 15 AD 632,634(1948); In re Ohlendorf and
Others, 1o Apr.1948, 15 AD 656,666(1948); In re Von Leeb
and Others, 2o Okt.1948, 15 AD 376(1948); Bernstein v.
Van Heyghen Frères, Cir.Ct.App.2nd Circ., 163 F.2d 246,
cert.den. 332 U.S. 772, 14 AD 11(1947); U.S. v. Valentine, Dist.Ct.Puerto Rico, 2o Aug.1968, 288 F.Supp.
957,986seq., 63 AJIL 345(1969). In the Eichmann case
both the District Court of Jerusalem, 12 Dec.1961, and
the Supreme Court of Israel, 29 May 1962, repeatedly
and extensively relied on the judgments of the International Military Court: 36 ILR 18,39seq.,295,311,317seq.

(2o3) Van V. v. Commissioner of Internal Revenue, 9 Dec.1969,
2 NYIL 226(1971).

(2o4) On pp.228 and 23o.

(2o5) Cf. also Den Breejen v. Lloyd Schleppschiffahrt A.G.,
before the District Court of Rotterdam, 2 Jan.1957, 4
NTIR 311(1957). The Court, in interpreting the Rhine-
Convention of Mannheim of 1868, relies on the "constant
legal practice of the Central Commission for Rhine
Navigation."

(2o6) Jenks, The Prospects, p.547seq.,728; Stoll, L'application et l'interprétation du droit interne par les
juridictions internationales (1962); van Panhuys,
Relations and interactions, p.19seq.; Batiffol, Droit
international privé Vol.I, p.29seq.(197o).

(2o7) Jenks, The Prospects, p.59oseq.,729; for the practice
of Administrative Tribunals of international organizations on this question see Seyerstedt, Settlement of
Internal Disputes of Intergovernmental Organizations by
Internal and External Courts, 24 ZaöRV 1,9oseq.(1964).
This problem arises in a similar way in federal States
to the extent that federal courts apply the law of
component states. In Erie Railroad Co. v. Tompkins, 3o4
U.S. 64, the U.S. Supreme Court found that federal
courts had to apply the law of a State as declared by
its legislature or by its highest court.

(2o8) PCIJ Ser.A., Nos.2o/21.

(2o9) On p.46. In the same sense also <u>Brazilian Loans Case</u>,
PCIJ Ser.A., Nos. 2o/21 p.93,124. Cf. also references to
the <u>Serbian Loans case</u> in English courts: <u>In re Société
Intercommunale Belge d'Electricité</u>, Chancery Division,
/1933/ 1 Ch.684 at 689; in the House of Lords sub.nom.
<u>Feist v. Société Intercommunale Belge d'Electricité</u>
/1934/ A.C.161 at 173; <u>Rex v. International Trustee for
the Protection of Bondholders Aktiengesellschaft</u>, Court
of Appeal, /1937/ A.C.5oo at 514.

(21o) /1953/ 1 Q.B. 248.

(211) <u>Arbitration between the Reparation Commission and the
Government of the United States of America under the
Agreement of June 7, 192o.</u> 5 Aug.1926, 8 BYIL 156,162.

(212) On p.271.

(213) For examples of decisions of domestic courts in which
international "precedents" are relied upon in conjunction with a comprehensive examination of international
authority see e.g.: <u>Anglo-Iranian Oil Co. v. Jaffrate</u>,
Supreme Court of Aden, /1953/ 1 WLR 246, where the
court, apart from two arbitral awards (p.256seq.),
relies on domestic precedents (p.254seq.), foreign
judicial decisions (p.255seq.), executive statements
(p.257seq.) and scholarly writings (p.259). In a similar
way the Austrian Supreme Court (4 Feb.196o, SZ XXXIII/15)
in interpreting the State Treaty of 1955, took account
of an advisory opinion of the PCIJ, of foreign judicial
decisions, of its own previous decisions, of parliamentary debates, of domestic law and scholary writings.
See also <u>Anglo-Iranian Oil Co. v. Idemitsu Kosan
Kabushiki Kaisha</u>, High Court of Tokyo, 1953, 2o ILR
312,313seq.(1953).

(214) Jenks, The Prospects, p.753. See, however, Sloan, The
Binding Force of a 'recommendation' of the General
Assembly of the UN, 25 BYIL 1,19(1948); Friedmann, The
Changing Structure, p.144 expresses the view that the
creative function of the ICJ is much greater in advisory
than in contentious proceedings. But see the authors in
note 231 below who seem to think that a judgment of the
European Human Rights Court is binding also for subsequent cases, but not a report of the Commission.

(215) In addition to the above-cited cases (notes 197-2o1 and
213) see the District Court of Jerusalem in the <u>Eichmann</u>
case, 21 Dec.1961, 36 ILR 5,33; <u>Bartolomei c. C.I.M.E.</u>,

Tribunale Napoli, 16 Sept.1966, 51 Rivista DI 143(1968); State of Saurashtra v. Jamadar Mohamad Abdulla and Others, Supreme Court of India, 3 Oct.1961, 3 IJIL 199,2o5(1963).

(216) Royal Holland Lloyd v. U.S., 7 Dec.1931, 73 Ct.Cls. 722, 6 AD 442 (1931-32).

(217) P.749.

(218) This is not to say that decisions adopted by marginal majorities or dissenting opinions are not also relied upon. See e.g. the references to the Lotus case by the District Court of Jerusalem in the Eichmann case, 36 ILR 57(1968) and to the dissenting opinion of Judge Moore to the same case by the Supreme Court of Israel on p.292.

(219) 16 Annuaire 1o6(1897).

(22o) On p.115. Cf. also 19 Annuaire 333(19o2).

(221) The Proceedings of the Hague Peace Conference 19o7 Vol.I, (J.B.Scott Ed.) p.436seq.,449seq.(1921).

(222) See esp. p.451seq. See however a similar solution incorporated into Art.2 of the French-Danish Treaty of Arbitration of 9.Aug.1911: "Les parties contractantes s'engagent à prendre ou, éventuellement, à proposer au pouvoir législatif, les mesures nécessaires pour que l'interprétation donnée par la sentence arbitrale dans les cas susvisés s'impose par la suite à leurs tribunaux." Martens, Nouveau Recueil Générale de Traités, 3d Ser., Vol.5, p.683.

(223) 2 AJIL Supp. 75(19o8). This solution was subsequently also adopted in Art.63 of the Statute of the Permanent Court of International Justice.

(224) Cf. also Giles, Uniform Commercial Law 21seq.(197o); Riese, Einheitliche Gerichtsbarkeit für vereinheitlichtes Recht?, 26 RabelsZ 6o4(1961).

(225) Conférence de la Haye en Droit International Privé, Actes des la Sixième Session, p.2o8(1928).

(226) On p.233,234.

(227) P.198seq.,222seq.; Cf. also Bartin, Principes de Droit international privé, p.1o9(193o); Julliot de la Morandière, La sixième conférence de la Haye de Droit international privé, 55 Clunet 281,294(1928).

(228) 35 Annuaire 184seq. 3o6(1929,II).

(229) 46 Annuaire 178seq., 367(1956).

(23o) Nadelmann, Uniform Interpretation of 'Uniform' Law: A Postscript, Unidroit Year-Book 63,68(1963).

(231) Sørensen, Principes de droit international public, 1o1 RC 119(196o, III); Golsong in his remarks on Scheuner, (note 233) p.27o distinguishes between decisions of the Commission which are not binding and judgments of the Court, which must be followed by domestic courts. To the same effect: Schorn, Die Europäische Konvention zum Schutze der Menschenrechte und Grundfreiheiten, p.4o5(1965).

(232) Janssen-Pevtschin et.al., La Convention, p.236seq.

(233) Buergenthal, The Effect of the European Convention on Human Rights on the Internal Law of Member States, ICLQ Suppl.No.11, p.95, 1ooseq.(1965); Pinto, Consequences of the application of the Convention in municipal and international law, in Human Rights in National and International Law, (Robertson, Ed.), p.281(1968); Scheuner, Comparison of the jurisprudence of national courts with that of organs of the Convention as regards other rights, op.cit. p.2o4,232seq.; ibid., An investigation of the influence of the European Convention on Human Rights and Fundamental Freedoms on national legislation and practice, in International Protection of Human Rights, (Eide/Schou, Ed.), p.2o4(1968); Schindler, Die innerstaatlichen Wirkungen der Entscheidungen der europäischen Menschenrechtsorgane, in Festschrift Guldener p.289(1973); Vogler, Spruchpraxis p.752.

(234) Buergenthal, The Domestic Status of the European Convention on Human Rights, 13 Buffalo LRev. 391(1964); Ermacora, Die Bedeutung von Entscheidungen der Menschenrechtskommission für die österreichische Rechtsordnung, 84 JBl 621(1962); Khol, Internationale Gesetzgebung und staatliche Rechtsanwendung, in Internationale Festschrift für Alfred Verdross, p.185,193(1971); Scheuner, An investigation, p.2o4seq.; Schindler, Die innerstaatlichen Wirkungen, p.289.

(235) Drzemczewski; The Authority of the Findings of the
Organs of the European Human Rights Convention in
Domestic Courts, Legal Issues of European Integration 1
(1973); Ress, Die Wirkungen der Urteile des Europäischen
Gerichtshofs für Menschenrechte im innerstaatlichen
Recht und vor innerstaatlichen Gerichten, Report to the
5th International Colloquy on the European Convention
on Human Rights, Frankfurt am Main, 9-12 April 1980.

(236) Vgl. Schreuer, The Interpretation of Treaties by Domestic
Courts, 45 BYIL 256(1971).

(237) Beddard, The Status of the European Convention on Human
Rights in Domestic Law, 16 ICLQ 206(1967); Lord Shawcross,
United Kingdom Practice on the European Convention on
Human Rights, 1 RBDI 297(1965).

(238) Jacobs, The European Convention on Human Rights in the
English Courts, 2 EuGRZ 569(1975); Drzemczewski, Euro-
pean Human Rights Law in the United Kingdom: Some
Observations, 9 Human Rights Journal 123(1976); Watson,
The European Convention on Human Rights and the British
courts, 12 Texas International Law Journal 61(1977);
Ress, die Wirkungen, op.cit., note 225.

(239) To this effect Buergenthal, The Effect of the European
Convention, p.104. Cf. also below X.A.

(240) Jenks, The Prospects, p.751.

(241) United Kingdom Association of Professional Engineers and
Another v. Advisory, Conciliation and Arbitration Service, House of Lords, 14 Feb.1980, /1980/ 2 WLR 266.

(242) 3 July 1965, Slg.5021.

(243) 15 Dec.1961, 4 Yearbook of the European Convention on
Human Rights 356(1961).

(244) 4 March 1968, Slg.5666.

(245) 2 Oct.1964, Application No.1931/63, 7 Yearbook of the
European Convention on Human Rights 212,222(1964);
8 March 1962, Application No.808/60 5 Yearbook 108,122
(1962); 1 Oct.1965, Application No.2145/64, 8 Yearbook
282,312(1965).

(246) E.g.: Dec. of 29 Sept.1970, Slg.6239; Dec. of 13 Oct.
1970, Slg.6275; Dec. of 1 Dec.1973, Slg.7210; Dec. of 6

March 1975, Slg.7494; Dec.of 15 Oct.1976, Slg.79o7; Dec. of 26 Jan. 1978, Slg.8234.

(247) Dec. of 24 Feb.1973, Slg.6995; Dec. of 13 March 1973, Slg.7o14; Dec. of 23 June 1973, Slg.7o68; Dec. of 29 June 1973, Slg.7o99; Dec. of 1 Dec.1973, Slg.72o8; Dec. of 7 Dec.1973, Slg.723o; Dec. of 5 March 1975, Slg.7492. Cf. also Dec. of 19 March 1974, Slg.7284.

(248) E.g.: Dec. of 11 Oct.1974, Slg.74oo.

(249) Cf. e.g. Dec. of 5 March 1975, Slg.7492.

(25o) 18 June 1975, 2 EuGRZ 492(1975).

(251) E.g.: Austrian Supreme Court, 16 June 1971, 27 ÖJZ 66(1972).

(252) Reichsgesetzblatt 1922 II p.238.

(253) Bundesgesetzblatt 1956 II p.1589. The Court terminated its activity in 1959.

(254) Art.177 EEC, Art.41 ECSC, Art.15o EURATOM. Art.6 of the Statute of the Benelux Court, 13 European Yearbook 262(1965) contains a similar provision on preliminary rulings. However, there is no obligation to request a preliminary ruling if the domestic court is able to rely on a previous decision of the Benelux Court.

(255) See esp. Bebr, Law of the European Communities and Municipal Law, 34 Modern LR 481,494seq.(1971); ibid., Article 177 of the EEC Treaty in the Practice of Natio- nal Courts, 26 ICLQ 241(1977); Holloway, Are you Satis- fied with Article 177?, in Symposium Europa, p.229, 24oseq.(1971); Miele, Les Organisations internationales, p.335seq.; Pescatore, Die unmittelbare Anwendung, p.66,79; Waelbroek, The Application of EEC Law by National Courts, 19 Stanford LR 1248(1967).

(256) Da Costa en Schaake N.V. et al. v. Niederländische Fi- nanzverwaltung, Slg.IX, p.63,8oseq.

(257) Rotterdam u. Puttershoek v. Minister für Landwirtschaft und Fischerei in Den Haag, Slg.X,p.1,26.

(258) The advantages of this policy are well illustrated by the practice of the Arbitral Tribunal established under Art.1o8seq. of the German-Austrian Property Treaty of

15 June 1957, Austrian BGBl.119/1958. This Tribunal
also has jurisdiction to hand down preliminary rulings.
A somewhat narrow interpretation of the Treaty, which
denied any legal relevance to rulings beyond the particular case, led to frequent, almost literal, repetitions
of previous preliminary rulings. See Seidl-Hohenveldern,
The Austrian-German Arbitral Tribunal pp.52seq.,96(1972).
Cf. also BGH 26 June 1963, Fontes A, II, 5 No.123.

(259) Bundesfinanzhof, 15 Jan.1969, 8 CMLRep. 221(1969);
Bundesgerichtshof, 27 Feb.1969, 8 CMLRep. 123(1969);
Bundesverfassungsgericht, 9 June 1971, BVerfGE 31,145;
Bundesverwaltungsgericht, 2 July 1975, 2o CMLRev 255
(1977); Bundesgerichtshof, 1o Oct.1977, NJW 1978, 1113;
State v. Cornet, Cour de cassation (Fr.), 29 June 1966,
6 CMLRep. 351(1967); Garoche v. Soc. Striker Boats,
Cour de cassation (Fr.), 8 May 1973, 13 CMLRep. 469
(1974); Ministero delle Finanze v. Isolabella e Figlio,
Corte di cassazione, 7 June 1972, 97 Il Foro Italiano
1963(1972); Schiavello v. Nesci, Corte di cassazione, 6
Oct.1972, 16 CMLRep. 198(1975).

(26o) Bundesfinanzhof, 18 July 1967, 6 CMLRep. 326(1967).

(261) 22 Dec. 1978, 27 CMLRep.543(198o).

(262) Cf. e.g. D. c/ Etat belge, Court of Appeal of Brussels,
9 March 1961, quoted from Bebr, Judicial Control of the
European Communities, p.198(1962); Grundig Nederland N.V.
v. Ammerlaan, Gerechtshof te's-Gravenhage, 2o Feb.1963,
3 CMLRep. 373(1964); Gerrit Hofma v. Grundig, Gerechtshof
Leeuwarden, 3o Sept.1964, 6 CMLRep. 1(1967).

(263) Saarknappschaft v. Freund & Martin, Cour d'Appel de
Colmar, 15 Nov.1967, 9 CMLRep. 82(1969).

(264) Finanzgericht Baden-Württemberg, 21 March 1967, AWB
2o5(1967); S.A.F.A. v. Amministrazione delle Finanze,
Court of Appeal Milan 12 May 1972, 12 CMLRep. 152(1973).

(265) S.A. en liquidation "Carrière Dufour" et autres c/ S.A.
en liquidation "Association générale des fabricants belges de ciment Portland artificiel" et autres, Belgian
Cour de cassation, 8 June 1967, 6 CMLRep. 25o,3oo(1967).

(266) Kantongerecht Amsterdam, F.I.V.A. v. Mertens, 28 June
1962, 2 CMLRep. 141,144(1963).

IV. THE LEGALITY OF INTERNATIONAL DECISIONS

The expectations concerning compliance attached to the
decision of an international institution are not only determined by its authority in the sense outlined in the previous
chapter. An international decision's legal relevance may be
decisively influenced by the question of its "legality" in
terms of the powers conferred upon the international institution and the limitations imposed upon it, both of a procedural and substantive kind. The allegation that irregularities
have occurred in making the decision is the most direct and
radical form of attack against it. Whereas arguments directed
at the degree of authority to be enjoyed by an international
decision often at least concede a limited amount of significance, an allegation of irregularity is almost invariably
made to support a claim of nullity.(1)

International decision-makers such as courts, arbitral
tribunals, or organs of international organisations, exercise
their jurisdiction on the basis of powers explicitly or
implicitly conferred upon them and within the framework of
procedural provisions regulating their conduct. Disregard
for these limitations can lead to defects exposing decisions
to claims of excess of power or of procedural irregularity.
The history of international arbitration is rich in disputes
concerning the alleged defectiveness of international awards,
(2) without yielding simple and generally satisfactory
solutions. Possible consequences of such defects are nullity,
voidability requiring an authoritative decision by a reviewing organ, and minor irregularities not affecting the validity of the international decision.

Reviews of the legality of international decisions by authoritative procedures specifically established for this task are
an exception in contemporary international law. Even where
such review procedures exist, their jurisdiction and effects
are usually no more than rudimentary. For instance, the law
governing employment by the United Nations and its Specialized Agencies offers a review system through administrative
tribunals. However, this system naturally only covers a
small fraction of the total bulk of decision-making activities of these organizations. Only the European Communities
have a comprehensive system of judicial review for Community
acts comparable to developed domestic legal systems.

The possibility to request advisory opinions from the International Court of Justic is, no doubt, an important way to
subject the legality of decisions of international organs to
an authoritative scrutiny. The significance of this procedure

is, however, considerably curtailed by two aspects. First, the request for the advisory opinion is conditional on a political decision normally by the very organ whose decision has given rise to misgivings concerning its regularity. Secondly, these opinions do not have the effect of invalidating the international decision under review, but are rendered only by way of an advice to the requesting organ, whose freedom of action remains unaffected.(3)

In the vast majority of cases, decisions of international institutions are not subject to any outside review. The international decision-maker is normally the sole guardian of the legality of its conduct. This lack of institutionalized review procedures should not lead to the conclusion that questions concerning the regularity or defectiveness of international decisions cannot arise before other decision-makers. Domestic courts confronted with international decisions of a judicial or "political" nature can easily be put into the position of having to answer the question of whether an international decision was adopted in accordance with the rules governing the international organ's activities, whether it is "valid", or whether it suffers from an irregularity justifying its disregard. Proceedings before domestic courts in which questions of this kind arise may be directed primarily at the review or implementation of the international decision or may just involve a preliminary point for which the international decision is material. In either situation, there can usually be no question of a formal review in the sense of an invalidation or reversal of the international decision, although there are odd examples of attempts by domestic courts to "invalidate" international decisions.(4) Nevertheless , the discretion enjoyed by domestic courts and their control over resources can have a decisive impact on the effectiveness of international decisions, that have been found defective by them.

A domestic court before which the legality of an international decision is challenged has several alternatives at its disposal. One possibility is a flat refusal to undertake a review of the international decision. This refusal to enter into the question of the international decision's legality may be based on the fundamental proposition that the decision, because of its international origin, is not subject to the review of domestic decision-makers, at any rate not of courts of law. This position is strongly reminiscent of the act of State doctrine and is, no doubt, based on similar policy considerations.(5) However, the act of State doctrine is far from universally accepted or acted upon by courts and could hardly be regarded as a general prescription of international law. Its unreflected extension by analogy to decisions of international institutions seems hardly advisable.

Nevertheless, domestic courts have adopted this technique in several cases in which the validity of international judicial decisions was challenged before them.(6) United States courts when faced with claims of nullity of international arbitral awards show a tendency to rely not so much on any principle of non-reviewability of these decisions as to retreat into the "political questions" doctrine. Not only attempts to challenge international arbitral awards, because of alleged defects rendering them void,(7) but also attempts to enforce international awards which were suspected of nullity(8) were disposed of simply by reference to executive prerogatives.

A decision by the German Reichsgericht was different in its reasoning but identical in its outcome.(9) In this case one party had alleged an excess of jurisdiction by the German-Japanese Mixed Arbitral Tribunal. The Reichsgericht held that the provisions of the Treaty of Versailles and of the Statute on the Mixed Arbitral Tribunals, providing for the finality and direct application of awards, necessarily implied that a review of these awards by German courts was inadmissible. This reasoning is not entirely convincing. The fact that the awards were not subject to any appeal procedure for their material review is no conclusive proof that other decision-makers must necessarily disregard any evidence of their nullity. The crucial question seems rather whether a domestic court is the appropriate organ to undertake this kind of review and, if so, what circumstances it should accept as rendering the award void.

These isolated instances in the practice of domestic courts, show no clear trend towards the development of an "act of international institutions doctrine" analoguous to the act of State doctrine. On the contrary, there is a considerably larger number of cases in which the courts dealt with alleged defects and irregularites of decisions of international institutions.

In one group of cases the regularity or validity of the international decision in question was scrutinized, but eventually confirmed. Thus, in some cases domestic courts looked into the question of whether official interpretations by the International Monetary Fund(1o) or by other international bodies(11) were *ultra vires*. In other cases, the courts found that the signing of a power of attorney by the Secretary-General of the United Nations (12) or the conclusion of a contract for the shipment of powdered milk by UNICEF(13) were part of the legitimate functions of the respective organs. In proceedings before an Australian court(14) the editor of a communist newspaper was charged with sedition in connection with various articles on the hostilities then taking place in Korea. The defendant contended, *inter alia*, that the entire United Nations operation in Korea was illegal since the crucial decision in the Security Council was invalid because of the Soviet Union's absence when it was taken. The judge hearing the appeal seemed worried by this argument, but, nevertheless, upheld the conviction after consulting with the Foreign Office. In a similar way, an American court,(15) applying Staff Rule 7 of the United Nations, came to the conclusion that this prescription was covered by the provisions of the United Nations Charter.

In these cases, in which the courts though examining the legality of the international decisions eventually confirmed them, the question of whether domestic courts should be endowed with the function of undertaking this kind of review appears somewhat theoretical. From a strictly procedural point of view the mere entry into the question of the international decisions' validity could be regarded as objectionable. On the other hand, this kind of reasoning can equally be regarded as nothing more than a decision-strategy in which the challenge to the international decision's validity is not rejected a *limine*, but is overruled on substantive grounds.

Only the cases in which domestic courts came to the conclusion that international decisions were, in fact, defective and hence had to be disregarded, fully raise the problem of the admissibility and desirability of such a scrutiny. Compared to the total number of available cases in which domestic courts dealt with the legal consequences of decisions of international institutions, the number of cases in which this radical strategy for their rejection was chosen is small. However, it should not be forgotten that courts have a wide range of far less spectacular arguments at their disposal for disregarding international decisions. (See above chapter II.A.2.).

A striking feature of these decisions of domestic courts, in which decisions of international organs were dismissed as illegal, is that all the international decisions involved touched upon important economic, territorial, or military interests of the forum State. It does not seem far-fetched to express the suspicion that national identifications may have played an important rôle in the choice of this radical

strategy to reject the international decisions. (See chapter
XIII.B.1. below). An obvious example is the decision of an
Iranian court in <u>National Iranian Oil Co. v. Sapphire International Petroleums Ltd.</u>(16) In this case an arbitration had
taken place between the National Iranian Oil Co. (an agency
of the State of Iran) and a foreign corporation. This arbitration was based on an agreement which had been ratified by
Parliament and had received the royal assent. When an award
was rendered which was unfavorable to Iran, the District
Court of Teheran acted in the manner of a court of cassation.
It examined the international award for procedural irregularities as well as for errors of substance. The Iranian court
"rejected" the arbitrator's reasoning, found his awards
ultra vires and "incorrect", and therefore declared it
"null" and "overruled". This decision by the Iranian court,
which is couched in extreme language and badly reasoned,
leaves little doubt that the court's main endeavor was to
rid the State agency of a troublesome international obligation. The decision's poor quality means that its contribution to the solution of the question of a review of international decisions by domestic courts will be minimal.

Other cases are not so spectacular, but still leave room for
doubt concerning the judiciousness and rationality of the
domestic decisions involved. They include: a judgment of the
German Reichsgericht(17) rejecting as illegal dispositions
made by an organ of the League of Nations which did not
regard the Saar territory as part of the German Reich; a
decision of a United States Court of Appeals(18) holding
that a resolution of the American Committee on Dependent
Territories of the Organization of American States on the
status of Puerto Rico "seems to have gone beyond the competence of the American Committee..."; and a statement by a
Rhodesian judge finding the introduction of the Rhodesian
question to the United Nations by the British government "of
doubtful validity in international law and under the Charter".(19) An Egyptian prize court(2o) in proceedings against
a vessel carrying Israeli cargo even cast doubt on the
competence of the General Assembly to adopt the partition
plan for Palestine:

> The General Assembly of the United Nations adopted a
> Resolution partitioning Palestine in spite of the fact
> that the Charter of the United Nations does not estab-
> lish in any of its Articles the competence of the
> United Nations to partition States and to distribute
> their territories among several sovereignties.

In none of these cases were the indications for irregularities rendering the international decisions invalid really

convincing. Rather, it appears likely that the allegations
of illegality made by the courts were based on an especially
strong endeavor to avoid the consequences of the international
decisions in question.

It would, however, be an overreaction to these cases, to
draw the conclusion that domestic courts must generally be
denied any power to review decisions of international institutions. As pointed out before, domestic courts have such a
multitude of decision-techniques at their disposal to frustrate the consequences of international decisions that the
prohibition of this most unequivocal and direct mode of rejecting them would not be of much help anyway. Moreover, and
more importantly, as long as there are no institutionalized
review procedures for decisions of international institutions,
an organ charged with their application or implementation
must surely also be granted the power to review their validity or legality.(21)

A doctrinaire postulate that decisions of international institutions must be accepted under all circumstances, even where
there is evidence of grave procedural irregularities or an
excess of power, lending support to the suspicion that the
international decision is void, does not seem acceptable.
This necessary review function can assume particular significance where international institutions show a tendency towards an irresponsible use of voting power by interest groups
to force through political desiderata which do not correspond
to the purposes of the organization, and which are neither
covered by the constitutive document nor by constitutional
developments carried by the entire membership.

On the other hand, the convincing refutation of an international decision because of an alleged illegality must be
based on a meticulous examination of all the relevant circumstances. Until solid proof for grave irregularities rendering
the decision void has been forthcoming, a presumption of validity must be upheld.(22) A frivolous rejection of the international decision, without cogent reasons, exposes the
court to the suspicion that the true motives for its decision
do not lie in the international decision's ostensible defects.

(1) Cf. also Virally, La valeur juridique, p.87.

(2) See esp. Schätzel, Rechtskraft und Anfechtung von
     Entscheidungen internationaler Gerichte (1928); Reis-
     man, Nullity and Revision; Matscher, Die Begründung,
     p.44o; Guggenheim, La validité et la nullité des actés
     juridiques internationaux, 74 RC 195,216(1949, I).

(3) See esp. E.Lauterpacht, The Legal Effect of Illegal
     Acts;

(4) Cf. the Sapphire case below note 16.

(5) Cf. also Schermers, International Institutional Law
     Vol.II, p.542.

(6) Cf. also the examples for "nondecisions" presented
     above II.A.3.

(7) The Brig "General Armstrong", Court of Claims, 17 March
     1856 and 1 Feb.1858, Moore, International Arbitration
     Digest Vol.II, 11o2,11o8; Z & F Assets Realization Cor-
     poration et al. v. Hull et al., Supreme Court, 6 Jan.
     1941, 311 U.S. 47o, 1o AD 424(1941-42). See also Lake
     Ontario Land Development and Beach Protection Associa-
     tion Inc. v. Federal Power Commission, Court of Appeals
     D.C., 29 Jan.1954, 48 AJIL 498(1954), where the court
     in an *obiter dictum* expresses doubts concerning its
     power to review a decision of an international boundary
     commission.

(8) Frelinghuysen v. Key, Supreme Court, 7 Jan.1884, 11o
     U.S.63; Boynton v. Blain, Supreme Court, 23 March 1891,
     139 U.S.3o6; La Abra Silver Mining Co. v. U.S., Supreme
     Court, 11 Dec.1899, 175 U.S.423.

(9) 24 May 1928, RGZ 121,18o.

(1o) International Bank for Reconstruction and Development &
     International Monetary Fund v. All America Cables and
     Radio Inc. et al., Federal Communications Commission,
     23 March 1953, 22 ILR 7o5,7o9(1955).

(11) Cf. the decision of the Swiss Zollrekurskommission of
     22 March 1961, quoted by Dominicé, La nature, p.259, on
     the "explanatory notes" of the "Nomenclature Committee"
     under Art.IV c of the Convention on the Nomenclature
     for the Classification of Goods in Customs Tariffs of
     15 Dec.195o, 347 UNTS 129.

(12) UN v. Canada Asiatic Lines Ltd., Superior Court of
     Montreal, 2 Dec.1952, 26 ILR 622(1958-II).

(13) Balfour, Guthrie & Co. Ltd. v. U.S., U.S.Dist.Ct.N.D.
     Calif., 5 May 1950, 90 F.Supp. 831, 17 ILR 323(1950).
     Cf. also Studio-Karten GmbH v. Deutsches Komittee der
     UNICEF e.V., BGH, 16 Jan.1976, UNJYB 247(1976).

(14) Burns v. The King, New South Wales Quarter Session
     Appeal Court, 6 Apr.1951, 20 ILR 596(1953).

(15) Keeney v. U.S., Ct.App.D.C., 26 Aug.1954, 20 ILR 382.

(16) District Court of Teheran, 1 Dec.1963, 9 ILM 1118(1970).

(17) 21 Jan.1930, RGSt 63,395.

(18) Ruiz Alicea v. U.S., Ct.App. 1st Circ., 10 March 1950,
     180 F.2d 870, 17 ILR 42,46(1950). Cf. also U.S. v. Vargas
     above p.84, where the Court cast doubt on the legality
     of activities of the U.N. Special Committee on Colonia-
     lism with respect to Puerto Rico.

(19) Madzimbamuto v. Lardner-Burke, Baron v. Ayre, Bezuiden-
     hout, Dupont & Lardner-Burke, Appellate Division of the
     High Court, 29 Jan.1968, 39 ILR 61 per MacDonald J.A.
     on p.338; cf. also R. v. Ndhlovu and others, Appellate
     Division of the High Court, 13 Sept.1968, 53 ILR 50 at
     86, 92(1979).

(20) The Inge Toft, 10 Sept.1960, 16 Revue Egyptienne de
     Droit International 118(1960), 31 ILR 509 at p.517(1966).

(21) On the capacity of domestic courts to review the legali-
     ty of decisions of the European Communities see e.g.
     Green, Political Integration by Jurisprudence, p.196seq.;
     Zuleeg, Das Recht der Europäischen Gemeinschaften im
     innerstaatlichen Bereich, p.349seq.; ibid., Fundamental
     Rights and the Law of the European Communities, 8
     CMLRev. 446,460(1971).

(22) Schermers, International Institutional Law Vol.II,
     p.543.

V. INTERNATIONAL DECISIONS IN THE COURTS OF THIRD STATES

As pointed out above, domestic courts when deciding cases involving questions of international law, perform a dual function. In rendering decisions in conformity with international law they perform tasks of the forum State, that is, a participant in international intercourse. Their judgments carry out the forum State's international duties or serve to enforce its international claims. At the same time domestic courts play an important rôle for the international community. The scarcity of enforcement organs in the international arena means that the international legal order is largely dependent on State organs for its implementation. A domestic organ applying and enforcing international prescriptions is, therefore, functionally also an organ of the international community.

These considerations apply fully also to a compliance with and deference to decisions of international institutions by domestic courts. In the vast majority of cases the two functions of the domestic courts coincide: The international decision is directed at the forum State and creates rights and duties for it. In applying the international decision, the domestic court discharges the forum State's rights or obligations and simultaneously renders the international decision effective.

There are, however, situations in which the functions of the State organ and that of the international decision-maker do not coincide. In a number of cases before domestic courts parties have invoked international decisions which had no or only very tenuous connections to the forum State. In cases in which the international decision is not directly addressed to the forum State, the question then arises whether a domestic court should, nevertheless, give deference to it.

There are several situations in which this question can arise. First, recommendations of international institutions are sometimes invoked before the courts of non-Members. Second, in connection with the prescribing function, the internal law of an international institution - not purporting to regulate the conduct of the forum State or of other Members - can play a rôle in domestic litigation. Third, the applying function of international institutions can give rise to all three types of claims mentioned above before courts of States which have no connecting point to the international decision: The court can be called upon to implement operative international decisions which create neither rights nor obligations for the forum State; the international decision may offer an answer to a preliminary question pending before the domestic court, although it is not addressed to the forum State; and an international judgment or award rendered in proceedings in which the forum State did not participate can afford a "precedent" for a question of international law relevant to the case before the domestic court.

A. RECOMMENDATION

Decisions of international institutions, which are directed at a wide range of addressees, usually the institution's entire membership, are rarely invoked in the courts of non-Members. With respect to decisions of organizations enjoying near universal membership, like the United Nations, such a situation can arise in very few countries only. Even for regional organizations, this contingency is usually rather theoretical.

Nevertheless, there is a group of decisions concerning the Universal Declaration of Human Rights rendered prior to the admission of the forum State to the United Nations. Among this group only the practice of the Austrian Constitutional Court contains the argument that the Human Rights Declaration is irrelevant for the courts of non-Members. In a decision of 1950 the Court rejects a reliance on the Universal Declaration because

> this decision of the U.N. does not, at present, form part of the Austrian legal order, since the Republic of Austria has not yet been admitted as a Member of the United Nations.(1)

This argument is not entirely convincing. A decision of the same court rendered two decades later(2) is, however, peculiar if not completely incomprehensible. In this case, the Constitutional Court, fifteen years after Austria's admission to the United Nations, not only repeats its opinion that the Human Rights Declaration does "not form part of the Austrian legal order" but also substantiates this formula by a reference to its earlier decision of 1950.

The practice of the courts of the Federal Republic of Germany, going back to as early as 1953, stands in marked contrast to the Austrian position. In a considerable number of cases the Universal Declaration is relied upon, especially for the interpretation of the basic rights guaranteed by the German Constitution.(3) In none of these cases did the courts see any difficulty in the lack of the Federal Republic's member-

ship in the United Nations. Even an attempt to explain this
practice by claiming that the contents of the Universal
Declaration was simply applied as part of general customary
international law, would be unconvincing: In several decisions
the courts specifically emphasized that the Human Rights
Declaration was not part of the "general rules of international law" as incorporated by Article 25 of the German
Constitution.

A judgment of the Swiss Federal Tribunal(4) also contains a
brief reference to the Universal Declaration of Human Rights.

The view expressed in the German and to a limited extent in
the Swiss practice is surely to be preferred. The Universal
Declaration of Human Rights, even though only adopted as a
recommendation and by a relatively limited group of States
by today's standards, represents the legal convictions and
expectations of the entire international community. It
contains no "binding rules" in a formal sense either for
Members or non-Members. As a "standard of achievement",
however, it enjoys a high degree of authority for all States
and all their organs and should, hence, be respected and
applied accordingly.

On the other hand, it would be inappropriate to draw any
hasty analogies from the Universal Declaration of Human
Rights to other international recommendations of a general
character. Decisions of international institutions can only
rarely be legitimately accepted as the expression of the
legal expectations of the entire international community in
the same manner as the Human Rights Declaration.

B. PRESCRIPTION

Decisions of international institutions regulating the
internal administration of organizations are prescriptions
of international origin with peculiar features. The internal
law created by international organizations is markedly
different from other areas of international law, both with
respect to the material contents of the prescriptions and in
its addressees. This holds true in particular for the law
governing the employment of staff by international organizations. This body of law is addressed to the internal relationship between the organization and its officials and
ostensibly does not affect the Member States. This has led
some authors to conclude that this type of international
prescription plays no rôle in the decisions of State-
organs.(5) A closer examination reveals that this conclusion
is not entirely accurate. There are several cases in which

conflict of laws principles have led domestic courts to apply internal prescriptions of international institutions, especially the law governing employment.(6)

Thus the procedures for the settlement of labor disputes between the international orgnization and its employees, as laid down in the organizations' "Staff Regulations", have repeatedly been accepted as decisive by domestic courts.(7) An American court(8) even relied on the substantive provisions of the United Nations "Staff Regulations" and "Staff Rules" which had been invoked by a defendant in criminal proceedings to justify her refusal to give evidence before a Congress Sub-Committee.

C. APPLICATION

1. Implementation or Review

a) Of Judicial International Decisions

It is commonly accepted that operative international decisions, especially judgments or awards, which require a specific performance, only create obligations for their immediate addressees, that is, the participants in the proceedings. With respect to the International Court of Justice, Article 59 of the Statute seems to be quite unequivocal to this effect. On the other hand, the invocation of international decisions of this kind before the courts of States that have not participated in the international proceedings is often a promising way towards their enforcement.

The question arises whether the absence of an "obligatory effect" of judgments and awards for third States means that the courts of these States should refuse to take notice of them and should decline applications to lend their hand in their enforcement.(9) The practice of courts shows no clear trend, but, nevertheless, deserves brief description.

In Steinberg et al. v. Custodian of German Property before the Israel Supreme Court(1o) the applicant had obtained an award against Germany before the German-Roumanian Mixed Arbitral Tribunal in 1926. He relied on an Israeli statute, the German Property Law of 195o, providing for payment of German debts by the Israeli Custodian of German property, *inter alia*, "under a judgment of a competent court". The Supreme Court refused to recognize the award holding that "competent court" only meant an Israeli court and not a foreign tribunal even if it is otherwise competent. The claim therefore had to be tried by the District Court on the merits.

By contrast, the United States District Court for the Southern District of New York in Société Vinicole de Champagne v. Mumm Champagne Co. Inc.(11) saw no obstacle to enforcing an international award under similar circumstances. In this case, a German owned company including its trademarks had been liquidated by France pursuant to the Treaty of Versailles and sold to the plaintiff. The efforts by the previous owners to assert the trademarks in the French courts and before the Franco-German Mixed Arbitral Tribunal were adversely decided. They nevertheless incorporated the defendant in New York and used the trademark. The court granted an injunction against their use finding that "...the judgments of the Mixed Franco-German Tribunal are *res iudicata* against defendant corporation..."(12)

Two more recent cases tried in Netherlands courts(13) are similar in their result. Both concerned the enforcement of arbitral awards rendered in favor of foreign companies against foreign States or State-owned enterprises. In both cases arguments concerning the sovereign immunity of the defendants were dominant, but were ultimately dismissed. (Cf. chapter XII.B.1. below). In both cases the courts also examined the question of whether a special connecting point to the forum State was necessary in order to enable Netherlands courts to enforce the arbitral awards. In both cases the requirement of a special domestic connection was rejected without any fundamental discussion of the effects of awards on third states. In one of the two cases, N.V.Cabolent v. National Iranian Oil Co., an attempt was made to enforce an international award in favor of a Canadian company against an Iranian Governmental body in the Netherlands courts. The District Court, rejecting the claim, pointed out that the agreement underlying the arbitration had no connection to the Dutch sphere of jurisdiction. The Court of Appeal, reversing the decision of the District Court, found that for jurisdiction over defendant's *acta iure gestionis* "...a so-called 'Binnenbeziehung' - a more or less close connection between the act and the country of the forum - is not required.(14)

This court practice is still too scarce to permit any firm conclusions concerning an obligation of domestic courts to enforce international judicial decisions unconnected with the forum State. From a policy-oriented perspective, there are, however, strong arguments in favor of an enforcement also by courts of third states.

Legal systems have developed basically two modes for enforcing claims to wealth between members of a community: Self-
help, that is to say, enforcement by the member who considers
himself entitled to the benefits, or, alternatively, enforcement by the community on behalf of the member. The measures
of enforcement can take the form either of indirect compulsion (*i.e.*, value deprivations aimed at persuading the
debtor to comply) or of direct compulsion (*i.e.*, depriving
the debtor of the benefits to which he is not entitled and
transferring them to the creditor). With the progressive
development of a system of law, self-help and indirect
compulsion tend to decline in importance and direct enforcement by community organs becomes dominant. Courts of law are
seen as a more reliable way to safeguard compliance with
community prescriptions than the application of force by the
aggrieved participant. Attachment of a debtor's property is
considered more economical to secure the transfer of assets
than imprisonment for debt.(15)

International law, like other legal systems at an early
stage of their development, has been largely characterized
by self-help and indirect compulsion or reprisals. With the
proscriptions of most forms of forcible self-help and an
increasing number of possibilities for the judicial settlement of international disputes, coupled with a growing
tendency of States and non-State entities to own assets
abroad, it may well be appropriate to take a fresh look at
the possibilities for the enforcement of obligations arising
from international wealth transactions.

Despite a relatively high degree of compliance with judgments
of the International Court and of other international judicial bodies, their lack of power to secure compliance with
these decisions remains one of the weakest points in international judicial settlement. An effective system of international adjudication will therefore ultimately depend on
the degree of cooperation shown by organs with a more immediate control over resources.

There is no reason why measures to implement an international
judgment or award should only be taken by courts of States
that were parties before the international judicial organ.
(16) It is true that the domestic court in a third country,
relying on the international judicial decision in order to
give relief to the judgment creditor out of the debtor's
property located within the court's sphere of effective
control, will not be able to derive any "binding force" from
the international decision based on the forum State's participation in the international proceedings. The domestic

court's position is here not that of an organ of a party having to comply with a judgment or award, but rather that of a community-organ. The effect of a final decision on an enforcement agency is quite different from that on the parties and cannot be reasonably dealt with in terms of participation. The domestic court enforcing an international judicial decision unconnected to the State of the forum will therefore neither "comply with the decision" nor exercise self-help, but perform the function of an international community-organ acting in accordance with considerations of international public policy.

Within the legal framework of the International Court, Article 94 of the UN-Charter and Article 59 of the Statute do not deal with the implementation of the Court's decisions by third States, but merely lay down the obligation of the Parties to comply with the verdict. The prescription applicable to third States and their organs is the general duty of all Members(17) to give every assistance in any action taken by the United Nations as laid down in Article 2(5) of the Charter. The duty to cooperate in the implementation of international obligations, as expressed in authoritative international decisions, and to prevent their frustration should be regarded as the responsibility of all States including their courts.(18)

A number of approaches appear feasible for the technical realization of these policy considerations. One would be the treatment of international judgments and awards by domestic courts in analogy to the conditions for the recognition and enforcement of foreign judgments and awards. The success of this method would, however, not least depend on the general policy of the local law towards recognizing foreign decisions. (Cf. chapter VII.E.1.a) below). It is therefore not without problems.

Another possibility would be statutory prescriptions regulating the enforcement of certain international judgments and awards. To set one's hope on this method would probably not be very realistic. The forum State usually has no special interest in the enforcement of international judicial decisions between third parties. There is hence no particular motive for passing this type of legislation.

Finally, there is the possibility of multilateral treaties providing for the enforcement of international judicial decisions in the courts of all States parties to it, even if they have not participated in the international judicial proceedings in a particular case. The Convention on the

Settlement of Investment Disputes between States and Nationals
of Other States embodies this idea. (Cf. chapter VII.E.1.a)
below). Apart from the duty of parties to abide by and comply
with awards rendered in pursuance of the Convention, there
is also an obligation on *all* Parties to the Convention and
their courts to recognize and enforce the pecuniary obligations imposed by such awards in their territories. (Art.54 of
the Convention).

b)   Of Non-Judicial International Decisions

As pointed out before, operative decisions of "political"
international organs are relatively rarely relied upon before
domestic courts for the purpose of their implementation or
review. Moreover, the recognition and implementation of these
decisions by domestic courts largely depends on the enactment
of implementing provisions by the States concerned. (Cf. chapter VII.E.1.b) below). An invocation of this type of international decision in the courts of third States, that is,
non-Members,(19) is not likely and does not appear promising.(2o) Deference to international decisions of this kind
by domestic courts is feasible in cases of a voluntary
submission to certain decisions or participation in certain
measures, like enforcement measures under Chapter VII of the
UN Charter, by non-Members.(21) An explicit declaration by
the forum State to this effect, and any implementing measures
taken by it, will, however, usually create a sufficient
connecting point to remove any problems for domestic courts.

2. Preliminary Questions

Courts are sometimes also referred to international decisions
without any particular relation to the forum State in connection with preliminary questions to be answered in cases
pending before them. This is particularly so with decisions
of international organs of a declaratory character. Declaratory decisions, even though they may formally only be addressed to the participants in international proceedings, enjoy
a certain authority *erga omnes* and can become relevant to
non-participants.(22)

An obvious example is an authoritative international decision
determining the status of a territory.(23) An international
decision finally settling a territorial dispute between two
contestants also determines the question of jurisdiction
over the disputed area with objective effect. Thus, it would
be futile for a third State and its courts to reject Norway's
method of drawing the base line for its fisheries zone on
the ground that the International Court of Justice's judgment of 1951 was *res inter alios acta*.

Similar considerations must apply to the authoritative
determination of the status of territories by other methods.
In its Advisory Opinion on the legal status of <u>Namibia</u>, the
International Court of Justice specifically dealt with the
legal position and duties of third States, that is, non-
Members of the United Nations:

> In the view of the Court, the termination of the Man-
> date and the declaration of the illegality of South
> Africa's presence in Namibia are opposable to all
> states in the sense of barring *erga omnes* the legality
> of a situation which is maintained in violation of
> international law... The Mandate having been terminated
> by decision of the international organization in which
> the supervisory authority over its administration was
> vested, and South Africa's continued presence in Namibia
> having been declared illegal, it is for non-member
> States to act in accordance with those decisions.(24)

An authoritative decision by an international organ possessing jurisdiction to pass a decision on the status of a
territory should, therefore, be recognized by the courts of
all States in cases in which preliminary questions concerning
this territory have to be answered. Preliminary questions of
this kind can arise in connection with: the nationality of a
person from that territory;(25) choice of law problems concerning facts with a connecting point in the territory;(26)
or the legality of an exercise of jurisdiction over the
territory.

Apart from territorial questions, international decisions
can also display a certain objective effect in other fields.
An authoritative determination of the legality or illegality
of measures of expropriation can decisively influence the
reaction of courts in third States towards claims based on
these measures.(27) The decision of an international organ
on property rights can be relevant for the courts of third
States. The admission of a new Member to an international
organization can offer an authoritative answer to the question
of the applicant's statehood not only *vis-à-vis* other Members
but also *vis-à-vis* non-Members and their courts.(28)

3. "Precedents" for Analogous Legal Questions

The authority of an international decision as a "precedent"
for subsequent decisions, is largely independent of its
consequences as an operative decision between the parties.
The purpose of the invocation of a precedent is the elucidation of a legal question *in abstracto* or the reliance on
general policies applied in the earlier case. To seek a

specific formal link between the case in which a precedent
is invoked and the parties to the original proceedings would
not appear to make much sense. Nevertheless, the requirement
of a formal connection to the forum State, establishing the
relevance and "binding force" of an international precedent,
is a recurrent idea in scholarly writings.

The simplest method limits the precedential effect of the
international judgment or award to the States which participated in the international litigation. Thus, it was argued
that, as between the Parties to the international proceedings,
the decision not only settled the particular disputes but
also determined the objective question of law with effect
for the future.(29)

This theory, resting on the Parties' alleged consent to be
bound in future cases, while possibly meeting certain demands
of derivational logic, cannot be considered particularly
satisfactory. Not only is the assumption of a submission to
the tribunal's verdict *pro futuro* artificial, but this
doctrine would also totally exclude any legal effect for
similar or identical cases if the forum State has not participated in the original international judicial proceedings.

A somewhat broader basis for an international decision's
effect on future domestic cases is seen in the forum State's
mere subjection to the international tribunal's jurisdiction
in respect of a particular question of law. Thus, even
without participation in the proceedings, the international
judicial organ's abstract competence in the subject-matter
and *vis-à-vis* the forum State was regarded as sufficient to
establish a link to the municipal court, making the international judgment or award binding in subsequent cases.(3o)
A decision concerning a multilateral treaty that vested
compulsory jurisdiction in the adjudicating international
organ to settle disputes arising from its interpretation
would, according to this view, be binding on the domestic
courts of all States Party to the treaty, even if they had
not taken part in the international proceedings. Where the
treaty did not contain such a jurisdictional clause, a
judgment or award between two parties would not display an
effect for other contracting parties.(31)

The drawback of this hypothesis lies in the fact that it
makes the application of substantive law dependent on the
contingencies of the international organ's extent of jurisdiction at a particular time. This may still be supportable
where the provision conferring jurisdiction on the international decision-maker is closely linked to a treaty to be

interpreted. To extend such a theory to the general jurisdiction of, say, the International Court and to make the relevance of its case-law dependent on the current extent of the individual forum State's submission to its jurisdiction is, however, manifestly absurd.

A more generous view of the weight to be attributed to international judicial decisions considers a treaty to which the forum State is a party binding on the domestic court as interpreted by any competent international judicial organ.(32) This effect seems to be derived from the binding force of the treaty, the acceptance of which is seen to embrace future interpretative decisions by international courts or tribunals.

Apart from the fact that such a wide construction of a State's acceptance of the treaty somewhat strains the limits of logic, it is by no means clear why this deference to past international decisions should apply only to treaties but not to other types of international law. The sole criterion for this privileged position of an international judgment or award interpreting a treaty seems to be the more manifestly consensual character of the prescriptions involved. It is difficult to understand why according to this theory general international law as interpreted by an international judicial organ should not also be "binding" on the domestic court.

What all the above theories have in common is the desire to establish the relevance of international precedents by way of a fictitious consensual element. The recognition of the obvious utility and necessity of resorting to the experience of past decisions is not matched by a theoretical framework capable of satisfactorily integrating the phenomenon of international judgments or awards into the system of "sources of law". Therefore, attempts are made to bridge the gap between the endeavor to justify the reliance on precedents and the impossibility to accommodate them among the traditional sources of law by way of a construed consent of the forum State to the international decision. The outcome of this construction would be a "binding force". Where the fictitious consent of the forum State cannot be construed, the international decision would be devoid of any authority.

All these constructions are based on the conception that international precedents constitute "rules" which are binding on certain States and their organs. As set out above in some detail, (Chapter III.E.3.b)) the legal significance of international practice for the subsequent conduct of decision-makers can be much more accurately perceived in

terms of the relative concept of authority. The construction
of a consensual link between the forum State and the international precedent appears superfluous. The existence of a
relationship between the international decision-maker and
the forum State may possibly be one of several elements
determining the degree of authority of the former's practice.

The legal policies expressed in an international judgment or
award can be significant for any decision-maker in a subsequent case involving similar sets of facts and policy questions. Every authoritative decision contributes to the
clarification and development of the law and creates legal
expectations for the future. These legal expectations can
show their effect in all areas of the international decision-
making process and are independent of any formal link to the
original decision.

(1)   5 Oct.195o, Slg.2o3o, ÖJZ 94(1951), 46 AJIL 161(1952),
      78 Clunet 622(1951).

(2)   6 Oct.197o, Slg.626o. Cf. also a decision of the Austrian
      Administrative Court, 16 Dec.1966, Slg.7o45A.

(3)   Bundesgerichtshof, 21 Jan.1953, 6 NJW 392(1953), 2o ILR
      37o(1953); Bundesgerichtshof, 12 July 1955, 8 NJW
      1365(1955), 22 ILR 52o, 524(1955); Bundesverwaltungsge-
      richt, 22 Feb.1956, BVerwGE 3,171, DVerBl. 378(1956);
      Bundesverfassungsgericht, 17 Jan.1957, BVerfGE 6, 55;
      Bundesverwaltungsgericht, 29 June 1957, BVerwGE 5,153;
      Kammergericht Berlin, 14 Sept.1961, 14 NJW 22o9,2211
      (1961); Oberlandesgericht Stuttgart, 5 Nov.1962, 1o
      Zeitschr.für das gesamte Familienrecht 39,41(1963);
      Bundesverwaltungsgericht, 16 Jan.1964, 83 DVerwBl.
      983,984seq.(1968); Bundesverfassungsgericht, 3o June
      1964, BVerfGE 18,112, 118; Bundesverfassungsgericht,
      15 Dec.1965, 19 NJW 243(1966); Bundesgerichtshof,
      1o Jan.1966, 19 NJW 726(1966); Bundesverfassungsgericht,
      3 Oct.1969, 23 NJW 235(197o); Bundesverfassungsgericht,
      4 May 1971, BVerfGE 31,58; Bundesverfassungsgericht,
      7 July 1971, BVerfGE 31,229. For references to further
      decisions of German courts relying on the Human Rights
      Declaration see 28 ZaöRV 131(1968).

(4)   Mejia v. Regierungsrat des Kantons Bern, 9 May 1963,
      32 ILR 192.

(5)   Skubiszewski, Legal Nature, p.195; ibid., Resolutions,
      p.83; Dominicé, La nature juridique, p.25o; See however
      Economides, Nature juridique, p.227 note 7.

(6)   Cf. also Seyersted, Settlement of internal disputes,
      p.84seq.; ibid., Jurisdiction over Organs, p.5o6;
      Jenks, The Proper Law, p.18seq.

(7)   Viecelli v. IRO., Tribunale Trieste, 2o July 1951, 49
      AJIL 1o2(1955); Maida v. Administration for Internatio-
      nal Assistance, Corte di cassazione, 27 May 1955, 23
      ILR 51o(1956), 39 Rivista DI 546(1956).

(8)   Keeney v. U.S., Court of Appeals, D.C., 26 Aug.1954,
      218 F.2d 843, 2o ILR 382(1953). Cf. also A.P.F.Eckhardt
      v. Eurocontrol, Local Court of Sittard (Netherlands),
      25 June 1976, 9 NYIL 276(1978) in which the court
      assumed jurisdiction on the merits in a dispute between
      an international organization and its former employee
      and applied the organization's pertinent regulations.

(9) In this sense: Simons, Verhältnis der nationalen Gerichtsbarkeit, p.44.

(1o) 7 March 1957, 24 ILR 771(1957).

(11) 13 Dec.1935, 13 F.Supp. 575, 8 AD 487(1935-37).

(12) 13 F.Supp.595.

(13) N.V. Cabolent v. National Iranian Oil Co., Court of Appeal The Hague, 28 Nov.1968, 9 ILM 152(197o); Société Européenne d'Etudes et d'Entreprises v. Yugoslavia, Supreme Court, 26 Oct.1973, 5 NYIL 29o(1974), 14 ILM 71(1975).

(14) 9 ILM 157(197o).

(15) Cf. Rosenne, The Law and Practice of the International Court, p.121.

(16) Generally on the question of the cooperation of third States in the enforcement of claims arising from international judgments see Rosenne, The Law and Practice of the International Court, p.142, and the oral argument of Sir Gerald Fitzmaurice in the Monetary Gold case, who argued that non-compliance with international judgments was a matter of concern to all members of the international community: Case of Monetary Gold removed from Rome, ICJ Pleadings, p.126(1954). See also Akehurst, Reprisals by Third States, 44 BYIL 1(197o); Jenks, The Prospects, p.7o3seq.

(17) With respect to non-Members of the United Nations participating in the work of the International Court, see Rosenne, The Law and Practice of the International Court, p.123seq.

(18) To the same effect see Reisman, Nullity and Revision, p.815seq.; cf. also Schachter, The Enforcement, p.12. On the enforcement of judgments of Administrative Tribunals of international organizations see Seyersted, Settlement of internal disputes, p.33seq.,54,93.

(19) It should be noted, however, that the Security Council has issued "decisions" and "orders" also to non-Members. See Seyersted, Is the International Personality of Intergovernmental Organizations valid vis à vis Non-Members?, 4 IJIL 233,237(1964). Cf. also Widdows, Security Council Resolutions and Non-Members of the United Nations, 27 ICLQ 459(1978).

(2o) But see the suggestions by Jenks, The Prospects, p.7o6
seq. to utilize domestic courts also of third States
for the recovery of debts to international organizations.

(21) Cf. v.Schenck, Das Problem der Beteiligung der Bundesrepublik Deutschland an Sanktionen der Vereinten Nationen,
besonders im Falle Rhodesiens, 29 ZaöRV 257(1969);
R.Bindschedler, Das Problem der Beteiligung der Schweiz
an Sanktionen der Vereinigten Nationen, besonders im
Falle Rhodesiens, 28 ZaöRV 1(1968).

(22) Cf. Rosenne, The Law and Pratice of the International
Court, p.126,628seq.; Jenks, The Prospects, p.712.

(23) Cf. Jenks, The Prospects, p.674seq.

(24) ICJ Reports, p.16,56(1971).

(25) Cf.e.g.: In re Krüger, Netherlands Council for the
Restoration of Legal Rights (Judicial Division), 13
Sept.1951, 18 ILR 258(1958).

(26) Cf. e.g.: Opinion of the Italian Consiglio di Stato
upon the Foreign Ministry's request, 9 Dec.1958, 43
Rivista DI 321(196o).

(27) Cf. e.g.: Anglo-Iranian Oil Co. v. S.U.P.O.R., Court of
Rome, 13 Sept.1954, 22 ILR 23,41(1955); Anglo-Iranian
Oil Co. v. Idemitsu Kosan Kabushiki Kaisha, District
Court of Tokyo, 1953, 2o ILR 3o5,3o8 (1953).

(28) Cf. e.g.: U.S.S.R. v. Luxemburg and Saar Company,
Commercial Tribunal of Luxembourg, 2 March 1935, 8 ILR
114(1935-37).

(29) Huber, Die Fortbildung des Völkerrechts, p.562; Lammasch,
Die Rechtskraft internationaler Schiedssprüche, p.97seq.;
ibid., Die Lehre von der Schiedsgerichtsbarkeit in
ihrem ganzen Umfange, p.187; Pinto, Le juge interne
français, p.88.

(3o) Batiffol, Droit international privé Vol.I, p.47seq.;
Waelbroek, Nature juridique, p.515; more cautiously in
respect of the European Human Rights Convention: Buergenthal, The Effect of the European Convention, p.1o3;
See also Partsch, Die Anwendung des Völkerrechts p.81
seq., where the rejection of this theory in relation to
the International Court of Justice is based on Article
94(1) of the U.N. Charter.

(31) Jenks, The Prospects, p.735seq.

(32) Cautiously Zorn, Das völkerrechtliche Werk, p.364;
     Sørensen, Principes, p.119; Jenks, The Prospects,
     p.745.

VI. INTERNATIONAL DECISIONS AND DOMESTIC LAW

A. TRADITIONAL THEORIES ON THE RELATIONSHIP OF INTERNATIONAL AND DOMESTIC LAW

The relationship of national and international law has attracted extensive scholarly attention from several genera-tions of international and constitutional lawyers and remains one of the most disputed areas of the entire discipline. No other area of international law has generated such a persis-tent controversy between different theories or schools of thought. Innumerable scholarly products have been devoted to the slogans of "monism" and "dualism". Their detailed presen-tation has become almost a ritual of every introduction to international law. A repetition and discussion of the respec-tive arguments appears neither necessary nor useful in this context.

A clear victory for either of the two constructions has not been achieved, if alone for the reason that the respective arguments often proceed from entirely different assumptions and are directed at completely different goals. Some, espe-cially the monists, concentrated their dialectic endeavors primarily on the construction of a unified theory of norms(1) or on the presentation of a coherent legal philosophy.(2) Others, especially the dualists, based their arguments, above all, on a description of factual phenomena.(3) Yet others were primarily concerned with the theoretical under-pinnings of certain policies concerning a preferred public order.(4) In view of the diverse methods employed, it is hardly surprising that the discussion often proceeded on entirely different levels and along different lines, and that the arguments of the respective adversaries were often regarded as completely futile.

Nevertheless, the controversy between these two prominent schools of thought has over the years lost much of its acrimony. Dualism in its more recent and milder variety(5) does not deny that there are, after all, points of contact between the two systems of law, and that international law is not exclusively concerned with the behavior of nation-States. The necessity of a harmonization of prescriptions in national and international law is therefore admitted. The nature of these measures of harmonization is, however, still not entirely agreed. Monism in its contemporary brand has abandoned the more radical postulates of its predecessors about an automatic mechanism of derogation of inconsistent norms within the entire united legal system and has retreated into a construction of delegation of prescriptive competences which is based more on theoretical considerations than on any empirical observations.(6) To the extent that international law is seen as the "superior" delegating legal order, the removal of material conflicts between international and national norms is not seen to take place through an automatic nullity of the domestic prescription, but either by way of its formal repeal or by way of a State's international responsibility. Here too, the necessity of measures of harmonization is admitted in order to supplement the theoretical unity of the legal order with an actual uniformity of substantive prescriptions.

This reciprocal moderation of standpoints has deprived the controversy between the two theories of much of its practical significance. The consequences for the actual conduct of decision-makers are often identical even though the theoretical foundations may differ. The pertinent provisions of nearly all modern constitutions and the practice of State-organs on questions of international law can be explained on the basis of either of the two theories in their moderate forms. Not infrequently, a preference for one construction over the other may depend on an observer's jurisprudential standpoint or practical perspective, especially on whether an international or constitutional lawyer is seized of the question. It is, therefore, hardly surprising that a growing number of writers entertain serious doubts on whether the controversy about monism and dualism leads to any meaningful results.(7)

The two theories in their moderate contemporary versions are thus largely neutral from an operational point of view, that is, they need not lead to divergent outcomes in specific decision-situations. Their psychological impact should, nevertheless, not be underestimated. Monism upholding the "supremacy" of international law is still closely associated with policies favoring the promotion of international community interests. Dualism is considered to uphold positions of sovereignty and special interests. Even though the two theories do not require divergent results in terms of specific value allocations, a decision-maker whose thinking is dominated by either of the two schools of thought may well be influenced by that theory in making a particular decision.

Notwithstanding the largely speculative character of the theoretical discusssion on monism and dualism in their more recent forms, this debate has still had some impact on efforts to find practical solutions for the harmonization of international and national law. The questions involved include the requirement and nature of implementing measures taken by domestic law for international prescriptions. They also include attempts to reconcile competing material prescriptions of national and international origin, often labelled with the somewhat simplistic term "supremacy". Finally, the theoretical debate on the relation of national and international law has also shown some impact on the status of individuals and corporations in international law. The following chapters will deal in some detail with all these questions to the extent that they are relevant to the treatment of international decisions by domestic courts.

The limits and shortcomings of both the monist and the dualist constructions lie in a premise which is common to both theories: The fiction of a homogeneous and static legal order exclusively composed of clearly defined norms. Only this highly abstracted conception permitted the evolution of these simplified all-embracing theories. These theories are governed more by an endeavor to achieve conceptual clarity and simplicity than by realism and the ability to solve practical problems. Simplicity and clarity are, no doubt, desirable properties also for scientific theories, but where simplicity is obtained at the cost of realism and practical utility its advantages become dubious.

A legal theory which is restricted to the notion of a system of static rules is unable to cope with questions of competing legal orders or decision processes in any other manner than in terms of normative hierarchies or mechanical operations between different sets of rules. This highly abstracted notion of the law only offers an imprecise and unsatisfactory description of the actual processes and interactions which manifest themselves in concrete decisions. It does not permit a detailed evaluation of the various factors influencing and determining the actual behavior of effective decision-makers.

The alternative of a theory viewing the law not as a static system of norms but as an authoritative process of effective decisions could remove most of these shortcomings. It would see international law and domestic law and their relationship not as one or several systems of norms, but as a multitude of decisions made by authorized actors, which in turn determine the behavior of other decision-makers.(8) It is true that these processes of decisions take place in distinguishable arenas and in the framework of different social processes, national and transnational. But they have numerous connecting points and are in constant interaction. A constructive contribution to the relationship of national and international law must focus on the details of this inter-

action in order to describe trends in decisions, to project
probable future developments, and to present policy alternatives for preferred solutions. The practical problems arising
in this context, especially in the treatment of international
prescriptions by domestic decision-makers, are numerous and
diverse. Their solution depends, among other factors, on the
type of international decision invoked, on the kind of
domestic organ involved, and on the claims put forward. The
different legal questions arising in these situations cannot
be answered with the help of stereotype general theories on
the relationship of national and international law coupled
with logical derivations. The diversity of interactions
between international and domestic decisions can only be
adequately described with the help of a differentiated and
problem-oriented approach. Specific solutions should be
judged not so much on the basis of their conformity with a
general theory as on their ability to contribute to the
solution of particular problems in accordance with the
policy considerations developed for them.

For these reasons the following parts of this investigation
into the treatment of decisions of international institutions
by domestic courts will follow neither of the two well-known
theories. Rather, an attempt will be made to present an
accurate picture of past practice together with policy
alternatives for the purpose of finding the best solution
for specific problems.

B.   PROCEDURES PROVIDED BY DOMESTIC LAW FOR THE IMPLEMENTA-
      TION OF INTERNATIONAL PRESCRIPTIONS

1. General Policies

Domestic legal systems know a variety of techniques to
safeguard the fulfillment of international obligations.
These techniques vary in their degree of specification and
range from general principles laid down in constitutions to
concrete administrative measures. A large part of these
techniques consists in general directions aimed at applying
organs, instructing them to make their decisions conform
with international prescriptions. The details of these
implementing techniques in different domestic legal systems
have been described repeatedly in detail in scholarly writings.(9)

The legal nature of these implementing techniques of domestic
law has been the object of some controversy.(1o) One school
of thought, strongly influenced by dualist ideas, regards
them as nothing less than a transformation of international

law into domestic law. A provision, once it has undergone
this process of transformation, would thus lose its international character and would have to be applied as part of
domestic law. This theory is based on the idea that the exercise of the prescribing function is a monopoly of certain
State-organs, namely the legislative branch. It is to some
extent supported by the participation of legislative organs
in the conclusion of treaties. The approval given by the
legislative organ to the provisions of the treaty is seen as
a constitutive act of prescription for domestic law. In
addition, the texts of treaties are usually promulgated in
official publication organs in a similar way to statutes.

This theory appears particularly convincing where legislative
approval of a treaty is independent of the international expression of consent to be bound or where the domestic legislature adopts detailed implementing provisions going beyond
the text of the treaty. This theory of transformation is
far less persuasive in other areas of international law
which do not depend on an explicit expression of consent to
international prescriptions and where there is, hence, far
less room for the intervention of State legislatures. Despite
this, even clauses in constitutions, referring to general
international law, have been construed as constitutive law-
making in the sense of a genuine transformation of international customary law into domestic rules.(11)

This theory of transformation is particularly popular in
England, West Germany, and Italy. Applied consistently, it
leads to unsatisfactory results. Especially in the context
of the interpretation of treaties(12) and the modification
or termination of prescriptions of international origin,(13)
the construction of a transformation of international law
into domestic law leads to unacceptable consequences.(14)

Another view, which takes account of these difficulties,
sees the techniques provided by domestic law for the fulfil-
ment of international obligations by domestic decision-makers
not in the sense of a reception of international prescriptions
into domestic law, but merely as an instruction to apply
international law as such. Under this theory the international prescriptions do not change their character, but are
interpreted and applied in their international context. This
solution, often termed "adoption",(15) seems to be gaining
support lately also in West Germany under the name *Vollzugs-
theorie*.(16) It regards the implementing measures of domestic
law as nothing more than directions to apply and implement
the prescriptions of international law without affecting
their international status.

This view of an application of international law as international law, but by virtue of a directive of domestic law, tends to lead to a conception of the relationship of the two legal orders strongly reminiscent of the conflict of laws. The application of international prescriptions is conditional on a mandate of domestic law; this mandate, however, is seen as a reference to the foreign, that is, international, law.(17)

A premise common to both these theories on the nature of domestic implementing measures is the absolute control of domestic law over whether and in what way international law is to be applied by State-organs.(18) The fact that internal decision-makers like domestic courts are created by the forum State's legal order leads to the ostensibly self-evident conclusion that they are, hence, exclusively subject to the directions of this legal order. The fact that many domestic legal systems provide directions for the application of international law, and that decisions touching upon questions of international law frequently refer to these directions, seems to support this assumption.

However, a closer examination reveals that the behavior of domestic decision-makers, especially courts, towards questions of international law cannot be attributed exclusively to domestic prescriptions.(19) Even in countries whose constitutions contain no provisions for the application of international law other than treaty law, such as the United States, the Netherlands and Switzerland, customary law is constantly applied without any misgivings.

The law of treaties also offers some indications which throw doubts on the assumption that domestic law controls the behavior of domestic courts exclusively: Even where treaty law has been made subject to specific measures of incorporation through domestic legislation, courts repeatedly have direct resort to the international agreement.(2o)

These examples alone suggest that the widely held assumption of the exclusive control of municipal law over the behavior of domestic courts on questions of international law must be seen subject to certain limitations. The question arises whether this entire assumption is not yet another consequence of the undifferentiated theories on the relationship of international law and municipal law as outlined above. Does the fact that applying organs like domestic courts have been established by domestic law and owe their authority to it, really lead to the necessary conclusion that their decision-making functions are exclusively directed by their domestic law? Is the idea of international law as a foreign law,

which must be made applicable through transformation into
the local law or through a choice of law rule of the local
law, really persuasive? Would it not, perhaps, be more
appropriate to view international law as a law common to the
international community rather than a foreign law?

If the law is not seen as a rigid and neatly encapsulated
system of rules, but as a process of authoritative decisions,
the entire question assumes a completely different shape.
What matters then is not the introduction of "foreign" legal
norms into the domestic legal order, but the division of
functions between different decision-makers. The crucial
question is not whether the "foreign" rules of international
law are valid and applicable within domestic law, but rather
which State-organs should take what decisions on the basis
of what prescriptions or decisions of international law.
These questions cannot usefully be answered on the basis of
doctrinaire assertions and logical derivations, but only in
a pragmatic way and in the light of the particular circumstances.(21)

The notion of the "internal validity" of international law,
which is conditional on prescriptions issued by certain
State-organs before it can be applied by others, is evidently based on the view that international law is only addressed
to certain State-organs that must then take further action
to make it mandatory for other internal decision-makers.
Questions of international law, however, arise in the most
diverse areas of social interaction and are by no means
restricted to the relations between nation-States or to
State-organs specialized in external relations. For this
reason, an a-prioristic conception of a so-called "internal
legal order of the State", for which prescriptions of international origin become relevant only if they have been trans-
planted by specific State-organs from an external or international legal order, does not appear meaningful.

It does by no means follow from these considerations, that
general measures of domestic law aimed at safeguarding a
behavior of internal decision-makers that is in conformity
with international law are superfluous or even contrary to
international law. An outright rejection of instructions to
apply international law or of domestic prescriptions implementing international obligations would only lead back to
the stereotype of extreme monism. These measures and provisions of domestic law have an eminently important function
and often exercize a decisive influence on the conduct of
domestic decision-makers in specific situations. This recognition must, however, not lead to the unreflected and ill-

judged conclusion that only the domestic implementing measures determine the validity and effective implementation of international law.

International law is not concerned with the details of domestic procedures for its implementation and does by no means require its "direct application". On the other hand, it is directed at a large variety of participants and decision-makers. Whenever the applying function of internal decision-makers on matters of international law is called for, the question is merely which types of State-organs are best equipped and appropriate for this task, and whether applying organs like domestic courts should wait for the intervention of other State-organs like the legislature and the executive.

Although a domestic court is the creation of domestic law, it is, nevertheless, faced with a demand for deference to international law. Whenever it implements and applies international law, it functionally also acts as an international decision-maker irrespective of whether there is a domestic prescription directing it to do so. (See also chapter I.B. above). Often a court will act without any conscious awareness of this dual function. The court thus employs the institutional authority conferred upon it by the local law to give effectiveness to the prescriptions of the international order, which lacks appropriate structures of its own for their enforcement.(22) The legal order setting up an organ is not necessarily identical with the legal order applied by it. Under this idea of *dédoublement fonctionnel*, the domestic court, therefore, should apply international prescriptions also by virtue of their own authority, and not necessarily because of any transformation into domestic law or the local law's direction to apply it.(23) The existence of local prescriptions supplementing or contradicting international prescriptions is, no doubt, a significant factor determining the behavior of domestic courts, but is not exclusively decisive.

In the terminology of the conflict of laws, this means that international law is not a unity with the local law as suggested by the proponents of monism, but is still also *lex fori*. It is the law of the entire international community, its application is neither restricted territorially to certain law districts nor to certain types of decision-makers. A reference of the local law to certain prescriptions or "sources" of international law is, therefore, not a necessary precondition for its application. It is neither a "superior" (as suggested by monism) nor an "external" law (as suggested by dualism), but a common law. A solution of

the relationship of national and international law modelled
on the principles of the conflict of laws would, therefore,
only make sense if the international prescription to be
applied in the particular case does not have universal currency and is not addressed to the forum State's organs or
subjects. Possible examples are treaties between third States,
regional international law and especially decisions of international organizations directed only at certain States or
other participants, such as, parties to international judicial proceedings or members of an international organization.
In situations of this kind, the references and "choice of
law rules" of the *lex fori* would not only have to be sought
in the local municipal law but also in general international
law.

In sum: Measures and prescriptions of the local law, whether
of a general or a specific nature, that direct internal
decision-makers to apply international law are an important
factor in the internal decision-making process concerning
international law and significantly affect the behavior of
domestic courts. In some cases, especially where detailed
directions on the mode of compliance with general international obligations are necessary or where the position of the
forum State on international prescriptions of doubtful authority appears significant, directives of domestic law are of
utmost importance for the effective application of international law. If the measures provided by the local law for
the implementation of international law are more by way of a
general declaration of principle, they can, at least, provide
an important supplementary element for a conduct of local
decision-makers that is in accordance with international law.
On the other hand, there is neither any conclusive theoretical reason nor any compelling factual evidence for the assumption that an explicit direction of the local law to
apply international law is the sole and exclusive factor
determining the behavior of domestic courts towards questions
of international law. In situations in which there are no
serious doubts neither about the existence nor about the
precise contents of international prescriptions, the intervention of legislative organs of the forum State is not a
necessary precondition for their implementation by domestic
applying organs.

2. Implementing Measures for Decisions of International
   Institutions

The techniques developed by domestic law, whereby deference
to international prescriptions by domestic decision-makers
is to be guaranteed, are settled and uncontroversial in

their essential aspects in most domestic legal systems as
far as treaty law and customary international law are concerned. They are frequently regulated by specific constitutional
provisions and have been the subject-matter of .extensive
practice and scholarly writings.(24) By contrast, the application of decisions of international institutions, apart
from the European Communities, has so far attracted very
little attention. Statements in scholarly publications on
this subject are usually sweeping and do not offer a differentiated treatment of the specific problems raised by different
types of international decisions and different types of claims
based upon them.(25) Legislative and executive measures trying to cope with this problem are neither uniform nor comprehensive. Under these circumstances, an investigation into
court practice can hardly be expected to yield clear and
simple results.

There are several techniques available to a domestic legislator to safeguard the application of international decisions. The simplest such technique is a general constitutional provision directing internal decision-makers to apply
them. This would follow the method employed by many constitutions for the implementation of treaty law and customary
international law. A search in contemporary constitutions
for the existence of such a general clause with respect to
decisions of international institutions is hardly fruitful.
(26) Although a number of constitutions contain references
to organized international cooperation, most of these provisions can hardly be construed as requiring the application
of decisions of international organs by domestic decision-
makers.

In a number of European countries membership in the European
Communities was regarded as necessitating constitutional
amendments.(27) The constitutions of some Members had already
previously contained similar provisions. The constitutions
of other Members were amended after their accession to the
European Communities. Thus, the Constitutions of the Federal
Republic of Germany (Art.24), of Italy (Art.11), of the
Netherlands (Art.67), of Belgium (Art.25bis), of Luxemburg
(Art.49bis), of Denmark (Art.2o(1)), but also of the non-
Members Norway (Art.93) and Sweden (Art.81(3)), contain
clauses providing for the transfer of sovereign functions
to international organizations or institutions.(28) France
had a similar provision in the preamble to the Constitution
of 1946.

Provisions referring to international institutions contained
in other constitutions are even less instructive to our

question. They appear in the form either of general declarations of principle(29) or of internal delimitations of competences.(3o) In still other countries constitutional problems arising from an accession to international organizations and the necessity of constitutional amendments are still under consideration.(31)

The literature on these constitutional provisions, which is particularly prolific with respect to Article 24 of the German Constitution,(32) clearly shows that these prescriptions are not primarily concerned with the deference to be accorded by domestic decision-makers to decisions of international institutions. They are directed at such constitutional problems as the exercise of sovereign powers by external organs,(33) the distribution of jurisdictions, and so forth. Any attempt to construe these provisions in the sense of a "transformation" or incorporation of international decisions or of a direction to apply them would be hardly convincing.

An important exception to these observations on the provisions of contemporary constitutions concerning international institutions is the Netherlands' Constitution. Unlike other constitutions, its Article 67 does not only provide for the transfer of certain functions to international institutions, but also gives a clear mandate to domestic decision-makers to implement and apply their decisions. Article 67 paragraph 2 provides:

> With regard to decisions made by organizations based on international law, Arts.65 and 66 shall similarly apply.

Article 65 declares that directly applicable treaty provisions shall be generally binding. Article 66 declares internal prescriptions inapplicable to the extent that they are incompatible with directly applicable treaty provisions. Historically this far-reaching constitutional provision concerning decisions of international institutions can be traced back to the deliberations in connection with the setting up of the European Communities. But there is no need to restrict its application to this particular institution. However, even this seemingly simple and unequivocal constitutional provision creates difficulties.(34) For instance, the concept of "decisions" may give rise to doubts in certain cases, especially in connection with recommendations issued by international institutions. Also the reference to the direct applicability of international decisions may create more difficulties than it solves.

In the absence of pertinent constitutional clauses providing
for the application of international decisions, other ways
are devised to construe an internal obligation for domestic
applying organs to give deference to them. One possibility
is to assimilate international decisions to other well established types of international legal prescriptions or "sources"
whose internal applicability is beyond doubt. Sometimes an
attempt is made to utilize treaties for this purpose. Their
applicability and authority for internal decision-makers is
well settled in most domestic legal systems. Thus, interpretations of international agreements by international organs
are construed to be indirectly incorporated into domestic
law as part of the wider complex of the treaty. (See chapter
VII.C.2. and VII.E.3. below). Another construction extends
the consent given to a treaty, which sets up decision-making
functions for an international organ, also to the "secondary
treaty law" subsequently generated by the international
organ.(35) Under this theory the direction of domestic law
to apply the treaty would also embrace a direction to apply
any decision of the international institution created by the
treaty. Yet another construction sees the submission to the
international agreement as an authorization to the international organ, created by it, to enact "regulations".(36)

All these constructions are highly formalistic and appear
somewhat strained. In all these cases of ficticious incorporation, the domestic legislature has no latitude to accept
or reject individual decisions of international organs.
Especially the construction of a provision concerning the
transfer of jurisdiction to an international institution
contained in a treaty as a simultaneous mandate to internal
decision-makers to apply any future decisions issued by that
international institution is highly artificial.

In addition to these attempts to introduce decisions of
international institutions into domestic legal systems under
the guise of treaties, efforts are sometimes made to link
them to customary international law in order to justify
their application by domestic decision-makers. Especially
the invocation of international decisions as "precedents"
for the elucidation of customary law (chapter VII.E.3 below)
and of recommendations of international organs of a general
character (chapter VII.B. below) were seen in the context of
the established "source" customary law.

Here too, the observations already made above in chapter I.
C.2. on the "types of sources" of international law must
apply. The attempt to force new phenomena in the international decision-making process into the traditional categories

of sources of international law, in order to justify their
observance by internal decision-makers, may lead to acceptable results in individual cases. However, constructions of
this kind will hardly lead to generally satisfactory solutions. Instead of looking for simple all-embracing theories,
it would be far more fruitful to analyse the problems and
the policy questions arising from the invocation of different
kinds of international decisions and from the different types
of claims based upon them in order to reach differentiated
practical results.

In addition to such general constitutional clauses and to
such attempted assimilations to the established sources of
international law, a widely employed technique for the implementation of international decisions consists of special
legislative or administrative measures to make individual
decisions or groups of decisions operative in the municipal
sphere. In some countries, especially in the United Kingdom,
this technique is also employed for ordinary treaty law.(37)
In practice, this means an adjustment or amendment of the
domestic law by the legislature to safeguard the observance
of the respective international obligations.

This method has unquestionable advantages: Doubts concerning
the authority and material contents of the relevant international prescription are removed. The international prescriptions are harmoniously integrated into the local legal system. A linguistic adaptation to local terminology and possible detailed implementing provisions facilitate their
application. On the other hand, the technique of specific
measures of implementation also has important disadvantages:
The internal legislative measure can conceal the international prescription underlying its adoption.(38) The internal
decision-maker may not even be aware of an international
origin. Implementing legislation may reproduce the international decision in a distorted and incomplete way or at
least out of context. The most important point militating
against an exclusive reliance on this technique is the fact
that a comprehensive and complete adjustment of domestic law
to every international decision that could conceivably become relevant for an internal decision-maker is quite impossible. Apart from the inevitable delays caused by parliamentary procedures, the multitude and variety of these decisions would defy any such attempt. In addition, it is practically impossible to predict which international decision
will be invoked in future proceedings before courts and
other internal decision-makers. It would, therefore, be
entirely ill-conceived to try to obtain the undeniable
advantages of certain specific implementing measures through

a rigid insistence on their exclusive relevance for domestic decision-makers.

States have, in fact, taken a variety of different measures to cope with the problems raised by decisions of international institutions in their legal systems and to ensure their observance. A comparative analysis of these measures would be worth a detailed investigation, but would go far beyond the limits of this study.(39) In order to convey an idea of the difficulties and problems arising from this relatively new international phenomenon for traditional constitutions drafted before the establishment of intensive organized international decision processes, we shall take a short look at the impact of international decisions on the Austrian constitutional order at at the end of this chapter. The subsequent section dealing with the behavior of the courts in some detail on a broad comparative basis makes reference to the peculiarities of local implementing measures whenever necessary.

3. Implementing Measures and Direct Applicability

Implementing measures for international prescriptions in different countries are not confined to overcoming the dualist notion that international law must be part of the local law before it can be applied by domestic decision-makers. The criterion of direct applicability or of the self-executing nature of international prescriptions is concerned with their material contents. Here the problem is not so much the prescription's non-national origin as its degree of precision and detail.

In the context of treaties this question is the subject-matter of numerous scholarly writings(4o) and of an extensive practice. Not infrequently the arguments put forward take the shape either of stereotype formulas or of circular conclusions.(41) Scholars who give detailed consideration to this problem usually do not offer a uniform concept of "self-executing" or "direct applicability", but refer to several different criteria affecting the ability and willingness of decision-makers to apply international prescriptions directly.

A rough survey of this rich material basically yields two approaches. A subjective variant regards the problem of direct applicability as a question of the intentions of the parties to the treaty (or other international decision-makers, as the case may be). Under this view, the international prescription may not be addressed to the general public or to the domestic applying organ. Rather, these interna-

tional prescriptions may be aimed at certain supreme organs
of the State, especially the legislature, which then have to
take the necessary steps to have them carried out.

The objective variant, on the other hand, regards the question
of direct applicability primarily as an epistemological problem. General or vague formulations in international prescriptions make it difficult or impossible for the internal applying organ to recognize their precise meaning. The solution
of these problems of recognition and interpretation is regarded as part of the prescribing and not of the applying function. Therefore, action by the legislature is demanded before the courts may become active.

In reality, the problem is frequently not so much the subjective intention of the international decision-maker or the
objective nature of the prescription involved, but the
judge's perspectives concerning his rôle in the decision-
making process. Whether an international prescription or
decision is directly applicable or self-executing is not
least determined by the court's readiness to act independently, to tackle complex problems of interpretation, and to
make policy choices. In addition, the decision whether a
prescription can be directly applied commonly depends not
only on its objective characteristics but also on the procedural context in which it is invoked, particularly on the
type of claim based upon it.(42)

The problems of direct applicability, as discussed widely
with treaties, arise in a similar way for decisions of international institutions. The concept of direct applicability
is, however, too ambiguous, vague, and heterogeneous to
justify its separate treatment in this study. Subjective
questions of direct applicability of international decisions,
to the extent that they affect the *locus standi* to rely upon
them, will be treated below in the section on participants,
especially individuals. (chapter XII.D.). Questions concerning the necessity of internal legislation to clarify and
specify international decisions will be considered, where
necessary, in the following chapters.

EXCURSUS III: The Impact of Decisions of International
              Institutions on the Austrian Constitutional
              System.(43)

Austria, like many other States, has adhered to a large
number of treaties granting far-reaching powers of decision-
making to international institutions. For a considerable
period of time, up to about 1960, the transfer of these

powers was not seen as creating any particular legal problems. In the last two decades the administration and some constitutional lawyers have become increasingly aware of the implications of the jurisdiction of international institutions on the Austrian Constitution. Two main areas of concern are distinguishable. One is the constitutional basis for the transfer of sovereign powers to non-Austrian institutions. The other is the modality of incorporation of international decisions into the Austrian legal system.

a) The Transfer of Sovereign Powers and Austrian Law

In the early post-World War II period Austria was admitted to a number of important organizations possessing far-reaching powers of decision. They include the World Health Organization, the International Civil Aviation Organization, the World Bank, the International Monetary Fund and the United Nations. In none of these cases was there any sign of an awareness of constitutional problems. The ratification of the Treaty establishing the European Free Trade Association(44) marked an important change in this respect. This treaty provides for a considerable number of decision functions by the Council, including the power to amend the Treaty itself. All these provisions were incorporated in Austria as constitutional amendments.

The reason for this procedure is the doctrine that the Austrian Constitution exhaustively prescribes the organs and procedures for the exercise of sovereign powers. Any transfer or delegation of these powers, therefore, has to take place by way of an amendment to the Constitution. Even international decisions adopted unanimously create the same constitutional problems, since the Austrian delegate voting in favor of the decision in the international body is regularly not the organ competent for the respective function (usually legislative) under the Austrian Constitution. This doctrine of constitutional completeness has found practically unanimous acceptance in Austria.

The doctrine permits three solutions:
1. The adoption of every treaty provision vesting an international organ with decision-making functions as a constitutional provision; or
2. The incorporation of every decision of an international organ by the appropriate Austrian procedure, usually legislative; or
3. The inclusion of a general clause in the Constitution providing for the transfer of sovereign power to international institutions, subject to certain limitations.

Austrian practice has so far followed the first and the
second procedure.

1. Numerous provisions contained in a large number of treaties ratified by Austria since 1960 have been approved in
the form of constitutional amendments. This has led to a
multitude (several hundred) of scattered constitutional provisions in treaties, which enjoy this privileged position
not because of their fundamental importance, but for purely
formal reasons.

The most frequent source of constitutional difficulties is
the power of international organs to adopt amendments to
treaties not requiring the ratification of Member States.
This alone has led to a large number of completely trivial
constitutional provisions. For example, whenever the headquarters of an international organization are mentioned in
the constitutive treaty and an organ is authorized to make a
decision for a transfer of headquarters, this provision requires a constitutional amendment in Austrian law, since
technically the change of headquarters is an amendment to
the treaty.

Not only the multitude of decision-functions of international organs but also their variety creates problems. The
difficulties in determining exactly which international
decision-functions affect Austria's sovereign powers have
led to arbitrary dividing lines between different categories
of international decisions and to insecurity even with relatively similar types of decisions. Thus, decision-functions
only affecting the "internal structure" of the international
organization are generally not regarded as creating problems.
However, delegations of functions from one international
organ to another are already a matter for the Austrian Constitution. A list of other marginal cases creating uncertainties would cover several pages. An attempt made in 1971
to clear up all these difficulties by compiling a full list
of all constitutionally relevant provisions in constitutive
instruments of international organizations had to be abandoned. The draft for this statute(45) only highlighted the
almost intractable situation which this practice of proli-
ferating constitutional provisions in treaties has created.
Not surprisingly, this practice is not even consistent New
constitutional problems are "discovered" all the time. Old
constitutional qualms are sometimes given up after a while.

2. Decisions of international organs not covered by treaty
provisions enjoying the rank of constitutional law in Austria
are frequently individually enacted. They are either subjec-

ted to a formal ratification procedure, like treaties, or adopted as statutes. In most cases these procedures are, of course, carried out for purely formal reasons, since the Austrian authorities normally have no discretion left after the international decision has been adopted. Even where the international decision leaves room for its subsequent acceptance or rejection by individual States, this procedure is usually meaningless since the parliamentary procedure takes longer than the time limits provided for this purpose. Sometimes the Austrian delegates are forced to make reservations to international decisions purely for the purpose of enabling Parliament to go through the necessary ratification formalities.

3. The third possibility would be to include a general clause into the Constitution providing for the transfer of sovereign powers to international institutions. In the light of the unfavorable experiences with the practice so far employed in Austria, this method would certainly offer considerable advantages. It would also follow the example of a number of other European countries.(46)

Such a general clause would, however, have to be framed subject to certain limitations. Already a few scholars have put forward the view that a general authorization to transfer sovereign powers to international organs would amount to a basic alteration of the Constitution requiring a referendum. At present, decision-functions of international organs, though far-reaching in formal authority, are limited to a very few specific areas of the law. Misgivings concerning a wholesale abdication of sovereign powers are hardly justified at this stage. An increase in integration could, however, lead to a rapid intensification of international decision-making processes. For example, in the European Community, of which Austria is not a member, a large and important section of legislative and executive functions has been handed over to international organs.

The proposed general clause should, therefore, attempt to state the limits for an informal transfer of powers by treaties. Any integration going beyond these limits should continue to require a constitutional amendment. This would dispose of the necessity to introduce constitutional amendments for purely formal reasons in connection with perfectly trivial treaty provisions, while reserving basic decisions concerning membership in international organizations with decision-making powers of unprecedented importance to a two thirds majority of Parliament. These limits should include the inviolability of the three leading principles of the

Austrian Constitution (democracy, federalism and the rule of
law), the permanent neutrality, and the inviolability of
human rights.

b) The Incorporation of International Decisions into Austrian
   Law

The incorporation of international decisions into Austrian
law has not been uniform. One method follows the treatment
of treaties and consists in a mere official promulgation.
The publication of decisions of international organs has
become a very frequent feature in the Austrian Federal Gazette.

Another method is the enactment of internal prescriptions
reflecting the contents of the international decision. This
method is sometimes used even for international decisions
which have already been published in Austria. As mentioned
above, the reason for this technique is not only the sometimes vague or abstract wording of the international decision but also the endeavor to integrate it harmoniously into
the system and terminology of Austrian law. Sometimes specific new statutes are framed to accomodate decisions of
international organizations; sometimes existing statutes are
amended. In other cases mere executive regulations are used
to incorporate the contents of international decisions.

The method of incorporation by executive regulation, however,
creates peculiar difficulties. Austrian doctrine requires
for every executive regulation a specific basis in an Austrian
statute. Since decisions of international institutions do
not qualify as statutes, this method often creates difficulties. The solutions of creating exceptional constitutional
authorizations for executive regulations without a statutory
basis or of always enacting the international decisions in
the form of a statute are highly impracticable.

Here too, a general constitutional amendment permitting executive regulations on the basis of international decisions
published in Austria appears appropriate.

(1)   See e.g. Kelsen, Die Einheit von Völkerrecht und staat-
      lichem Recht, 19 ZaöRV 234(1958).

(2)   Verdross, Die Einheit des rechtlichen Weltbildes auf
      Grundlage der Völkerrechtsverfassung (1923).

(3)   See e.g. Triepel, Völkerrecht und Landesrecht (1899).

(4)   See e.g. Scelle, Précis, p.345.

(5)   See e.g. Rudolf, Völkerrecht und deutsches Recht (1967).

(6)   Cf. e.g. Verdross, Die normative Verknüpfung von Völker-
      recht und staatlichem Recht, in Festschrift für Adolf
      J.Merkl, p.425(197o).

(7)   See already Borchard, The Relation between International
      Law and Municipal Law, 27 Virginia LRev. 137(194o);
      Parry, The Sources, p.13; Fitzmaurice, The General
      Principles of International Law, 92 RC 1,71seq.(1957,
      II); McDougal, The Impact of International Law upon
      National Law. See also the list of references cited by
      Wildhaber, Treaty-Making Power and Constitution, p.4
      note 2(1971).

(8)   Cf. McDougal, The Impact, p.37.

(9)   See e.g. the bibliography by Wagner, Monismus und
      Dualismus, 89 AöR 239(1964) note 98; in addition see
      McDougal, The Impact, p.75; Mosler, L'application,
      p.636seq.; Seidl-Hohenveldern, Transformation or Adop-
      tion of International Law into Municipal Law, 12 ICLQ
      88(1963); van Panhuys, Relations and Interactions,
      p.37seq.; Lillich, The Proper Role, p.13seq.

(1o) For a recent contribution see Lord Denning in Trendtex
      Corpn. v. Central Bank of Nigeria, /1977/ 2 W.L.R.
      356,364seq.

(11) See esp. Rudolf, Völkerrecht und deutsches Recht,
      p.239seq. with further references; Schlochauer, Das
      Verhältnis, p.18; Thieme, Das Grundgesetz, p.55.

(12) Cf. Schreuer, The Interpretation, p.256seq.

(13) Cf. the unusual provision of Article 28 of the French
      Constitution of 27 Oct.1946, which provided for a
      parliamentary participation also in the termination of
      treaties.

(14) For comprehensive treatment see esp. Partsch, Die
     Anwendung, p.9oseq.; Cf. also Jenks, The Prospects,
     p.745seq.

(15) See Seidl-Hohenveldern, Transformation or Adoption;
     Morgenstern, Judicial Practice and the Supremacy of
     International Law, 27 BYIL 42,61seq.(195o).

(16) Partsch, Die Anwendung; Boehmer, Der völkerrechtliche
     Vertrag im deutschen Recht (1965).

(17) Wengler, Réflexions, p.924seq.; Strebel, Das Völkerrecht
     als Gegenstand von Verweisungen und Begriffsübernahmen,
     von Kollisionsregeln und Rezeption im nationalen Recht,
     28 ZaöRV 5o3(1968).

(18) Wengler, Réflexions, p.924; van Panhuys, Relations and
     interactions, p.45; Mosler, L'application, p.64o;
     Kraus, Der deutsche Richter und das Völkerrecht, in
     Festschrift für Rudolf Laun, p.223(1953).

(19) Partsch, Die Anwendung, p.84,157; van Panhuys, Rela-
     tions and Interactions, p.46; Mosler, L'application,
     p.689; Morgenstern, Judicial Practice, p.52; Seidl-
     Hohenveldern, Transformation or Adoption, p.9oseq.;
     Alexandrowicz, International law in the Municipal
     Sphere, p.92.

(2o) Alexandrowicz, International law in the Municipal
     Sphere, p.87seq.; Schreuer, The Interpretation, p.257
     seq. with a survey of English court practice. For the
     practice of French courts on treaties which had not
     been promulgated domestically see Ruzié, Les procédés
     de mise en vigueur des engagements internationaux pris
     par la France, 1o1 Clunet 562,57o(1974).

(21) Cf. also McDougal, The Impact, p.72: "The fact is that
     such terms as 'transformation', 'incorporation' and
     'adoption' are but metaphors of ill-defined reference,
     deriving whatever meaning they have from the limiting
     conception of law, international and national, as
     abstracted rules."

(22) Cf. esp. Scelle, Le phénomène, p.331seq.

(23) Cf. the analogous situation in federal states in which
     organs of component states apply federal law. See
     Panhuys, Relations and interactions, p.8,37; see also
     the related problem described by Jessup, The Doctrine

of Erie Railroad v.Tompkins applied to International
Law, 33 AJIL 74o(1939).

(24) See the references above note (9).

(25) See e.g. Papacostas, Nature juridique; Sørensen, Principes, p.12oseq.; Zacklin, The United Nations and Rhodesia,
p.76seq.; Skubiszewski, Enactment, p.267;

(26) Generally see Mangoldt, Das Völkerrecht in den neuen
Staatsverfassungen, 3 Jahrb.IR 11 (195o/51); Wildhaber,
Treaty-Making Power, p.384seq.; P.de Visscher, Les
tendances internationales des constitutions modernes,
8o RC 515, 545seq.(1952, I); Miele, Les Organisations
internationales et le domaine constitutionel des états,
p.388seq.; Stein, Application and Enforcement of International Organization Law by National Authorities and
Courts, in Schwebel (Ed.), The Effectiveness of International Decisions, p.66(1971).

(27) Wildhaber, Treaty-Making Power, p.384seq.; Hunnings,
Constitutional Implications of joining the Common
Market, 6 CMLRev. 5o(1968-69); Gaudet, The European
Communities, in Schwebel (Ed.), The Effectiveness of
International Decisions 3o9,32o(1971).

(28) For the text of these provisions see especially Peaslee,
Constitutions of Nations Vol.III(1968).

(29) Cf. e.g. Art.11 of the Algerian Constitution.

(3o) See Art.8(1) of the Constitution of Brazil; Art.246 § 1
of the Seventh Schedule (12) a. (13) of the Constitution
of India; Art.56 of the Constitution of South Korea;
Art.67 of the Constitution of Togo; Art.76(1)(a) of the
Constitution of Malaysia.

(31) For Switzerland see esp. Schindler, Supranationale
Organisationen und schweizerische Bundesverfassung, 57
Schw.Jur.Z. 197(1961); Guggenheim, Organisations supra-
nationales, indépendance et neutralité de la Suisse, 97
Zeitschr.f.Schw.R. 221(1963 II); Wildhaber, Vorschläge
zur Verfassungsrevision betreffend den Abschluß inter-
nationaler Verträge, 65 Schw.Jur.Z. 117,122seq.(1969);
ibid., Treaty-Making Power, p.395; Botschaft des Bundes-
rates an die Bundesversammlung über die Neuordnung des
Staatsvertragsreferendums vom 23.Okt.1974. For the
United States see esp.: Nathanson, The Constitution and
World Government, 57 North-western University LRev.355

(1962); Hay, Federalism and Supranational Organizations
p.2o5seq.(1966); Henkin, Foreign Affairs, p.189seq.;
Wildhaber, Treaty-Making Power, p.384.

(32) Klein, Die Übertragung von Hoheitsrechten (1952);
Inst.f.Staatslehre und Politik der Univ.Mainz, Der
Kampf um den Wehrbeitrag, 3 Vol.(1952-58); Mosler,
Internationale Organisation und Staatsverfassung;
Bernhardt, Der Abschluß völkerrechtlicher Verträge im
Bundesstaat, p.182seq.(1957); Glaesner, Übertragung
rechtsetzender Gewalt auf internationale Organisationen
in der völkerrechtlichen Praxis, 12 Die öffentliche
Verwaltung 653(1959); Maunz-Dürig, Kommentar zum Grund-
gesetz (1964); Mangoldt-Klein, Das Bonner Grundgesetz,
p.655seq.(1966,1974).

(33) See also Münch, Internationale Organisationen mit
Hoheitsrechten, in Festschrift Wehberg, p.3o1(1955).

(34) Cf. also Sørensen, Principes, p.12oseq.

(35) Dominicé, La nature, p.256; Dubouis, Le juge administratif, p.55; Henkin, Foreign Affairs, p.195; Bianchi,
Security Council Resolutions, p.84seq.

(36) Economides, Nature juridique, p.231,235seq.

(37) Cf. Schreuer, The Interpretation, p.256seq.

(38) Cf. the critical remarks about attempts to "incorporate"
EEC regulations by Bebr, Community Regulations and
National Law, 1o CMLRev. 87,95seq.(1973).

(39) See the brief survey of the situation in France by
Ruzié, Les procédés, p.565; for Greece see Economides,
Nature juridique, p.231seq.; for Spain see the note in
19 Revista Esp.DI 452(1966) and 2o Revista Esp.DI
5o4(1967).

(4o) See esp. Bleckmann, Begriff und Kriterien der innerstaatlichen Anwendbarkeit völkerrechtlicher Verträge
(197o); Koller, Die unmittelbare Anwendbarkeit völkerrechtlicher Verträge und des EWG-Vertrags im innerstaatlichen Bereich (1971), and the references cited by
these authors. Especially on European Community Law see
Bebr, Directly Applicable Provisions of Community Law:
The Development of a Community Concept, 19 ICLQ 257(197o).

(41) See the pertinent criticism by McDougal, The Impact,
p.76seq.

(42) Bleckmann, Begriff und Kriterien, p.66seq.; Schlüter,
     The Domestic Status, p.13o.

(43) For a more detailed and fully documented analysis see
     Schreuer, Beschlüsse internationaler Organe im österrei-
     chischen Staatsrecht, 37 ZaöRV 468(1977) and the lite-
     rature cited there.

(44) BGBl 196o/1oo.

(45) "Erstes Staatsverträge-Sanierungsgesetz". 122 Blg.NR
     XIII GP.

(46) See above p. 168.

VII. IMPLEMENTING MEASURES IN THE PRACTICE OF COURTS

The preceding chapter has given some indication of the diverse, and sometimes haphazard, nature of implementing measures for decisions of international institutions taken by the legislative and executive branches of States, and of the variety of formal or substantive motives underlying them. Usually these measures do not offer any clear and uniform guidance for domestic courts. Therefore, a detailed investigation into the problems encountered by domestic courts in this context and of the solutions chosen by them is indispensible. This investigation will follow the outline as used above, by decision-functions of international institutions and, where appropriate, by types of claims based on the international decisions. For not infrequently the attitude of courts towards the necessity of measures of incorporation is decisively influenced by the kind of international decision invoked and the type of claim based upon it.

In examining the behavior of domestic courts on these questions, it should always be borne in mind that the rejection of an international decision based on the ostensible reason of its lack of incorporation into domestic law can be one of several methods to ward off the consequences of the international decision. The argument of non-incorporation may often be no more than a welcome strategy to avoid the undesirable consequences which would otherwise arise from the international decision. Some inconsistencies of court practice on the requirement of specific measures of incorporation may well be explained from this perspective.

A survey of court practice reveals several situations which permit conclusions of varying degrees concerning the attitude of courts towards the necessity of measures of implementation or incoporation. In cases in which there are, in fact, specific measures of incorporation of a legislative or executive kind, problems normally do not arise. The reliance on the international decision takes place on the basis of and by reference to the implementing measure. Where an international decision has not been specifically incorporated into the domestic law, the internal decision-maker has several possibilities at his disposal. He can flatly refuse to give deference to it. Alternatively, he can rely on the international decision by adopting one of several justifications for doing so: He can construct a ficticious incorporation through one of the methods as described above in chapter VI.B.2.; he can deny the necessity of specific implemen-

ting measures; and, finally, he can rely on the international
decision without discussing the question of its incorporation.

A. INTELLIGENCE

In the relatively few cases in which the exercise of the intelligence function by international institutions has played
a rôle in the decisions of domestic courts (see chapter III.
A. above), problems of incorporation into the local law never seem to have arisen. A look at the type of materials
used in these cases shows that this is hardly surprising.
The relevant information usually concerned either factual
evidence or preparatory works to conventions or to formal
decisions by international organs. Although it is obvious
that this kind of material, such as the deliberations in
the International Law Commission, does command a certain
degree of authority and may even constitute an independent
factor in the development of the law, it was not seen as "rules of law", but simply as "evidence". Measures of incorporation for this type of source were not regarded as necessary.

B. RECOMMENDATION

Recommendations by international organizations cover a wide
range of subject-matters, including a number of questions
which can affect the behavior of internal decision-makers
and the legal position of litigants before domestic courts.
(See chapter III.B. above). Their limited authority, however,
sets them apart from other types of prescriptions of international origin, such as, treaties or regulations. Legislative
measures to implement international recommendations would
usually go beyond the expectations of compliance created by
them and are not normally regarded as an obligation of States to which they are addressed. Their formal incorporation
into domestic law would almost certainly divest them of
their nature as recommendations.

The implementation of international recommendations in
internal law has only received scant attention in scholarly
writings. Their non-binding character evidently disqualifies
them from being treated as "norms" in the eyes of most
authors.(1) Incorporation or transformation of these prescriptions of dubious legal nature, in order to make them
applicable to domestic litigation, is usually not contemplated.(2) The practical questions, however, are considerable.

A search for examples of a direct incorporation of general
international recommendations into domestic law yields
hardly any results. On the other hand, the indirect influence

of these recommendations on domestic legislation is difficult
to assess. Thus, the Universal Declaration of Human Rights
has served as a model for the human rights provisions of a
number of national constitutions.(3) It was, however, probably
used more as a help in the drafting work of legislatures
than as the object of implementing measures. General clauses
in constitutions referring to the Human Rights Declaration(4)
are probably to be interpreted not so much as measures of
incorporation but as declarations of principle.

Even the practice of certain States to promulgate the Universal Declaration of Human Rights officially, leaves room for
considerable doubt in the light of pertinent court decisions.
In a dispute over copyrights, the Cour d'Appel de Paris(5)
came to the conclusion that the Human Rights Declaration's
official promulgation in France made it equivalent to a
French statute:

> ...la Déclaration Universelle des Droits de l'Homme
> votée le 1o décembre 1948 par l'Assemblée des Nationas
> Unies et publiée aux 'Journal Officiel' du 19 février
> 1949, ce qui en fait une loi de l'Etat français, sti-
> pule...(6)

The French Conseil d'Etat, on the other hand, emphatically
rejects this view. It held in two decisions,(7) given before
and after the decision of the Cour d'Appel de Paris, that
the publication in the *Journal Officiel* did not justify the
assumption that the Universal Declaration of Human Rights
had the force of law in France, since the Constitution only
provides this for treaties properly ratified and published.
(8) In a similar vein, the Belgian Conseil d'Etat rejected a
reliance on the Universal Declaration notwithstanding its
promulgation in the *Moniteur Belge*.(9)

The absence of any formal measure of incorporation in most
countries for recommendations, such as, the Universal Declaration of Human Rights, has in only relatively few cases before domestic courts led to a refusal to give deference to
them. The cases were mostly decided in countries like Ireland,(1o) Ceylon,(11) and Mauritius(12) with a strong British constitutional influence. They can probably be explained by the English tradition requiring a transformation of
treaty provisions by way of special statutes.(13) However,
there are also decisions by the Austrian Constitutional
Court and Administrative Court(14) which declare that the
Universal Declaration "is not part of the Austrian legal
order".(15)

The reference to a lack of implementing measures for a recommendation can, of course, be nothing more than a welcome strategy to forestall undesirable consequences which would follow from its application.(16) A comparison of cases in which reliance on international recommendations was rejected by domestic courts, however, reveals that the argument of their non-binding character (see chapter III.B.1. above) is a considerably more popular reason for their non-application.

In the vast majority of available cases, the absence of specific measures of transformation or implementation by the States concerned has not prevented the courts from relying on and referring to recommendations, especially the Universal Declaration of Human Rights. Here too, we can sometimes find constructions attempting to introduce the Universal Declaration into internal law. Especially Italian courts, faithful to their dualist tradition, have adopted fictions of this kind. One method used the reference to the Universal Declaration of Human Rights in the preamble to the European Convention on Human Rights, which is incorporated into Italian law.(17) More frequently, the Universal Declaration was brought under the heading of "norme dell diritto internazionale generalmente riconosciute", which are recognized in Italian law in accordance with Article 1o of the Constitution.(18) In a similar way, a decision of the Supreme Court of the Philippines(19) applies the Human Rights Declaration as part of the generally accepted principles of international law that are adopted by the Constitution.

A number of decisions from the Federal Republic of Germany stand in marked contrast to these cases.(2o) The German decisions specifically emphasize that the Human Rights Declaration is not part of the "general rules of international law" as accepted by Article 25 of the Constitution. This has not prevented German courts from relying on the Universal Declaration and on other recommendations in a number of decisions. (See chapter V.A. above). In some of them, the courts refer to the provisions of international recommendations as *ordre public international*,(21) as an "eternal law of nature",(22) or as "principles inherent in every legal order".(23) A specific incorporation of such fundamental international principles into the local law is evidently not regarded as a pre-condition for their acceptance by internal decision-makers.

The majority of cases in which domestic courts refer to international recommendations, as set out in chapter III.B. above, contain no reference to an awareness of any difficulties arising from the relationship of international and na-

tional law. In numerous cases the courts simply rely on the
Universal Declaration of Human Rights, especially as an aid
for the interpretation of domestic law.

C. PRESCRIPTION

The prescribing function of international institutions bears
the closest resemblance to the traditional concept of legislation. It is, therefore, not surprising that the problem of
the incorporation or transformation of this type of international decisions has figured most prominently both in scholarly writings and in the practice of courts. This is not to
say that different types of international prescriptions have
always given rise to the same sorts of solutions. As outlined
above in chapter III.C. the prescribing techniques employed
by international institutions deviate from traditional treaty
procedures, but all retain certain connections with treaty
law. It is, therefore, not surprising that attempts to justify their direct application by reference to the underlying
treaties are frequent. The incorporation of the original
treaty itself is then often regarded as embracing any attendant decisions of international organizations.

1. Amendments to Treaties

Amendments to treaties adopted by international organs without the traditional procedures of ratification by all Members are frequent.(See chapter III.C.1. above). These amendments are not always subjected to the same internal implementing procedures as the original treaties. Despite this,
there are no known cases in which courts have refused to
apply these treaties as amended because of a lack of measures
of incorporation for the amending decisions. In most cases,
it seems likely that courts are unaware of the novel proceedings which have led to the amendment of the treaties before
them and have simply applied the treaty in its current
version.

2. Official Interpretations

Of the various provisions conferring the power to adopt
official auhoritative interpretations on international
organs, as set out above in chapter III.C.2., only the
competence of the International Monetary Fund's Executive
Directors under Article XXIX (Formerly Article XVIII) of the
Fund Agreement has shown an impact on the activities of domestic courts. The official interpretation to Article VIII/
2(b) of the Bretton Woods Agreement is a frequent issue in
litigation involving foreign currencies. But the practice of

Member States shows no awareness of this fact. There are no known instances of attempts to incorporate or implement the Executive Directors' official interpretation of Article VIII/ 2(b). In some countries only certain legislative measures were taken to comply with the obligations under the Fund Agreement or only certain parts of the Agreement were endowed with "force of law". In England(24) and in the United States (25) these measures do not cover Article XVIII (now Article XXIX). Even in coutries where Article XVIII was incorporated and promulgated as part of the Fund Agreement, the effect of this practice on the legal status of the official interpretation subsequently adopted is by no means clear. In Austria, for example, the authority of external organs to pass "interpretative regulations" has given rise to constitutional misgivings.(26) Even in the Netherlands, where the Constitution specifically provides for the application of decisions of international organzations, there are difficulties since the requirement of the decision's local promulgation has not been fulfilled.(27)

From a traditional standpoint, the logical consequence of this situation would probably be the non-application of the official interpretation to Article VIII/2(b) by domestic courts. This undesirable result is avoided in scholarly writings with the help of the usual constructions. One theory is that the internal validity of Article XVIII (now Article XXIX) of the Fund Agreement should also safeguard the internal application of any international decisions taken under this provision.(28) As stated above, the construction of provisions vesting international organs with decision-making powers as simultaneously incorporating these international decisions into domestic law is rather artificial. Furthermore, this fiction is useless in countries which have not even incorporated Article XVIII (now Article XXIX). Another theory is that where Article VIII/2(b) is clearly applicable, (29) it should only be applied as interpreted by the Executive Directors.(3o) This view too, does not provide a convincing solution to the official interpretation's "internal validity". An official interpretation is an autonomous part of the international decision-making process. Even though it is based on an existing prescription, the official interpretation is part of the prescribing function. The problem of incorporation or internal validity, which is so cherished in traditional scholarly writings, cannot suddenly be explained away with the help of the assertion that the official interpretation is declaratory only and is,thus, really only a part of the treaty provision which is already incorporated.

The practice of the courts, as set out in chapter III.C.2. above, shows no trace of theoretical misgivings of this kind. In none of the cases in which the official interpretation of Article VIII/2(b) was applied, did the courts see any difficulty in the absence of its incorporation into the local law. The cases in which the official interpretation is disregarded give no reasons for doing so. It should be pointed out that even the absence of an incorporation of Article XVIII (now Article XXIX) of the Fund Agreement does not seem to have exercised any influence on the courts. A number of cases in United States courts(31) show this well enough. In England(32) there is an early case,(33) decided before the Executive Directors' Official Interpretation, in which the court apparently looked for an official interpretation of Article VIII/2(b) and regretted its absence. A later English judgment(34) seems to follow the official interpretation without mentioning it specifically.

3. Regulations

Of all the different types of international decisions, general mandatory prescriptions (regulations) adopted by international organs bear the closest resemblance to the traditional concept of "rules". This is probably the reason why these prescriptions have figured most prominently in the discussion on the problem of the incorporation of international decisions into domestic law. General and detailed prescriptions adopted by international organizations are not easily introduced into domestic law with the help of fictions or under the guise of other accepted "sources of law". Consequently, scholars are generally agreed that regulations originating from traditional international institutions, that is, excluding the European Communities, such as, the Annexes to the Chicago Convention on International Civil Aviation, must be incorporated into the internal law of Members before they can be applied.(35) Sometimes this requirement is understood subject to the reservation that certain regulations, such as, those regulating flights over the High Seas in accordance with Article 12 of the Chicago Convention, shall be directly applicable even without implementing measures by Member States.(36) Otherwise, a direct effect for internal decision-makers or individuals of regulations emanating from international decision-makers is generally denied - except for the European Communities.(37)

The constitutive instruments of the international organizations concerned usually give no clear guidance on the method of implementation required for the regulations adopted by them.(38) Nevertheless, the organizations themselves sometimes

indicate that they regard general implementing measures necessary. Thus, in a resolution of 1948 the ICAO Council
called upon Members "in complying with ICAO standards, which
are of a regulatory character, to introduce the text of such
standards into their national regulations, as nearly as possible, in the wording and arrangement employed by ICAO."(39)
This call was repeated in the forewords to subsequent Annexes, but has since been abandoned in favor of a more flexible
approach under which only those provisions should be incorporated into domestic law which are regarded as appropriate
for implementing legislation.(4o)

The practice of States, as far as it can be ascertained, in
incorporating this type of international decision, is by no
means uniform. One method, which is sometimes applied, is a
general reference in a domestic statute to the international
regulations, or parts of them, in the version as currently
adopted by the international organizations. This method was
chosen by a number of States to give internal effect to the
Annexes to the Chicago Convention.(41) In countries with a
developed body of law in the field of aviation, such a wholesale introduction of the Annexes would create difficulties.
Another method, therefore, adopted by a number of countries,
including the USA,(42) the United Kingdom,(43) Canada,(44)
Australia,(45) West Germany,(46) and Austria,(47) is enabling
legislation authorizing the executive to issue the necessary
regulations in order to adjust the internal provisions to
the requirements of the Annexes. Yet another method is the
adoption of legislation from time to time in order to adjust
the domestic law to regulations issued by international
organizations.(48) In France various Annexes to the Chicago
Convention were made applicable with the help of "décrets",
"arrêtés", "circulaires", and "instructions ministérielles".
(49) There is no evident objective reason for this diversity
of implementing measures. Yet another method to "incorporate"
the international prescriptions is simply their official
promulgation. This method is used primarily for the International Sanitary Regulations of the World Health Organization,(5o) sometimes for decisions of the Council of the
European Free Trade Association,(51) and in Austria for the
frequent decisions of the Mixed Committee established by the
Agreement between Austria and the European Communities.

Not surprisingly, the practice of domestic courts concerning
the requirement of implementing measures for this type of
international prescriptions is neither uniform nor consistent. In cases in which the courts were able to rely on
local implementing measures there were usually no problems.
The international prescriptions were simply applied by reference to the domestic implementing measures.(52)

Explicit refusals by domestic courts to apply prescriptions adopted by international organizations because of a failure of the local law to incorporate them are rare: In a dispute concerning a building permission for a tower close to an airport, the Belgian Cour de cassation(53) rejected an attempt by counsel for the State to rely on Annex 14 to the Chicago Convention, since the appropriate national legislation to make the provisions of Annex 14 applicable had not yet been passed.

A statement to the same effect by the Cour d'appel de Paris (54) concerning the International Sanitary Regulations was evidently an *obiter dictum*. The required measures had been taken, there was, therefore, no obstacle to the application of the regulation.

The Swiss Federal Court, when confronted with the problem of the internal validity of a decision passed by the OECD Council, evaded the question by declaring the international prescription too vague to be self-executing:

> The meaning of Subsection 5 of the Council's decision is not sufficiently specific to provide the basis for its application to a particular case. The Federal Court is therefore unable to apply it directly. The provision is only directed at the political authorities. This is probably also the reason why it was never officially promulgated.(55)

The scarceness of these domestic decisions refusing to apply international regulations because of their lack of incorporation into the local law should not be given too much significance. The available sample of cases is probably too small to be truly representative. It must be suspected that in a much larger number of cases international prescriptions of this kind would have been applicable, but were passed over with silence, because they had not been incorporated into the local law.

In contrast to these cases, there are others in which courts do not seem to have given much attention to the existence or not of domestic implementing measures. In two French cases the courts, including the Cour de cassation,(56) had no misgivings concerning the application of Annex 9 to the Chicago Convention, although this Annex had been neither incorporated into French law nor even published locally. In a similar way, the Oberlandesgericht Frankfurt/Main applied provisions of Annexes 11 and 15 to the Chicago Convention without any reference to German implementing measures.(57) However, it would probably be misleading to draw any far-reaching conclu-

sions from these cases. It is quite likely that the courts
were unaware of the true origin of these "Annexes" and simply
regarded them as parts of the Convention. Nor can other isolated examples(58) of cases in which prescriptions adopted
by international organs were apparently relied upon without
implementing legislation be regarded as a reliable indicator
of a general practice.

A specialised area for the prescribing function of international organs is the so-called internal law of international
institutions. Especially the law governing employment by
international institutions is the object of a rich regulatory
activity by international organizations. At first sight an
incorporation into domestic law of prescriptions of this
kind would appear entirely inappropriate and superfluous,
since it is, after all, international organs which have to
apply this body of law. A closer look at everyday practice,
however, reveals that even in this field the doctrinaire
separation of different legal orders does not always do
justice to the realities of the international decision-
making process. Of course, it is true that the application
of these prescriptions is primarily in the hands of the
international organizations which have adopted them. Nevertheless, there are cases in which the rules governing employment by international organizations have played a role in
proceedings before domestic courts.

Italian courts have relied on the Staff Regulations of the
International Refugee Organization, in order to resolve the
procedural problem of how to delimit their jurisdiction from
the concurrent competence of the dispute settlement procedures created within the organization.(59) An American case
Keeney v.U.S. is particularly instructive since it even
involved the application of substantative provisions of
United Nations employment regulations by a domestic court.
In this case the defendant had declined to testify before a
Senate Subcommittee by refusing to answer questions concerning her employment by the United Nations. She relied on her
obligation under the organization's "Staff Rules" not to
communicate unpublished information without official authorization. The District Court before which she was tried rejected this defence:

> The United Nations is not clothed with the power to
> legislate on matters in the realm of municipal law of
> the United States.(6o)

On appeal the conviction was reversed. The Court of Appeals
(61) held that the defendant was entitled to rely on Staff
Rule 7 which laid down the obligation not to disclose unpublished information.

All these cases demonstrate clearly that the domestic decision-
maker can find itself in a position of having to rely on
international prescriptions that have not been incorporated
into its local law, in order to decide legal questions pending before it. A rigid insistence on legislative measures
implementing international prescriptions could lead to unacceptable outcomes.

D. INVOCATION

The relatively few instances in which the invoking function
in connection with international organizations has played an
important role in domestic litigation (see chapter III.D.
above) have not given rise to any difficulties concerning
their incorporation. Like with intelligence, invocation is
not viewed as belonging to the traditional concept of "rules
of law". Problems of incorporation or implementation are
consequently not contemplated.

E. APPLICATION

The frequency and variety of the applying function by international organizations has given rise to a relatively large
number of cases before domestic courts in which international decisions of this kind have been invoked. A variety of
claims (implementation or review, clarification of preliminary questions, "precedent") have been based on them. The
problems arising from the question of their implementation
or incorporation are consequently somewhat complex.

1. Implementation or Review

a) Of Judicial International Decisions

Claims brought before domestic courts for the implementation
or review of decisions of international courts or tribunals
are promising primarily if the international decisions are
concerned with wealth allocations. Claims for wealth are
part of the usual activities of domestic courts. Their
enforcement is normally within their range of effective
power.

An obvious parallel to the treatment of international judicial decisions is, of course, the enforcement of foreign
judgments and awards. The treatment of foreign judgments and
awards is not perceived in terms of their "transformation"
or "incorporation" into the local law, but in terms of their
recognition on the basis of local procedural prescriptions
or of international agreements.(62) In many countries this

recognition of foreign judgments and awards is granted in formal decisions of the local courts often termed *exequatur*. Even where no formal recognition procedures are provided in the courts, the execution of a foreign judgment or award directed at payment or specific performance requires some sort of formal decision, like an order of enforcement or writ of execution.(63) In these situations it is thus up to the local courts themselves to take the necessary steps to secure the implementation of the foreign decision. An application by analogy of these procedures to international judgments and awards would, therefore, not appear to lead to any difficulties arising from dualist notions of the relationship of national and international law.

Not surprisingly, the practice of domestic courts on the implementation of international judicial decisions dealing with wealth allocations shows similarities to the treatment of foreign judgments and awards. The absence of legislative or executive implementing measures, or even the active opposition by other State organs, has not prevented the courts from declaring decisions of Mixed Commissions or of international arbitral tribunals enforceable, for instance, by granting an *exequatur*.(64) Sometimes the opposite course is taken and the international decision is reviewed on the merits.(65) But this practice, too, would be difficult to reconcile with strictly dualist ideas. In those cases in which courts refused to get involved with international judicial decisions by reference to their international character, the aspect which seemed to worry the courts was not any theory of dualism, but a reluctance to enter into "political questions". (See also chapter II.A.3. above).

On the other hand, the fact that the initiative in these cases is with the courts and not with the legislature or the executive does not automatically solve all problems. The provisions on the treatment of foreign judgments and awards differ widely from one country to another and are by no means always equally favorable to recognition.(66) Their mere transfer by analogy to international decisions could, therefore, easily lead to a conflict with the forum state's international obligations and with our preferred policy of according effectiveness to international decisions.

Obviously, there should be no objection against granting an *exequatur* to an international decision as long as this serves to facilitate its implementation. It should, however, not be forgotten that the granting of an *exequatur* is subject to different conditions in different countries. They range from a mere confirmation of the foreign decision's

authenticity to far-reaching powers to review foreign decisions on the merits, like in France.(67) The formal requirement of a writ of execution or order of enforcement can,
therefore, under certain circumstances, serve as a means to
frustrate the international decision's implementation.

A case decided by the French courts offers an instructive
example. In proceedings to obtain an *exequatur* for an arbitral award against Yugoslavia, the applicant's claim was
examined on the merits and led to protracted litigation right
up to the Cour de cassation.(68)

A well-known case concerned an attempt to implement a judgment of the Permanent Court of International Justice in the
Belgian courts. In Soc. commerciale de Belgique c. Etat hellénique et Banque de Grèce,(69) the Belgian enterprise had
initially obtained an arbitral award in its favor against
Greece. When Greece refused to comply with its obligations
under the award, Belgium, in the exercise of diplomatic
protection, took the case before the PCIJ. The Permanent
Court in its judgment found "that the arbitral awards made
on January 3rd and July 25th, 1936, between the Greek Government and the *Société commerciale de Belgique* are definitive
and obligatory".(7o) The Belgian corporation then tried to
institute proceedings for the enforcement of the international decisions against Greece. The Civil Court of Brussels
was not impressed by Greece's plea of State immunity, but,
nevertheless, refused a writ of execution. Apart from the
applicant's lack of privity in relation to the judgment of
the Permanent Court, (see chapter XII.D.1. below) the enforcement was also refused because no *exequatur* had been
obtained for the international decision:

> Attendu que la demanderesse fait observer qu'il ne se
> conçoit pas de faire exéquaturer par nos tribunaux un
> arrêt émanant de cette Cour internationale, statuant
> sur des litiges nés entre Etats;
>
> Attendu que si, *de lege ferenda* semblable dispense
> d'exéquatur apparaît concevable, voire légitime, il
> n'en est pas moins constant qu'à l'heure présente aucun
> arrangement international n'est venu introduire, dans
> nos institutions, semblable consécration;
> ...
> Attendu qu'elle ajoute que les arrêts de la Cour per-
> manente seraient affranchis de la formalité de l'exe-
> quatur, cette Cour ne constituant pas une "juridiction
> étrangère" mais, en réalité, une "juridiction supérieure
> commune à tous les pays qui sont parties à son organisa-
> tion et à son statut"...

Attendu qu'en l'absence d'un pouvoir d'exécution propre,
appartenant à cette Cour, et permettant aux parties
litigantes de réaliser, *de plano*, l'exécution de ces
arrêts, ceux-ci ne sont point, à cet égard, affranchis
des servitudes qui s'attachent, sur le territoire national aux décisions qui n'émanent pas d'une juridiction
nationale;(71)

This decision has rightly been severely critisised.(72) The
simple equation of a judgment of the Permanent Court of
International Justice, of the International Court of Justice,
or of other international decision-makers with a foreign
judgment or award makes little sense. The unreflected application of the principles of the local conflict of laws concerning foreign decisions to international decisions of this
kind becomes all the more dubious if the local requirements
for the recognition of these decisions are restrictive. The
fact that Belgium could not be held internationally responsible for the failure of its courts to enforce the international decision, which it had itself obtained for its national, does not really affect the policy considerations which
should govern this case. A revision of international decisions by refusing to recognize them is not justified merely
because the international decision creates no direct obligations for the forum State.(73) If, and to the extent that,
the *exequatur* procedure only serves to authenticate the international decision, it can expedite proceedings and is
unobjectionable. If, however, it is used openly or covertly
to review the international decision on the merits, then the
general reservations against a revision of international
decisions by domestic courts as set out above in chapter II.
A.2. must apply.(74)

An equation of international with foreign judicial decisions
for the purpose of their enforcement by domestic courts is,
therefore, only of limited practical value. The clear differences between international judgments, for example of the
International Court of Justice, and foreign judgments do not
normally create any problems of delimitation and also underline the need for a differentiated treatment. Arbitral
awards, on the other hand, can create difficulties when it
comes to determine whether they are truly "international" or
merely "foreign".(75) Especially in so-called mixed arbitral
proceedings between States and non-State participants, chiefly commercial enterprises, there are often marginal cases.
On the one hand, there can be little doubt that arbitrations
under certain agreements between States and foreign conces-
sionaires have strong public order features and cannot be
regarded simply as foreign commercial arbitrations.(76) On

the other hand, States display an increasing tendency to
enter the international market place in the rôle of ordinary
traders and, consequently, submit to the normal settlement
procedures of international commercial intercourse. The
application of the well-known distinction between *acta iure
imperii* and *acta iure gestionis* not only to the question of
State immunity but also to the problem of the enforcement of
international arbitral awards may be a possible answer. It
should, however, be borne in mind that this distinction has
created considerable difficulties of delimitation in preci-
sely the instant areas where clarity and precision is most
needed to solve our problem. (See also chapter XII.B.1. below).

The attempt to draw a line between truly international and
foreign awards would of course be futile if it could be
demonstrated that the same policies should prevail for both
types of cases. An investigation of this question would,
however, involve a considerable digression into the law
governing transnational commercial transactions and would go
beyond the limits of this study. Nevertheless, there are
practical implications for such a distinction. In the area
of commercial arbitration there are, apart from bilateral
treaties, a number of important multilateral conventions on
the reciprocal recognition and enforcement of foreign arbitral awards.(77) The most important ones are: the Geneva
Protocol on Arbitration Clauses of 24 September 1923 (27
LNTS 158); together with the Geneva Convention on the Execution of Foreign Arbitral Awards of 26 September 1927 (92
LNTS 3o2); the United Nations Convention on the Recognition
and Enforcement of Foreign Arbitral Awards of 1o June 1958
(33o UNTS 38); and the European Convention on Internatonal
Commercial Arbritration of 21 April 1961 (484 UNTS 364).
The purpose of these treaties is to safeguard the execution
of private commercial arbitral awards. Nevertheless, their
application to arbitrations in which States participate(78)
cannot be excluded.(79) Jenks(8o) has suggested a new convention along the general lines of the UN Convention of 1958
to facilitate the enforcement of truly international awards.

In some situations, the question of the implementation of
decisions of international judicial organs is not left to
the discretion of domestic courts, but is regulated in
treaties or statutes providing specifically for the imple-
mentaiion of certain types of international judicial decisions. The technique used is usually to put the international judicial decision on the same footing as a final judgment of a municipal court of the forum State. Early examples
of this method can be found in a number of bilateral treaties

between Chile, on one side, and Great Britain and France, on the other, for the settlement by arbitration of certain claims arising from belligerent actions by Chilean troops.(81)

The Peace Treaties after the First World War did not specifically provide for the implementation of awards rendered by the Mixed Arbitral Tribunals, which were established by them. Article 3o1 paragraph g of the Treaty of Versailles merely provided:

> The High Contracting Parties agree to regard the decisions of the Mixed Arbitral Tribunal as final and conclusive and to render them binding upon their nationals.(82)

Implementing legislation to this treaty provision in several countries,(83) including Germany,(84) provided for the execution of these international awards in the same way as for judgments of domestic courts.

After the Second World War this method was again used to safeguard the direct implementation of international decisions. The Convention on the Settlement of Matters Arising out of the War and the Occupation,(85) concluded between the Federal Republic of Germany and the Western Allied Powers, provided for several judicial international organs whose decisions were to be regarded as directly binding on German courts and authorities.(86) Similar provisions apply under the London Agreement on German External Debts of 1953.(87)

The most important contemporary example for a "direct enforcement" of international decisions concerning wealth allocations is, undoubtedly, provided by the European Communities. Decisions or judgments of the Council, the Commission,(88) and the Court of Justice(89) that involve a pecuniary obligation on persons other than States are directly enforceable. Although enforcement is governed by the local rules of civil procedure, an order of enforcement must be given without any review of the international decision except for a verification of its authenticity.(9o)

An important step forward in the enforcement of international arbitral awards by domestic decision-makers, especially courts, is the World Bank Convention of 18 March 1965 on the Settlement of Investment Disputes between States and Nationals of other States.(91) Article 54 of this Convention, too, provides for the treatment of these international awards like local judgments:

> (1) Each Contracting State shall recognize an award rendered pursuant to this Convention as binding and

> enforce the pecuniary obligations imposed by that award
> within its territories as if it were a final judgment
> of a court in that State...

Any review of the merits of the international award is specifically excluded by Article 53 of the Convention.

A number of countries, including the Federal Republic of
Germany,(92) the United Kingdom,(93) and the United States,
(94) have adopted implementing legislation for this treaty
provision.(95) Article 54(2) of the Convention also provides
for the advance designation of the court or authority competent for the recognition or enforcement of the international
awards. A survey compiled by the Secretary General of the
International Center for the Settlement of Investment Dis-
putes(96) shows that Member States have in most cases desig-
nated courts, often district court, but also appelate courts,
including the supreme courts, for the task of enforcing these
awards. In a few countries this task has been conferred upon
executive departments, especially the foreign ministry. At
present there is not yet any practice available on Article
54 of the ICSID Convention.

International judgments and awards not dealing with wealth
allocations are not likely to be implemented by domestic
courts by applying the local conflict of laws rules concerning foreign judicial decisions. A call for measures to incorporate them into the local law would, therefore, seem more
appropriate. On the other hand, domestic courts are not often
in a position to implement international judicial decisions
dealing with values other than wealth. Possible examples
would be cases in which domestic courts make use of a jurisdiction which has been found to appertain to them by an
international court.(97) In situations of this kind, Moroccan and French courts(98) have not hesitated to rely on the
International Court's Judgment on the Rights of Nationals of
the United States in Morocco.(99) They do not seem to have
regarded any domestic implementing measures for the application of the International Court's judgment as being necessary.(1oo)

This corresponds to a view held in scholarly writings that
the duty to implement a decision of an international judicial organ is incumbent on all organs of the State including
the courts.(1o1) No difference is made between claims to
wealth and other values.(1o2)

b) Of Non-Judicial International Decisions

While domestic courts are frequently regarded as the appropriate organs to take the necessary steps for the implemen-

tation of international judgments and awards, especially
where claims to wealth are involved, a look at court practice on operative decisions of so-called political international organs yields a completely different picture. Domestic
courts are only rarely in a position to participate in the
implementation or application of this type of international
decision. Even where there is room for a judicial intervention, the courts give much weight to the existence of
implementing legislation.

This cautious attitude can be traced back already to the
League of Nations. The Polish-German Convention of 1922 concerning Upper-Silesia conferred on the Council of the League
of Nations the right to give final decisions on certain
questions arising from transfers of assets of social security
organizations in territory transferred to Poland. After the
League Council had given such a decision on 9 December 1924,
a social security organization tried to rely on it in court
proceedings. The Supreme Court of Poland(1o3) rejected this
invocation, since the decision of the Council of the League
of Nations had not been officially published and had, hence,
"not yet become a statute forming part of the Polish law of
the land".

The German Reichsgericht when faced with the same decision
of the League Council made its recognition dependent on similar conditions:
> The decision of the Council of the League of Nations
> has only obtained internal validity if its contents has
> been enacted as domestic law.(1o4)
In the particular case the official promulgation in the
"Reichsgesetzblatt" was, however, regarded as sufficient.

Within the framework of the United Nations, it is primarily
incumbent upon the Security Council to take operative measures in concrete situations. Enforcement of these decisions
is not often within the sphere of effective control of domestic courts but, as pointed out in chapter II.A.1., there
are cases in which their cooperation can be essential for
the maintenance of economic sanctions.(1o5) The pertinent
decisions of the Security Council are normally phrased at a
high level of abstraction. Specific implementing measures by
individual UN Members are usually desirable or necessary
before Security Council decisions can be put into effect.(1o6)
Such implementing measures are, in fact, frequently taken.

A number of States have passed general enabling legislation
providing the basis for specific steps to implement Security
Council decisions, in particular, measures not involving the

use of armed force under Article 41 of the Charter.(1o7) Thus,
the United Nations Participation Act of the United States(1o8)
authorizes the President to take the necessary measures for
the implementation of sanctions, especially by executive
orders (Sec.5(a)). At the same time the Act provides for
criminal sanctions in the case of violations of these presi-
dential orders (Sec.5(b)).

The example of the boycott resolutions of the Security Council against Rhodesia shows that a large number of Member
States have found detailed implementing legislation necessary
in order to carry out their obligations under the various
Security Council resolutions.(1o9) These implementing measures
are designed to help to solve the often complicated economic
and trade problems arising from the international decisions
and, simultaneously to overcome any misgivings in connection
with the non-domestic nature of the prescriptions involved.
(11o) Whatever the motives underlying the implementing
measures, courts are in a position to rely on domestic prescriptions when giving effect to the decisions of the Security Council and have actually done so in numerous cases.(111)
Nevertheless, the problems confronting courts in these situations can be considerable. American and Australian cases are
apt illustrations of these difficulties.

In a case before the US Federal Courts, Diggs v. Shultz,(112)
a group of persons, who had grievances against the regime in
Southern Rhodesia, sued the Secretary of Treasury to enjoin
him from issuing import licences for chromium from Southern
Rhodesia in violation of Security Council Resolution 232 of
December 16,1966 and Security Council Resolution 253 of May
29,1968. Two executive orders had implemented these resolutions in the United States.(113) The Court of Appeals for
the District of Columbia dismissed the claim because a
subsequent statute had abrogated the terms of the Security
Council decisions. In looking at the subsequent statute the
court repeatedly declared that it was in blatant disregard
of the United States' *treaty obligations*. This would permit
the conclusion that the Security Council resolutions were
regarded as "supreme law of the land".(114) On the other
hand, it is worth noting that the Security Council had subsequently repeated and reconfirmed its decisions to impose
sanctions against Rhodesia,(115) a fact which passed entirely
unnoticed in the judgment.

In a subsequent case decided by the same court, Diggs v.Ri-
chardson(116) plaintiffs relied on Security Council resolutions to obtain an injunction prohibiting the U.S. government from continuing to deal with South Africa concerning

the importation of seal furs from Namibia. The court applied
the test of the self-executing nature of treaties, found
that the provisions of the Security Council resolutions invoked were not addressed to the judicial branch and, hence,
were unenforceable in the absence of implementing legislation.

In the Australian case of <u>Bradley v. Commonwealth of Australia and the Postmaster-General</u>(117) there were no implementing measures to rely upon. In this case it was the Government which attempted to enforce the UN Sanctions against
Rhodesia. The plaintiff was an employee of the Rhodesian
Department of Information who ran a Rhodesia Information
Centre in Sydney. The Postmaster-General had acted in pursuance of Security Council resolutions against Southern Rhodesia, in particular Resolution 277 of March 18,197o, which
> 11. *Requests* member States to take all possible further
> action under Article 41 of the Charter to deal with
> the situation in Southern Rhodesia, not excluding any
> of the measures provided in that Article.

He had taken a literal reading of Article 41, which, *inter
alia*, provides for the interruption of postal, telegraphic,
and other means of communication, and he had given instructions to disconnect plaintiff's telephone, to stop mail, and
telegrams passing to and from him and to deregister a publication issued by the plaintiff, which was registered for
postal transmission. Plaintiff thereupon instituted proceedings mainly to obtain an injunction against the continuation
of such actions and for damages.

The highest Australian court took a rather narrow view of
the international questions involved. It treated the question
of the Postmaster-General's discretion to take the action,
as described above, as a matter of statutory interpretation
under the Post and Telegraph Act and found that he had no
authority to give the directions he had given. In its treatment of the Security Council resolution, the court, although
recognizing the obligation of Member States under Article 25,
defeated its effect by a strictly dualist approach:
> Since the Charter and the resolutions of the Security
> Council have not been carried into effect within Austra-
> lia by appropriate legislation, they cannot be relied
> upon as a justification for executive acts that would
> otherwise be unjustified or as grounds for resisting an
> injunction to restrain an excess of executive power,
> even if the acts were done with a view to complying
> with the resolutions of the Security Council. It is
> therefore unnecessary to consider whether the resolutions
> of the Security Council, properly construed, would
> require the Commonwealth as a member nation to take the
> action that has been taken against the Rhodesia Infor-
> mation Centre.(118)

This extension of the requirement of specific measures of incorporation to decisions of the Security Council has led the
Court to extraordinary consequences. The Australian Government's action had been directed against the agent of an illegal foreign regime in fulfillment of what it considered
its international obligations. The mere fact that this action
had taken place on Australian territory apparently prompted
the Court to review its legality under the local domestic
law, while disregarding the situation under international
law. This policy stands in marked contrast to the tendency
of American courts to stand aloof from executive acts on
international questions. The Australian Court not only
refused to concern itself with the international legality of
the government's conduct but actively intervened to compel
the executive department to act contrary to its international obligations. It, thus, seems to imply that detailed statutory authorization for the conduct of foreign affairs is
required whenever their consequences make themselves felt on
Australian territory.

The effect of the combined policies of disregarding international decisions for lack of their incorporation into the
local law and of a stringent review of government action
trying to implement them could seriously affect organized
international cooperation. It could largely immobilize the
work of executive departments in the framework of international organizations until implementing legislation has been
enacted to carry out international decisions in every case.

This case aptly demonstrates how a rigid insistence on domestic implementing legislation can amount to a functional revision of international decisions. This revision may well be
the side-effect of a doctrinaire position on the relationship
of national and international law. In some cases the refusal
to give deference to international decisions, because they
have not been incorporated into the domestic law, can, however, be a welcome strategy to avert their undesirable consequences on the domestic level. The judgment of an Israeli
military court on the occupied West Bank seems a fairly obvious example. It rejected a defense motion challenging the
court's jurisdiction, based on the Security Council's call
on Israel to withdraw from occupied territories. The court
relied not only on the resolution's allegedly non-obligatory
character (see p.83 above) but also on the fact that it had
not been incorporated by the Knesset.(119)

2. Preliminary Questions

In cases in which international decisions are relied upon in
domestic proceedings merely for the purpose of elucidating

preliminary questions of international law, the domestic
courts' behavior is usually not decisive for the international decisions' effectiveness. (See chapter II.B.3. above).
Disregard shown by the domestic court for an international
decision in a situation of this kind would not normally expose the forum State to international responsibility. The
international decision in question may be such that the
executive or legislature sees no reason to take any measures
for its implementation or, at any rate, not for instructions
to the courts to give deference to it. This is particularly
so where the international decision does not require any
specific conduct or performance but merely declares or establishes a status or situation which is internationally relevant. An incorporation or instruction of compliance for international decisions of this kind is hardly conceivable. On
the other hand, domestic court proceedings not infrequently
raise international questions which are decisive for the
outcome of the case and which can only be answered by having
resort to an international decision. The application of a
previous decision to answer a preliminary point is an application of the law no less than the application of general
prescriptions. A consistently dualist approach would, therefore, have to insist on an incorporation into the local law
in the same manner as for other types of international
decisions or for other types of claims based upon them. It
would not be convincing to try to get around this problem by
presenting the international decision as a mere fact, which
would enjoy exemption from the alleged requirement of "transformation".

A survey of the not inconsiderable international practice on
this question is startling in its uniformity. There is no
indication that domestic courts ever entertained any doubts
about the applicability of international decisions for the
clarification of preliminary questions just because they had
not been incorporated into the local law by implementing
legislation. This observation holds true for different kinds
of international decision-makers and different types of international decisions, including some highly "political
questions". Thus, judgments of the International Court of
Justice and of other judicial international organs on questions of the extent of a State's jurisdiction(12o) and on
the legality of expropriations(121) were relied upon by
domestic courts to clarify preliminary points in both civil
and criminal proceedings. Decisions admitting new Members to
the League of Nations(122) and United Nations Security Council decisions(123) were accepted as conclusive on the question of whether a territorial entity enjoyed the quality of
statehood. In a whole series of cases, decisions of the

United Nations General Assembly on territorial questions,(124) especially in the context of newly independent States,(125) were relied upon by domestic courts in determining their territorial jurisdiction. In none of these cases are there any indications that the courts were aided by an incorporation of such international decisions into domestic law, or any other implementing measures. An attempt to derive the "trans- formation" of these international decisions into the local law from the forum State's original consent by treaty to the international organs' decision functions(126) is too artifi- cial to be convincing.

Perhaps even more significant is the fact that, even in the cases in which courts refused to accept the arguments based on the international decisions, the reasons given for their refusal were never the absence of the international decisions' incorporation into domestic law. The reasons given in these cases were either a lack of jurisdiction on the part of the international organ,(127) the incorrectness of the interna- tional decision(128) or the irrelevance of the decision for the question before the domestic court.(129) A refusal to recognize an international decision, which had been invoked merely to settle a preliminary question, on the basis of dualist arguments was evidently not regarded as meaningful.

3. "Precedents" for Analogous Legal Questions

In the case of an invocation of an international decision, usually of a judicial organ, for the purpose of having its policies applied by analogy, the connection between the international decision and the domestic case is even more remote than with preliminary questions. An incorporation of international "precedents" into domestic law for the purpose of their application by domestic courts is not a realistic possibility. There are no known examples for attempts of this kind.

The discussions mentioned in chapter III.E.3.c) on specific provisions dealing with the effects of international judi- cial decisions on subsequent cases, also touched upon the applicability of these "precedents" to domestic litigations. In the debates at the Peace Conferences in The Hague on the relevance of arbitral awards as "precedents" for subsequent disputes their direct application by domestic courts was merely discussed.(13o) When the same question was mooted with reference to the uniform interpretation of conventions for the unification of private law, there seemed to be con- sensus that legislative measures were necessary to make the- se interpretations binding for internal decision-makers.(131)

Of the numerous cases in which domestic courts rely on international "precedents" for the resolution of questions of international law, as set out in chapter III.E.3., only a few display misgivings prompted by dualist attitudes. In most cases
courts never even deal with this question and do not attempt
to rely on a fictitious or construed incorporation of the
international practice. Of these relatively few cases, in
which dualist arguments were specifically put forward in
relation to international "precedents",(132) a decision of a
Tangier court is probably the most outspoken example.(133)
In this case the court had to decide whether its jurisdiction was ousted by arrangements creating consular courts
for disputes involving American citizens. The International
Court of Justice had shortly before decided the virtually
identical question with respect to the French Zone of Morocco.(134) The Tangier court refused to follow the International
Court's interpretation. First it denied the propriety of
looking at analogous cases on principle (see p.88 above) and
then added:

> ...the judgments of the International Court of Justice
> resolve differences arising between States, which dif-
> ferences usually refer to conflicting interpretations
> of treaties between the two nations concerned. The ju-
> ridical value of such judgments is centred on the dif-
> ferences with which they deal, and the judgments are
> binding upon the High Contracting Parties, who must
> then take the necessary internal legislative measures
> to carry out the decisions of that high Court. For the-
> se reasons, those judgments cannot have an obligatory
> character on individuals who might litigate on similar
> matters.(135)

The necessity to look at the practice of international organs when determining questions of international law makes
the impracticability of a rigid adherence to a dogmatic
dualism(136) particularly evident. To require international
decisions to be incorporated by legislation into domestic
law before they can be applied as "precedents"(137) is quite
unrealistic. Any attempt to keep abreast of international
judicial practice by continuous implementing legislation
before internal decision-makers are allowed to take note of
them would be entirely ineffectual.

Scholarly writings have often tried to overcome these difficulties with the help of various fictions and constructions.
Sometimes the forum State's submission by treaty to the international organ's jurisdiction was interpreted as an incorporation of that organ's later practice.(138) Another method
was to argue that, where the international decision concerned

a treaty applicable before domestic courts, the treaty should
simply be accepted by domestic courts in the way it had been
interpreted by the international organ.(139) Likewise, the
usual constitutional provisions concerning the wholesale incorporation of customary international law were interpreted
to cover any international decisions clarifying questions of
general international law:(14o)

> Where the doctrine of incorporation applies and interna-
> tional law is accepted as part of the law of the land
> the clarification of international law by an internatio-
> nal court or tribunal may be self-executory not only in
> the sense that it determines the point of law at issue
> between the parties to the particular case but equally
> in the sense that the law as clarified becomes a part
> of the law applicable as the law of the land in virtue
> of the doctrine of incorporation.(141)

Here too, we find the attempt to justify the application of
international decisions by domestic courts by assimilating
them to the established sources of international law. These
theories are, indubitably, well-meaning and the policies
underlying them accord with our professed goal of giving effect
to international decisions. The question is just whether
these rather artificial fictions are really necessary to
justify the direct application of international decisions as
"precedents". Especially the idea of a direct application of
international decisions under the guise of the international
prescriptions which these decisions purport to interpret
seems to regard the international judicial decisions as purely declaratory. As mere "evidences of the law", these decisions would even under dualist doctrine not require any incorporation into domestic law. As pointed out before, such a
distinction between "sources and evidences" of the law does
not accord with reality. In the international arena more
than elsewhere judicial practice is an important element in
the development of the law. The notion that the application
of international judicial practice on treaties and other
international prescriptions is nothing more than the application of these prescriptions themselves is, therefore,
highly fictitious.

F. SUMMARY AND POLICY ALTERNATIVES

The above survey of court practice on the requirement of
measures of implementation for decisions of international
institutions clearly shows that this question can only be
answered in a differentiated manner. An undifferentiated
dualist attitude, generally denying the applicability of
international decisions for domestic courts unless they have

been incorporated into the local law by implementing legislation, would lead to entirely unsatisfactory results and
does not correspond with the majority of past practice of
domestic courts. On the other hand, a simplistic monist solution generally dismissing legislative or executive implementing measures would be equally unrealistic.

The question of whether implementing measures under domestic
law are required for decisions of international organs should
be not so much a problem of doctrine or theory but of practicability and common sense. As indicated by the practice of
courts, the necessity of implementing measures is determined
both by the kind of international decision invoked and by
the type of claim based upon it. Specific implementing measures of the local law only make sense if the forum State is
left with some latitude over whether or in what way it wishes
to have the international decision implemented.

This applies in particular to international decisions which
are couched in such vague terms that the details of their
application require further specification. The argument militating for implementing measures in these cases is not based
on any dogmatic consideration of their "validity" in internal law, but on the practical problem of the courts' ability
to apply them. Obviously there is no clear criterion determining how specific a presciption or decision must be before
it can be applied by the courts. Especially in the realm of
internal constitutional law, courts have demonstrated their
ability to construe and apply highly abstract prescriptions
and to give a concrete meaning to general principles through
their practice. On the other hand, a harmonised or uniform
policy on questions of international interest in the courts
of different countries may often be preferable to a slow
haphazard step-by-step development of practice. Implementing
measures can be an effective means to achieve this goal.

Where, however, the requirement of a clear obligation to act
in conformity with an international decision and the requirement of sufficient specification of that decision's contents are met, local implementing measures appear redundant,
except to allay any formal misgivings arising from internal
constitutional law.

The utility and desirability of internal implementing measures in many situations should not lead to the conclusion
that domestic courts must refuse to give deference to international decisions in cases in which the legislature or
executive have failed to take such measures. Especially the
question of an international decision's direct applicability

or "self-executing" character should be treated with flexibility. Not infrequently a prescription which appears obscure
at first sight can be interpreted with the help of external
criteria, in particular the international or foreign practice concerning it. Whether a prescription or decision is
directly applicable or not, cannot be ascertained by looking
at its wording *in abstracto*, but only from the circumstances
of a specific decision-situation. It is true that the problem of so-called non-self executing provisions has so far
played a relatively small role in the practice of domestic
courts on decisions of international institutions. The reliance on this argument may, however, one day become an important obstacle to their effective implementation.

Any a-prioristic notion that decisions of international organs are only directed at certain State organs, which must
then take the necessary measures to pass them on to the
courts and other decision-makers, is arbitrary and leads to
unnecessary impediments to their application. Any inactivity
by the legislature in implementing the international decisions would then prevent their potential beneficiaries, especially individuals, from invoking them before domestic
courts.(142)

These general policy considerations lead to the following
conclusions concerning the different international decisions
and claims as outlined above: Recommendations adopted by
international organs are an appropriate subject for implementing measures by Member States, both because of their limited international authority and because of their often abstract and general phrasing. These implementing measures
will normally consist not in a direct incorporation of their
texts but in the adjustment of domestic prescriptions. An
extensive practice of domestic courts shows that, even in the
absence of implementing measures, recommendations can and
should be directly applied - especially for the purpose of
interpreting prescriptions in statutes and treaties.

Amendments to treaties adopted by international organs do
not require any formalized proceedings to incorporate them
into domestic law. The practice of courts shows no difficulties in this area.

Similar considerations apply to official interpretations by
international organs, like those under Article XXIX (formerly
Article XVIII) of the Fund Agreement: There are no difficulties concerning their authority. They are directly applicable
as far as their degree of precision is concerned, since
their very purpose is to clarify and set out in detail the

meaning of treaty provisions. There is, consequently, no necessity for any special implementing procedures in domestic
law.

Regulations, especially as issued by some Specialized Agencies of the United Nations, create difficulties for several
reasons. Although their material contents are often sufficiently clear and specified, their international authority can be
subject to doubts, due to escape clauses in favor of Members
and also because of a widespread practice of non-compliance.
(See chapter III.C.3. above). To the extent that they affect
complicated technical problems, a harmonization with and
adjustment of related local prescriptions is often necessary.
Both these aspects strongly militate in favor of a clarification by local legislation or executive decrees. In addition,
the international organs concerned evidently expect general
implementing measures by Members when issuing these regulations.

A glance at the law of the European Communities reveals that
this solution for regulations is not prompted by theoretical
but purely practical considerations. Article 189 of the EEC
Treaty refers to prescriptions in the form of regulations
and directives. Regulations apply generally and take direct
effect in each Member State.(143) Nevertheless, there can be
a need for implementing measures in particular instances.(144)
Directives, on the other hand, are directed at Member States,
stating the result to be achieved, but leaving States with
the choice of form and methods. Nevertheless, their direct
application is a possibility if the forum State has failed
to enact the necessary implementing measures and a party
would otherwise be deprived of its benefits.(145) The application of this flexible and pragmatic practice - as developed
in European Law - to regulations adopted by traditional international organs would be a promising possibility.

Operative international decisions, arising from the application function of international organs, that concern wealth
allocations are suitable for direct application by domestic
courts. A formal recognition of these decisions, such as,
via an *exequatur*, should be limited to a review of their
authenticity. An intervention by the legislature or executive is only necessary in exceptional cases.

International decisions requiring specific action by domestic
organs, like resolutions imposing economic or other sanctions
which require complicated economic, political, and military
measures, can hardly be left to an autonomous implementation
by the courts. The scope for individual measures by the

forum State is usually considerable and the possibilities for implementation are diverse. A direct enforcement of these decisions by domestic courts would usually not be practicable. The only possibility for direct action by the courts appears to be a refusal to enforce transactions that are contrary to the international decision.

Deference to an international decision that determines or establishes a status with effect *erga omnes* should not depend on any implementing measures in domestic law. Typical examples would be territiorial decisions by international judicial or non-judicial organs. Practice clearly demonstrates that a reliance on decisions of this kind for the determination of preliminary questions pending before domestic courts can take place directly and irregardless of any incorporation into domestic law.

The same policy must apply to references to the development of international law by the practice of international organs, especially courts and tribunals. Any attempt to make international "precedents" applicable by implementing legislation would be unrealistic. Their rejection because of a lack of implementing measures would be inappropriate.

(1)   But see Waelbroek, Nature juridique p.5o4seq.

(2)   But see Sloan, The Binding Force, p.3o; Kiss, Nature
      juridique, p.269seq.

(3)   Cf. McDougal and Bebr, Human Rights in the United
      Nations, p.639; Schwelb, The Influence of the Universal
      Declaration, p.223; Skubiszewski, Legal Nature, p.2o4.

(4)   Art.11 of the Algerian constitution: "La République
      donne son adhésion à la Déclaration universelle des
      droits de l'Homme..." Cf. also Art.7 of the Constitution
      of Somalia, as well as the Preambles to the Constitutions
      of Dahomey, Ivory Coast, Gabon, Guinea, Cameroon, Mada-
      gascar, Mali and Senegal.

(5)   Stê Roy Export and Charlie Chaplin c/ Société Les Films
      Roger Richebê, 29 Apr.1959, 87 Clunet 128(196o).

(6)   On p.136.

(7)   Elections de Nolay, 18 Apr.1951, 17 AFDI 24(1971);
      Re Car, 11 May 196o, 88 Clunet 4o4(1961), 39 ILR 46o.

(8)   This view is supported by French scholary writings:
      Dehaussy, Les conditions d'application des normes
      conventionelles sur le for interne français, 87 Clunet
      7o3,715(196o); Ruziê, Le juge français, p.11o.

(9)   De Meyer c. Etat belge, 9 Feb.1966, 4 RBDI 569(1968),
      47 ILR 196. Cf. also Manderlier v. UN & Belgium, Tribu-
      nal civil Brussels, 11 May 1966, 45 ILR 446,451. In
      this case the claim failed primarily due to the immuni-
      ty of the United Nations. The court relied on the lack
      of incorporation as an additional argument.

(1o) In re O'Laiglêis, Supreme Court, 3 Dec.1957, 8 BILC
      853,864; The State v. Furlong, High Court, 24 Jan.1966,
      9 BILC 369,372; Re Woods Supreme Court, 19 Dec.1967, 53
      ILR 552(1979).

(11) The Queen v. Liyanage, 65 New Law Reports 73,82(1964).

(12) Roussety v. The Attorney General, High Court, 3o March
      1967, 44 ILR 1o8, 13o; but see the ambiguous reference
      to the Universal Declaration in Director of Public Pro-
      secutions v. Labavarde and Another, High Court, 9 March
      1965, 44 ILR 1o4,1o6.

(13) Generally see Schreuer, The Interpretation of Treaties, p.256seq.; but see R. v. Romano before the English Court of Criminal Appeal, 15 July 1963, 8 BILC 79o. In this case the court found it pointless to make a recommendation for the deportation of a person with dual citizenship, which included British citizenship, since the Home Secretary had indicated that he felt precluded from deporting such persons in view of the Human Rights Declaration.

(14) Const. Ct.: 5 Oct.195o, Slg.2o3o, 46 AJIL 161(1952), 78 Clunet 622(1951); 6 Oct.197o, Slg.626o. Admin. Ct.: 16 Dec.1966, Slg.7o45A.

(15) See above also chapter V.A. and compare the numerous cases in which the courts of the Federal Republic of Germany have relied on the Universal Declaration.

(16) Cf. Military Prosecutor v. Halil Muhamad Mahmud Halil Bakhis and Others, Israeli Military Court in Ramallah, 1o June 1968, 47 ILR 484. See above p.83.

(17) Ministry of Home Affairs v. Kemali, Corte di cassazione, 1 Feb.1962, 4o ILR 191,195; see also the somewhat unclear references to implementing legislation in Fallimento Ditta Maggi c/ Ministero del tesoro, Tribunale di Roma, 27 July 1959, LXXXIII Il foro italiano 196o, I, 5o5,5o7 28 ILR 6o7,6o9.

(18) Cf. above note 58 on p.113.

(19) *Loc.cit.*

(2o) Bundesverwaltungsgericht, 22 Feb.1956, BVerwGE 3,171, DVerw Bl 378(1956); Bundesverwaltungsgericht, 29 June 1957, BVerwGE 5,153; Kammergericht Berlin, 14 Sept.1961, 14 NJW 22o9,2211(1961).

(21) Bundesgerichtshof, 22 June 1972, BGHZ 59,83. See also below chapter XI.B.2.

(22) OLG Stuttgart, 5 Nov.1962, 1o Zeitschr.f.d.gesamte Familienrecht 1963, 39(41) *[7]*.

(23) Bundesverwaltungsgericht, 16 Jan.1964, 83 Deutsches Verwaltungsblatt 983(1968).

(24) Bretton Woods Agreement Act, 1945; Lachmann, The Articles of Agreement of the International Monetary Fund

and the Unenforceability of Certain Exchange Contracts,
2 NTIR 148,153(1953).

(25) Gold, Interpretation by the Fund, p.34; Meyer, Recognition of Exchange Controls, p.883. In the U.S. the official interpretation was published by the Chairman of
the National Advisory Council on International and
Financial Problems: 14 Fed.Reg. 52o8(1949), quoted from
Meyer, p.869.

(26) Seidl-Hohenveldern, Probleme der Anerkennung ausländischer Devisenbewirtschaftungsmaßnahmen, p.92; cf. also
Aufricht, Das Abkommen des Internationalen Währungsfonds
und die Unerzwingbarkeit bestimmter Verträge, 6 ÖZöR
529,539(1955). See also EXCURSUS III above.

(27) Lachmann, The Articles of Agreement, p.154.

(28) Hexner, Interpretation, p.353.

(29) On this point Nussbaum, Exchange Control, p.422,428seq.

(3o) Gold, Certain Aspects, p.88; Skubiszewski, Resolutions,
p.88; *ibid.*, Legal Nature, p.2oo; Meyer, Recognition,
p.884.

(31) Note 95 on p.118 above.

(32) Cf. Mann, The Private International Law of Exchange
Control under the International Monetary Fund Agreement,
2 ICLQ 97,1o4(1953), who doubts the legal effects of
the official interpretation for England. See also *ibid.*,
Der Internationale Währungsfonds und das internationale
Privatrecht, JZ 442,445(1953). *Contra:* Gold, The Interpretation by the International Monetary Fund, p.272;
ibid., Interpretation by the Fund, p.4o.

(33) Kahler v. Midland Bank Ltd., Court of Appeal, 19 Apr.
1948,/1948/ 1 All E.R. 811,819.

(34) Sharif v. Azad, Court of Appeal, 4 Oct.1966,/1967/ 1
Q.B.6o5, 41 ILR 23o.

(35) Mosler, Internationale Organisation und Staatsverfassung,
p.286; Skubiszewski, Enactment, p.267 with further
references; *ibid.*, Legal Nature, p.197; Erler, Rechtsfragen der ICAO, p.148seq. with further references;
Manin, L'organisation de l'aviation civile internationale, p.148seq.; Stein, Application and Enforcement,

p.69; Ruziê, Le juge français, p.1o6; *ibid.*, Les procé-
dês, p.574; on the OECD see Hahn, Die Organisation für
Wirtschaftliche Zusammenarbeit und Entwicklung, 12
Jahrb.des öff.R. 1,27(1963); Hanreich, Die Beschlüsse,
p.187,194seq.

(36) FitzGerald, The International Civil Aviation Organization, p.166seq. Schermers, International Institutional
Law, p.534; *contra*: Manin, L'organisation de l'aviation
civile internationale, p.153seq.

(37) Not entirely clear: Miele, Les organisations internationales, p.347seq.

(38) Manin, L'organisation de l'aviation civile internationale, p.156 attempts to derive a duty to enact implementing measures from Art.38 of the Chicago Convention.

(39) Quoted by Buergenthal, Law-Making in the ICAO, p.1o2seq.;
cf. also Merle, Le pouvoir rêglementaire, p.359; Manin,
L'organisation de l'aviation civile internationale,
p.153.

(4o) Buergenthal, Law-Making in the ICAO, p.1o3seq., Manin,
L'organisation de l'aviation civile internationale,
p.156. Cf also the statements by Member States to this
effect cited by Detter, Law Making by International
Organizations, p.255seq.

(41) Buergenthal, Law-Making in the ICAO, p.1o5 cites Sudan,
Laos, Libya and El Salvador as examples.

(42) Federal Aviation Act (1958), quoted from Erler, Rechtsfragen der ICAO, p.152.

(43) Sec.8 of the Civil Aviation Act 1949, quoted from
Shawcross and Beaumont on Air Law Vol.2, p.B63(1966-
74).

(44) Sec.4 of the Aeronautics Act 1952, quoted from Erler,
Rechtsfragen der ICAO, p.152.

(45) Sec.26(1)(b) of the Air Navigation Act 196o, quoted
from Buergenthal, Law-Making in the ICAO, p.1o6.

(46) § 32 Abs.3 Luftverkehrsgesetz, BGBl.1959 I, p.16.

(47) Luftfahrtgesetz, BGBl.253/1957. For a detailed analysis
see Bernard, Die Transformation der Normen der ICAO in
die österreichische Rechtsordnung, p.355seq.

(48) This method is used in the majority of Members for decisions of the EFTA Council. See the anonymous note: Die Ausführung der Ratsbeschlüsse in den Mitgliedstaaten in 12 EFTA Bulletin Nr.2, p.9(1971).

(49) See the detailed analysis by Manin, L'organisation de l'aviation civile internationale, p.161seq.; cf. also Merle, Le pouvoir réglementaire, p.358.

(5o) In Austria the formula introducing the publication of the International Sanitary Regulations, BGBl.97/1953, indicated that these Regulations had already entered into force in Austria as a consequence of their adoption by the WHO. The Swiss Parliament when invited to approve the International Sanitary Regulations like a treaty refused to deal with them since they were already binding by virtue of Art.21 of the Constitution of WHO. They were published in Switzerland in ROLF 1952, 861. Cf. Dominicé, La nature juridique, p.255; cf. also Huber, Die internationale Quasilegislative, p.28. The procedure in Belgium was similar: Waelbroek, Nature juridique, p.5o4. In the Federal Republic of Germany the International Sanitary Regulations were "published with force of Law". BGBl. 1955 II, p.1o62. On the treatment of the International Sanitary Regulations in France see Ruzié, Le juge français, p.1o7seq.

(51) Mori, Rechtssetzung, p.118seq. On Swiss practice see Bindschedler, Die Vollziehung völkerrechtlicher Verträge in den EFTA-Staaten, Schweiz, 12 EFTA Bulletin No.9, p.8,1o(1971). In Austria these decisions are also simply promulgated in the Federal Gazette. Cf. two cases in which Art.7 of the EFTA Treaty is applied as amended by the Council: Const.Ct. Slg. 5935, 6 June 1969; Administrative Court 6 Nov.197o, Österr.Steuer Zeitung Beilage 112(1971).

(52) E.g.: Hurwits v. State of the Netherlands, District Court, The Hague 12 June 1958, 6 NTIR 195(1959), 26 ILR 6o2, on the Code of Liberalization of OEEC; K.F.O. v. Public Prosecutor, Supreme Court of the Netherlands, 15 June 1971, 3 NYIL 296(1972) and Verenigde Tankrederij N.V. v. Willem Geervliet, Supreme Court of the Netherlands, 25 Feb.1972, 4 NYIL 413(1973) on the Police Regulations of the Central Commission for Rhine Navigation; Decisions of 7 July 1964 and 27 April 1965 of the Spanish Tribunal Económico-Administrativo Central, 19 Revista Esp.DI 452(1966), 2o Revista Esp.DI 5o2(1967) on recommendations of the Customs Cooperation Council.

(53) Belgium v. Marquise de Croix de Maillie de la Tour Landry et al., 3 Oct.1957, 24 ILR 9(1957); cf. also Régie des voies aériennes et Etat belge c. Verhoeven et commune de Steenokkerzeel, Cour d'appel de Bruxelles, 15 June 1965, 5 RBDI 385(1969).

(54) Dame Maury et Pivert c/ Ministère public, 18 Nov.1967, 48 ILR 231, 14 AFDI 866(1968), 95 Clunet 728(1968): "...le Règlement sanitaire international adopté par l'Organisation mondiale de la Santé n'est pas de plein droit applicable au droit interne des pays membres de ladite organisation; que pour ce faire, il était né-cessaire que des mesures réglementaires interviennent dans chacun des pays signataires;" cf. Ruzié, Le juge français, p.1o7seq.

(55) 12 July 1974, EuGRZ 14(1974).

(56) Public Prosecutor and Customs Administration v. Schrei-ber and Air France, Court of Appeals of Dakar, 15 May 1957, 24 ILR 54(1957), confirmed by the Cour de cassa-tion, 8 Nov.1963, Dalloz Somm. p.38(1964), cf. also Ruzié, Le juge français, p.1o7; Re Males, Cour de cassa-tion, 29 June 1972, 1o1 Clunet 142(1974), 19 AFDI 979 (1973), in this case the Foreign Ministry, in reply to an enquiry concerning the interpretation of the provi-sion, pointed out that the Annex was not directly applicable.

(57) 25 Feb.1965, 16 Zeitschrift f.Luftrecht u.Weltraumrechts-fragen 185, 188(1967).

(58) Staatsanwaltschaft des Kantons Thurgau v. Lang u.Legler, Swiss Federal Court, 27 Jan.195o, BGE 76 IV 43, 17 ILR 3o6(195o) concerning the Annexes to the Paris Convention relating to the regulation of Aerial Navigation; Swiss Zollrekurskommission, 22 March 1961, concerning the "explanatory notes" of the "Nomenclature Committee" under Art.IVc of the Convention on the Nomenclature for the Classification of Goods in Customs Tariffs, 347 UNTS 129, Dominicé, La nature juridique, p.256; Deci-sions of 24 Sept.1963 and 14 Jan.1964 of the Spanish Tribunal Económico-Administrativo Central, 18 Revista Esp.DI 225(1965), 19 Revista Esp.DI 79(1966), in which the "criteria" formulated by the Valuation Committee under Art.V of the Convention on the Valuation of Goods for Customs Purposes of 15 Dec.195o are applied.

(59) Viecelli v. IRO, Tribunale Trieste, 2o July 1951, 36
     Rivista DI 47o(1953), 49 AJIL 1o2(1955); Maida v. Admi-
     nistration for International Assistance, Corte di
     cassazione, 39 Rivista DI 546(1956), 23 ILR 51o(1956).

(6o) 17 March 1953, 11 F.Supp. 233, 47 AJIL 715(1953).

(61) Court of Appeals, D.C., 26 Aug.1954, 218 F.2d 843, 2o
     ILR 382(1953).

(62) Cf. Riezler, Internationales Zivilprozeßrecht und
     prozessuales Fremdenrecht, p.5o9seq., 627seq.(1949);
     Szászy, International Civil Procedure, A Comparative
     Study, p.523seq.,627seq.(1967); Condorelli, La funzione
     del riconoscimento di sentenze straniere (1967); Fou-
     chard, L'arbitrage commercial international, p.5o6seq.
     (1965); Fasching, Schiedsgericht und Schiedsverfahren
     im österreichischen und im internationalen Recht,
     p.174seq.(1973); Müller, Zum Begriff der "Anerkennung"
     von Urteilen in § 328 ZPO, 79 Zeitschr.f.Zivilprozeß
     199(1966); Matscher, Zur Theorie der Anerkennung auslän-
     discher Entscheidungen nach österreichischem Recht, in
     Festschrift für Hans Schima, p.265(1969).

(63) Riezler, Int.Zivilprozeßrecht, p.512,563,57o; Szászy,
     Int.Civil Procedure, p.551seq.

(64) Myrtoon Steamship Co. c/ Agent judiciaire du Trésor,
     Cour d'appel de Paris, 1o Apr.1957, 85 Clunet 1oo3(1958);
     Galakis c/ Trésor public, Cour d'appel de Paris, 21
     Feb. 1961, 9o Clunet 156(1963), confirmed by the Cour
     de cassation, 2 May 1966, 93 Clunet 648(1966); N.V. Cabo-
     lent v. National Iranian Oil Co., Court of Appeal, The
     Hague, 28 Nov.1968, 9 ILM 152(197o); Musulman c/ Banque
     Nationale de Grèce, Civil Court Saloniki, 1937, 65
     Clunet 9o8(1938).

(65) Cf. e.g. Republic of Colombia v. Cauca Co., 18 May
     193o, 19o U.S. 524.

(66) Cf. Szászy, Int.Civil Procedure, p.549seq.

(67) Szászy, Int.Civil Procedure, p.576. Recent French court
     practice shows a trend towards exercising more restraint
     in the review of foreign decisions. Cf. Schütze, Die
     Berücksichtigung der Rechtshängigkeit eines ausländi-
     schen Verfahrens, 31 RabelsZ 233,236(1967).

(68) Yougoslavie c/ Stê européenne d'études et d'entreprises, 98 Clunet 131(1971), 1o3 Clunet 136(1976), 1o4 Clunet 864(1977).

(69) Tribunal de Bruxelles, 3o Apr.1951, Sirey 1953, I, IV, p.1seq., 79 Clunet 244(1952), 18 ILR 3(1951), 47 AJIL 5o8(1953).

(7o) PCIJ Series A./B., No.78, p.178.

(71) Sirey 1953, I, IV, p.5.   *

(72) Rosenne, The Law and Practice of the International Court, p.13oseq.; Jenks, The Prospects, p.7o8seq.; Reisman, Nullity and Revision, p.817seq.

(73) Cf. also above V.C.1.a) and below XII.D.1.

(74) See also Ruziê in 1o2 Clunet 297(1975), who finds the granting of an exequatur to an international decision inappropriate.

(75) Cf. Pinto, Juge interne français, p.82seq.

(76) Generally see Fischer, Die internationale Konzession, p.417seq.

(77) See especially Fasching, Schiedsgericht und Schiedsver- fahren p.174seq.; Reisman, Nullity and Revision, p.824 seq.; Spofford, Third Party Judgment, p.211.

(78) Art.II of the last mentioned Convention specifically refers to "legal persons of public law".

(79) On the applicability of the U.N. Convention of 1958 to arbitrations in which States or State-controlled enter- prises participate see Reisman, Nullity and Revision, p.8o5. In Société Européenne et d'Entreprises v. Yugos- lavia the Netherlands Supreme Court, 26 Oct 1973, 5 NYIL 29o(1974) found the U.N. Convention of 1958 appli- cable to an arbitral award rendered in Switzerland against Yugoslavia in favor of a French enterprise. Cf. also Stuyt, Misconceptions about international (commer- cial) arbitration, 5 NYIL 35,56(1974).

(8o) The Prospects, p.711.

(81) Art.7 of the Chilean-French Treaty of 2 Nov.1882, Martens, N.R.G., 2nd ser.vol.9, p.7o6; Art.7 of the

Chilean-British Treaty of 4 Jan.1883, *ibid*. vol.9,
p.246; Art.6 of the Chilean-British Treaty of 26
Sept.1893, *ibid*. vol.21, p.65o; Art.6 of the Chilean-
French Treaty of 17 Oct.1894, *ibid*. vol.23, p.154.

(82) 13 AJIL Supplement 327(1919). Cf. also Art.256g of the
Treaty of St.Germain; Art.239g of the Treaty of Tria-
non; Art.188g of the Treaty of Neuilly.

(83) Cf. the Belgian statute of 25 March 1928, Pasinomie,
5.Ser.XIX, p.71, No.122(1928). The Czechoslovak statute
No.146 of 28 Apr.1922, quoted in a decision in 4 AD
174(1927-28). Concerning France see the reply of the
Foreign Minister of 7 Feb.192o: "Pour l'exécution en
France, l'agent général du gouvernement français inscrit
sur l'expédition du jugement la formule exécutoire et,
dans ce cas, la sentence est exécutée contre toute
partie comme un jugement français ordinaire." Journal
officiel (Chambre-Debats) p.49o(1928). See also Schätzel,
Die gemischten Schiedsgerichte der Friedensverträge, 18
Jahrb. des öff.Rechts 378,446(193o); Carabiber, Les
Juridictions internationales de droit privé, p.2ooseq.
(1947).

(84) Statute of 1o Aug.192o, RGBl.192o, p.1569. Cf. also the
judgment of the Reichsgericht of 24 May 1928, RGZ
121,18o.

(85) BGBl. 1955 II, p.4o5.

(86) Annex to Part Three, Art.9, par.3; Part Five, Art.7,
par.5; Part Ten, Art.12, par.5.

(87) BGBl. 1953 II, p.336; Art.29, par.7; Art.32, par.8

(88) Art.192 EEC, Art.164 EAEC, Art.92 ECSC.

(89) Art.187 EEC, Art.159 EAEC, Art.44 ECSC.

(9o) Runge, Die Zwangsvollstreckung aus Entscheidungen der
europäischen Gemeinschaften AWB 337(1962); Schütze, Die
Nachprüfung von Entscheidungen des Rates, der Kommission
und des Gerichtshofes nach Art.187, 192 EWG Vertrag, 16
NJW 22o4(1963); Valentine, The Court of Justice of the
European Communities Vol.I, p.8oseq.(1965); Green,
Political Integration by Jurisprudence, p.197seq.(1969).

(91) 4 ILM 532(1965). Cf. especially Sutherland, The World
Bank Convention on the Settlement of Investment Disputes, 28 ICLQ 367 at p.395(1979).

(92) BGBl. 1969 II, p.369.

(93) Arbitration (International Investment Disputes) Act 1966.

(94) Convention on the Settlement of Investment Disputes Act of 1966, 5 ILM 82o(1966). See esp. Sec.3 of the Act. See also the statement of the U.S. Department of State, 5 ILM 821(1966).

(95) For a survey of legislative measures see Annex 5 to Document No.8 issued by the International Centre for the Settlement of Investment Disputes.

(96) ICSID/8, Annex 4.

(97) Cf. also Rex v. Cooper, 24 Oct.1953, 2o ILR 166(1953), 82 Clunet 451(1955). In this case the Supreme Court of Norway relied on the ICJ's judgment in the Anglo-Norwegian Fisheries case.

(98) Cf. above II.B.1.

(99) ICJ Reports, p.176(1952).

(1oo) Cf. the comments by Laubadère in 42 RCDIP 16o(19$3), who attempts to derive the direct applicability of ICJ decisions for French courts from France's submission to the jurisdiction of the International Court.

(1o1) Jenks, The Prospects, p.715; Rosenne, The Law and Practice of the International Court, p.132seq.; Seidl-Hohenveldern, Internationale Präjudizentscheidungen, p.484; see however Kiss, Nature juridique, p.266seq., · who also envisages not directly applicable international judicial decisions.

(1o2) But see Jenks, The Prospects, p.719seq.

(1o3) Landesversicherungsanstalt Schlesien v. Rybnickie Gwarectwo Weglowe and Others, 5 Apr.1929, 5 AD 345(1929-3o).

(1o4) RGZ 131, 25o, 2 Feb.1931.

(1o5) See also a decision in which an implementing order for League of Nations sanctions against Italy is applied: G.L. v. A.M.C. van L., District Court of Breda (Netherl.) 3 Dec.1935, 8 AD 476(1935-37). See also the cases above III.E.1.b).

(1o6) Sørensen, Principes, p.121; Stein, Application and
Enforcement, p.68; Zacklin, The United Nations and
Rhodesia, p.76.

(1o7) The British United Nations Act 1946 provides for orders
in Council for the implementation of Security Council
decisions taken under Art.41 of the Charter. The Greek
statute No.92 of 1967 provides for executive orders
implementing not only Security Council decisions under
Art.41 but also certain General Assembly resolutions:
Economides, Nature juridique, p.232. The Austrian
Foreign Trade Act, BGBl. 314/1968 in its §5(1) provides
for a licensing system for trade with certain countries
on the basis of "international obligations." Trade
boycotts, like the one imposed by the Security Council
against Rhodesia, are enforced by subjecting all trade
with the country concerned to a license. Licenses are
then refused to the extent that this appears necessary
in order to comply with the international sanctions.

(1o8) 22 U.S.C. § 287-287c. Cf. also Bianchi, Security Council
Resolutions, p.1o4seq.

(1o9) For a survey of these implementing measures see esp.
the report of the Secretary General UN Doc.S/7781, in
Security Council, Official Records, 22nd Year, Supplement for January, February and March 1967; UN Doc.S/
8786, in Security Council, Official Records, 23rd Year,
Supplement for July, August and September 1968.

(11o) See especially the extensive and detailed British
measures reproduced in UN Doc.S/7781 and S/8786. By contrast see the Brazilian Decree No.62,98o of 12 June
1968, reproduced in UN Doc.S/8786, p.181, which simply
orders the application of Resolution 253(1968). For a
detailed analysis of the implementation of the sanctions
by Great Britain see Zacklin, The United Nations and
Rhodesia, p.78seq.

(111) See especially the cases in which penalties were imposed
for the violation of the boycott on the basis of domestic implementing measures: R. v. The Super Heater Co.
Ltd. Liverpool Stipendiary Magistrate, 1o Jan.1968, The
Times, 11 Jan.1968 p.4; cf. also the references to
similar convictions in the United Kingdom in Fourth
Report of the Sanctions Committee UN Doc.S/1o229 par.36
and 38. References to convictions by U.S. courts are
contained in a report of the United States to the
Sanctions Committee of 1o July 1972, UN Doc. S/1o852.

For convictions under Netherlands provisions for the
implementation of the Boycott against Southern Rhodesia
see Public Prosecutor v. J.S. and J.S., District Court
of Amsterdam, 13 June 1974, 6 NYIL 373(1975); Public
Prosecutor v. Etablissement Zephyr Holland Transito,
District Court of Amsterdam, 13 June 1974, 6 NYIL
373(1975); Public Prosecutor v.A.W., District Court of
Rotterdam, 3 July 1975, 7 NYIL 348(1976); O.M.v.C.S.,
District Court of Rotterdam, 3o Sept.1975, 7 NYIL
348(1976); Public Prosecutor v. C.S., Court of Appeal
of Amsterdam, 28 Oct.1976, 8 NYIL 3o5(1977).

(112)Court of Appeals D.C.Cir., 31 Oct.1972, 47o F.2d 461,
cert.den. 411 U.S. 931. See also the case comment in 14
VaJIL 185(1973).

(113)Executive Order No.11322 of 5 Jan.1967, 4 Fed.Reg.119;
Executive Order No.11419 of 29 July 1968, 33 Fed.Reg.
1o837.

(114)Cf. Art.VI(2) of the U.S.Constitution:"...all treaties
made, or which shall be made under the authority of the
United States, shall be the supreme law of the land;
and the judges in every State shall be bound thereby,...".

(115)Res.314 of 28 Feb.1972 and 318 of 28 July 1972.

(116)555 F.2d 848(1976).

(117)High Court of Australia, 1o Sept.1973, 1 Australian Law
Reports, 241(1973), 1o1 Clunet 865(1974), 52 ILR 1(1979).

(118)52 ILR 3(1979).

(119)Military Prosecutor v. Halil Muhamad Mahmud Halil Bakhis
and Others, Military Court in Ramallah, 1o June 1968,
47 ILR 484.

(12o)Rex v. Cooper, Supreme Court of Norway, 2o ILR 166(1953),
82 Clunet 451(1955); see also the already mentioned
cases before Moroccan and French courts concerning the
judgment of the ICJ on Rights of Nationals of the United
States of America in Morocco, above chapter II.B.1.

(121)Anglo-Iranian Oil Co. v. Idemitsu Kosan Kabushiki Kaisha,
District Court Tokyo, 1953, 2o ILR 3o5,3o8(1953);
Anglo-Iranian Oil Co. v. S.U.P.O.R., Civil Court of
Rome, 22 ILR 23,4o(1955).

(122)U.S.S.R. v. Luxemburg and Saar Company, Commercial
     Tribunal Luxembourg, 2 March 1935, 8 ILR 114(1935-37).

(123)Madzimbamuto v. Lardner-Burke, Appelate Division,
     Rhodesia, 29 Jan.1968, 39 ILR 61,2o9; Attorney-General
     of the Republic v. Mustafa Ibrahim and Others, Supreme
     Court of Cyprus, 1o Nov.1964, 48 ILR 6.

(124)Attorney General of Israel v. El-Turani, District Court
     of Haifa, 21 Aug.1951, 18 ILR 164,166(1951).

(125)Mbounya, Conseil d'Etat (Fr.), 3 Nov.1961, 8 AFDI
     942(1962) with references to more cases; Union des Po-
     pulations du Caméroun, Conseil d'Etat (Fr.), 24 Jan.
     1962, 9 AFDI 1o1o(1963); Passi c. Sonzogno, Corte di
     cassazione, 5 March 1953, 37 Rivista DI 579(1954);
     Cassa di risparmio della Libia c. Dainotto, Corte di
     cassazione, 18 Aug.1959, 44 Rivista DI 295(1961);
     Ministero degli esteri etc. c. S.A.I.C.E.S., Appello
     Roma, 23 June 1965, 5o Rivista DI 694(1967).

(126)Ruziê, Le juge français, p.111seq.; *ibid.*, Les pro-
     cédês, p.575.

(127)The Inge Toft, Egyptian Prize Court, 1o Sept.196o, 31
     ILR 5o9,517(1966); Ruiz Alicea v. U.S., U.S. Court of
     Appeals 1st Cir., 1o March 195o, 17 ILR 42,46(195o);
     U.S. v. Vargas, U.S.Dist.Ct., D.Puerto Rico, 29 Jan.
     1974, 37o F.Supp.9o8.

(128)RGSt 63,395, 21 Jan.193o.

(129)Willis v. First Real Estate and Investment Co. et al.,
     U.S.Court of Appeals 5th Circ., 24 Jan.1934, 68 F.2d
     671; Eichmann case, District Court of Jerusalem, 12
     Dec.1961, 36 ILR 5,58seq.

(13o)The Proceedings of the Hague Peace Conferences 19o7
     (J.B.Scott ed.) Vol.II, p.45oseq.

(131)Conférence de la Haye en Droit International Privé,
     Actes de la Sixième Session, p.2o8,233seq.; see also
     Resolution of the Institut de Droit International of
     1929 in 35 Annuaire 3o6(1929, II).

(132)See also the quotation from Pavia c. Amministrazione
     Finanze, Appello Genova, 5 Jan.1965, 49 Rivista DI
     395,399(1966) above p.88.

(133) Mackay Radio and Telegraph Co. v. Lal-la Fatma and others, Court of Appeal of the International Tribunal (a domestic court), 13 Aug.1954, 21 ILR 136(1954).

(134) ICJ Reports, p.176(1952).

(135) 21 ILR 137(1954).

(136) For examples of this rigid attitude see: Anzilotti, Il diritto internazionale nei giudizi interni, p.45(1905); Walz, Völkerrecht und staatliches Recht, p.229(1933); Makowski, L'organisation actuelle de l'arbitrage international, 36 RC 257,377(1931, II); Simons, Verhältnis der nationalen Gerichtsbarkeit, 35,5o; Kaufmann, *loc.cit.* on p.58.

(137) To this effect: Huber, Die Fortbildung des Völkerrechts auf dem Gebiete des Prozeß-und Landkriegsrechts durch die II. internationale Friedenskonferenz im Haag 1907, 2 Jahrb.des öff.R. 470,563(1908); Wehberg, Kommentar, p.152; Limburg, L'Autorité, p.585; Heise, Internationale Rechtspflege, p.86seq.,153seq.

(138) Waelbroek, Nature juridique, p.515; Dominicé, La nature juridique, p.262; more cautiously with respect to the Convention on Human Rights: Buergenthal, The Effect of the European Convention, p.103; cf. also Partsch, Die Anwendung des Völkerrecht, p.81seq., where this argument is rejected by reference to Art.94(1) of the U.N. Charter.

(139) Zorn, Das völkerrechtliche Werk der beiden Haager Konferenzen, 2 Zeitschr.f.Politik 321,364(1909); Sørensen, Principes, p.119; Jenks, The Prospects, p.745; Dominicé, La nature juridique, p.261seq.

(14o) Seidl-Hohenveldern, Transfomation or Adoption, p.98; Waelbroek, Nature juridique, p.515.

(141) Jenks, The Prospects, p.69o.

(142) Cf. also Schermers, International Institutional Law, p.619. For a detailed treatment of individual rights arising from international decisions see below XII.D.

(143) Cf. especially Bebr, Directly Applicable Provisions of Community Law: The Development of a Community Concept, 19 ICLQ 257(197o); *ibid.*, Community Regulations and National Law, 1o CMLRev. 87(1973); Kovar, L'applicabili-

té directe du droit communautaire, 1oo Clunet 279,289
(1973). Nevertheless, there have been repeated attempts
in Italy to "incorporate" regulations. Cf. Maestripieri, The Application of Community Law in Italy in 1972,
1o CMLRev 34o,346seq.(1973). The EEC Court has repeatedly confirmed the direct applicability of regulations:
Politi v. Finanzministerium der Italienischen Republik,
14 Dec.1971, Slg.XVII, p.1o39; Marimex v. Finanzministerium der Italienischen Republik, 7 March 1972, Slg.XVIII,
p.89; Leonesio v. Ministerium für Landwirtschaft und For-
ste der Italienischen Republik, 17 May 1972, Slg.XVIII,
p.287; Kommission v. Italienische Republik, 7 Feb.1973,
Slg.XIX, p.1o1. The Italian Corte Constituzionale also
rejects a transformation of EEC regulations: Decision
of 3o Oct.1975 in 3 EuGRZ 54(1976).

(144) Cf. Winter, Direct Applicability and Direct Effect. Two
Distinct and Different Concepts in Community Law, 9
CMLRev. 425(1972); on French practice see Ruzié, Les
procédés, p.566seq.

(145) See the references at the end of chapter XII.D.2. below.

VIII. THE PUBLICATION OF INTERNATIONAL DECISIONS

A. GENERAL POLICIES

An adequate promulgation of prescriptions is a basic policy requirement in any decision process. Predictability and stability of decisions can only be safeguarded under a system which provides the necessary information to participants and decision-makers. Most domestic legal systems extend the requirement of an official publication of all written prescriptions also to treaty law.

The same policies must apply, in principle, also to decisions of international institutions. Obviously this does not extend to decisions which are only directed at individual parties, such as wealth allocations in judgments or awards. But even international decisions which have general implications for an indefinite number of participants cannot always meet the requirement of a formal publication in accordance with the formalities of the local law. This is particularly so for international decisions which are to be consulted by internal decision-makers on preliminary questions. Decisions determining or establishing an international status *erga omnes* can hardly be subjected to a formal publication in all countries of the world.

Similar difficulties arise with international "precedents". An insistence on their domestic publication would be just as unrealistic as a call for their incorporation into the local law.

With official interpretations,(1) regulations, and recommendations a formal domestic publication is feasible. The relatively large freedom of action left to States under regulations and recommendations means that a publication of these international decisions in their official journals could actually change their legal nature. Normally texts appearing in these official journals are accepted as "binding" prescriptions.

An alternative to a reproduction of international decisions in the official journals of States is their promulgation in an official publication of the international organization. If this official publication is easily accessible to the general public, or at least to those affected by the decisions, there are no objections to this promulgation technique. However, at present, only the Official Journal of the European Communities appears to meet the requirements of adequate international publication.

B. DOMESTIC PRESCRIPTIONS ON THE PUBLICATION OF INTERNATIONAL
   DECISIONS

The French Decree of 14 March 1953 on the Ratification and
Publication of International Obligations assumed by France (2)
takes the possibility of an international publication into
account. In principle, Article 3 of this Decree provides for
the local publication of all documents binding on France, to
the extent that they can affect the legal position of individuals, in the *Journal Officiel* or in a "Bulletin officiel
spécial". However, it adds the following exception:

> Les dispositions du présent article ne sont pas appli-
> cables aux règlements émanant d'une organisation inter-
> nationale lorsque ces règlements sont intégralement
> publiés dans le Bulletin officiel de cette organisation,
> offert au public, et lorsque cette publication suffit,
> en vertu des dispositions expresses d'une convention
> engageant la France, à rendre ces règlements opposables
> aux particuliers. (3)

In Austria the Statute on the Federal Gazette in its original
version, (4) in § 2(2) only had a general clause on "other
promulgations" by the Federal Government or Federal Minist-
ries. An amendment to this Statute (5) of 1972 now refers specifically to decisions of international organs:

> § 2. (1) The Federal Gazette shall contain for publi-
> cation:
>
> ...
>
> (c) prescriptions, including their translation
>   into the German language, issued by inter-
>   national organs on the basis of special con-
>   stitutional authorization with direct effect
>   for Austria, unless their contents is exclu-
>   sively directed at administrative authorities.
>
> ...
>
> (5)   The Federal Chancellor can determine by
>   executive order that the prescriptions men-
>   tioned in para. 1 lit. c are not to be pub-
>   lished in the Federal Gazette, but in another
>   appropriate way.

In the preparatory works to this statute it is pointed out
that the proper publication of international decisions is
dictated by the principle of certainty of the law. At the
same time, the assurance is given that this publication has
always taken place, a statement which is probably over-opti-
mistic. A look at the Austrian Federal Gazette does, in

fact, reveal a large number of decisions of international
institutions.(6) They include WHO regulations, decisions of
the Council of EFTA, decisions of the Mixed Committee established by the Agreement between Austria and the EEC, and
other international decisions.

C. THE PRACTICE OF COURTS

Court practice on the requirement of local publication for
decisions of international organs is contradictory. In some
cases an official publication by the forum State was regarded as a sufficient basis for a court application.(7) In
other cases an application was rejected notwithstanding an
official publication.(8) In yet another group, international
decisions were relied upon in spite of an absence of local
publication.(9)

This inconsistency of practice is particularly manifest where
the application of the same international decision is rejected in countries where it has been officially published,(1o)
while it is applied without hesitation in countries where
it has not been published.(11)

D. POLICY ALTERNATIVES

A maximum of publicity for decisions of international institutions, which have effects on the position of individuals
and on the activities of the courts, is unquestionably important. In many cases an official promulgation would also satisfy a call for their "incorporation". The present practice
of States in this respect certainly leaves room for improvement. The method of an appropriate publication and dissemination by international organisations themselves could also be
employed to a larger extent than at present. Particularly in
highly specialized areas, in which the group of persons affected is small and relatively easily accessible, this method
of publication seems feasible.

On the other hand, only a flexible approach of the courts
can do justice to the special problems arising from the
publication of international decisions. State practice concerning publication and the practice of courts clearly show
that a rigid insistence on a formal promulgation by the
forum State would often be unrealistic. In many cases a formal publication must yield to an examination of actual publicity. In the absence of a system of organized and comprehensive publication in the international arena, domestic courts
in their capacity as functional international decision-makers
will often have to be satisfied with a general knowledge about

decisions and presciptions of international origin. The most
obvious example for this proposition is the practice on the
Universal Declaration of Human Rights. Knowledge of this
decision of the United Nations General Assembly is extremely
wide, even though it has not been promulgated in the official
journals of many States. Nevertheless, courts have frequently relied upon its principles.

(1)   In <u>Banco do Brasil, S.A. v. A.C. Israel Commodity Co.Inc.</u>,
       the Court of Appeals of New York, 4 Apr.1963, refers to
       the publication of the official interpretation to Artic-
       le VIII 2(b) of the Articles of Agreement of the Inter-
       national Monetary Fund in 14 Federal Register 52o8,52o9
       (1949). 32 ILR 371,373.

(2)   Journal Officiel, 15 March 1953, p.2436, quoted from
       Kiss Vol.I, No.522.

(3)   Cf. also Merle, Le pouvoir réglementaire, p.358; Søren-
       sen, Principes, p.121seq.; Skubiszewski, Enactment,
       p.268seq.; *ibid.*, Resolutions, p.86; Kiss, Nature
       juridique, p.261seq.; Ruziê, Le juge français, p.1o5;
       Ruziê, Les procédés, p.564. Cf. also the case <u>Dlle Sca-</u>
       <u>rabel Livia</u>, Cour de Dijon, 28 Oct.1965, 12 AFDI 887
       (1966), in which the court discusses this publication
       technique.

(4)   BGBl. 33/192o.

(5)   BGBl. 1o6/1972.

(6)   Cf. Hanreich, Die Beschlüsse p.185seq. and Schreuer,
       Beschlüsse internationaler Organe im österreichischen
       Staatsrecht, 37 ZaöRV 468(1977).

(7)   RGZ 131,25o of 2 Feb.1931; VerfGH Slg. 5935, 6 Juni
       1969 and VwGH 6 Nov.197o, Österr.Steuer Zeitung Beilage
       112(1971); <u>Sté Roy Export and Charlie Chaplin c/ Socié-</u>
       <u>té Les Films Roger Richebé</u>, Cour d'Appel de Paris, 29
       Apr.1959, 87 Clunet 128(196o); German Bundesverwaltungs-
       gericht, 16 Sept.1977, NJW 1759(1978).

(8))   <u>Elections de Nolay</u>, Conseil d'Etat (Fr.), 18 Apr.1951,
       17 AFDI 24(1971); <u>Re Car</u>, Conseil d'Etat (Fr.), 11 May
       196o, 88 Clunet 4o4(1961); <u>De Meyer c. Etat belge</u>,
       Conseil d'Etat (Belg.), 9 Feb.1966, 4 RBDI 569(1968).
       All these cases concerned the Universal Declaration of
       Human Rights. Cf. Above VII.B.

(9)   E.g.: <u>Mbounya</u>, Conseil d'Etat (Fr.), 3.Nov.1961, 8 AFDI
       942(1962); <u>Re Males</u>, Cour de cassation (Fr.), 29 June
       1972, 1o1 Clunet 142(1974), cf. also the decision of
       the Swiss Federal Court <u>Staatsanwaltschaft des Kantons</u>
       <u>Thurgau v. Lang u. Legler</u>, 27 Jan.195o, BGE 76 IV 43,
       where the Court found it doubtful whether the publica-
       tion of an Annex to the Paris Convention on Air Naviga-
       tion in the "Aero-Revue" was sufficient. The question
       was not decided.

(1o) See the treatment of the Universal Declaration of Human Rights by the French and Belgian Conseils d'Etat. Above VII.B.

(11) See the treatment of the Universal Declaration of Human Rights by German courts. Above V.A.

IX. SUBSTANTIVE PRESCRIPTIONS OF DOMESTIC LAW AND INTERNATIONAL DECISIONS

A. GENERAL POLICIES

In any specific decision situation, an applying organ is confronted not only with the question whether a particular prescription should be applied to the facts before it, but also which of several prescriptions (which may supplement each other but may also compete with each other) are to be applied. The answer to this problem depends, first, on the extent to which different competing prescriptions are regarded as applicable to the facts and, second, on their relative authority.

Disputes before domestic courts raising questions of international law almost invariably also involve questions of domestic law. The court trying to reach a decision has to put the prescriptions of international and domestic law into a meaningful relation. In situations of joint application of different prescriptions, a certain degree of antithetical tendencies is inevitable. This antithetical tendency need not be a clear contradiction of evidently incompatible presciptions, as is often assumed in studies concerned with the "primacy of norms". In fact, situations of clearly conflicting prescriptions are rather exceptional. On the other hand, every situation in which decisions are different, depending on whether international prescriptions are applied or the case is determined purely on the basis of domestic law, creates a situation of competition and poses the question of the prescriptions' relative authority.

This problem is made even more complex by the fact that both international law and domestic law have prescriptions of different degrees of authority. In international law, a prescription's authority is often determined more by its contents than by its form and is frequently disputed. In domestic law, a prescription's rank in a hierarchy of norms is usually determined by the procedure establishing it and its classification as "constitutional law", "statute", or "executive order".

Many domestic legal systems have attempted to solve this problem by conferring a certain degree of authority on international law in relation to domestic law, in other words, by assigning a particular rank to it. This is done by classification into types of international prescriptions, such as, "general principles of international law" or "treaties" or *ad hoc* for individual groups of prescriptions, like particular treaties or parts of treaties. Thus, the international prescriptions are either put on a par with certain types of domestic prescriptions or they are given precedence over domestic law.

The details of these internal constitutional arrangements for international law have been the object of much scholarly attention. (1) There is a tendency to overrate them, which is based on the assumption that only the domestic prescriptions purporting to govern the relative authority of international *vis-à-vis* domestic prescriptions are decisive for the behavior of internal decision-makers, especially domestic courts. But the distribution of powers between inclusive and exclusive decision processes determining the relative authority of presciptions emanating from them is not dictated just by the constitutive prescriptions of the exclusive process. Domestic constitutional provisions on the "rank of international law in domestic law" are, therefore, only of limited significance, representing no more than a claim to authority by domestic law in relation to international law. Whether a decision-maker will accede to this claim will depend on its institutional position and its perspectives. A domestic court is an organ created by the forum State's law, but it is often functionally also an international decision-maker confronted with claims which are directly based on international prescriptions and decisions. The extent to which a domestic court is able to comply with competing claims arising from the internal and the international decision processes will depend very much on the circumstances of the particular case. Where a conflict between international and domestic presciptions arises from the forum State's clear intention to act contrary to its international obligations, a domestic court will often identify with the forum State and will act accordingly. Where a contradiction is of a more technical kind and does not affect any values vital to the forum State, deference to international obligations can be expected more easily. Obviously, courts do not openly profess to act contrary to their domestic law, but use other techniques to put international prescriptions into effect. These techniques may consist in a generous "harmonizing interpretation", (2) or a finding that the international presciptions are "materially applicable" to the case. The readiness to use these or similar decision-techniques in favor of international law not only depends on the circumstances of the case, especially the values affected by the decision, but also varies from country to country and from one type of court to another.

Any attempt to solve the question of an international decision's authority in relation to domestic law exclusively

with the help of internal constitutional provisions is doomed
to failure, if alone for the reason that these internal prescriptions rarely, refer to decisions of international institutions.(3) Any assertion that this question must be solved
by reference to the forum State's rules governing the relationship of international and domestic law would, therefore,
be of little help.

A suggestion sometimes put forward in scholarly writings is
the equation of decisions of international institutions with
the treaties establishing these institutions. We have already
repeatedly come across this attempt to solve problems created
by international decisions by assimilating them to the "established sources of international law". Under this theory, the
international decision should be treated by internal decision-
makers in exactly the same manner as the treaty setting up
the international organ.(4) The problem of the "rank" of
treaties *vis-à-vis* domestic law is usually solved, at least
in principle.

This extension of the solution adopted for treaties to international decisions has the advantage of simplicity, but is,
of course, based on a fiction. It is true that the international organ has been established by a treaty and has been
endowed with decision-making powers by a treaty. But the
activities of the international organ are not simply treaty-
law, but the result of an autonomous jurisdiction, which can
attain a high degree of independence through a generous interpretation of its implied powers and other constitutional
developments. The activities of the organ can be partly or
wholly independent from the wishes of the original Parties
to the treaty. Thus, there can be an obligation to comply
with its decisions even against the wishes of a State participating in it. The fact that the original consent to the
international organ's establishment has been given in the
form of a treaty does not offer any clue to the authority of
this institution's decision. International obligations arising from decisions of international organs enjoy independent
authority in the international decision-making process and
cannot simply be explained by reference to the forum State's
consent given to a treaty. An attempt to derive the degree
of authority enjoyed by decisions of international organs in
relation to domestic law from the fact that, historically,
the establishment of the international institution has taken
place through a treaty is not convincing.

The only instances where it appears appropriate to treat international decisions as being analogous to treaties are
amendments to treaties and official interpretations to treaties adopted by international institutions.(5)

B. THE PRACTICE OF COURTS

A detailed empirical investigation of court practice dealing
with the competition of domestic prescriptions with international decisions would have to follow the system, used above,
of looking at different kinds of international decisions by
decision functions and at the different types of claims based
upon them. These would then have to be related to different
types of domestic prescriptions, like constitution, statutes,
executive orders. However, it seems doubtful whether such an
investigation proceeding from formal characteristics of the
international and domestic prescriptions involved would really
permit any general conclusions on the relative authority of
international decisions and domestic prescriptions for the
work of domestic courts. In any case, the scarcity of cases
offering clues on this question does not permit this line of
investigation. The reason for this scarcity of practice is
not a lack of opportunities for courts to deal with this
question, but rather, their tendency to avoid the issue. Neither the explicit rejection of an international decision because of a conflicting domestic prescription nor the opposite
solution of openly disregarding domestic law in order to comply with an international obligation are attractive options
for a domestic court.

The court has a number of strategies at its disposal to
avoid an open decision on conflicting internal and international prescriptions or decisions. Where a court anticipates
a conflict of this kind, it can, first of all, forestall it
by pointing to the international decision's lack of authority (see chapter III. above) or lack of incorporation into
the local law (chapter VII. above) or non-self executing
character. (chapter VI.B.3. above) (6) If the court does not
adopt one of these techniques, it will often be able to find
a "harmonizing interpretation". Sometimes the international
decision is simply applied by the domestic court without
any mention of the fact that domestic law would otherwise
require a different solution of the case.

Accordingly, the following survey can only offer a brief
description of the techniques employed by domestic courts
when confronted with competing precepts from domestic prescriptions and decisions of international institutions.
Roughly speaking, the method of avoiding conflicts through
harmonizing interpretation and the method of deciding either
in favor of the domestic or international precepts can be
distinguished.

1. Avoiding Situations of Conflict

A situation of "competition" between domestic prescriptions and international decisions is relatively undramatic where domestic courts are able to find that they are in harmony with each other. Statements of this kind are relatively frequent where attempts have been made to challenge domestic law by relying on the Universal Declaration of Human Rights (7) or on other resolutions of the United Nations General Assembly.(8) It would, however, be misleading to draw any far-reaching conclusions from these cases concerning the courts' readiness to scrutinize the conformity of domestic law with these international decisions. The fact alone that in some of the cases domestic courts when referring to the Universal Declaration emphasize its non-obligatory charac- ter(9) contradicts such an inference. Moreover, there is no known case in which a domestic court has found a provision of its internal law incompatible with the Universal Declara- tion and has, therefore, refused the application of the lo- cal law.(1o)

In the opposite situation, in which attempts were made to prevent the application of international decisions by rely- ing on alleged obstacles in domestic law, domestic courts were sometimes content to point out that the international decisions were not incompatible with the law of the forum State, especially the Constitution.(11) In an Indian case(12) a group of persons tried to stop the government from handing over a previously Indian administered area, which had been awarded in an international arbitration to Pakistan. They argued that under the Indian Constitution the cession of Indian territory could only be effected by constitutional amendment. The Supreme Court of India rejected this conten- tion. It held that the handing over was no cession, since, due to the declaratory nature of the international award, the disputed area had never been Indian territory.

A somewhat more active role is admitted by domestic courts where they profess to reconcile the competing precepts of domestic law and international decisions by a harmonizing interpretation. In these cases, it is at least admitted that the application of domestic law without reference to the international decision could have led to a different judg- ment. Where international decisions of limited authority, such as, recommendations, are invoked, an attempt to argue in favor of their "supremacy" would not be particularly promising. A harmonizing interpretation, therefore, appears to be the only way to take account of the international de- cision. In fact, nearly all the known examples for this

technique concern the Universal Declaration of Human Rights.
It is used, above all, in interpreting the fundamental freedoms enshrined in domestic constitutions.(13) Sometimes provisions of ordinary statutes affecting nationality,(14) extradition,(15) the position of aliens,(16) labor law,(17) refugees,(18) matrimonial law,(19) and retroactive criminal le-
gislation(2o) are also interpreted with its help. In a similar way, courts sometimes also interpret treaties, especially
the European Human Rights Convention,(21) with the help of
the Universal Declaration.

2. Solving Situations of Conflict

a) In Favor of Domestic Law.

The relatively few cases in which courts feel compelled to
refuse to apply international decisions openly because of
conflicting provisions of domestic law, permit no clear general conclusion. In a number of cases, in which precedence
was given to domestic law, the international decision in
question was only a recommendation. In these cases, the court
simply held that the recommendation did not affect the validity or applicability of the conflicting internal provision.
(22) In an Indian case,(23) the legality of expropriation
laws was challenged, although they were covered by the Constitution. The court held:

> Doubtless if there were no express provision in the
> Constitution like Art 31 or 31(a) the provisions of the
> Charter of the United Nations and the Universal Declara-
> tion of Human Rights might possibly be invoked in favor
> of the petitioners, on the doctrine of wise use of pub-
> lic policy... but where Art 31 expressly bars the juris-
> diction of the Court to question the adequacy of compen-
> sation it is futile to rely on Art 17(2) of the Univer-
> sal Declaration of Human Rights. Hence though an argu-
> ment of this type...is attractive and requires serious
> consideration, I must hold that the provisions of the
> Declaration of Human Rights where they conflict with
> the provisions of the Constitution will be of no avail
> in municipal courts.(24)

The only known case involving a clear and deliberate conflict
between a decision of an international organ and a domestic
statute is the already mentioned case Diggs v. Shultz.(25)
The United States Congress had adopted legislation for political reasons, which was intended partially to frustrate the
United Nations Security Council's boycott resolutions against
Rhodesia in the United States.(26) Under these circumstances,
the decision of the Court of Appeals for the District of Co-

lumbia to uphold the statute at the cost of the Security
Council sanctions' effectiveness did not come as a surprise.
It should, however, be noted that the court based its decision on the ground that the Statute had to be regarded as an
abrogation of existing treaty obligations.(27) Evidently,
the resolutions were regarded as "supreme law of the land"
which had subsequently been superseded by the Statute. It
seems doubtful whether this application of the *lex posterior*
principle is a felicitous attempt to solve this problem of
conflicting legal precepts. In fact, the Security Council,
reacting to the United States' measures had subsequently repeated and reconfirmed its resolutions.(28) Under a consistent
application of the *lex posterior* method these later international decisions should in turn have superseded the Statute.
This aspect is not discussed in the judgment, and it is not
unlikely that the later Security Council resolutions had not
come to the Court's knowledge.(29)

Finally, the most radical method open to domestic courts to
resolve a conflict in favor of internal prescriptions is
simply to ignore the international decision without even
mentioning it. Obvious examples for this strategy are judgments of the Supreme Court of Israel(3o) concerning the
status of Eastern Jerusalem and of the occupied West Bank
and a decision of a South African court(31) in connection
with "South-West Africa". However, any conclusions from these decisions should be treated with great caution. In the
absence of any reasons offered by the courts for ignoring
the international decisions, these cases could equally well
be explained on the basis of strictly dualist doctrines. A
look at the values affected by these cases lends support to
the suggestion that the true motives for the courts' behavior were not considerations concerning the relative authority of internal and international prescriptions, but the
endeavor to support the forum State's political position on
a highly controversial international question. (See also
chapter XIII.B.1. below).

b)   In Favor of International Decisions.

The cases in which courts decide in favor of applying international decisions at the cost of domestic prescriptions are
difficult to analyse. An explicit dismissal of the local law
in favor of the international decision can hardly be expected. Such a solution would only appear acceptable if the
local law grants precedence to international decisions either
directly like the Netherlands Constitution or with the help
of a construction extending a "supremacy" of treaty law also
to international decisions as "secondary treaty law".(32)

A better method is to tackle the problem of competing precepts arising from domestic prescriptions and international decisions not with the help of a "hierarchy of norms" but from the perspective of inclusive and exclusive jurisdictions. The authority of the international decision vis-à-vis domestic courts is the result of a shifting of jurisdiction from an exclusive (domestic) to an inclusive (international) decision-process. In case of competing directions given by the domestic prescription and by the authoritative decision of an international organ acting in accordance with the powers conferred upon it, the international organ's inclusive jurisdiction should, in principle, be given preference. This would obviate the need to resort to the construction of a derogation.

The already mentioned decision of the Court of Appeals for the District of Columbia, Keeney v. US,(33) is a good example for this approach. In this case the defendant had refused to comply with a domestic obligation to testify before a Congressional Subcommittee. Her acquittal was based on the United Nations Staff Rules which imposed an obligation of secrecy upon her.

The behavior of courts is similar in cases in which prescriptions governing labor disputes created by international institutions are accepted in place of otherwise applicable domestic law,(34) or where the Rhine Police Regulations adopted by the Central Commission for Rhine Navigation are applied in place of otherwise applicable penal law of the forum State.(35) In these cases, the decisions of international institutions are not given deference because of any supremacy conferred upon them by the local law, but because of their autonomous jurisdiction over certain inclusive matters.

This kind of solution is preferable to any formalistic construction placing domestic prescriptions and decisions of international institutions into a rigid hierarchy of norms. The questions arising from the interaction of different decision-processes taking place in different, but not wholly unconnected, arenas cannot be settled adequately by a system of subordination or precedence of rules in which conflicting norms abrogate each other, depending on their respective rank. The prescriptions and decisions involved have their origin in heterogeneous social processes and have been adopted by different kinds of decision-makers. The principles developed within a relatively homogeneous domestic legal system to deal with conflicting prescriptions cannot lightly be transferred to situations of competing precepts of different origins. These principles, applied to our problem, would lead to random results and are unable to sustain a policy of effective implementation of international decisions.

These shortcomings are particularly evident in the application of the principle of *lex posterior*.(36) This principle proceeds from the assumption of a coherent prescribing organ whose latest expression of will is to be regarded as authoritative. In situations of several prescribing organs with conflicting intentions, the application of *lex posterior* is likely to lead to a game of legislative "leap frog" with each organ trying to supersede the decision of the other by later action.(37)

C. POLICY ALTERNATIVES

The most promising starting point for the development of a theory dealing with situations of competition between domestic prescriptions and international decisions is to see the problem as a question of delimitation of inclusive and exclusive jurisdiction. In those areas in which decision-making powers have been conferred upon international organs their decisions should be regarded as the materially applicable law. This does not imply any "supremacy" for the international decision in terms of a hierarchy of norms. Any conflicting internal prescription will not be "abrogated". It does, however, mean that in cases of doubt internal decision-makers, like domestic courts, should decide in accordance with the decisions of international institutions. This approach would conform to one of our basic postulated policies, namely, that of effectiveness for international decisions, without falling into the trap of doctrinaire monism.

It must, however, be realistically admitted that there are situations in which domestic courts will favor internal prescriptions at the cost of international decisions conflicting with them. These include, in particular, instances in which the forum State makes a conscious political decision to act contrary to the international decision and passes legislation to this effect.(See chapter XIII.B.1. below). Especially in crisis-situations or in cases affecting values which are given high national importance, States may feel compelled not to comply with obligations arising from their membership in international organisations. Under these circumstances, a strong tendency of domestic courts to behave in conformity with domestic prescriptions must be expected.

Similar situations can arise where decisions of international institutions conflict with the forum State's basic structure of value distribution. This structure is often seen to have its basis in the country's constitution and often affects fundamental rights of the individual. A checking function of the courts can be a valuable contribution to the preservation

of human rights also with respect to international decisions.
This is not to say that international decisions should be
subjected to a scrutiny of constitutionality in individual
Member States similar to domestic statutes. On the other
hand, the accepted goal of cooperation through organized
international decision-making should not lead to an integration euphoria at the cost of other recognized goals - notably
the protection of individual liberties. Thus, the traditional
supervisory function of the courts can be put to good use in
this area by ensuring that international decisions conform
to certain basic policies of Member States. Where necessary,
the courts can become the last barrier to safeguard the individual against decisions of international organs violating
basic rights.

A glance at European Community Law reveals that the policies
expressed here for the activities of more traditional international institutions have already found a certain measure
of acceptance.(38) At the earlier stages of the discussion
on the relationship between Community Law and domestic law
arguments were frequently based on the provisions of constitutions of Member States concerning international law, especially treaties. Under these arguments, any precedence of
Community Law over domestic law could only be based on arrangements in the domestic law of Members ganting "supremacy" to
treaties. In the meantime, a different view appears to prevail, especially under the influence of the Court of Justice
of the European Communities.(39) It is accepted that the EEC
Treaty created its own legal order as a result of the partial transfer of public functions from the Member States to
the Community. Consequently, Community Law is applicable
even where it conflicts with domestic law. This priority of
application of Community Law is not based on any higher rank
and a resultant abrogation of domestic law, but simply on
the competence of the Community organs for the subject-matter
assigned to them and on the necessity to safeguard their effective functioning. This theoretical basis offers a sufficient guarantee for the effectiveness of Community Law.

The protection of individual liberties within the framework
of Community Law has been the subject of a heated controversy. The Community Court has repeatedly given assurances that
human rights, although not mentioned in the Treaties, are an
indispensible part of Community Law and will be upheld in
all proceedings before the Court.(4o) Nevertheless, the German Constitutional Court does not appear to be satisfied by
the existing safeguards for human rights on the Community
level and has reserved the right to review Community decisions for their conformity to the guarantees for basic rights

contained in the German Constitution.(41) The dispute surrounding the attempts of domestic courts to examine whether Community Law complies with the requirements of domestic human
rights guarantees is directed not so much at the basic question
of whether individual liberties should be protected in the
framework of Community Law. The necessity of such a protection is generally admitted. The controversial issue is merely
whether domestic courts are the proper guardians. The misgivings of those writers who see a danger for the slowly emerging priority of Community Law, if this function is conceded
to domestic courts, are probably exaggerated. The endeavor
to protect the effectiveness of Community Law is, no doubt,
commendable. However, the protection of human rights and individual liberties by all accepted means and in all fora
should be regarded as a goal of at least equal importance.

The considerations outlined in this chapter for a possible
solution of problems arising from a competition between
domestic prescriptions and international decisions do not
offer a simple reply to all the detailed questions arising
in this area. They can only offer a general framework of
policy alternatives.

The technicalities and theories for the solution of problems
arising from conflicting prescriptions differ from one legal
system to another. It would be neither realistic nor desirable
to demand a completely uniform practice in this area. The
important point is not the theoretical construction adopted
to resolve the problems arising from the concurrent application of internal prescriptions and international decisions,
but the observance of the basic policies of effectiveness
for the international decision and adequate protection of
individual rights.

(1)   For some of the most important studies see: Morgenstern,
       Judicial Practice and the Supremacy of International
       Law, 27 BYIL 42(195o); Guggenheim, Völkerrechtliche
       Schranken im Landesrecht (1955); Mosler, L'application
       p.639seq.; McDougal, The Impact, p.8oseq.; Partsch, Die
       Anwendung des Völkerrechts p.57seq.

(2)   On the question of an interpretation of domestic law in
       the light of international Law see Mosler, L'application,
       p.681; Bleckmann, Begriff und Kriterien, p.85seq. with
       further references.

(3)   See however Art.67/2 of the Netherlands Constitution
       which extends the precedence for treaties under Art.66,
       also to decisions of international institutions. The
       provisions concerning international institutions in the
       Norwegian (Article 93) and Swedish (Article 81(3))
       Constitutions contain reservation clauses for internal
       constitutional law. Cf. also Hambro, The New Provision,
       p.571. For French law Sørensen, Principes, p.122 assumes
       a rank below ordinary statutes. For Belgian law Ganshof
       and Vanwelkenhuyzen, La Constitution Belge, p.589 find
       a rule giving priority to international decisions
       desirable.

(4)   Scheuner, Die Rechtssetzungsbefugnis, p.235,241; Skubi-
       szewski, Legal Nature, p.198seq.; Dominicê, La nature
       juridique, p.257.

(5)   Skubiszewski, Resolutions, p.88seq.; *ibid.*, Legal
       Nature, p.2oo.

(6)   Generally on the tendency of courts to declare inter-
       national prescriptions "non-self executing" in order to
       evade a conflict with domestic law see Bleckmann,
       Vorrang, p.528.

(7)   In re Hauck, Voigt and Others, Cour de cassation (Fr.),
       3 June 195o, 17 ILR 388(195o); German Bundesverwaltungs-
       gericht, 22 Feb.1956, BVerwGE 3,171; Bundesverwaltungs-
       gericht, 29 June 1957, BVerwGE 5,153; High Court of
       Mauritius, Director of Public Prosecutions v. Labavarde
       and Another, 9 March 1965, 44 ILR 1o4,1o6; Israel
       Supreme Court, American European Beth-El Mission v. Mi-
       nister of Social Welfare, 12 Nov.1967, 47 ILR 2o5,
       2o7,2o8seq.; Administrative decision of the Crown
       (Netherlands) in I.C. v. Minister of Justice, 4 March
       197o, 2 NYIL 238(1971).

(8) Chile, Special Copper Tribunal, <u>Excess Profits of Natio-</u>
<u>nalized Copper Companies</u>, 11 Aug.1972, 11 ILM 1o13,1o46,
1o59(1972). The Court found that internal prescriptions
providing for the expropriation of foreign companies
without compensation did not conflict with the General
Assembly Resolution on "Permanent sovereignty over
natural resources". On this decision see also Schreuer,
Unjustified Enrichment in International Law, 22 AJCompL
281,285(1974).

(9) See the two decisions of the Bundesverwaltungsgericht
in note 7.

(1o) A case cited to this effect by Skubiszewski, Recommen-
dations, p.363, is probably based on a misinterpretation
of the source cited by that author. But see the decisions
below XI.B.2. refusing the application of foreign law
which is in conflict with the provisions of the Univer-
sal Declaration.

(11) <u>Lake Ontario Land Development and Beach Protection Asso-</u>
<u>ciation, Inc. v. Federal Power Commission</u>, US Ct.of
Appeals, D.C., 29 Jan.1954, 48 AJIL 498(1954); German
Bundesverwaltungsgericht, 16 Sept.1977, NJW 1759(1978).

(12) <u>Maghanbhai Ishwarbai Patel and Others v. Union of India</u>,
1969, 9 IJIL 234(1969). For the decision of the lower
court see 8 IJIL 267(1968).

(13) <u>Public Prosecutor v. F.A.v.A.</u>, Supreme Court of the
Netherlands, 1951, UN Yearbook of Human Rights 251(1951);
<u>Isabel Rodriguez v. Rafael Pantoja</u>, Supreme Court of
Bolivia, 3o Apr.1951, UN Yearbook of Human Rights
16(1951), in this case the recommendation relied upon
was the League of Nations' "Declaration of the Rights
of the Child"; <u>Fallimento Ditta Maggi c. Ministero del</u>
<u>tesoro</u>, Tribunale di Roma, 27 July 1959, 28 ILR 6o7;
<u>Kennedy v. Mendoza-Martinez</u>, US Supreme Court, 18 Feb.
1963, 372 U.S. 144,161; Bundesverfassungsgericht, 17
Jan.1957, BVerfGE 6,55; Bundesverfassungsgericht, 3o
June 1964, BVerfGE 18,112,118; Bundesverfassungsgericht,
15 Dec.1965, 19 NJW 243(1966); Bundesverfassungsgericht,
3 Oct.1969, 23 NJW 235(197o); <u>Choithram Verhomal Jeth-</u>
<u>wani v. A.G.Kazi and Others</u>, India, 1966, 6 IJIL 247,
251(1966); see also the dissenting opinion in <u>Satwant</u>
<u>Singh Sawhney v. Assistant Passport Officer, New Delhi</u>,
Supreme Court of India, 1967, 7 IJIL 542,55o(1967).

(14) Ministry of Home Affairs v. Kemali, Corte di cassazione,
1 Feb.1962, 4o ILR 191,195; Re Tovt, Court of Taranto,
2o March 1954, UN Yearbook of Human Rights 169,171(1954).

(15) Bundesgerichtshof, 21 Jan.1953, 6 NJW 392(1953), 2o ILR
37o(1953); Bundesgerichtshof, 12 July 1955, 8 NJW
1365(1955), 22 ILR 25o,254(1955); Hackstetter v. State
of Israel, Supreme Court of Israel, 1972, 2 Israel YBHR
344(1972), 51 ILR 331(1978).

(16) Fuji v. California, California Dist.Ct.Appeal, 24
Apr.195o, 44 AJIL 59o(195o).

(17) American Federation of Labor v. American Sash and Door
Co., US Supreme Court, 3 Jan.1949, 335 U.S. 538,549.

(18) Bundesverwaltungsgericht, 16 Jan.1964, 83 DVerwBl.
983(1968).

(19) Vanderginste v. Sulman, Court of Courtrai, Belgium, 26
Apr.1956, UN Yearbook of Human Rights 23(1956); Miriam
Streit v. Nissim, the Chief Rabbi of Israel, Israel
Supreme Court, 1o July 1964, 18 Piskei Din 598,612(1964).

(2o) Waddington v.Miah, House of Lords, 1 May 1974,/1974/ 1
WLR 692 at 694.

(21) Mejia v. Regierungsrat des Kantons Bern, Swiss Federal
Court, 9 May 1963, 32 ILR 192; Hackstetter v. State of
Israel, above note 15. A.J.K.v. Public Prosecutor,
Dist.Ct.Maastricht, 27 Jan.1959, 7 NTIR 73(1961);
Ministry of Home Affairs v. Kemali, above note 14;
Bundesverfassungsgericht, 4 May 1971, BVerfGE 31,58.

(22) Cf. In re Best and Others, Supreme Court of Denmark, 17
March 195o, 17 ILR 434(195o). This was an unsuccesful
attempt to oppose retroactive penal provisions against
war criminals with the help of the Universal Declaration. X. v. Minister of Defence, Netherlands administrative decision, 14 Nov.1968, 1 NYIL 219(197o). This was
an attempt to invoke a resolution of the Consultative
Assembly of the Council of Europe on conscientious
objectors against the Military Service Act.

(23) Biswambhar Singh v. State of Orissa, High Court of
Orissa, 27 Apr.1957, 24 ILR 425(1957).

(24) P.427.

(25) Court of Appeals D.C.Cir., 47o F.2d 461.

(26) The so-called Byrd amendment to the Strategic and Critical Materials Stock Piling Act of 1971. See also the references by Henkin, Foreign Affairs and the Constitution, p.436, note 11, and Zacklin, The United Nations and Rhodesia, p.82seq.

(27) On p.466. Generally on the constitutional implications see Bianchi, Security Council Resolutions, p.88,1o7seq.

(28) SC Res. 314 of 28 Feb.1972 and 318 of 28 July 1972.

(29) Cf. also Brand, Security Council Resolutions: When do they give rise to Enforceable Legal Rights?, 9 Cornell International Law Journal 298(1976); Schweitzer, The United Nations as a Source of Domestic Law: Can Security Council Resolutions be Enforced in American Courts?, 4 Yale Studies in World Public Order 162(1978).

(3o) Avalon Hanzalis v. Greek Orthodox Patriarchate Religious Court and Constandinos Nicola Papadopoulos, 1o March 1969, 48 ILR 93; Muhammad Abdullah Iwad and Zeev Shimshon Maches v. Military Court Hebron District, and Military Prosecutor for the West Bank Region, I.D.F., 13 Oct.1970, 48 ILR 63.

(31) S. v. Tuhadeleni and Others, Appellate Division, 22 Nov.1968, 18 ICLQ 789(1969), 52 ILR 29(1979).

(32) Staatsanwaltschaft des Kantons Thurgau v. Lang und Legler, Swiss Federal Court, 27 Jan.195o, BGE 76 IV 43, cf. also Dominicé, Nature juridique, p.257. Kiss, Nature juridique, p.259seq. interprets Article 55 of the French Constitution, which gives priority to treaties over domestic law, in this sense.

(33) 26 Aug.1954, 218 F.2d 843.

(34) Viecelli v. IRO, Tribunale Trieste, 2o July 1951, 36 Rivista DI 47o(1953); Profili v. International Institute of Agriculture, Corte di cassazione, 26 Feb.1931, 23 Rivista DI 386(1931); Marrê c/ UNIDROIT, Tribunale di Roma, 26 June 1965, 5o Rivista DI 149(1967); Dame Klarsfeld c/ Office franco-allemand pour la jeunesse, Cour d'Appel de Paris, 18 June 1968, 15 AFDI 865(1969); A.P.F.Eckhardt v. Eurocontrol, Local Court of Sittard (Netherlands), 25 June 1976, 9 NYIL 276(1978).

(35) <u>K.F.O. v. Public Prosecutor</u>, Netherlands Supreme Court,
15 June 1971, 3 NYIL 296(1972).

(36) For a criticism of attempts to resolve problems arising
from the relationship of national and international law
with the help of *lex posterior* see the remarks by Sohn
in 63 ASIL Proceedings 18o(1969).

(37) For a pertinent example see the disagreement between
the Security Council and the U.S. Congress notes
26-28 above.

(38) The scholarly writings and the decisions of domestic
courts on this aspect of Community Law are far too numerous to be covered in this short note.

(39) See esp. <u>Van Gend & Loos v. Niederländische Finanzver-</u>
<u>waltung</u>, 5 Feb.1963, Slg.IX, p.1; <u>Costa v. ENEL</u>, 15 July
1964, Slg.X, p.1251; <u>Walt Wilhelm v. Bundeskartellamt</u>,
13 Feb.1969, Slg.XV, p.1; <u>Marimex v. Finanzministerium</u>
<u>der italienischen Republik</u>, 7 March 1972, Slg.XVIII,
p.89; <u>Kommission v. Italien</u>, 13 July 1972, Slg.XVIII,
p.529.

(4o) Cf. <u>Stauder v. Ulm</u>, 12 Nov.1969, Slg. XV, p.419; <u>Inter-</u>
<u>nationale Handelsges.m.b.H. v. Einfuhr und Vorratsstelle</u>
<u>für Getreide und Futtermittel</u>, 17 Dec.197o, Slg.XVI,
p.1125; <u>J.Nold, Kohlen und Baustoffgroßhandlung v. Kom-</u>
<u>mission</u>, 14 May 1974, Slg.XX, p.491. In <u>Rutili v. Fran-</u>
<u>zösisches Innenministerium</u>, 28 Oct.1975, 3 EuGRZ 2(1976),
the Court of Justice of the European Communities for
the first time explicitly applied the European Convention of Human Rights. See also the Joint Declaration of
the European Parliament, the Council and the Commission
of 5 Apr.1977 concerning the protection of human rights
in European Community Law: 16 ILM 729(1977).

(41) See especially the controversial decision of 29 May
1974, BVerfGE 37,271, 14 CMLRep. 54o(1974). But see
already previous decisions of 18 Oct.1967, BVerfGE
22,293 and 9 June 1971, BVerfGE 31,145. In a similar
manner the Italian Constitutional Court reserves the
right to examine Community Law for its conformity with
human rights: <u>Frontini v. Ministero delle Finanze</u>, 27
Dec.1973, 14 CMLRep.372(1974).

X. EXISTING INTERNAL JUDICIAL DECISIONS AND INTER-NATIONAL DECISIONS

Judgments and other judicial decisions have an important place in the internal decision-making process of States. Their influence on the subsequent behavior of domestic courts justifies a separate examination of situations in which they conflict or at least compete with international decisions. The authority of judicial decisions on the subsequent activities of the courts manifests itself in two ways: Through the creation of precedents for similar cases and through the finality of judgments for the particular case.

A. INTERNAL PRECEDENTS

Not surprisingly, the question of a possible collision between international obligations and precedents of the local courts has attracted attention primarily with respect to common law countries. Scholarly opinion is practically unanimous in the rejection of the principle of *stare decisis* for decisions of domestic courts dealing with questions of international law.(1) Jenks(2) has suggested to solve this problem for English law by treating domestic decisions on international law like judgments on a point of foreign law which are not subject to the doctrine of precedent. This analogy is unobjectionable as long as the equalization of international law and foreign law remains restricted to the question of the domestic decisions' value as precedents.

The reason for the rejection of internal precedents on questions of international law is not only the continuous development of international law, which takes place largely independently of the court practice of individual States. Even at the moment of the judgment by a domestic court on an international legal question, this decision does by far not command the same degree of authority as, for example, the judgment of a domestic court of last instance on the law of the forum State.

English court practice on this question is not entirely clear. Cases dealing with the immunity of foreign States have thrown some light on this question. In a number of cases courts simply followed internal precedents without addressing themselves to the underlying question of principle.(3) Two recent decisions in the Court of Appeal are clearly contradictory on this point. In the first, Thai-Europe Ltd. v. Pakistan Government,(4) two of the judges dealt with the question in some detail and came to the conclusion that:

> A rule of international law, once incorporated into our
> law by decisions of a competent court, is not an infe-
> rence of fact but a rule of law. It therefore becomes
> part of our municipal law and the doctrine of stare
> decisis applies as much to that as to a rule of law
> with a strictly municipal provenance.(5)

Two years later in <u>Trendtex Corp. v. Central Bank of Nigeria</u>
(6) only one of the judges found that he had to "stand
loyally but reluctantly on the old doctrine and the old
decisions".(7) The majority was clearly in favor of a more
flexible approach. They held that "international law knows
no rule of stare decisis"(8) and that international law as
applied in old domestic precedents could not be preserved
"in a sort of judicial aspic".(9)

Situations of competition between local precedents and international decisions are most likely to arise in situations
involving a parallel interpretation and application of
treaties. In other words, the international decision concerned is likely to be an "international precedent". (See
chapter III.E.3. above) The rather reserved attitude of
domestic courts towards openly discussing international
practice, for example, on the European Convention on Human
Rights, (see EXCURSUS I above) has so far not made any
difficulties of this sort apparent. On the other hand, a
facile assumption that courts in countries not adhering to
the principle of *stare decisis* would lightly dismiss internal precedents in favor of pertinent international practice
(1o) may be misguided. This is borne out by a decision of
the Court of Appeal of Brussels(11) which rejects an invocation of the practice of the Human Rights Commission and
the Human Rights Court, pointing out that it could see no
justification for preferring the international practice to
the contrary practice of the Cour de cassation.

The degree of international authority enjoyed by the international decision is also significant when it collides with
domestic precedents. In a case before a United States federal court(12) an attempt was made to interpret an extradition treaty in accordance with resolutions of the United
Nations General Assembly favoring the extradition of persons
suspected of war crimes. The court did not accept this view:

> We have examined the various United Nations Resolutions
> and their background and have concluded that they have
> not sufficient force of law to modify long standing
> judicial interpretations of similar treaty provisions.
> (13)

By way of summary we can say that a rigid adherence to local
precedents conflicting with decisions of international
institutions would, no doubt, lead to entirely unacceptable
results and would moreover, be contrary to the professed
policy of ensuring the effectiveness of international decisions. This should not lead to the opposite extreme of unre-
servedly postulating a higher authority for international
decisions than for domestic precedents. Especially in cases
where the international decision concerned is itself invoked
as a "precedent", whose authority is influenced by a number
of variables, (see chapter III.E.3.b) above) it is feasible
that a consistent practice of domestic courts on a question
of international law is more authoritative than isolated
unrepresentative international decisions.(14)

B. FINAL JUDGMENTS

The irrevocability of final court decisions is an important
element of stability and security of the law. Exceptions
allowed to this principle by domestic procedural provisions
are usually very restrictive. The cancellation of a final
judgment through the subsequent decision of a court is only
admitted in the presence of exceptional circumstances pre-
scribed by the local law.

A clear conflict between a final judgment of a domestic
court and an international decision is most likely in cases
in which the domestic judgment has been reviewed by the
international organ and found defective. A large part of the
cases brought before the international organs supervising
the observance of the European Convention on Human Rights
deal with decisions of domestic courts. The requirement of
the exhaustion of local remedies before the Convention-
organs can be seized of a complaint usually means that the
domestic decisions challenged on the international level are
final and not subject to review under municipal law. This,
in turn, is liable to create a certain amount of difficulties
when the necessity arises for the forum State to remove the
consequences of a violation of the Convention. A government
wishing to comply with a decision of the Human Rights Court
or the Committee of Ministers, or attempting to forestall an
adverse decision against it, will not always find it easy to
wipe out violations by restoring the *status quo ante*. Redress for a breach of the obligations laid down in the Convention by a final decision of a civil or criminal court is
likely to encounter considerable obstacles: Non-execution of
a final judgment is often impossible under domestic law. In
a civil case a successful third party will have an enforceable
right to execution. Where the victim has unsuccessfully

sought to enforce rights guaranteed by the Convention in the
domestic courts, a final decision will normally preclude him
from raising the claim again. In the case of criminal proceedings under circumstances contrary to the Convention, an
administrative pardon or amnesty will by no means remove all
consequences of a conviction.(15)

In situations such as these, the only real possibility for a
restitutio in integrum will lie in a rehearing of the case.(16)
The provisions for the reopening of cases in the light of
new circumstances, contained in the rules of procedure for
domestic courts, obviously suggest themselves for this
purpose. In the absence of known precedents it must, however,
remain a matter of speculation whether courts will actually
make use of them in cases where an international organ has
found the domestic decision faulty. Since the conditions for
a retrial tend to be rather narrowly circumscribed, it seems
doubtful whether courts will resort to this procedure without specific legislation instructing or enabling them to do
so.(17) Besides, where the reopening of a case is conditional
on the disclosure of "new facts", a decision of an international organ will hardly suffice. It will usually have to be
considered as merely a new opinion on a point of law unless
the violation of the Convention involved irregularities in
the taking of evidence.

The question has been mooted to some extent for German law,
though with somewhat conflicting results. Even advocates of
an analogous application of the pertinent procedural provisions for a retrial to cases involving adverse finding by
Convention-organs(18) have expressed doubts as to whether
the courts will follow this course without pertinent legislation.(19)

As mentioned above, there are no known cases in which courts
have directly dealt with this problem. A judgment of the
Austrian Supreme Court(2o) refers to the possibility of a
reopening of proceedings under these circumstances by way of
an *obiter dictum*. This case concerned proceedings in which a
divorce had been granted on the basis of defendant's conviction for murder of her mother-in-law. The defendant claimed
that she had lodged a complaint against her conviction with
the European Commission on Human Rights and that it was,
therefore, not yet final. The Supreme Court rejected her
complaint, but found:

> If a violation of the Convention should be established
> in the future by the European Court /of Human Rights7
> the possibility of setting aside any court measure or
> court decisions affected by this violation would have

to be examined. The setting aside of the criminal
conviction would open the possibility to the defendant
to have the civil proceedings reopened.

The drafters of the European Human Rights Convention were
evidently aware of the difficulties arising from the finality of domestic decisions which are found to be in violation
of the Convention by its international organs. They inserted
Article 5o to cope with some of the questions arising from a
conflict between a decision of the Human Rights Court and
domestic law. Article 5o provides:

> If the Court finds that a decision or measure taken by
> a legal authority or any other authority of a High
> Contracting Party is completely or partially in conflict
> with the obligations arising from the present Conven-
> tion, and if the internal law of the said Party allows
> only partial reparation to be made for the consequences
> of this decision or measure the decision of the Court
> shall, if necessary, afford just satisfaction to the
> injured party.

In the application of Article 5o the injured party's right
to redress is, thus, simply transformed into a claim for
wealth which is not likely to come into conflict with the
formal validity of the internal measure, which the international decision has found to be defective. In some cases, it
may, moreover, be impossible to remove an already completed
violation of the Convention by remedial action, so that
financial indemnity remains the only possible form of compensation. The amount of this just satisfaction to be determined by the Court is not limited to damages, strictly
speaking, but includes compensation for the "moral injury"
inflicted by the breach of the Convention.(21)

It is not easy to predict whether States will actually go so
far as to expose themselves to domestic judicial proceedings
by refusing to comply with a decision affording just satisfaction under Article 5o. It must be hoped that courts of
the defendant State, or even of third States, will not
hesitate to enforce these decisions of the Human Rights
Court. This question was raised at a Parliamentary Conference
on Human Rights in October 1971.(22) A draft recommendation
suggesting the drawing up of a "European agreement rendering
the decisions pronounced by the European Court of Human
Rights enforceable in internal law" was adopted by the
Consultative Assembly of the Council of Europe by unanimous
vote in October 1972.(23)

International decisions that do not refer to a specific

domestic judgment, but only express general policies which happen to conflict with a domestic judgment are even less likely to serve as a basis for its cancellation. This is all the more so if the international decisions concerned are recommendations: A Netherlands,(24) a Belgian,(25) and a Bavarian(26) case all demonstrate that domestic courts are not prepared to accept the Universal Declaration of Human Rights as a reason for a reopening of proceedings, for a "recours en annulation", or for a constitutional complaint against domestic judgments.

(1) See the anonymous note to <u>In re Piracy Jure Gentium</u>, 16
    BYIL 199(1935); Jenks, The Prospects, p.75oseq.; Morgen-
    stern, Judicial Practice, p.8oseq.; Erades, Is stare
    decisis an impediment to the enforcement of international
    law by British courts?, 4 NYIL 1o5(1973); Schreuer, The
    Applicability of Stare Decisis to International Law in
    English Courts, 15 NILR(1978).

(2) The Prospects, p.75oseq.

(3) For references see Schreuer, note 1 above.

(4) /1975/ 1 W.L.R. 1485.

(5) Per Scarman L.J. at p.1495.

(6) /1977/ 2 W.L.R. 356.

(7) Stephenson L.J. at p.381.

(8) Lord Denning M.R. at p.365.

(9) Shaw L.J. at p.388.

(1o) Buergenthal, The Effect of the European Convention,
     p.1o2.

(11) 12 Dec.1967, in Collection of Decisions of National
     Courts referring to the Convention, published by the
     Directorate of Human Rights of the Council of Europe,
     Art.31, p.1.

(12) <u>Karadzole et al. v. Artukovic</u>, Court of Appeals, 9th
     Dist., 24 June 1957, 247 F.2d 198, 24 ILR 51o.

(13) 24 ILR 516. The judgment was subsequently quashed by
     the Supreme Court 355 U.S. 393.

(14) Cf. also Schreuer, The Authority, p.7o5seq.

(15) For detailed treatment of these questions see Schreuer,
     The Impact, p.63seq. with further references.

(16) Buergenthal, The Effect of the European Convention,
     p.99; Miele, Les organisations internationales et le
     domaine constitutionnel des Etats, p.386.

(17) Guradze, Die Europäische Menschenrechtskonvention,
     p.248; Schindler, Die innerstaatlichen Wirkungen, p.284;
     Scheuner, Comparison of the Jurisprudence, p.234.

(18) Schlosser, Das völkerrechtswidrige Urteil, p.186seq.; Schorn, Die Europäische Konvention, p.4o5; Schumann, Verfassungs- und Menschenrechtsbeschwerde gegen richterliche Entscheidungen, p.324.

(19) Schumann, Menschenrechtskonvention und Wiederaufnahme des Verfahrens, p.754. For an opinion opposed to a rehearing under these circumstances see Müller, Die Anwendung der Europäischen Menschenrechtskonvention in der Schweiz, 94 Zeitschrift für Schweizerisches Recht 373,4o4(1975).

(2o) 29 Jan.1963, 18 ÖJZ 327(1963).

(21) For a more detailed analysis of Art.5o including the pertinent practice, see Schreuer, The Impact, p.66seq. with further references.

(22) Consultative Assembly of the Council of Europe Doc.3161 (1972).

(23) Recommendation 683.

(24) In re Rauter, Special Court of Cassation, 16 AD 546(1949).

(25) De Meyer c. Etat belge, Conseil d'Etat, 9 Feb.1966, 4 RBDI 569(1968).

(26) Bayrisches Verfassungsgericht, 3 July 1961, 14 NJW 1619(1961).

XI. INTERNATIONAL DECISIONS AND THE CONFLICT OF LAWS

Litigation before domestic courts involving foreign elements often raise legal questions commonly described under the label of conflict of laws or, more narrowly, private international law. This area of the law involves basically two types of problems. One is the question whether the courts of a country have jurisdiction over a particular case. The other is the question of the law applicable to a particular case. Decisions of international institutions can offer guidance for the solution of both types of problems.

A. THE JURISDICTION OF THE FORUM STATE AND ITS COURTS

Domestic decision-makers investigating the limits of their activities, that is, the extent of their jurisdiction vis-à-vis other States, usually first look at their domestic law. The delimitations provided by international law for the jurisdiction of States are usually reflected in the internal prescriptions concerning court procedure. A reference to international prescriptions by a domestic court may serve to underline the forum State's claim to a particular jurisdiction. Sometimes there are international decisions and prescriptions which are not sufficiently reflected in domestic law. In order to decide the preliminary question whether it is entitled to make a decision on the merits a domestic court may have to resort to international law.

In this context international organs can play a role in the settlement of border or other territorial disputes, in deciding the material or personal jurisdiction of internal decision-makers, or in participating in the creation of new States.

The most obvious examples are cases in which the decision of an international judicial organ has denied the jurisdiction of the forum State over a disputed territory, and the court, consequently, denies its competence for that area.(1) Similar situations arise where the United Nations General Assembly has declared colonial territories independent. The Italian Corte di cassazione(2) and the French Conseil d'Etat(3) entertained no doubts that the resolutions of the General Assembly which had declared Libya, Ethiopia-Eritrea, and Cameroon independent, had terminated the jurisdiction of the courts of the former mother-countries for these territories.

Sometimes domestic courts rely on international decisions in the opposite sense to confirm their territorial or personal jurisdiction. The judgments of the International Court of

Justice concerning the <u>Rights of Nationals of the United States of America in Morocco</u>(4) and in the <u>Anglo-Norwegian Fisheries Case</u>(5) respectively confirmed the jurisdiction of Moroccan and Norwegian courts in the disputed spheres. The courts of these countries were, therefore, subsequently able to rely on these international judgments in order to justify their exercise of jurisdiction.(6) In a similar way, the District Court of Haifa(7) relied on the United Nations General Assembly's Partition Plan for Palestine. It found that it had jurisdiction to try certain offences, *inter alia,* by reference to the fact that the place of commission was Israeli territory under the State's declaration of independence, which in turn relied on the Partition Plan.

There are, however, also cases in which courts refuse to accept pertinent international decisions pointing towards limitations of the forum State's jurisdiction.(8) The motives for the rejection of the international decisions in these cases do not appear to lie so much in their consequences for the particular case as in an endeavor to submit to the political aspirations of the forum State on controversial territorial questions. (See also chapters XIII.A.3. and XIII.B.1. below).

B. THE APPLICABLE LAW

1. Choice of Law

There are also situations in which decisions of international organisations are relevant for the question which of several municipal legal systems is applicable to a case. Here too, the answer can lie in a territorial decision of an international organ. The jurisdiction over the locality, which constitutes the connecting point for the case, can be decisive for the applicable law.(9)

A good example is afforded by a judgment of a United States federal court,(1o) which concerned the effects of an international territorial decision on private property rights. After a change in the course of the Rio Grande, the boundary river between the United States and Mexico, in 1898, a Boundary Commission established by treaty eventually found in 193o that "the dominion and jurisdiction of this banco /the territory in question/ shall pass to the United States of America...". This was in spite of the fact that effective control over the land had since long before been exercised by Texas. The plaintiff tried to enforce a title to a parcel of land, in the relevant strip of territory, that he had bought in 1927 under Mexican law, that is, at a time when in

the Commission's opinion the land had still been Mexican.
The court rejected the claim, holding that the Boundary
Commission's decision had only settled the dispute between
the Governments, but had no effects on private rights.

The foreign law applicable under the prescriptions governing
the conflict of laws is not necessarily the law of another
State. It can be the so-called internal law of an international organization. This applies in particular to cases
before domestic courts involving the law governing employment by international organizations. (See chapters V.B. and
VII.C.3. above).

To the extent that international institutions exercise functions of territorial administration, the prescriptions adopted by them for the administered territory can become applicable like foreign law in the proper sense. A topical example
are the efforts of the United Nations Council for Namibia to
gain control over the territory which is still occupied by
South Africa. In a Decree(11) of 23 September 1974, the
Council not only prohibited any unauthorized export of natural resources from Namibia but also threatened the seizure
of any illegal exports. It was intimated that the enforcement of these provisions with the help of domestic courts
was under consideration.(12)

Although there is little doubt concerning the international
authority of the Decree, it is by no means certain that
domestic courts would actually apply the decision of the
United Nations Council for Namibia as the applicable law
under the conflict of laws. It appears not unlikely that
courts will prefer to apply South African law as the effective law prevailing in the territory.

2. Ordre Public

The majority of cases in which international decisions
become relevant in the application of foreign law do not
concern the question of choice of law in the strict sense,
but the conformity of the applicable foreign law with certain standards set in international decisions. The problem
is usually referred to under the label of *ordre public*. Mere
findings of conformity, like those made by Japanese(13) and
Italian(14) courts about the Iranian Statute nationalizing
the oil industry in relation to the General Assembly Resolution on the "Right to exploit freely natural wealth and
resources",(15) are probably only of limited significance.
On the other hand, there are a number of cases demonstrating
that especially the Universal Declaration of Human Rights is

an appropriate standard for the examination of foreign law before its application.(16) Netherlands(17) and Belgian(18) courts have refused to recognize foreign nationality laws which, in their eyes, conflict with Article 15 of the Universal Declaration of Human Rights. A German court(19) based its recognition of a marriage concluded abroad on Article 16/1 of the Universal Declaration, even though the law of the place of conclusion, which is normally the relevant law, did not recognize it. The German Federal Constitutional Court(2o) has held that a compliance with the prohibition under Spanish law against a Spaniard marrying a German divorcee would be unconstitutional, relying, *inter alia*, on Article 16 of the Universal Declaration.(21)

A decision of the German Federal Supreme Court(22) of 1972 demonstrates that decisions of international organisations can also work the other way. A prescription of foreign law not normally applicable under the conflict of laws can become applicable if it is clear from decisions of international institutions that transactions violating the foreign prescription are against public policy. The Federal Court dismissed an action arising from an insurance contract covering the export of cultural objects from Nigeria. The transaction underlying the insurance contract was illegal under Nigerian law, but this foreign prohibition would not normally have been applicable to a case before German courts. Nevertheless, the court concluded that it was clear from several decisions adopted by the General Conference of UNESCO and from a Convention adopted by it, though not yet in force for Germany, that practices of this kind were contrary to the "*ordre public international*":

> The deliberations of UNESCO and the adoption of the Agreement by the General Conference show clearly that this organization, competent for international cultural cooperation, has for a long time regarded the export of cultural objects contrary to the prohibition of a State as conduct which is prejudicial to public interests and an impediment to an understanding between nations... Within the international community there are, therefore, certain basic convictions concerning the right of every country to protect its cultural heritage and concerning the reprehensibility of "practices"..., which adversely affect it and which must be checked. In the interest of the preservation of decency in international trade with artistic objects the export of cultural objects, contrary to a prohibition of the country of origin, therefore, deserves no civil law protection...(23)

(1) La Ninfa (Whitelaw v. U.S.), Court of Appeals, 9th
     Circuit 29 June 1896, 75 F. 313, where the court held
     that an Act of Congress prohibiting the killing of seals
     in the Bering Sea could not be applied to a U.S. vessel
     outside the three-mile zone. The decision was based on
     the award in the Bering Sea Arbitration between the
     U.S. and Great Britain (Martens, N.R.G., 2nd ser.,
     Vol.21, p.439), which had denied an exclusive jurisdic-
     tion of the United States over waters of the Bering Sea.
     See also Y. v. Public Prosecutor, Dist.Ct.of Breda
     (NL), 11 Feb. and 2o March 1957, 7 NTIR 282(196o). In
     this case the court refused to make a finding on its
     territorial jurisdiction, since a dispute concerning
     the territory in question was pending before the ICJ

(2) Cassa di risparmio della Libia c. Dainotto, 18 Aug.1959,
     44 Rivista DI 295(1961); Passi c. Sonzogno, 5 March
     1953, 37 Rivista DI 579(1954).

(3) Mbounya, 3 Nov.1961, 8 AFDI 942(1962); Union des Popula-
     tions du Caméroun, 24 Jan.1962, 9 AFDI 1o1o(1963).

(4) ICJ Reports 176(1952).

(5) ICJ Reports 116(1951).

(6) Ministère public c/ Mohamed Ben Djilalli Ben Abdelkader,
     "Teignor", Tribunal Criminel de Casablanca, 6 Nov.1952,
     8o Clunet 666(1953); Administration des Habous c/ Deal,
     Cour d'appel de Rabat, 12 Nov.1952, 42 RCDIP 145(1953).
     Cf. also the judgment of the French Cour de cassation
     in Re Bendayan, 4 March 1954, 49 AJIL 267(1955). Rex v.
     Cooper, Supreme Court of Norway, 24 Oct.1953, 82 Clunet
     451(1955).

(7) Attorney-General of Israel v. El-Turani, 21 Aug.1951,
     18 ILR 164(1951). Confirmed by the Supreme Court on 31
     Dec.1952.

(8) German Reichsgericht, 21 Jan.193o, RGSt 63,395; Ruiz
     Alicea v. U.S., Court of Appeals 1st Cir., 1o March
     195o, 18o F.2d 87o; U.S. v. Vargas, US Dist.Ct. Puerto
     Rico, 29 Jan.1974, 37o F.Supp. 9o8; D.Tomás G.M./Minis-
     terio de la Gobernación, Supreme Court of Spain, 5 May
     1965, 2o Revista Esp.DI 478(1967); Military Prosecutor
     v. Halil Muhamad Mahmud Halil Bakhis and Others, Israel
     Military Court, 1o June 1968, 47 ILR 484; Madzimbamuto
     v. Lardner Burke etc., Appellate Division, Rhodesia, 29
     Jan.1968, 39 ILR 61; S. v. Tuhadeleni and Others,

Appellate division, South Africa, 22 Nov.1968, 18 ICLQ
789(1969), 52 ILR 29(1979).

(9) De Bodinat v. Administration de l'Enregistrement, Cour
de cassation (Fr.), 3 July 1939, 11 AD 52(1919-42). In
this case the Court relied on a "resolution" of the
League of Nations (probably the Mandate Agreement) in
order to determine whether French tax legislation was
applicable to Cameroon. See also the Opinion of the
Italian Consiglio di Stato of 9 Dec.1958, 43 Rivista DI
321(196o), where the status of Jerusalem played a role
for the application of Israeli law to a lease of an
object situated there. In Occidental Petroleum Corp. v.
Buttes Gas & Oil Co., US Dist.Ct., C.D.Calif., 17 March
1971, 331 F.Supp.92, a case arising from a dispute
between two oil companies, the question of sovereignty
over the territory which both companies claimed for
exploitation arose as preliminary question. The court
refused a decision on this point and found that only an
international court could settle the territorial issue.

(1o) Willis v. First Real Estate and Investment Co. et al.,
Court of Appeals, 5th Cir., 24 Jan.1934, 68 F.2d 671,
11 AD 94(1919-42).

(11) Namibia Gazette No.1, Decree No.1 for the Protection of
the Natural Resources of Namibia.

(12) The Times, 3o Jan.1975, p.6. Cf. also Shockey, Enforce-
ment in United States Courts of the United Nations
Council for Namibia's Decree on Natural Resources, 2
Yale Studies in World Public Order 285(1976); Booysen &
Stephan, Decree no.1 of the United Nations Council for
South West Africa, 1 South African Yearbook of Interna-
tional Law 63, 72(1975); Schermers, The Namibia Decree
in National Courts, 26 ICLQ 81(1977), Brooks, Security
Council Decisions and Private Contracts in Conflict of
Law Situations, 3 South African Yearbook of Interna-
tional Law 33(1977).

(13) Anglo-Iranian Oil Co. v. Idemitsu Kosan Kabushiki Kaisha,
District Court of Tokyo, 27 May 1953, 2o ILR 3o5,3o9,
Higher Court of Tokyo, 1953, 2o ILR 312.

(14) Anglo-Iranian Oil Co. v. S.U.P.O.R., Court of Rome, 13
Sept.1954, 22 ILR 23,4o.

(15) GA Res. 626(VII).

(16) Cf. also Lerebours-Pigeonnière, La Déclaration universelle, p.262seq.

(17) In re Krüger, Netherlands Council for the Restoration
of Legal Rights (Judicial Division), 13 Sept.1951, 18
ILR 258(1951).

(18) Re Pietras, Cour civil de Courtrai, 16 Nov.1951, UN
Yearbook of Human Rights 14(1951); In re Jacqueline-
Marie Bukowicz, Cour civil de Courtrai, 1o Oct.1952, UN
Yearbook of Human Rights 21(1953).

(19) OLG Stuttgart, 5 Nov.1962, 1o Zeitschrift für das
gesamte Familienrecht 39(1963).

(2o) 4 May 1971, BVerfGE 31,58, NJW 15o9(1971).

(21) See, however, the decision of the Kammergericht Berlin
of 14 Sept.1961, 14 NJW 22o9,2211(1961). In this case
the Court held that if there was an Iranian law prohibiting a marriage between an Iranian and a non-Iranian,
it would have to be honored in spite of the contrary
provision in Article 16(1) of the Universial Declaration.

(22) 22 June 1972, BGHZ 59,83. See also the note by Bleckmann 34 ZaÖRV 112(1974).

(23) BGHZ 59,86.

XII. THE PARTICIPANTS IN PROCEEDINGS BEFORE DOMESTIC COURTS

The position of different types of litigants in court proceedings is a general procedural problem. Typical questions arise in connection with a litigant's standing or with procedural privileges. In proceedings before domestic courts involving points of international law, the most important procedural questions arise from claims to immunity by foreign States or their representatives and by international organizations. In addition, the question arises to what extent individuals and corporations are entitled to pursue claims originating from the international arena. These questions are of a general nature and are by no means restricted to decisions of international institutions. Nevertheless, the specific problems arising from an invocation of international decisions justify a separate treatment of the position of the parties in the context of this study.

This chapter will look at some of the questions raised by four typical participants. First, we shall examine problems arising from the participation of the forum State itself in domestic litigation. Secondly, we shall turn to foreign States and, thirdly, to the participation of international organizations themselves in domestic litigation. Finally, we shall look at some of the questions arising when individuals and companies participate in judicial proceedings involving decisions of international institutions.

A. THE FORUM STATE

The forum State is a frequent participant in judicial proceedings. This participation can occur in the exercise of its sovereign authority or as a consequence of private law transactions, usually commercial. A typical "official" participation in court proceedings are the functions of the public prosecutor, or the fiscus in litigation involving taxes and duties, or the executive branch in disputes involving the public administration. Jurisdiction over some of these issues is often exercised by specialized courts. In private law transactions, the State's right to sue and be sued was not always admitted everywhere, but this capacity seems to be largely accepted nowadays.

Decisions of international organs can arise in domestic litigation involving the forum State as a party as a consequence of all the decision functions outlined above (namely, intelligence, recommendation, prescription, invocation and

application and in the context of all the claims based upon
them (implementation or review, preliminary questions, and
"precedents"). In the majority of cases involving international decisions, there is no perceptible causal connection
between the forum State's participation and the behavior of
the courts.

In certain cases involving the implementation or review of
international decisions rendered in the framework of the
applying function by international organs, the position of
the forum State as a party in the litigation can, however,
exercise an influence on the course and outcome of the proceedings. They concern either claims to wealth against the
forum State on the basis of an international arbitral award,
usually as a result of international commercial transactions
with non-State participants, or attempts to enforce international claims to values other than wealth on the basis of
general international decisions.

The participation of the forum State in domestic judicial
proceedings, of course, immediately raises the question of
the court's impartiality. It would be mistaken to regard the
procedural aspect of the forum State's participation alone
as a danger to the objectivity of a court. A danger to the
unbiased conduct of an internal decision-maker lies much
more in the substantive question whether there are important
special national interests of the forum State in the disputed
claims. These special interests need not and frequently do
not coincide with a formal participation of the forum State.
In a large number of situations the ability of courts to
decide unaffected by special national interests is not impaired by the forum State's position as a party in the
case. The important question as to the limits of judicial
impartiality in the face of international problems will,
therefore, be dealt with in a separate section of this
study. (Chapter XIII.B.1.)

1. Claims to Wealth

Domestic courts confronted with claims against the forum
State arising from commercial transactions or other pecuniary
obligations are usually perfectly capable of discharging
their functions in a fair and objective manner. An impartial
behavior in a situation of this kind is based not least on
the realization that the long-term economic benefits for the
forum State of a faithful discharge of obligations arising
from international judgments and awards concerning wealth
transactions by far outweigh the short-term benefits of non-
payment in a particular case.

There are, however, exceptions. An example is the decision
of the Court of First Instance of Teheran in National Iranian
Oil Co. v. Sapphire International Petroleums Ltd.(1) The
Court purported to set aside the forum State's obligation to
pay compensation as laid down in an international arbitral
award by declaring the international decision void.

As against this example of an evidently partisan judgment of
a domestic court, there are a number of other cases in which
courts have proved to be effective agencies for the enforcement of pecuniary obligations arising from international
decisions against the forum State. A series of French cases
illustrate this point:(2) In Myrtoon Steamship Co. c/ Agent
judiciaire du Trésor(3) the Greek plaintiff attempted to
enforce an international arbitral award which had been
rendered in pursuance of a charterparty concluded with the
French government. The government agent pleaded invalidity
of the award on the ground that according to Articles 83 and
1oo4 of the French Code of Civil Procedure the State of
France is not permitted to submit to arbitration.(4) This
argument was rejected by the Court of Appeals of Paris: the
domestic prescription invoked only applied to internal contracts. In the particular case the proper law of the contract
was English law. There was consequently no reason to refuse
an *exequatur*. Apart from these more formalistic reasons, the
judgment also gives a hint at the underlying policy considerations:

> ...il serait contraire aux intérêts de l'Etat de défendre
> à ses représentants d'accepter un mode de règlement de
> ses différends conformes aux usages du commerce inter-
> national, alors que son refus entraînerait souvent la
> rupture des pourparlers engagés;(5)

The Court's reliance on the proper law of the contract,(6)
while yielding satisfactory results in the particular case,
seemed a somewhat narrow base for the decision. Dependence
on the vagaries of conflict law is an unreliable guideline
in questions of basic international policy. The critisism
directed at this solution for this reason(7) found a positive response with the Court of cassation: In Trésor public
v. Galakis(8) - the facts of this case were almost identical
to Myrtoon - it refrained from the previous references to
the proper law. The State's pleas of immunity were simply
rejected on the ground that the special protection of the
State was not a question of capacity and did not apply to
international contracts concluded in conformity with maritime
commercial usage.

The French Conseil d'Etat displays a similarly reserved

attitude towards attempts by the executive to ward off court
supervision of its conduct in complying with international
decisions concerning wealth transactions. In <u>Ministre de l'Economie et des Finances c/ Sieur Canino</u>(9) the foreign plaintiff had demanded interest for the late payment of a sum
adjudicated in his favor by an international arbitral tribunal. The Conseil d'Etat found in the plaintiff's favor and
rejected the contention that the Government's refusal to pay
was an "acte se rattachant à la conduite des relations
extérieures", which was exempt from scrutiny of the courts.

This group of French cases supports the assumption that, in
a majority of cases before domestic courts for the implementation or review of international decisions concerning
wealth transactions, the participation of the forum State in
the proceedings exercises no decisive influence on their
outcome. The procedural privileges claimed by the forum
State were rejected. A bias in favor of the forum State in
deciding the merits of the cases is not apparent.

2. Claims to Values Other Than Wealth

Attempts to have so-called political decisions of international organizations enforced or revised by domestic courts
are relatively rare. (See chapter III.E.1.b.) above). The
responsibility for their implementation is generally regarded to lie with the executive branch of government. Attempts
to bring disputes concerning their implementation before the
courts must often fail because the courts have no jurisdiction to review the forum State's pertinent implementing
measures. The relatively few available cases in which courts
deal with this question are all from countries with a common
law tradition. In these countries the ordinary courts enjoy
much wider powers to supervise the executive's conduct in
areas of public administration than under continental legal
systems.

The relevant court decisions are outlined elsewhere in this
book. They include the unsuccessful attempt to enlist the
help of Indian courts to prevent the Government's compliance
with an international territorial decision.(1o) Unsuccessful
attempts undertaken before the United States federal courts
to force the Government to comply with sanctions imposed by
the United Nations Security Council.(11) Finally, a successful attempt before Australian courts to prevent the Government's compliance with similar obligations arising from
international sanctions.(12)

This sparse court practice permits of no general conclusions.

In the first case the court complied with the international
decision in accordance with the forum State's intentions; in
the second group of cases the courts did not comply with
the international decisions in accordance with the forum
State's intention; in the third case the court refused to
comply with the international decision contrary to the forum
State's intention. At present there is no example for the
fourth and probably most interesting possibility of an
enforcement of the international decision contrary to the
forum State's intention.

At any rate, this divergent court practice demonstrates that
there does not appear to be a simple single factor, like the
position of the defendant government, determining the behavior of domestic courts in these situations. The possibility
of forcing the forum State to comply with an international
decision with the help of its own courts can, therefore, not
be dismissed outright. At present, predictions concerning
future trends in decisions concerning the behavior of courts
are hardly possible. Obviously much will also depend on the
peculiarities of the local law, especially on the procedural
possibilities against the forum State.

EXCURSUS IV: Responsibility of the Forum State for Decisions
             and Activities of International Institutions

In a number of cases actions against the forum State were
not aimed at altering its position towards the implementation
of an international decision. Rather, the target of the
action is the international institution itself or one of its
decisions or activities. The procedural difficulties in
pursuing a claim against the international organization
induced the plaintiffs, who felt aggrieved by the international decision or activity, to turn to the forum State
either as co-defendant, or exclusively, in view of the
evident hopelessness to recover satisfaction from the international organization.

Of course, these attempts to claim "responsibility by proxy"
on the part of a Member State or host State of an international organization raise basic theoretical questions concerning the legal personality, especially the capacity to
incur liabilities, of international organizations.(13) Procedural difficulties in pursuing a claim against the participant primarily responsible are not necessarily a sufficient
basis to allow an action against another participant. On the
other hand, important policy considerations militate against
depriving aggrieved individuals of their rights of action
for purely procedural reasons. It is not clear whether the

plaintiffs in these cases advanced any arguments of this
kind. The decisions of the courts, at any rate, contain
hardly any references to basic questions of theory or policy.

The courts almost uniformly reject a substitution of the
international organization by the forum State as defendant.
Depending on the peculiarities and traditions of the local
law, the grounds given for these decisions are either more
formal or more directed at the merits. Both the French(14)
and Belgian(15) Conseils d'Etat dismissed actions against
the forum State arising respectively from labor disputes
with an international organization or from a decision of the
United Nations High Commissioner for Refugees, simply for
lack of competence. A New York court(16) reacted similarly
when it had to decide on the action of a private tax-payer
against the Secretary-General of the United Nations and
against New York. A judgment was sought declaring invalid:
the grant of land and easements to the United Nations for
the headquarters site, the allocation of funds for improvement of the streets in the area around the headquarters,
the exemption of the site from taxation and other privileges.
The action, in so far as it was directed against New York
was dismissed on the ground that it failed to state a cause
of action.

In a case before the Court of Appeals of Athens(17) the
plaintiff felt aggrieved by a decision of the Greek-Bulgarian
Mixed Emigration Commission. The action was directed against
a member of the Commission and against the Greek State. The
Court dismissed the action on the ground that the international Commission was an independent body and that its
decision could, therefore, not be attributed to the Greek
State.

A difficult question of topical importance is the responsibility for the activities of military units in the service of
the United Nations.(18) Cases arising from certain incidents
in the former Belgian Congo clearly show that the enforcement
of claims against the organization involves considerable
difficulties. The attempts of an injured person to enlist
the help of the Belgian courts(19) to obtain compensation
were not successful: The claim against the United Nations
itself was rejected on the ground of the organization's
jurisdictional immunity; the claim against the Belgian State
failed because the actions of United Nations troops were, in
the eyes of the court, not attributable to it.

There is only one English decision, Attorney-General v. Nissan,(2o) in which the House of Lords found the Crown respon-

sible for damages inflicted by United Nations troops. The peculiar circumstances of the case may offer a partial explanation for this surprising decision. First, the unit involved was a British contingent, which had injured the British plaintiff. Secondly, the injurious activity - the occupation of a hotel - had already commenced before the subordination of the unit to the United Nations' command. Nevertheless, the conclusion of the court that it is not the organization but the participating States which bear responsibility for their troops operating in the service of the United Nations (21) leaves some doubts.

For an individual pursuing a claim, a State is almost certainly a more promising adversary in court proceedings than an international organization whose procedural immunity is almost impenetrable. Nevertheless, the general extension of a State's responsibility to army units which are beyond its command and control does not appear advisable. It could seriously affect the readiness of Members to put troops at the disposal of the United Nations.

In the long run, an improvement of the procedural position of persons, who have suffered damages inflicted by international organizations, will probably not be achieved by replacing the organization's responsibility by a liability of a State more or less connected to its activity. The majority of the available court practice evidently rejects this construction. A more promising solution would lie in the direction of an improvement of procedural protection against international institutions, either through a limited reduction of their procedural privileges (see chapter XII.C.2. below) or through the establishment of appropriate international machinery for the enforcement of individual claims.

B. A FOREIGN STATE

1. Claims to Wealth

The participation of foreign States in domestic proceedings directed at the implementation of international decisions can raise difficult problems of immunity. The steadily growing participation of States and State-controlled enterprises in international commerce has created considerable difficulties in the area of the settlement of disputes arising from commercial transactions. The effectiveness of the traditional dispute settlement procedure before domestic courts was seriously impaired by an insistence of States on their procedural privileges. More recently, however, the court practice in most States shows a clear trend to treat

State immunity not as a question of sovereign status but by
reference to the public or non-public function involved in
the particular dispute.(22)

States and State-controlled enterprises have also followed
the trend towards an arbitral settlement of disputes in
international commerce. Part of the reasons for this trend
may have been the difficulties arising from a participation
of foreign States in domestic litigation. However, the
submission to international arbitration by no means solves
all procedural problems. Arbitral tribunals regularly have
no means at their disposal to make their decisions controlling. At critical stages of the proceedings they depend on
the help and cooperation of State organs, usually the courts.
These critical stages usually arise when the arbitral proceedings are to be instituted and when an award is to be enforced.

This means that a domestic court called upon to implement an
international arbitral award against a foreign State is
faced with problems similar to those of a court having to
make a decision on the merits. It may, therefore, appear
obvious to extend the widely accepted distinction between
acta iure imperii and *acta iure gestionis* also to this
question. On the other hand, there are also arguments in
favor of applying specific criteria to cases involving the
enforcement of international awards against foreign States.
One such argument sees the submission to arbitration as a
general waiver of immunity,(23) which would include proceedings for the enforcement of awards and would obviate the
usual distinction between official and commercial activities.
Another argument,(24) pointing in the opposite direction,
distinguishes between immunity from jurisdiction on the
merits and immunity from execution, the latter of which
would be more extensive or even absolute. Since the implementation of international decisions involves measures of
execution, or at any rate steps preparatory to it, this view
would practically exclude any intervention on the part of
domestic courts. A preferable solution would probably be to
try to develop specific policies taking account of the fact
that an authoritative international decision has been rendered on the merits. The basic preference for the effectiveness of international decisions would offer a sufficient
basis for a special limitation of State immunity.

The practice of courts is not entirely unanimous but still
offers certain clues. The results of the "classic" principle
of absolute immunity on attempts to enforce international
judicial decisions against foreign States is best exemplified by an English case. Duff Development Ltd. Comp. v.

Kelantan(25) arose from an agreement between the plaintiff
company and the Government of Kelantan containing an arbitration clause that incorporated the English Arbitration Act,
1889, so far as applicable. After an award had been rendered
in favor of the Company, the Government of Kelantan, relying
on the Arbitration Act, applied to the Chancery Division to
have the award set aside. The application was refused. The
Company thereupon sought leave to enforce the award in
accordance with other provisions of the same Act. After
receiving an official communication from the Secretary of
State for the Colonies to the effect that Kelantan was an
independent sovereign, the Court of Appeal, whose decision
was in turn upheld by the House of Lords, found that the
Company's application had to be dismissed. In the Court's
opinion, the Government of Kelantan had not submitted to the
jurisdiction of the English courts for the purpose of the
proceedings to enforce the award, either by assenting to the
arbitration clause or by applying to the Court to set aside
the award.

Such a general policy of non-enforcement against foreign
States must be regarded as highly unsatisfactory. The foreign
Government had been found to be in default of its obligation
under the agreement by the arbitral tribunal and had specifically consented to the enforcement of an award by the English courts by incorporating the Arbitration Act into the
contract. The refusal to implement international decisions
under such circumstances must detract much from the value of
any arbitration clause in an international government contract and will introduce a paralysing element of uncertainty
into transactions of non-State entities with foreign governments.(26) In view of the recent changes of English law with
respect to sovereign immunity(27) this infelicitous case is
probably only of historical significance today.

The readiness of courts to apply a more restricted concept
of State immunity in connection with the implementation of
international decisions has been hesitant and by no means
uniform. In a case that concerned a decision of a Mixed
Arbitral Tribunal under the Peace Treaties after the First
World War, the Supreme Court of Czechoslovakia(28) was
seized of an attempt to enforce an award rendered in favor
of a Czechoslovak national against the Hungarian State. A
Czechoslovak law specifically provided for the execution of
these decisions. Although the court found that the law only
applied against private individuals and not against the
Contracting Parties, it held that this was otherwise in
respect of immovable property situated in Czechoslovakia.
The immovable property of a foreign State situated in the

country was found to be subject to execution in the same way
as the immovable property of nationals.(29) Of course, this
rather arbitrary limitation of State immunity does not offer
a general solution to the problem.

Subsequent cases before Belgian and French courts yielded
remarks on the immunity of foreign States in connection with
the enforcement of awards which were *obiter dicta*, but,
nevertheless, throw some light on the attitude of the courts.
In the case Soc. commerciale de Belgique c. Etat hellénique
et Banque de Grèce(3o) the attempt to enforce the international decision failed for other reasons. Nevertheless, the
defendant's attempt to invoke immunity was curtly dismissed
by the Tribunal de Bruxelles:
> ...la souveraineté de l'Etat étranger s'arrête à sa
> frontière, sous la réserve des exceptions imposées par
> le libre exercice de sa représentation diplomatique à
> l'extérieur;...(31)

In Yougoslavie c/ Sté. européenne d'études et d'entrepri-
ses(32) the Tribunal de grande instance de Paris, although
refusing implementation of the award against Yugoslavia for
other reasons, rejected the plea of sovereign immunity.(33)
It found that by accepting the compromissary clause the
Yugoslav State had renounced its immunity from jurisdiction
with respect to the arbitrators and their award. This renunciation had to be regarded as including the procedure for
securing an *exequatur*, necessary to give the award its full
effect. The court added, however, that the renunciation of
immunity from jurisdiction did not affect Yugoslavia's
immunity from execution. The order of *exequatur* was not to
be taken as a measure of execution but merely as a preliminary step to such an act. This fine distinction between
measures of execution and steps preliminary to it is not
very convincing. The result is the same as in the Duff
case discussed above. An order of *exequatur* seems a rather
pointless administrative exercise if immunity from execution
is upheld in spite of it.

In two more recent Netherlands cases the courts attempted to
apply the widely accepted distinction between *acta iure gestionis* and *acta iure imperii* also to the enforcement of international arbitral awards against foreign States. One case
was an attempt to enforce the award rendered in favor of the
Sapphire Company against the National Iranian Oil Company
(NIOC)(34) with the help of the Netherlands Courts.(35) The
other case(36) concerned the same award as the above-mentioned case between Yugoslavia and the Sté. européenne.

In both cases the district courts first came to the conclusion
that the transactions underlying the arbitrations were not
commercial and that the pleas of immunity, therefore, had to
be upheld. In the case against the NIOC the District Court
of The Hague based its findings on the

> primordial economic and social interests of the State
> of Iran in the oil industry on her territory, which
> promotion that State has made part of its public respon-
> sibility... (37)

Upon appeal, the method of distinguising between *acta iure
imperii* and *acta iure gestionis* was retained but the decisions were reversed. In the case against the NIOC(38) the
court examined its corporate character, the nature of its
commercial activities, and, particularly, the agreement
underlying the arbitration. It found that the parties entering
into it were of equivalent status, and that it consequently
could not be classified as an act *iure imperii*. NIOC's ties
with the State of Iran and the significance of petroleum for
that country were held to be irrelevant. In the case against
Yugoslavia(39) the appellate courts came to the conclusion
that a contract for the construction of a railway line with
a foreign company was a private transaction, even if the
railway line was of possible strategic importance.

In both cases the courts also dealt with the separate plea
of immunity of foreign States from execution. In the case
against the NIOC the Court of Appeal of The Hague held:

> A judicial award is, by its nature, enforceable; and if
> immunity constitutes no bar to jurisdiction, it can in
> principle neither constitute a bar to enforcement.(4o)

This view was shared by the Supreme Court in the case against
Yugoslavia. It declared categorically that there was no rule
of international law which prohibited an execution against
State-owned property situated abroad.(41)

The apparent ease with which the courts arrive at opposite
results, both seemingly logical, by applying the same *acta
iure gestionis - iure imperii* test, must raise serious doubts
as to whether this method is really a panacea for all problems of State immunity. This undoubtedly important and useful method to curtail sovereign privileges in international
commerce presents important difficulties in its practical
application. Although the extension of the widely accepted
distinction between the two types of State activity also
to our type of problem is sometimes advocated(42) and obviously suggests itself to the domestic judge, it is questionable whether this method is really the best solution in

cases where a final judicial determination of the respective
rights and duties has already taken place on the international level. The court practice so far available shows no
evidence of an awareness that the existence of an authoritative international decision on the merits could offer an
independent criterion for a limitation of immunity in proceedings directed at their enforcement.

The distinction, rejected by the Netherlands courts, between
a (limited) immunity from jurisdiction and an (absolute)
immunity from execution would, in effect, be a total bar to
the intervention of domestic courts in the enforcement of
international decisions. Quite apart from the specific
problems of international awards, the acceptance of an
unlimited immunity of States from execution would largely
neutralize the progress made in limiting immunity from jurisdiction. Decision-making by internal as well as international organs can only be effective in the presence of stable
expectations concerning appropriate procedures to make the
decisions controlling. Qualifications may be appropriate
with respect to the kind of State-owned property open to
execution. Installations which directly serve the public
interest would obviously have to be kept exempt from enforcement measures. These policies are reflected in two recent
statutes governing the law of state immunity, the U.S.
Foreign Sovereign Immunities Act of 1976 (28 USC 1609-1610)
and the United Kingdom State Immunity Act 1978 (Section 13).

The construction of a waiver of immunity by way of a submission to international arbitration is not entirely convincing. The parties may have specifically wished to avoid
adjudication by a domestic court and, therefore, agreed to
submit a dispute to an international judicial organ. On the
other hand, a submission to international arbitration by no
means implies that an intervention of domestic courts in the
implementation of the award is contrary to the common intention of the parties. Moreover, the fiction of a waiver of
immunity from execution by way of a submission to international adjudication could hardly be extended to purely inter-
State litigation. An implementation of pecuniary obligations
adjudicated by the International Court of Justice or another
international judicial or non-judicial organ could hardly be
based on a construed waiver of immunity through submission
to the international organ's jurisdiction. On the other
hand, domestic courts could play an important role in the
enforcement of pecuniary obligations arising from inter-
State disputes where a decision by an authoritative international decision-maker has been forthcoming.(43)

None of the traditional theories, therefore, offers a truly
satisfactory answer to the problem of immunity of foreign
States in proceedings for the enforcement of international
decisions directed at wealth. The most rational solution
would appear to be a further exception to the principle of
State immunity which is to be applied in addition to the
widely accepted distinction between *acta iure imperii* and
acta iure gestionis. Under this policy domestic courts should
reject pleas of immunity made in proceedings for the implementation of an authoritative international decision which
unequivocally determines the obligation of the foreign State.(44) The existence of an international decision on the
merits largely invalidates the arguments otherwise militating against proceedings instituted against foreign States
in domestic courts. An arbitrary or partisan behavior towards
the foreign State is no longer a real danger at the enforcement stage. The violation of the foreign State's "dignity"
can hardly be accepted as a serious argument in this kind of
situation. The refusal to comply with clear obligations as
laid down authoritatively by an international decision-maker
cannot be regarded as belonging to the prerogatives of a
sovereign, which have to be respected by the organs of other
States.

In comparison to attempts to achieve compliance with international decisions of this kind through "political" or
"diplomatic channels", the intervention of the courts has
much to commend itself. Their relatively independent status
enables them to proceed in a more objective and impartial
manner than a government which is often hampered by everyday political considerations. In addition, courts are especially equipped to deal with problems arising in connection
with authoritative wealth allocations. They have the appropriate enforcement machinery at their disposal and can deal
with any attendant legal problems arising in connection with
the enforcement.

The realization of these policy suggestions will largely depend on the readiness of domestic courts to adjust their as
yet unsettled practice accordingly. Important progress could
also be expected from multilateral treaties excluding pleas
of State immunity in proceedings directed at the enforcement
of certain types of international decisions. Unfortunately,
the relevant treaties concluded in recent years show no
clear step in this direction.

The United Nations Convention of 1958 on the Recognition and
Enforcement of Foreign Arbitral Awards (330 UNTS 38) was
quite evidently drafted with a view to non-State partici-

pants.(45) Consequently, it does not contain any provisions
on the immunity of foreign States.

The World Bank Convention of 1965 on the Settlement of Investment Disputes between States and Nationals of Other
States(46) provides for the enforcement by domestic courts
of the awards rendered in the framework of the Convention
(Article 54). However, at the same time there is an explicit
reservation concerning any provisions existing in individual
Member States on the immunity of both the forum State and
foreign States (Article 55).(47) This limitation of the
powers of domestic courts is all the more regrettable since
difficulties are most likely to arise in the implementation
of the international awards against State parties. Of course,
this means that in most cases at least the distinction between *acta iure imperii* and *acta iure gestionis* will be
applied. But, in view of the difficulties of delimitation
engendered by this widely accepted method, its application
to awards rendered under the Convention is not entirely
satisfactory.

Even the European Convention on State Immunity of 1972(48)
stops short of ruling out immunity in proceedings for the
enforcement of international awards. Article 12 lists several
types of proceedings relating to arbitration in which a State
may not claim immunity from the jurisdiction of courts of
other Contracting States. However, the enforcement of awards
is not included in this list.

2. Claims to Values Other Than Wealth

An intervention of domestic courts for the implementation of
international decisions solely concerned with values other
than wealth against foreign States is hardly feasible. However, in certain situations they could be instrumental in
implementing or at least adding effectiveness to international decisions with strongly "political" overtones, that is
to say in situations in which values other than wealth play
a significant part. This would include claims to indemnity
for illegal acts adjudicated by international organs or
obligations towards international organizations as determined
by their proper organs. For instance, the right to seize
natural resources illegally exported from Namibia, as laid
down in the Decree for the Protection of the Natural Resources of Namibia,(49) is also applicable against States and
could be enforced in domestic courts against foreign States.

C. AN INTERNATIONAL INSTITUTION

Every participation of an international institution in proceedings before domestic courts necessarily raises questions
concerning decisions and activities of that institution. However, procedural situations of this kind are rare. Usually
international organizations avoid getting drawn into proceedings before domestic courts. Often they establish an alternative machinery for the settlement of disputes. Where
attempts are made to sue international organizations before
domestic courts, an invocation of their immunities, as
granted in treaties, usually forestalls a decision on the
merits.

These grave procedural limits explain the relative scarcity
and lack of variety of domestic cases involving the organizations themselves as parties. The procedural possibilities
of courts are very restricted. Contending against an international decision through domestic litigation against its
author, the international institution, is rarely promising,
both from the position of plaintiff and defendant. Most
cases involving the direct participation of international
institutions in proceedings before domestic courts concern
decisions of international institutions only in connection
with the invoking function as exercised by them before the
domestic court.

1. The International Institution as Plaintiff

In the few cases in which international organizations or
their organs acted as plaintiffs before domestic courts the
central issue was usually their right to sue. The defendant
normally contested either the organization's capacity to act
in court proceedings or its representative's power of agency.
In other words, the act of the international organization
under scrutiny was the court action itself. The claims underlying these actions were usually of a private law character,
sometimes arising from terminated contracts of employment.

In none of the known cases did the courts entertain doubts
concerning the capacity and power of the respective international organization or its representative to act in proceedings before domestic courts.(5o) The right to sue was
either based on particular treaty provisions(51) or regarded as belonging to the organization's implied powers.(52)

Situations are, however, feasible, in which international
institutions themselves invoke one of their previous decisions before domestic courts and demand its implementation.

One example is the action discussed above, p.74, by the International Bank for Reconstruction and Development and the International Monetary Fund against a number of telegraph companies(53) to enforce certain rights granted to them in their constitutive treaties. Both plaintiffs underlined their claims with the help of official interpretations of their constitutive treaties. These authoritative international decisions in the organizations' own cause were accepted by the domestic deciding agency.

The United Nations Council for Namibia has indicated that it plans to enforce the Decree for the Protection of the Natural Resources of Namibia with the help of domestic courts.(54) In proceedings of this type the action would be directed at the implementation of the international decision. Formally the domestic court would merely enforce the UN Council for Namibia's claims to possession of the natural resources involved. However, the true objective of such an action would, of course, not be the enforcement of claims to wealth but the acquisition of control over the disputed territory in accordance with the pertinent decisions of the General Assembly, the Security Council, and the International Court of Justice's advisory opinion.

2. The International Institution as Defendant.

The immunity of international institutions from lawsuits in domestic courts is the object of detailed prescriptions. These prescriptions are contained in the international organizations' constitutive instruments,(55) in multilateral conventions on the privileges and immunities of international organizations,(56) in headquarters agreements,(57) and in domestic statutes.(58) The details of these prescriptions have been described extensively in scholarly writings.(59) A typical example of this kind of provision on immunity from domestic lawsuits is Section 2 of the Convention on the Privileges and Immunities of the United Nations:

> The United Nations, its property and its assets wherever located and by whomsoever held, shall enjoy immunity from every form of legal process except in so far as in a particular case it has expressly waived its immunity.

Identical or similar provisions can be found in numerous pertinent international conventions. With respect to third States, that are neither members of the organization nor parties to a treaty providing for immunities, some writers postulate a customary rule to the same effect.(60)

Only some international organizations recognize certain

limits to their immunity from lawsuits and admit certain
actions for particular purposes.(61) Thus the International
Bank for Reconstruction and Development in accordance with
Article VII Section 3 of its Articles of Agreement, admits
actions under certain conditions.(62) The Treaties establishing the European Communities(63) admit lawsuits against
the Communities in domestic courts unless the Court of
Justice of the European Communities has jurisdiction to hear
the case.

The policy underlying this far-reaching protection of international institutions against interventions by domestic
courts is evident. The purpose is to provide optimum conditions for the functioning of the organizations. Although the
pertinent provisions confer immunity in terms of status,
their effect is also to grant non-reviewability to the activities and decisions of the respective international organs
in actions directed against them.

The organization's interest in maximum independence in the
exercise of its functions is antithetical to the interests
of its adversaries in judicial protection. The position of
parties having claims against international institutions is
severely impaired by the curtailment of court proceedings.
For this reason many organizations have established alternative dispute-settlement-machinery.(65) They include, in
particular, administrative tribunals for the settlement of
disputes arising from contracts of employment(66) and arbitrations for other contractual relations of international
organizations.(66) Nevertheless, these procedures are far
from comprehensive and do by no means offer a full and
satisfactory substitute for the judicial protection normally
afforded by domestic courts.

The ostensibly unequivocal positive prescriptions concerning
the immunity of international organizations before domestic
courts would serve to support the assumption that the pertinent practice of domestic courts must show little variation.
A closer look at court practice, nevertheless, reveals some
interesting aspects. The grounds on which the dismissals of
actions against international organizations are based are
not always uniform. Moreover, there are individual attempts
by courts to find limits to these immunites.

Actions against international organizations concerning their
primary functions have invariably been unsuccessful: In a
lawsuit against the United Nations for damages caused by UN
troops the dismissal of the action was based on Article 1o5
of the UN Charter and Section 2 of the Convention on the

Privileges and Immunities of the United Nations.(67) In a
somewhat older English case(68) the Court of Appeal found it
necessary to perceive an international organ as a union of
sovereign States in order to derive its immunity from the
sovereign immunity of its component Members. In a case before
the US federal courts against the Inter-American Development
Bank Section 3, Article XI of its constitution, permitting
actions against the bank in principle, was construed as a
general waiver of immunity.(69) The court, therefore, reviewed the decisions of the bank in granting loans, as demanded by the plaintiff, but eventually dismissed his claim on
the merits.

The immunity of international organizations was also usually
recognized in areas of activities outside their primary functions, such as, road traffic(7o) or the establishment of
headquarters.(71) A particularly important area of dispute
settlement arising from the activities of international organizations is the law governing the employment of international officials. The procedures specially created by international organizations for the settlement of employment disputes are not always regarded as satisfactory by their employees. Therefore, actions before the ordinary domestic
courts are sometimes preferred. The courts seized of disputes of this kind were usually not prepared to admit actions
against the organizations.(72) The rejection of the actions
was either based on the organizations' immunity under international law(73) or on a lack of jurisdiction *ratione mate-
riae*,(74) which precluded domestic courts from entering into
internal questions of the organizations.

The practice of Italian courts deserves a brief separate
treatment in this context. First, it is comparatively extensive. Second, it shows tendencies towards a more differentiated treatment of the right to sue international organizations. This attitude is already manifested in an inclination
not to reject actions arising from employment disputes because of the organization's immunity but on the ground of
the domestic courts' lack of material jurisdiction over
questions of this kind, which are to be settled autonomously
by the organizations themselves.(75) Pleas of immunity were
sometimes explicitly rejected in these cases.(76) The claimant was referred to the dispute settlement procedures existing within the organization's framework.(77) In one case
the Court of Cassation even reached the conclusion that a
reference to material Italian law, contained in the organization's conditions of employment, established the jurisdiction of the Italian labor courts.(78)

Another remarkable phenomenon in Italian court practice is
an inclination to extend the distinction between *acta iure
imperii* and *acta iure gestionis* to the immunity of international organizations.(79) In the area of employment disputes
this led to a distinction between different categories of
employees: The legal relationship to officials in higher
positions, who directly serve the purposes of the organization, is to be exempted from the jurisdiction of domestic
judiciaries. Contracts with manual workers rendering auxiliary services are not to be covered by the organization's
immunity.(8o) More recently the criterion adopted by the
Italian Court of cassation for distinguishing between employment contracts of a public and of a private nature is the
permanency and continuity of the relationship. Contracts
with persons providing irregular or casual services would
thus not fall into the category of public employment and
would hence not give rise to the organisation's immunity.(81)
In a similar way, a contract for the running of a canteen
for the organization's employees is not *ratione imperii* and,
therefore, subject to the jurisdiction of the courts.(82)
In proceedings against the FAO the court specifically emphasized that the provisions of the headquarters agreement,
which granted judicial immunity to the organization in general terms, could only be understood subject to the distinc-
tio between "public law activities" and "private law activities".(83)

This practice of Italian courts, although it may not always
be entirely consistent, at least offers an attempt to balance,
on the one hand, the justified interests of the organizations
in the independent exercise of their functions and, on the
other hand, the equally justified interests of their adversaries in judicial protection. Here too, we should beware of
simple rules ostensibly offering general solutions. Thus,
the distinction, sometimes adopted in scholarly writings,(84)
between the organization's "internal domain" and its "external relations" is probably too vague and arbitrary to serve
as a general standard for courts determining the limits of
their jurisdiction. This distinction may have some descriptive value, but in specific decision situations it can
probably offer no more than a smoke screen for a decision
reached by other criteria.

The adoption of the distinction between *acta iure imperii*
and *acta iure gestionis*, as applied to State immunity, evidently commends itself in view of the similarity of problems.
Nevertheless, it is not unproblematic. In view of the nation-
State's dominating position in internal as well as external
arenas, a reduction of sovereign privileges is often in

accordance with preferred community policies. With international organizations problems are often exactly the opposite.
Their position is still tenuous and requires additional
support. Participation in ordinary transactions may often
not be a satisfactory criterion to find limits for the
procedural protection accorded to them. A participation in
transactions which are governed by substantive domestic law
and not the organization's "internal law" is often an essential part of its functions. To subject these transactions to
the scrutiny of domestic courts as "private activity" could
seriously affect the functioning of international organizations.

Contracts of employment have strong private features. On the
other hand, their contents are often determined by the organization's so-called internal law. The distinction between
different contracts of employment, as undertaken in the
above-mentioned cases, in order to classify them as "public"
or "private" does not offer a convincing solution.

These difficulties in the application of general standards
like "internal domain" or "acts of a public nature" suggest
that it may be more promising not to look for simple rules
but to try to elaborate the policy considerations militating
in favor or against an intervention of domestic courts.

The independence and freedom of international organizations
from intervention by State organs is often an essential
condition for the effective discharge of their functions.
The importance of their functions justifies a certain degree
of privileges and immunities in the public interest even if
this involves limited infringements of the rights of individuals to judicial protection. However, this special procedural protection of international institutions should stop
where its adverse effects become disproportionate to the
public interest in safeguarding the independent functioning
of the organization. A complete shield against judicial
action, even for an international organization's most trivial
transactions, without the establishment of alternative dispute settlement procedures is difficult to justify and is
probably not even in the organization's long-term interest.

The decision-making organs, set up or utilized by many organizations to deal with employment disputes (esp. administrative tribunals) are sufficiently independent to guarantee
impartial decisions. They conform with both the organizations' desire for freedom from outside interference and the
individuals' interest in judicial protection. Where such a
decision organ exists, there are no serious policy arguments

against a recognition of immunity in domestic courts. Where
such an independent international decision organ does not
exist and where there is a danger of unilateral and arbitrary
action against an international official, situations are
feasible in which the individual's interest in judicial
protection is not offset by an equally strong interest of
the organization in "independence". Occasional decisions by
domestic courts in labor disputes are not likely to affect
seriously the independent functioning of international
organizations.

These policy considerations should not make us lose sight of
the fact that they may remain purely hypothetical for many
cases before domestic courts. Most of the pertinent prescriptions in treaties and statutes are quite unequivocal in
granting unlimited immunity to international organizations.
It is doubtful whether courts of other States will follow
the example of the Italian courts in searching for limits to
this immunity.

D. INDIVIDUALS AND CORPORATIONS

As indicated, the problems arising from a participation of
States and international organizations in domestic litigation touching upon international decisions, arise mainly
from the procedural privileges of these parties. The questions
arising from the participation of individuals and corporations in litigation of this kind are entirely different.
Notwithstanding the increasing participation of actors without "international legal personality" in the traditional
sense in international transactions, the dependence of these
non-State participants on the countries of their nationality
is still considerable. Since these non-State participants do
not have access to certain important international arenas,
they cannot directly participate in some international decision processes. Even where they have access, they often
depend on the help and cooperation of State organs in efforts
to implement international decisions in their favor. The
question is to what extent individuals and corporations can
invoke international decisions before domestic courts giving
rise to direct rights for them.

International decisions concerning wealth transactions, usually judgments and arbitral awards, specifically designate
the parties deriving rights and obligations from them. These
parties are usually identical with the participants in the
international proceedings. Some international courts and
tribunals, however, are not open to non-State participants.

In cases in which States have acted before these international decision-makers in the exercise of diplomatic protection, the question can arise whether, and to what extent, individuals and corporations are entitled to benefits arising from these international decisions.

With respect to international decisions not concerned with claims to wealth, the situation is somewhat different. Decisions of this kind, whether they are directed at individual States or at an indeterminate circle of addressees, rarely specify the rights of particular individuals. Individuals and corporations may, however, acquire rights and obligations from international decisions of this kind, which are enforceable in domestic courts, as members of a general group to which the international decision is addressed.

1. Claims To Wealth

Traditional international law only admitted States as actors in international procedures to pursue rights of their nationals. The question arose whether individuals and corporations were able to invoke international judgments and awards, in spite of the fact that they had not themselves participated in the international proceedings. The total procedural submission of the individual claim to the control of the State of the claimant's nationality often led to the conclusion that the exercise of diplomatic protection actually changed the nature of the claim, and that only the protecting State was entitled to any proceeds arising from the international decisions.(85) This view was further supported by the State's complete discretion whether or not to exercise diplomatic protection.(86) It seemed to follow that a claim to wealth successfully pursued before an international decision- maker belonged only to the State itself and not to its protected national.(87)

A typical example of this attitude is offered by the case of Soc. Commerciale de Belgique c. Etat Hellénique et Banque de Grèce.(88) In this case arbitral awards in favor of the Company against Greece had been confirmed by the Permanent Court of International Justice in proceedings instituted by Belgium. In proceedings to enforce the arbitral award in Belgian courts, the Company also attempted to invoke the Permanent Court of International Justice's judgment. This attempt was rejected on the ground that the Company had not itself participated in the international proceedings before the Permanent Court:

> ...la demanderesse prétend que l'arrêt, rendu le 15 juin 1939 dans le litige, opposant l'Etat hellénique et

l'Etat belge - prenant, devant la Court de la Haye,
fait et cause pour elle, - ferait titre pour elle, qui
n'était point partie à ces débats; qu'il ne se conçoit
pas qu'une partie qui, par définition, n'est pas admise
à la barre d'une Court internationale, puisse se récla-
mer d'une décision judiciaire, à laquelle elle n'était
point partie litigante. (89)

The Belgian court by relying on the lack of the Company's
direct representation before the Permanent Court evidently
implied that Article 24 of the International Court's Statute,
limiting access to States, must be taken as determining the
personal allocation of substantive rights and obligations
under the Court's decisions. (9o)

Other actions in domestic courts in which individuals or
corporations attempted to rely on inter-State adjudications
were not directed against the foreign creditors but against
the home-State which had successfully pursued the plaintiff's
claim on the international level. (91) The purpose of the
action was to compel the home-State to hand over the assets
obtained in the exercise of diplomatic protection to the
aggrieved individual. The courts were not prepared to uphold
claims of this kind. (92)

The United States Supreme Court has never reacted favorably
to such efforts to make it intervene in the executive's
distribution of these resources. Two awards rendered by a
United States-Mexican Commission in 1875 in favor of Benjamin
Weil and the La Abra Silver Mining Company led to disputes
that gave the Supreme Court occasion to elaborate its views
on this point. (93) After allegations that the awards had
been procured by fraudulent means, payments to the American
beneficiaries of the awards were stopped by the United States
authorities. In a series of lawsuits the Supreme Court repeatedly rejected their claims to the distributable amounts.
(94)

The factual evidence suggests that the Supreme Court was
correct in holding the international awards void for fraud.
What is, however, worrying about the cases is the Court's
strong inclination to use the participation of the United
States in the international proceedings as justification for
the executive's refusal to distribute the funds. There was
consequently no extrastatutory right of nationals to the
assets adjudicated by the arbitral tribunal. The Supreme
Court held that:

As between the United States and Mexico indeed as between the United States and American claimants, the

money received from Mexico under the award of the
Commission was in strict law the property of the United
States and no claimant could assert or enforce any
interest in it so long as the government legally withheld
it from distribution.(95)

Although the outcome of these cases was most probably justified, the reasoning offered by the United States Supreme
Court is unsatisfactory. The notion that a State pursuing
its national's claims in the international arena acts on its
own behalf, can easily lead to denying private claims to
such funds even where no irregularity of the international
proceedings is alleged.

In a relatively recent decision(96) the French Conseil d'Etat
has refused to accept the fiction, that the State exercising
diplomatic protection pursues its own rights, under circumstances which would have been detrimental to the protected
individual. In this case the Italian State had been awarded
a sum of money in an inter-State arbitration against France
on behalf of its national Canino. When France was in arrears
with its payments, Canino himself sued for interest. The
Conseil d'Etat rejected the usual arguments based on the
plaintiff's non-participation in the international litigation
and proceeded to pierce the veil of diplomatic protection.
It came to the conclusion that Canino must be treated as the
true beneficiary of the inter-State proceedings:

> ...le collège arbitral franco-italien,...a alloué au
> sieur Canino personellement l'indemnité mise à la
> charge du Gouvernement français; que cette indemnité
> n'a été payée au Gouvernement italien qu'en qualité de
> mandataire du sieur Canino; qu'ainsi ce dernier était,
> bien que le Gouvernement italien fût seul habilité à
> agir devant le collège arbitral, titulaire d'un droit
> propre à l'égard de l'Etat français;(97)

The view, prevalent in the older American cases and also in
the mostly older scholarly writings, of the States' "ownership" of the assets obtained in the exercise of diplomatic
protection is the result of a failure to distinguish between
substantive rights and the capacity to participate in proceedings for their enforcement. The fiction that the State
when protecting its national in the international arena is
only asserting its own rights may be necessary or, at any
rate, useful for the pursuit of claims through inter-State
procedures.(98) It does not make sense to carry this fiction
into the post-adjudicative phase to govern the subsequent
relationship between the original holder of the right, its
protecting State, and the judgment debtor.

The test of *res judicata* with its traditional requirements
of identity of claim, persons, and cause(99) will only afford
a poor touchstone for domestic courts when called upon to
give effect to international decisions involving material
rights of non-State entities.(1oo) The solution chosen by
the French Conseil d'Etat, which is not determined by formalistic criteria of participation in international proceedings,
is clearly preferable. This method, which has been suitably
termed the principle of mutable privity,(1o1) is also supported by the overwhelming majority of more recent scholarly
writings.(1o2)

The argument that individuals are unable to derive claims
from international proceedings in which they have not participated seems to have been used as a convenient strategy to
ward off claims against the forum State or a foreign State.
A look at cases raising similar legal problems, but involving
claims against other defendants, clearly shows that the
courts were not prepared to draw the full consequences from
this theory.

Consistently applied this theory would have removed the
international claim from the estate of the individual concerned, who would, thus, only have a "moral right" to it.
Consequently, internationally protected claims up to their
actual payment would not be inheritable, liable to attachment, or part of a bankrupt's estate. As a voluntary grant
by the government, any individual claim to proceeds from
diplomatic protection would, thus, not be subject to the
normal dispositions of private law.

A look at court practice reveals that individual claims
arising from international proceedings were in fact treated
as legal assets. Delarbre v. Chedeville(1o3) before the
French Cour de cassation arose from the murder of a French
national by a group of soldiers in Mexico. A French-Mexican
Commission adjudicated a sum of money as indemnity to his
heirs. One of the heirs died before the award was rendered.
The defendant, a creditor of the deceased heir, obtained an
attachment of part of the sum. The surviving heirs applied
to have the attachment set aside, claiming that the sum in
question did not represent a true debt or indemnity under
civil law of which all heirs would benefit from the time of
the murder, but a voluntary contribution (*libéralité*) by
the French government to which only the principles of international law should apply. The Cour de cassation rejected
these contentions, reiterating the position of the Commission
that the allocation of damages to the heirs was not a voluntary contribution but one in pursuance of strict law. In the

absence of any provision to the contrary, the law provided
that the indemnity was due to all heirs as of the day of the
murder; therefore, also to the heir who subsequently died.
The liquidated indemnity was consequently held to be subject
to attachment by the creditors of the deceased heir.

Cases involving competing private claims, each alleging to
be entitled to the assets adjudicated in international decisions, seem to have caused much less difficulty than the
more sensitive question of State control over the validity
of private claims. The available evidence suggests that
courts found no difficulty in examining the question who of
several claimants was entitled to a wealth allocation where
no problems of validity and revision of the international
awards arose.(1o4)

The suspicion that the behavior of domestic courts, when
dealing with the enforcement of international decisions of
this kind, is not so much governed by the formal aspect of
the individual's participation in the international proceedings as by an endeavor to preserve the affected State's
freedom of action is supported by further evidence. In cases
in which the claims of nationals against their governments
were not directed at enforcement but at revision of the
international decision, the courts also showed no readiness
to intervene.(1o5) Thus, in Z & F Assets Realization Corporation v. Hull(1o6) the plaintiffs held awards by the German-
American Mixed Claims Commission. They sued the Secretary of
State to abstain from certifying and the Secretary of the
Treasury to abstain from paying later awards that would de-
plete the available funds to their detriment. The claim was
mainly based on the allegation that, since the German Commissioner had withdrawn from the Commission, the later awards
were null and void. The United States Supreme Court, upholding the decision of the courts below,(1o7) pointed out that
the suit was the subject-matter of an international controversy and, therefore, a political matter. The proceedings
before the Commission had been between governments and the
plaintiffs had not been directly party to them. Congress,
therefore, had complete power to decide what payments to
make out of the funds. A certification by the Secretary of
State under the Settlement of War Claims Act,1928 was not a
mere authentication of the awards. Congress had vested him
with the authority to pass upon the regularity and validity
of the awards. His certificate must, therefore, be deemed
conclusive.

Again little can be said against the outcome of the decision.
But it is deplorable that the courts found it necessary to
substantiate their refusal to review the awards not so much

by reference to their intrinsic finality as by asserting
executive discretion. The Supreme Court's deference to the
Mixed Claims Commission's decision must be considered more
than off-set by its confirmation of the executive's power to
pass upon the "regularity and validity" of the awards.

Finally, there is evidence of interference and control by
the State of the beneficiaries' nationality even in cases in
which individuals and coroporations had directly participated
in international arbitrations. In Republic of Colombia v.
Cauca Co.(1o8) the United States federal courts intervened
to review an award in favor of a United States citizen and
against Colombia just like appellate courts. The only feasible justification for this revision of the international
award was the nationality of its beneficiary.

An attempt by the State to exercise control over international
claims of its nationals can be made even before an international award has been rendered. Yougoslavie v. Stê. européenne
d'études et d'entreprises concerned a dispute between the
French Company and Yugoslavia that arose from an agreement
between the two parties. The French State had intervened and
exercised diplomatic protection in favor of the Company. The
Company cooperated in the negotiations which led to an
agreement between the two governments in 195o. After receiving the sums due to it under the intergovernmental agreement, the Company invoked an arbitration clause in the
original contract alleging that its claims were not fully
covered by the settlement negotiated between the two governments. The Yugoslav government refused to cooperate in the
arbitration, and an award was rendered in the Company's
favor. The Company obtained an *exequatur* for the award and
Yugoslavia appealed. The court of first instance(1o9) and the
Paris court of appeal(11o) held that the 195o agreement had
settled the claims between the parties. The Company had
accepted the terms of the intergovernmental settlement,
therefore it had to be regarded as having the authority of
res judicata against it. The courts therefore revoked the
exequatur. The Cour de cassation(111) overturned this decision. It found that a State exercising diplomatic protection only acted in the pursuit of its own rights. Consequently the inter-State settlement, waiving part of the claim,
did not deprive the protected national of his right to pursue other means to obtain full redress.

In an attempt to enforce this award in the Netherlands
courts, the Supreme Court found in favor of the Company on
the point of Yugoslavia's immunity.(112) The Court of Appeal
of The Hague to which the case was referred back, however,

relied on the agreement between France and Yugoslavia and dismissed the action on the ground of "ordre public".(113)

It seems doubtful whether the Company, after availing itself successfully of diplomatic protection, should have been permitted to institute the arbitral proceedings.(114) It is true that the French cour de cassation's strict separation of the inter-State settlement and the company's claim worked to the benefit of the protected private rights. On the other hand, allowing private claimants a "second bite" after successful diplomatic protection is not likely to be accepted as a general policy by State debtors in situations of this kind. Both the protecting and the debtor State will find means to obtain unequivocal waivers by protected individuals and corporations to forestall any attempts to obtain supplementary compensation in addition to the sums agreed in the inter-State arrangements.

This survey indicates that any difficulties for individuals and corporations relying on international judgments and awards concerning wealth transactions lie not so much in the apparent problem of their lack of participation in inter-State proceedings. While this argument may have some significance, a frequent motive of domestic courts appears to be the endeavor to preserve maximum freedom of action for the private claimant's home State. This means a submission of individual claims to the control and disposition of the home State for the purpose of: (a) distributing the proceeds of successful inter-State proceedings; (b) opposing unfavorable international decisions; and even (c) sometimes reviewing and revising international decisions which directly and explicitly favor the individual or corporation.

Many of these interferences with the claims of nationals arising from international decisions may be justified by special circumstances. But in view of the steadily growing participation of non-State actors in international transactions, it appears necessary, as a general policy, to call for an increased protection of individual claims arising from international decisions independently of the home State's discretion and control. The basic policy preference for the effectiveness of international decisions should also be reflected in procedures which make them controlling vis-à-vis private beneficiaries.

2. Claims to Values Other Than Wealth

Attempts to base individual claims on international decisions which do not offer specific wealth allocations raise different problems. In cases of this type the plaintiff does not attempt to rely on an individual international value allocation in his favor, but merely argues that the international decision has generally created enforceable rights also for non-State parties. The domestic court is confronted with the question whether the international decision has in fact created rights which can be pursued by individuals.

This question is relatively uncontroversial in cases in which the invocation of the international decision is not directed at the enforcement of a specific duty to act. References made by individuals to international decisions for the purpose of elucidating preliminary points pending before the court, or to international "precedents" or to official interpretations by international organs, are not regarded as problematic by domestic courts. In these situations the invocation of the international decision by the individual or corporation is not seen as an attempt to claim a subjective right but as an argument on a question of law.

The situation becomes more difficult where an attempt is made to enforce an international decision not directed at any particular participants but generally prescribing or prohibiting a certain line of conduct. The general nature of the international decision often gives no clear indication of its addressees. It may be directed at the governments of all member States or even all States, but may also be addressed at anybody dealing with its subject-matter. The absence of a formal participation of individuals and corporations in procedures leading to the international decision offers no answer to the question of whether the decision establishes individual rights and duties.

More specifically then, what are the consequences for individuals and corporations of enforcement action ordered by the United Nations Security Council or of other international resolutions condemning certain practices in international trade? Can individuals and corporations demand compliance with these international decisions before domestic courts, or, conversely, can they be held responsible for non-compliance?

This question arose directly in Diggs v. Shultz(115) where private plaintiffs tried to force the United States Secretary of Treasury to comply with the boycott resolutions against Rhodesia. Their interest in compliance with the boycott consisted in a number of personal grievances against the regime in Southern Rhodesia. Nevertheless, the Court of Appeals for the District of Columbia Circuit confirmed their

standing:
> United Nations Security Council Resolution 232 was -
> and is - an attempt by means of concerted international
> pressure to turn the Rhodesian Government away from the
> course of action which has resulted in the adverse cir-
> cumstances experienced by appellants. They are unquesti-
> onably within the reach of its purposes and among its
> intended beneficiaries.
> ...to persons situated as are appellants, United Nations
> action constitutes the only hope; and they are perso-
> nally aggrieved and injured by the dereliction of any
> member state which weakens the capacity of the world
> organization to make its policies meaningful.(116)

In Diggs v.Richardson,(117) plaintiffs sought to enjoin the
U.S.government from continuing to deal with South Africa
concerning the importation of seal furs from Namibia. Their
reliance on Security Council Resolution 3o1 was brushed
aside in a tersely worded judgment of the same court which
had previously admitted individual standing in Diggs v.
Shultz:
> ...The U.N. resolution underlying that obligation does
> not confer rights on the citizens of the United States
> that are enforceable in court in the absence of imple-
> menting legislation.(118)

In a German case the Bundesgerichtshof(119) substantiated
the application of recommending decisions of the General
Conference of UNESCO to private transactions by applying the
concept of *ordre public*. (See also chapter XI.B.2.above) The
contract which violated the international decisions was
held unenforceable since it was contrary to the international *ordre public*.

These cases, offer no clear indication that domestic courts
will grant a general *ius standi* to individuals for actions
directed at the implementation of international decisions,
(12o) or will generally hold individuals and corporations
responsible for their violation. The far-reaching verbal
concessions made by the Court of Appeals in Diggs v.Shultz
towards a right of action for individuals arising from
United Nations Security Council decisions imposing sanctions
are largely neutralized by the fact that the Court was able
to dismiss the action for other reasons. Moreover the Court
has since abandoned this doctrine. The use of the concept of
ordre public, as demonstrated in the German case, in order
to apply important decisions of international institutions
to private transactions is, no doubt, a promising technique

to make them controlling. However, this technique is only feasible for certain international decisions and only in certain decision situations before domestic courts. It is by no means clear that courts will generally apply international decisions of the kind contemplated here to individuals and corporations.

In the application of regulations emanating from international institutions similar problems must be expected as with treaties. The direct applicability of treaties to individuals is the subject-matter of intensive scholarly attention and court practice, usually under the term of "self-executing". (121) There is as yet no conclusive court practice concerning the existence or not of directly enforceable individual claims arising from international regulations. This is primarily due to the fact that there are usually detailed implementing measures in domestic law for these regulations. The few cases in which courts dealt with the applicability of these regulations center on the question of their "internal validity" and specificity, but not on whether they established individual rights. (See chapter VII.C.3. above).

It is significant that an invocation by individuals of general recommendations, especially the Universal Declaration of Human Rights, does not seem to have met with any difficulties.(122) This may be due partly to the fact that usually the recommendations were not the main basis of the individual claims but were only utilized as ancillary arguments, often as an aid for the interpretation of domestic prescriptions protecting basic rights. Moreover, it would have been particularly unconvincing to base a denial of individual rights arising from the Universal Declaration on its allegedly purely inter-State character.

In looking for solutions to the question, largely unanswered by court practice, to what extent individual claims and obligations can arise from international decisions, it seems advisable not to proceed from doctrinaire and formalistic criteria but to adopt a pragmatic and policy-oriented approach. In particular, no useful conclusions concerning the possible addressees of international decisions can be derived from such notions as the traditional subjects of international law or the non-admission of individuals to the international arena. The decisive question in a particular case is the authority of the international decision, the policies pursued by it, and its intended beneficiaries or obligors. Where these questions have been clarified, it would not make sense to postulate for dogmatic or formal reasons that decisions of international institutions concern

only the legislative or executive branches of States, and
that their invocation by or against individuals or corporations is inadmissible.

A glance at the law of the European Communities shows revea-
ling parallels with respect to regulations, directives and
decisions: EEC regulations are generally applicable and
directly affect also individuals and corporations in each
Member State. Directives, on the other hand, are only binding as to the results to be achieved upon Member States,
leaving to national authorities the choice of form and
methods to make them applicable to individuals and corporations. Decisions are binding upon those to whom they are
directed, Member State, or individual, or corporation. (Article 189 EEC). This classification, thus, follows the
traditional distinction between self-executing and non-self-
executing presciptions: The effects of the international
decisions on individuals and corporations are intended to
depend on their form.

In actual practice this rigid formal distinction between
Community decisions which are directly applicable to every-
body and those which are only directed at Member States(123)
has not always proved feasible. The dividing line between
regulations, on one hand, and directives and decisions
directed at States, on the other, has become blurred. The
Court of Justice of the European Communities has held in a
number of cases that also directives and decisions directed
at States can have direct effects for individuals and can be
invoked by them before the courts.(124) The decisive criterion is "not only the form of the measure in issue but also
its substance and its function in the system of the Treaty".
(125) Domestic courts have followed this practice in a
number of cases: A direct applicability for individuals of
directives and decisions aimed at States was specifically
recognized.(126)

(1)   1 Dec.1963, 9 ILM 1118(197o), cf. above p.139; cf. also
      the remarks of the Supreme Court of Czechoslovakia in
      Enforcement of International Awards (Czechoslovakia)
      Case, 26 Apr.1928, 4 AD 174,176(1927-28). The Court
      flatly denied the possibility of an enforcement of
      international arbitral awards against the forum State
      with the help of domestic courts. However, the instant
      case concerned an award against a foreign State. The
      Court's remarks were therefore clearly *obiter*.

(2)   Cf. also Batiffol, Arbitration Clauses between French
      Government Owned Enterprises and Foreign Private Par-
      ties, 7 Columbia Journal of Transnational Law 32(1968).

(3)   Cour d'appel de Paris, 1o Apr.1957, 85 Clunet 1oo3(1958),
      24 ILR 2o5(1957).

(4)   For a comparative analysis on the question of the
      capacity of States to enter into private law arbitra-
      tions see Carabiber, L'immunité de juridiction, p.28seq.

(5)   85 Clunet 1oo8(1958).

(6)   This reasoning was adopted a few years later also by
      the Cour de cassation: In Office Nationale Interpro-
      fessionel de Céréales c/ Capitaine du S/S San Carlo,
      14 Apr.1964, 92 Clunet 646(1965) the French public
      owned corporation tried to circumvent the arbitral
      proceedings by instituting proceedings before the
      French courts.

(7)   Cf. Goldman in 92 Clunet 647(1965).

(8)   Tribunal de grande instance de la Seine, 25 June 1959,
      87 Clunet 489(196o); Cour d'appel de Paris, 21 Feb.1961,
      9o Clunet 156(1963), 41 ILR 452; Cour de cassation, 2
      May 1966, 93 Clunet 648(1966), 48 ILR 329.

(9)   29 Nov.1974, 1o2 Clunet 294(1975).

(1o) Maghanbhai Ishwarbhai Patel and Others v. Union of India,
      Supreme Court of India, 1969, 9 IJIL 234(1969). Cf.
      above p. 239.

(11) Diggs v. Shultz, Court of Appeals D.C., 31 Oct.1972,
      47o F.2d 461. Cf. above p. 2o1 and p.24o; Diggs v. Dent,
      Dist.Ct.D.C., 13 May 1975, 14 ILM 797(1975), affirmed
      sub nom. Diggs v.Richardson, Court of Appeals D.C., 17

Dec.1976, 555 F.2d 848; Kangai v.Vance, Court of Appeals
D.C., 6 Oct.1978, 73 AJIL 297(1979).

(12) Bradley v. The Commonwealth of Australia and the Postmaster-General, High Court, 1o Sept.1973, Australian
Law Reports. I 241(1973), 52 ILR 1(1979), Cf. above p.
2o2.

(13) Generally on this question see esp. Ginther, Die völkerrechtliche Verantwortlichkeit internationaler Organisationen gegenüber Drittstaaten (1969).

(14) Sieur Weiss, 2o Feb.1953, 81 Clunet 745(1954).

(15) Kare-Merat et Kabozo c. Etat belge, min. de la Justice
et délégué du Haut Commissariat pour les réfugiés, 25
Sept 197o, 8 RBDI 675,687(1972).

(16) Curran v. City of New York et al., Supr.Ct.of N.Y.
Queens County, 31 Dec.1947, 42 AJIL 5o8(1948).

(17) X. v. Y. and the Greek State, 1934, 7 AD 387(1933-34).

(18) Cf. Ginther, Die völkerrechtliche Verantwortlichkeit,
p.163seq.

(19) Manderlier v. UN & Belgium, Tribunal civil Brussels,
11 May 1966, 45 ILR 446, 5 RBDI 374(1969); confirmed by
the Cour d'appel Brussels, 15 Sept.1969, 98 Clunet
843(1971), 7 RBDI 743(1971).

(2o) 11 Feb.1969, /197o/ A.C.179, 44 ILR 359, 43 BYIL 217
(1968-69).

(21) See especially Lord Morris of Borth-y-Gest /197o/ A.C.
221seq., and Lord Pearce on p.223. Cf. also Bridge, The
Legal Status of British Troops forming Part of the
United Nations Force in Cyprus, 34 Modern Law Review
121(1971).

(22) For further references to the vast literature on this
topic see: Sucharitkul, State Immunities and Trading
Activities in International Law (1959); Sweeney, The
International Law of Sovereign Immunity (1963); Panebianco, Giurisdizione interna e immunità degli stati
stranieri (1967); Schaumann und Habscheid, Die Immunität ausländischer Staaten nach Völkerrecht und deutschem Zivilprozeßrecht, 8 Berichte der Deutschen Gesellschaft für Völkerrecht (1968); Sucharitkul, Immunities

of Foreign States Before National Authorities, 149 RC 87(1976,I). See also the recent United States Foreign Sovereign Immunities Act of 1976. For the recent changes in English law see note 27 below.

(23) Cf. United States decisions dealing mostly with the institution of arbitral proceedings: <u>Victory Transport Inc. v. Comisaria General de Abastecimientos y Transportes</u>, Court of Appeals 2d Cir., 9 Sept.1964, 336 F.2d 354, cert.den. 381 U.S.934; <u>Petrol Shipping Co.</u>, Court of Appeals 2nd Cir., 21 Apr.1966, 36o F.2d lo3, cert. den. 385 U.S.931; <u>Ipitrade International, S.A. v.Nigeria</u>, U.S.Dist.Ct.D.C., 25 Sept.1978, 17 ILM 1395(1978). The French Cour de cassation rejects this doctrine of a waiver of immunity through arbitral agreement: <u>Faure et Association des Porteurs Français de Scripts Lombards c/ Etat italien et Comité des Obligataires de la Compagnie des Chemins de Fer Danube-Save-Adriatique</u>, 5 Oct. 1965. 45 ILR 83(1972); <u>Société Transshipping v. Federation of Pakistan</u>, 2 March 1966, 47 ILR 15o.

(24) Carabiber, L'immunité de juridiction, p.38seq.; Spofford, Third party judgment, p.215seq.

(25) /1924/ A.C. 797, 1o Apr.1924.

(26) Cf. also Reisman, Nullity and Revision, p.813.

(27) English practice has recently abandoned the principle of absolute immunity. See especially <u>Trendtex Trading Corporation v. Central Bank of Nigeria</u>, Court of Appeal, 13 Jan.1977, /1977/ W.L.R. 356. The British State Immunity Act 1978 in Section 9 specifically denies immunity in proceedings which relate to arbitration.

(28) <u>Enforcement of International Awards (Czechoslovakia) Case</u>, 26 Apr.1928, 4 AD 174 (1927-28).

(29) The fact that the property in question was the diplomatic legation of a foreign country caused some dismay: cf. Deak in 23 AJIL 582(1929) and Bosco in 8 Rivista DI 48(1929). The Supreme Court of Czechoslovakia corrected its judgment in a subsequent decision: 4 AD 37o(1927-28).

(3o) Tribunal de Bruxelles, 3o Apr.1951, 79 Clunet 244(1952).

(31) 79 Clunet 258(1952).

(32) 6 July 197o, 98 Clunet 131(1971). This judgment was
confirmed by the Cour d'appel de Paris, 29 Jan 1975,
1o3 Clunet 136(1976) whose decision was in turn set
aside by the Cour de cassation, 14 June 1977, 1o4
Clunet 864(1977). Both appellate decisions did not
address the question of immunity.

(33) An attempt to enforce this award in Uruguay failed due
to Yugoslavia's immunity: Société européenne d'êtudes
et d'entreprises c. Yougoslavie, Corte suprema, undated,
93 Clunet 175(1966).

(34) See above p.139.

(35) N.V.Cabolent v. National Iranian Oil Co., Dist.Court
The Hague, 15 Apr.1965, 5 ILM 477(1966), Court of
Appeal The Hague, 28 Nov.1968, 9 ILM 152(197o). The
Sapphire Co. had transferred its claim arising from the
arbitration to its Netherlands subsidiary N.V.Cabolent.

(36) Société Européenne d'Etudes et d'Entreprises v. Yugoslavia, Rotterdam Dist.Ct., 9 Nov.1971, 3 NYIL 294(1972),
Court of Appeal The Hague, 8 Sept.1972, 4 NYIL 39o
(1973), Supreme Court, 26 Oct.1973, 5 NYIL 29o(1974),
14 ILM 71(1975).

(37) 5 ILM 478(1966). Cf. the criticism directed at this
decision by Reisman, Nullity and Revision, p.813seq.

(38) 9 ILM 152(197o).

(39) Court of Appeal, 4 NYIL 39o(1973). However, the Court
found that the arbitral award was void. The Supreme
Court, 5 NYIL 29o(1974) found in favor of the company
on all counts and referred the case back to the Court
of Appeal. The Court of Appeal in a subsequent decision
of 25 Oct.1974, 6 NYIL 374(1975) refused the enforcement of the award since the claim had been settled in a
treaty between France and Yugoslavia.

(4o) 9 ILM 161(197o).

(41) 5 NYIL 294(1974).

(42) Seidl-Hohenveldern, Commercial Arbitration and State
Immunity, in International Trade Arbitration (Domke,
Ed. 1958), p.87; Domke, International Aspects of Com-
mercial Arbitration in the Americas, 8 Academia Inter-
americana de Derecho Comparado e Internacional, Cursos
Monograficos 481,483(196o).

(43) Concerning the ICJ see Jenks, The Prospects, p.71oseq., Schachter, The Enforcement, p.13seq. But see the reply by the French Minister of Justice in 1931 to a question by a Senator whether measures to enforce the judgment of the PCIJ in the Brazilian Loans case were feasible:

> En raison des immunités diplomatiques /sic!/, aucune mesure d'exécution ne peut être employée contre un gouvernement étranger sur le territoire français. Il ne saurait donc appartenir aux tribunaux français de ramener à exécution l'arrêt rendu le 12 juillet 1929 par la Cour Permanente de Justice Internationale. Ces tribunaux ne peuvent être saisis à cet effet, ni par les particuliers, ni par l'Etat, et il en résulte qu'il n'y a pas lieu d'examiner si l'arrêt de la Cour de la Haye a été rendu au profit des porteurs ou au profit du Gouvernement français.

Kiss, Vol.5 No.147.

(44) See also Schachter, The Enforcement, p.13seq.; Jenks, The Prospects, p.71oseq.,72o; Reisman, Nullity and Revision, p.82oseq.

(45) The preparatory works to this Convention contain indications that States were meant to be excluded from its application (cf. Reisman, Nullity and Revision, p.8o5). Nevertheless, its text permits extension of its provisions also to States.

(46) 4 ILM 532(1965).

(47) Cf. Coll, United States Enforcement of Arbitral Awards Against Sovereign States: Implications of the ICSID Convention, 17 HarvILJ 4o1 (1967).

(48) ETS No.74. Cf. also the Explanatory Reports to the Convention (1972) p.91.

(49) Adopted by the United Nations Council for Namibia on 27 Sept.1974, approved by the General Assembly on 13 Dec.1974. Promulgated as Namibia Gazette No.1.

(5o) UN v. B., Tribunal Civil Brussels, 27 March 1952, 19 ILR 49o(1952); Pan American Union v. American Security and Trust Company, U.S.Dist.Ct.D.C., 6 May 1952, 18 ILR 441(1951); UN v. Canada Asiatic Lines Ltd., Superior Court of Montreal, 2 Dec.1952, 26 ILR 622(1958-II).

(51) UNRRA v. Daan, District Court Utrecht, 23 Feb.1949, 16
     AD 337(1949), 82 Clunet 885(1955); IRO v. Republic S.S.
     Corp., US Ct.of Appeal, 4th Cir., 11 May 1951, 189 F.2d
     858, 46 AJIL 146(1952).

(52) Balfour, Guthrie & Co.Ltd. v. U.S., US Dist.Ct.N.D.Cal.,
     5 May 195o, 9o F.Supp. 831, 17 ILR 323(195o).

(53) International Bank for Reconstruction and Development
     and International Monetary Fund v. All America Cables
     and Radio Inc. et al., Federal Communications Commis-
     sion, 23 March 1953, 22 ILR 7o5.

(54) The Times, 3o Jan.1975, p.6.

(55) Cf. e.g. Art.1o5 UN Charter, Art.4o of the Statute of
     the Council of Europe, Art.139 of the OAS Charter.

(56) See e.g. the Convention on the Privileges and Immuni-
     ties of the United Nations, 1 UNTS 16; Convention on
     the Privileges and Immunitities of the Specialized
     Agencies, 33 UNTS 261; General Agreement on Privileges
     and Immunities of the Council of Europe, ETS No.2
     including Supplementary Agreement and four Protocols.

(57) Cf. the survey by Cahier, Etude des accords de siège,
     p.431.

(58) Cf. e.g. the United States International Organizations
     Immunities Act of 1945, 4o AJIL Off.Doc. 85(1946); and
     the German Verordnung über die Gewährung von Vorrechten
     und Befreiungen an die Vereinten Nationen BGBl.197o II,
     p.669.

(59) See Nguyen Quoc Dinh, Les privilèges et immunités;
     Cahier, Etude des accords de siège; Jenks, Internatio-
     nal Immunities (1961); Seyersted, Jurisdiction over
     Organs; Merkatz, Les privilèges et immunités; Beitzke,
     Zivilrechtsfähigkeit; Schlüter, Die innerstaatliche
     Rechtsstellung, p.167,seq., and the references cited by
     these authors.

(6o) Seyersted, Settlement of internal disputes, p.21; cf.
     also the references by Schlüter, Die innerstaatliche
     Rechtsstellung, p.174,seq., who himself doubts such a
     general rule. Also Beitzke, Zivilrechtsfähigkeit,
     p.114.

(61) Some writers are of the opinion that there is a general trend in favor of more limited and functional immunities of international organizations: Merkatz, Les privilèges et immunités, p.148; Schlüter, Die innerstaatliche Rechtsstellung, p.17o.

(62) See also the almost indentical Section 3, Article XI of the Charter of the Inter-American Development Bank.

(63) Art.4o/3 ECSC, Art.183 EEC, Art.155 EAC.

(64) Zemanek, Das Vertragsrecht der internationalen Organisationen, p.138seq.; Jenks, International Immunities, p.41seq.; Seyersted, Settlement of internal disputes; ibid., Jurisdiction over Organs, p.5o8.

(65) See especially Akehurst, The Law governing Employment, p.11seq.

(66) Harpignies, Settlement of disputes of a private law character.

(67) Manderlier v. UN & Belgium, Tribunal civil Brussels, 11 May 1966, 45 ILR 446.

(68) Godman v. Winterton, 13 March 194o, 11 AD 2o5(1919-1942).

(69) Lutcher S.A. Celulose e Papel Candoi v. Inter-American Development Bank, US Ct.App.D.C., 13 July 1967, 382 F.2d 445, 42 ILR 138.

(7o) Schaffner v. IRO, US Ct.App. in occupied Germany, 3 Aug.1951, 18 ILR 444(1951); see however Westchester County v. Ranollo, City Court of New Rochelle, N.Y., 8 Nov.1946, 41 AJIL 69o(1947).

(71) Curran v. City of New York et al., Supr.Ct.of N.Y. Queens County, 31 Dec.1947, 42 AJIL 5o8(1948); Procureur Général of the Court of Cassation v. Syndicate of Co-Owners of the Alfred Dehodencq Property Company, Cour de cassation (Fr.), 6 July 1954, 21 ILR 279(1954), 83 Clunet 136(1956).

(72) See, however, a number of Arab court decisions against UNRWA: 13 Whiteman 53seq, and A.P.F. Eckhardt v.Eurocontrol, Local Court of Sittard (Netherlands) 25 June 1976, 9 NYIL 276(1978).

(73) Bergaveche v. UN Information Centre, Labor court,
Argentina, 19 March 1958, 26 ILR 62o(1958-II); Dame
Klarsfeld c/ Office franco-allemand pour la jeunesse,
Cour d'appel de Paris, 18 June 1968, 15 AFDI 865(1969);
Supreme Court of Chile, 8 Nov.1969, UNJYB 237(1969);
Jakesch v. IAEA, Labor court, Vienna, 8 July 1971,
UNJYB 2o8(1972). In Schuster v. UN Information Centre,
Supreme Court of Argentina, 2o Dec.1951, cited from
Seyersted, Jurisdiction over Organs, p.5o9,512seq., the
Court came to the conclusion that the Organization had
waived its immunity.

(74) Chemidlin v. International Bureau of Weights and Measures, Tribunal civil de Versailles, 27 July 1945, 12
AD 281(1943-45); Díaz Díaz v. UN Economic Commission
for Latin America, Supreme Court of Mexico, 28 Apr.1954,
cited from Seyersted, Jurisdiction over Organs, p.5o9;
J.C. Meira Coelho c/ Asociacion latinoamericana de libre
comercio, Cour suprême Uruguay, 29 Dec.1965, 94 Clunet
972(1967).

(75) Profili v. International Institute of Agriculture,
Corte di cassazione, 26 Feb.1931, 23 Rivista DI 386
(1931), 5 AD 413(1929-3o).

(76) Viecelli v. IRO, Tribunale Trieste, 2o June 1951, 36
Rivista DI 47o(1953), 49 AJIL 1o2(1955).

(77) Marrê c/ UNIDROIT, Tribunale Roma, 12 June 1965, 5o
Rivista DI 149(1967), 95 Clunet 386(1968).

(78) Maida v. Administration for International Assistance,
27 May 1955, 39 Rivista DI 546(1956), 23 ILR 51o(1956).

(79) The application of this dinstinction to international
organizations is generally rejected in scholarly writings: Zemanek, Das Vertragsrecht der internationalen
Organisationen, p.142; Jenks, International Immunities,
p.45,151; Beitzke, Zivilrechtsfähigkeit, p.113seq.;
Seyersted, Settlement of internal disputes, p.21.

(8o) Mazzanti c. HAFSE e Ministero Difesa, Tribunale Firenze,
2 Jan.1954, 38 Rivista DI 353(1955), 22 ILR 758(1955);
Conte c. HAFSE, Tribunale Napoli, 28 Sept.1967, 51
Rivista DI 714(1968); C. v. ICEM, Corte di cassazione,
7 June 1973, UNJYB 197(1973).

(81) CIME v.Chiti, Corte di cassazione, 7 Nov 1973, 2
Italian YBIL 348(1976); Luggeri v.CIME, Corte di cassazione, 11 Nov 1974, 2 Italian YBIL 347(1976); CIME v.Di
Banella Schirone, Corte di cassazione, 8 April 1975, 2
Italian YBIL 351(1976); NATO v.Capocci Belmonte, Corte
di cassazione, 5 June 1976, 59 Rivista DI 824(1976), 3
Italian YBIL 328(1977). For further samples of the
prolific recent Italian court practice in this field
see 3 Italian YBIL 31o-347(1977).

(82) Branno c. Ministero Difesa, Corte di cassazione, 14
June 1954, 38 Rivista DI 352(1955), 22 ILR 756(1955).

(83) Porru v. FAO, Tribunale Roma, 25 Jan.1969, UNJYB 238
(1969).

(84) Ago, Die internationale Organisation, p.2o; Seyersted,
Settlement of internal disputes, p.8o; Waelbroek,
Nature juridique, p.5o3; Schlüter, Die innerstaatliche
Rechtsstellung, p.176seq.

(85) Vattel, Le droit des Gens (1758), liv.II, Chap.6,
para.71; Anzilotti, La responsabilité internationale
des états, 13 RGDIP 5,8(19o6); Clark, Legal Aspects
Regarding Ownership and Distribution of Awards, 7 AJIL
382,389(1913); Lammasch, Die Rechtskraft der internationalen Schiedssprüche, p.11,115; Heise, Internationale
Rechtspflege, p.68; cf. also the judgment of the Swiss
Bundesgericht of 17 June 1926 in 3 AD 244(1925-26).

(86) Witenberg, L'Organisation judiciaire, la procédure et
la sentence internationales, p.149seq.(1937).

(87) Borchard, The Diplomatic Protection of Citizens Abroad,
p.356seq.(1915); see, however, the same writer in The
Access of Individuals to International Courts, 24 AJIL
359,361(193o); Rundstein, La justice internationale et
la protection des intérêts privés, 1o RDILC 431,438
(1929); Wolff, Die internationalen Gerichte und die
privaten Interessen, p.982.

(88) Tribunal de Bruxelles, 3o Apr.1951, 18 ILR 3(1951);
Sirey 1953 I. IV,p.1.

(89) Sirey, 1953 I. IV.p.6.

(9o) Cf. also the criticism by Reisman, Nullity and Revision,
p.818.

(91) For cases in which the government had received payments
     under lump-sum agreements see Lillich, International
     Claims: Their Adjudication by National Commissions,
     p.23seq.(1962); Coerper, The Foreign Claims Settlement
     Commission and Judicial Review, 5o AJIL 868(1956).

(92) Cf. also the old English Baron de Bode's case, (1844-
     46) 8 Q.B. 2o8, 6 BILC 397.

(93) For more detailed treatment see Clark, Legal Aspects
     Regarding Ownership and Distribution of Awards, 7 AJIL
     382,389(1913).

(94) Frelinghuysen v. Key, 7 Jan.1884, 11o U.S. 63; Boynton
     v. Blain, 23 March 1891, 139 U.S. 3o6; La Abra Silver
     Mining Co. v. U.S., 11 Dec.1899, 175 U.S. 423. Cf. also
     the following cases in which claims were rejected under
     similar circumstances: Great Western Insurance Co v. U.S.,
     1o Nov.1884, 112 U.S. 193; Alling v. U.S., 4 May 1885,
     114 U.S. 562; but see U.S. v. Weld, 16 Apr.1888, 127
     U.S. 51. In Angarica v. Bayard, 3o Apr.1888, 127 U.S.
     251, a claim for interest based on a delay in the
     disbursement of money, which had been awarded in inter-
     national proceedings, was rejected.

(95) La Abra Silver Mining Co. v. U.S., 175 U.S. 458.

(96) Ministre de l'Economie et des Finances c/ Sieur Canino,
     29 Nov.1974, 1o2 Clunet 294(1975). But see the older
     decision Re Reitlinger, 1o March 1933, 7 AD 489(1933-
     34), where a private claim based on an international
     award failed since the award was classified as "acte de
     gouvernement".

(97) 1o2 Clunet 295(1975).

(98) Some writers have carried this fiction so far to declare
     that even in cases in which an individual has access to
     an international forum, the individual could only be
     regarded as acting in the name of his home State: Strupp,
     Theorie und Praxis des Völkerrechts, p.8(1925); Schmid
     u. Schmitz, Der Paragraph 4 der Anlage zu Sektion IV
     des Teils X des Versailler Vertrags, 1 ZaöRV Teil 1,
     p.251,285(1929); Kaufmann, Règles générales du droit de
     la paix, 54 RC 3o9,424(1935, IV).

(99) Cf. Judge Anzilotti's dissenting opinion to Judgment
     No.11 of the PCIJ, Ser.A, No.13, p.23.

(1oo) Limburg, L'Autorité de chose jugée, p.563seq.; Teneki-
des, Rapports de droit interne et de droit international en matière de chose jugée, 15 RDILC 683,698(1934);
Rosenne, The Law and Practice of the International
Court, p.13o,seq.

(1o1) Reisman, Nullity and Revision, pp. 9o, 134.

(1o2) Rosenne, Reflections on the Position of the Individual
in Inter-State Litigation in the International Court of
Justice, in International Arbitration Liber Amicorum
for Martin Domke, p.24o; H.Lauterpacht, International
Law and Human Rights, p.48(195o); Ralston, The Law and
Procedure of International Tribunals, p.138(1926); C.
de Visscher, Notes sur la responsabilité internationale
des états, 8 RDILC 245,259seq.(1927); to the same
effect see in (1932) Annuaire: C. de Visscher 481,
Politis 487, Higgins 495 and Dumas 496; Dunn, The
Protection of Nationals, p.174(1932); Feller, The
Mexican Claims Commission 1923-1934, p.83seq.(1935);
Eagleton, International Organisation and the Law of
Responsibility, 76 RC 319,369seq.(195o); Sinclair,
Nationality of Claims, 27 BYIL 125,126seq.(195o);
Grassi, Die Rechtsstellung des Individuums im Völker-
recht, p.336seq.,351(1955); Katzarov, Hat der Bürger
ein Recht auf diplomatischen Schutz?, 8 ÖZöR 434,444
seq.(1957/58); Doehring, Die Pflicht des Staates zur
Gewährung diplomatischen Schutzes p.19(1959); Blaser,
La nationalité et la protection juridique internationale de l'individu p.27(1962); Hallier, Völkerrechtliche Schiedsinstanzen, p.131seq.; Jenks, The Prospects,
p.72o; Reisman, Nullity and Revision, p.89seq.,134seq.;
Kiss, La condition des étrangers en droit international
et les droits de l'homme, in Miscellanea W.J.Ganshof
van der Meersch, vol.I, p.499,5ooseq.(1972); International judicial practice does not offer any clear
guidance on this question. See esp.: PCIJ, Ser.A.,
No.17, p.28, but see also the remarks of Judge Nyholm
on p.96; Ser.A/B, No.76, p.16; Ser.A, No.2o/21, p.16
seq.; ICJ Reports 1955, p.24, ICJ Reports 197o, p.44;
6 RIAA 2o8; Moore, International Arbitrations Digest
Vol.III, p.24oo; 2 RIAA 634; 4 RIAA 32 and 37; 7 RIAA
26 and 153.

(1o3) 16 Aug.187o, Dalloz périodique 1871. I. 279; for US
cases to the same effect see: Clark v. Clark, 1854, 58
U.S. 315; Judson v. Corcoran, 8 March 1855, 58 U.S.
612; Phelps v. McDonald, 5 May 1879, 99 U.S. 298;
Williams v. Heard, 25 May 1891, 14o U.S. 259.

(1o4) Hill v. Reardon, Court of Chancery (Engl.), 1826/27, 6
BILC 367,376; but see Burnand v. Rodocanachi in the
Common Pleas Division, 1 June 188o, 1 BILC 259; US
Supreme Court: Comegys et al. v. Vasse, 1828, 26 U.S.
193; Frevall v. Bache, 184o, 39 U.S. 95; Doerschuck v.
Mellon, US Ct.App.D.C., 21 Dec.1931, 55 F.2d 741;
American-Mexican Claims Bureau Inc. v. Morgenthau, US
Dist.Ct.D.C., 6 Jan.1939, 26 F.Supp.9o4, 9 AD 336(1938-
4o); Luckhardt v. Mooradian, Calif.Dist.Ct.App., 21
June 1949, 16 AD 339(1949); German Reichsgericht 26
Sept.193o, 6o JW 15o(1931), 5 AD 184(1929-3o); D.O. v.
Greek State, Civil Court of Athens, 14 Nov.193o, 58
Clunet 124o(1931); see also the decisions of the Ger-
man-US Mixed Claims Commission, 1 Nov.1923, 7 RIAA
23,27seq.

(1o5) See already the case of The Brig "General Armstrong",
in which a request to review an international arbitral
award dismissing the American claim was based on charges of mismanagement by the US and of *excès de pouvoir*
by the arbitrator. The request was rejected by the
Court of Claims since the claim "was political in its
nature, and is entirely independent of the judiciary."
J.B. Moore, 2 International Arbitrations Digest 1o71 at
11o8; also in Lapradelle-Politis, 1 Recueil des Arbitra-
ges Internationaux 635. The claim was nevertheless
subsequently paid under an act of Congress, 2 Moore
1113.

(1o6) Supr.Ct., 6 Jan.1941, 311 U.S. 47o, 1o AD 424(1941-42).

(1o7) 31 F.Supp. 371; 114 F.(2d) 464.

(1o8) US Supr.Ct., 18 May 19o3, 19o U.S. 524.

(1o9) 98 Clunet 131(1971).

(11o) 1o3 Clunet 136(1976).

(111) 1o4 Clunet 864(1977).

(112) Cf. above p. 275.

(113) 25 Oct.1974, 6 NYIL 374(1975).

(114) See also the comments by Kahn in 98 Clunet 134,139(1971).

(115) US Court of Appeals, D.C., 31 Oct.1972, 47o F.2d 461,
cert.den. 411 U.S. 931.

(116) 47o F.2d 464,465.

(117) Court of Appeals D.C., 17 Dec.1976, 555 F.2d 848.

(118) 555 F.2d 85o.

(119) 22 June 1972, BGHZ 59,83. See also the comment by
Bleckmann in 34 ZaöRV 112(1974).

(12o) But see Schermers, International Institutional Law,
p.62oseq., who regards the invocation by individuals of
international decisions imposing sanctions before
domestic courts as feasible. Cf. also Lord, Individual
Enforcement of Obligations arising under the United
Nations Charter, 19 Santa Clara L.Rev.195(1979); Brand,
Security Council Resolutions: When do they give rise to
Enforceable Legal Rights?, 9 Cornell International Law
Journal 298(1976).

(121) See especially Bleckmann, Begriff und Kriterien, p.157seq.
and the references cited there.

(122) For the practice of courts see III.B.2., V.A., VII.B.,
IX.B.1.

(123) In this traditional sense see e.g.: Finanzgericht
Rheinland Pfalz, 14 Oct.197o, 1o CMLRep. 733(197o);
Court of Appeal of Milano, S.A.F.A. v. Amministrazione
delle Finanze, 29 May 1972, 12 CMLRep. 152(1973), 1o
CMLRev. 9o(1973).

(124) Grad v. Finanzamt Traunstein, 6 Oct.197o, Slg. XVI,
p.825,837seq.; Transports Lesage v. Hauptzollamt Frei-
burg, 21 Oct.197o, Slg. XVI, p.861,873seq.; Haselhorst
v. Finanzamt Düsseldorf-Altstadt, 21 Oct.197o, Slg.XVI,
p.881,893seq.; SACE v. Finanzminsterium der Italienischen Republik, 17 Dec.197o, Slg. XVI, p.1213,1221seq.;
van Duyn v. Home Office, 4 Dec.1974, Slg. XX, p.1337,
1348.

(125) 1o CMLRep.132(1971).

(126) Finanzgericht Hessen, 15 Feb.1973, 12 CMLRev. 299(1975);
Bundesverwaltungsgericht, 3 May 1973, 9 Europarecht
164(1974); Bundesgerichtshof, 6 June 1973, 13 CMLRep.
251(1974); Finanzgericht Baden Württemberg, 21 May
1974, 16 CMLRep. 326(1975).

XIII. PERSPECTIVES: DEMANDS AND IDENTIFICATIONS

Perspectives are subjective factors determining the behavior
of participants in the decision-making process. Any realistic
perception of decision-making will quickly realize that the
influence of these perspectives is considerable. The most
important aspects of perspectives for our purposes are the
value demands involved in litigation before domestic courts
and any identifications with interests dominating the case,
common or special. By common interests we mean interests
common to the international community; whereas by special
interests we mean those which only benefit a particular
community, normally the forum State.

A glance at domestic court practice touching upon questions
of international law creates the strong impression that
these perspectives, value demands and identifications, play
a very important part in the behavior of the courts. However, it would be an overreaction to this realization to
fall into the extreme of an exaggerated "realism" by concluding that it is only these subjective elements which determine the behavior of courts, and that the strictly "legal"
arguments, as traditionally understood, serve the sole
purpose of disguising the courts' true motives. In many
cases formal legal arguments will truthfully reflect the
courts' motives or are at least an important contributing
factor to the decisions. Some cases, on the other hand,
create the impression that the value demands and interests
involved play a dominating rôle. A careful examination,
thus, reveals that these subjective factors are but one of
several groups of determinants for the conduct of the court.
Each group can differ in its importance depending on the
particular circumstances of the case. Not infrequently the
perspectives of decision-makers will also importantly influence their choice of formal reasons given for particular
decisions.

The readiness of courts to deal openly with these several
factors determining decisions differs widely and depends not
least on the local legal tradition and the views held by
judges concerning their proper functions. American and
English judges can be expected also to refer to values,
interests, and policies. French, Italian, and Austrian
judges usually carefully refrain from dealing with aspects
that are not strictly "legal" in their opinion. German
judges normally take a middle path between these two traditions.

A. DEMANDS FOR VALUES

The different values at stake in domestic litigation involving decisions of international institutions have repeatedly
been pointed out above in various contexts. Their significance for the behavior of courts is evident. It, therefore,
appears appropriate to focus on this aspect in this short
separate chapter. The pertinent case material has already
been presented above. A detailed documentation, therefore,
appears to be dispensible in this section.

For the purpose of this survey, the value demands apparent
in the available case material can be conveniently grouped
into four categories. The first category concerns demands
for wealth, mostly in the form of pecuniary claims. The
second category concerns demands of individuals for protection against State interference, in other words, individual
liberties or human rights. These two areas are typical and
traditional spheres of court activity, and decisions of
international institutions affect them in a variety of ways.
On the other hand, decisions of international institutions
are also invoked in domestic litigation to support demands
which do not traditionally fall within the cognizance of the
courts. The third category, thus, concerns questions of
State jurisdiction, including territory. The fourth category
concerns community measures taken by international institutions in the common public interest. This grouping cuts
across the accepted value categories of power, wealth, en-
lightenment, skill, well-being, affection, respect, and
rectitude to a certain extent. It is chosen for pragmatic
reasons to deal with the actual demands as they appear in
the available case material.

Any attempt to identify value demands in particular disputes
must beware of too simple categories which make the allocation of cases to them arbitrary and artificial. Not infrequently several types of values are involved in one and the
same dispute. The different values can simply arise cumula-
tively, but can also appear in a relation of rivalry. For
example, the case of the alleged infiltrator apprehended in
a frontier zone can give rise to competing value demands.
The accused invokes his individual rights to freedom of
movement. The prosecution emphasizes aspects of public
security. In addition, the area in question may be the
subject-matter of an international territorial dispute.(1)
The court must decide to which aspect of the case preference
should be given, that is to say, which value deserves more
protection. The scholarly observer analysing the decision
has to find out which value has dominated the court's moti-

ves, irrespective of its vocal behavior.

1. Wealth

Decisions on wealth allocations fall within the usual domain
of court activity and do not normally create particular
difficulties. The effects of decisions are usually limited
and foreseeable. There are normally no overriding public
interests affecting these decisions even if the forum State's
fiscus is directly involved. It is true that the courts show
a certain tendency to subject the implementation of international decisions concerning wealth to the control of
executive departments. (See chapter XII.D.1. above) On the
whole, however, we can conclude that domestic courts dealing
with arbitral awards or other international decisions concerning wealth allocations discharge their functions in an
impartial manner.

Some cases dealing with disputes concerning demands for
wealth, however, give rise to complications which can seriously affect the readiness and capability of courts to reach
independent decisions. As soon as a dispute concerning
wealth involves "political" consequences going beyond the
particular case, the courts' task can become extremely
difficult.

These "political" implications can concern international
territorial questions which have to be considered as preliminary questions to claims for immovable property.(2) More
frequently complications arise in connection with extensive
measures of expropriation. Disputes arising in consequence
of these measures can have important effects on the national
economy of the State concerned, both because of the size of
the claims involved and because of their nature as test
cases for subsequent litigation. The impact on the behavior
of the courts is evident.(3)

A further difficulty in connection with demands for wealth
arises when basic questions of the enforceability of the
claim against the debtor or defendant are involved. In these
cases the substantive wealth allocation may have been made
by the international organ, the defendant, however, claims
that due to his special "public" status enforcement against
him is against the public interest and hence, should, be
inadmissible. This demand is couched in terms of a claim to
immunity. (See chapter XII.B.1. above) The policy behind
this claim to immunity is the assertion that the dispute
should not be treated like a normal demand for wealth but,
that due to the public functions of the debtor, other over-

riding values are also involved. The attempt to distinguish between *acta iure imperii* and *acta iure gestionis* is expressive of an endeavor to find a dividing line between those cases which involve pure demands for wealth and those which also involve other values. An intervention by the courts is only regarded as desirable in the first category of disputes. The reaction of courts to claims to State immunity is a particularly clear example of their differentiated reactions to different value demands. It is, however, only one aspect of a much wider problem. Another common reaction of courts confronted with conflicting value demands with which they are either unwilling or unable to cope is to retreat into a "political questions" doctrine and refuse a decision on the merits.

2. Human Rights

The protection of individual liberties against undue State interference is another essential task of the courts in many countries. Depending on the peculiarities of the local judicial system, this function is discharged either by the ordinary courts or by specialist courts like administrative or constitutional courts. Compared to demands for wealth the situation is different here, inasmuch as the demands made by individuals are not countered by corresponding value demands but by the State's endeavor to exercise its public functions as effectively and economically as possible. In spite of this actual or assumed interest of the State, which is often in conflict with an effective protection of individual liberties, the courts in countries with a democratic structure of government have turned out to be highly important and successful in safeguarding human rights.

This active and assertive role of the courts in defending individual liberties can also be observed in cases involving decisions of international institutions concerning human rights. The readiness of courts to rely on international decisions of this kind is remarkably great and is contrasted by a much more reserved attitude towards similar international decisions involving values other than human rights. A particularly conspicuous feature of this practice is the tendency of courts to disregard formal objections: they rely on recommendations, that is, international decisions whose authority could be subjected to doubt (chapter III.B.2. above); they are often unperturbed by a lack of the international decisions' incorporation into the local law. (chapter VII.B. above) This practice creates the impression that the endeavor to further the protection of individual liberties also with the help of international decisions concerning

human rights has largely superseded formal considerations
like the proper "sources of law" or dualism.

There are, however, also limits to this readiness of domestic
courts to utilize international decisions for the protection
of human rights. In cases in which the individual liberties
to be protected run counter to important public interests,
(4) especially where far-reaching constitutional implications beyond the particular case were expected,(5) the
courts were considerably more reserved towards the pertinent
international decisions. The well-known formal arguments,
such as, lack of binding force or absence of measures of
incorporation for the Universal Declaration of Human Rights,
were utilized more frequently in these cases.

3. State Jurisdiction

In contrast to demands for wealth and for individual liberties, questions concerning internationally controversal
claims to jurisdiction are not part of the normal business
of domestic courts. Not surprisingly, courts confronted with
questions of this kind show a certain reluctance to make
decisions on the extent of the jurisdiction of States, especially territorial disputes.(6) There are, however, exceptions to this cautious attitude.

Where an international question of State jurisdiction has
been authoritatively determined on the international level
with the consent of all the parties involved, especially by
an international judicial decision but sometimes by the
decision of a non-judicial international institution, courts
normally display no misgivings in relying on an effective
and recognized international decision. In situations of this
kind the question of jurisdiction has ceased to be controversial, and a decision of the domestic court in accord with
the international decision is not likely to give rise to
"political" complications.

In these cases the invocation of international decisions is
usually not the central point of the litigation before the
domestic court(7) but serves to clarify preliminary questions. (See also chapter XI.A. above). The values primarily
at stake in the disputes are, therefore, affected by, but
usually not identical with, the question of State jurisdiction. The determination of a court's own jurisdiction is
part of its normal functions and can, in exceptional cases,
take place on the basis of decisions made by international
organs.

The pertinent practice indicates that where the international decision in question has been recognized by the States concerned, especially by the forum State, courts do not seem particularly worried by formal aspects, such as lack of incorporation. A good example is the termination of the forum State's jurisdiction over a territory with its consent by the decision of an international organization. A refusal of a domestic court to recognize this reduction of its territorial jurisdiction because of a lack of the international decision's formal incorporation would not make much sense. The courts simply acknowledge their newly restricted competence by reference to the international decision. (Chapter VII.E.2. above).

Another exception to the reserved and cautious attitude of domestic courts towards questions of international jurisdiction arises from the diametrically opposite type of situation. Where the forum State is actively engaged in an international territorial dispute, the courts almost invariably adopt its position. Pertinent international decisions are frequently adduced by the courts, but whenever possible they are interpreted in the forum State's favor; where this is not possible, they are rejected for a variety of reasons. In these situations, the pertinent international decisions do not appear to be an important factor determining the outcome of decisions. The more general problem of a strong identification of courts with important interests of the forum State and their resulting behavior will be dealt with below in chapter XIII.B.1.

4. Community Measures.

As observed (chapter II.A.1. and VII.E.1.b), domestic courts can be effective agencies to make international enforcement measures, especially economic sanctions, controlling. On the other hand, the implementation of concerted measures taken by the international community in the common public interest through international organizations is certainly not part of the normal tasks of domestic courts.

An examination of the case material, which is still somewhat scarce, indicates that courts have shown little readiness to play an active rôle in furthering these community measures. (8) They have largely failed to contribute to the enforcement of international sanctions, not least because they do not seem to regard the promotion of the community interest in the effective pursuit of coordinated international action as part of their proper functions. Reasons advanced for this failure often present the well-known formal arguments like dualism or *lex posterior*. This negative attitude towards cooperating with international community measures is particularly evident where it is persisted in even against the express intentions of the forum State. The political interests of the forum State, therefore, do not give a plausible explanation for this uncooperative stance of the courts towards community measures.

Attempts to enlist domestic courts for the implementation of international economic enforcement measures are, therefore, likely to encounter considerable difficulties. Plans which have been repeatedly suggested to overcome these difficulties (Cf. chapters II.A.1. and XI.B.1. above) envisage a conversion of the claim put forward in the domestic litigation into a demand for wealth, since this value is more likely to be successful than a claim overtly concerned with power. Nevertheless, in the light of the experience gained so far, it appears doubtful whether domestic courts will cooperate in attempts to confiscate goods originating from territories which have been put under international economic sanctions. The courts have a considerable arsenal of formal arguments at their disposal to reject claims of this kind. This arsenal ranges from doubts in the authority of the international decision, its lack of incorporation into the local law, the absence of sufficiently detailed prescriptions for it to be directly applicable, the lack of a right of action or standing of the plaintiff, the existence of a contrary provision of the local law, to conflict of laws problems concerning the law applicable to the question of ownership in the disputed goods. In view of the attitude so far displayed by the courts towards international enforcement measures, it is not likely that a mere presentation of the claim as an ostensible demand for wealth will suffice to win the cooperation of domestic courts. Given the present understanding of courts of their rôle, an effective intervention to support international community measures will probably only be achieved through detailed legislative guidance, which takes account of all these difficulties and leaves relatively little discretion to the courts.

B. IDENTIFICATIONS: SPECIAL VERSUS COMMON INTERESTS

The impact of the forum State's national interests or of international community interests on the behavior of courts is closely related to the value demands involved. The extent to which these interests are taken into account is often difficult to ascertain in individual cases, especially where the courts rely primarily on formal reasons. Courts do not

lightly expose themselves to the charge of "political"
decisions. However, a critical evaluation of the ascertainable circumstances of the cases often permits conclusions to
what extent courts have been influenced by considerations of
this kind.

1. Special Interests of the Forum State

The reluctance of domestic courts to hand down decisions
which are contrary to the forum State's political intentions
is a phenomenon which has often been observed and described.
(9) It is by no means restricted to questions of international concern but is particularly evident in this area. The
tendency of the courts to refuse decisions on the merits
which could affect the forum State's foreign policy is
particularly marked in the United States and is usually referred to under the label of the "political questions doctrine".

Apart from this hands-off policy, another typical behavior
on the part of the courts can be observed. Especially in
cases with a particularly strong political involvement of
the executive, the courts tend to adopt an active course
following the lead of their government. The steady shift of
international decision processes into organized arenas
increases the probability of controversial decisions of
international institutions. Not infrequently courts are
drawn into controversies between the forum State and the
international institution. The apprehension of courts about
a possible discrepancy with the position taken by their
government is highlighted by the fact that courts sometimes
specifically point out that the forum State has voted for a
United Nations General Assembly resolution(1o) even though
the authority of the resolution does not depend on its
consent.(11)

The question of the forum State's attitude towards an international decision creates no problems in cases in which the
international organ has decided in accordance with the forum
State's interests, or where the government has indicated its
willingness to abide by that decision.(12) The court is then
in a position to give deference to the international decision. Where the issue remains controversial even after the
decision in the international organ the court usually gives
preference to its national loyalty and identifies with the
interest of the forum State.

This is not to say that the position taken by the government
of the forum State towards an international decision will

invariably determine the behavior of domestic courts. The
values at stake for the national community play a decisive
role. Where the subject matter of the dispute does not
affect any basic interests of the forum States but, for
example, only involves a limited pecuniary obligation, a
dispassionate and unbiased behavior can be expected of the
courts. The cases in which forum States themselves participated in domestic litigation dealing with demands for wealth
arising from international decisions vividly illustrate this
point. (Chapter XII.A.1. above).

The situation is quite different in cases in which the international decision affects important public interests of the
national community. These interests are usually related to
demands for power and often affect territorial disputes,
questions of national security, or fundamental economic
issues. The existence and extent of a crisis situation also
plays an important part. No doubt, an independent and objective behavior of courts also in these areas of "political
questions" would be desirable. Experience shows, however,
that it would be unrealistic to expect courts in these cases
to act in contradiction to the position taken by their
government in the international arena. The publicity surrounding the issues at stake often makes a special executive
intervention or "advice" dispensable.

The problem of identification cannot be solved with any
formal legal techniques. The domestic court is faced with
the difficulty of presenting the decision corresponding with
the national community's overriding interests in a "legally"
acceptable form. It has a number of decision techniques at
its disposal to reach this result.

The most radical of these strategies in dealing with an
international decision which is incompatible with the forum
State's interests is to cast doubts on its legality and to
claim that it is void or *ultra vires*. We have already come
across a number of examples for this method of rejecting
international decisions in chapter IV. These cases concerned
the reaction of an Iranian court(13) to an international
arbitral award dealing with Iranian expropriation measures,
of the German Reichsgericht(14) to the finding of a League
of Nations organ that the Saar territory was not part of the
German Reich, of a United States Court(15) to an OAS Resolution concerning Puerto Rico, and of an Egyptian Court(16)
referring to the United Nations Partition Plan for Palestine.

Other strategies to avoid deference to unacceptable international decisions do not consist in such "frontal attacks" on

these decisions. They can consist in references to the non-binding character of the international decision or to the lack of incorporation into the local law. A good example is the above-quoted reaction of an Israeli court(17) to an invocation of a United Nations Security Council Resolution concerning Israel's duty to withdraw from occupied territories.

Sometimes the attempt is made to counter a politically unacceptable international decision by reference to other decisions of international organs. This was how the District Court of Jerusalem in the <u>Eichmann</u> case(18) reacted to the attempt of counsel for the defense to rely on the United Nations Security Council Resolution which had been censorious of the defendant's abduction from Argentina. The response of the District Court of Puerto Rico(19) to the activities of the United Nations Special Committee on Colonialism concerning Puerto Rico was similar.

Another method is simply to ignore the international decision altogether.(2o) In a South African case(21) in 1968 the question was whether legislation by South Africa for "South-West Africa" could be reviewed by domestic courts in the light of South Africa's obligations under the mandate. The Court, although it was referred to United Nations General Assembly Resolution 2145 (XXI) of October 27, 1966, apparently found it unnecessary even to deal with the question of whether the mandate had been revoked by the General Assembly's decision.

The approach which is most honest is an admission by the court that it will not accede to a claim because of the political implications involved. Thus an invocation of Security Council Resolution 253 on Rhodesia in an attempt to prevent the issuance of a visa to Ian Smith was rejected by the Court of Appeals for the District of Columbia by reference to the political questions doctrine.(22)

Finally, in a Rhodesian case(23) the Court had to decide the question of Rhodesia's statehood in order to determine the validity of legislation enacted subsequent to the minority regime's Unilateral Declaration of Independence. One judge actually managed to turn the Security Council Resolutions directed against the regime in Southern Rhodesia into an argument for Rhodesia's independence:

> Today, she is a *State* which has rebelled, but nevertheless she still continues to possess the characteristics of a State. That this is so is implicit in the various resolutions passed by the U.N.Organisation dealing with

the present Government. See Security Council Resolution
No.216 of Nov. 12, 1965, No. 217 of Nov.2o, 1965,
No.221 of April 9,1966, No.232 of Dec.16,1966. These
resolutions certainly cannot be construed as any form
of international recognition but it is implicit in them
that the Organisation must have regarded Rhodesia as
possessing the characteristics of a *State* because the
actions which these resolutions have set in train are
actions, which in terms of the United Nations Charter,
can only be taken against another State. The wording of
Art.4o and in particular the use of the words "parties
concerned" in the context of Chapter VII, makes this
plain enough.(24)

Although one cannot deny a certain amount of ingeniousness
to this piece of bizarre logic, there is really nothing to
support it. Quite apart from the fact that none of the four
resolutions cited do in fact refer to Article 4o, there is
nothing in the Charter of the United Nations to support the
view that enforcement action under Chapter VII can only be
directed against "States".

These examples are sufficient to demonstrate that domestic
courts will almost invariably uphold the interests of the
forum State's government in critical situations involving
acute or potential international conflicts. In these situations the domestic court becomes strongly aware of its
function as an organ of the State. Its role as a functional
international decision-maker becomes largely ineffective.(25)

The behavior displayed by courts in these situations does
not, however, warrant a generally pessimistic or cynical
attitude towards the activity of domestic courts in cases
involving decisions of international institutions or other
questions of inclusive concern. Such a reaction would be
just as mistaken as a naive belief that courts are immune
from identifying with special interests. The case material
set out here only outlines the outer margin of the area within which objective and dispassionate decisions of domestic
courts can be expected, that is to say, where they are
capable of discharging also their function as international
decision-makers. Disputes before domestic courts involving
controversial international questions which directly affect
the forum State are by no means the rule. It would be quite
out of place to draw general negative conclusions concerning
the capability of domestic courts to apply international
decisions from this limited number of decisions arising from
atypical situations.

2. Common Interests of the International Community

The interests of the international community to regulate common problems do not always correspond to the interests of individual States. Individual States may be indifferent or even opposed to the furtherance of certain interests of the international community as a whole. The dual function of domestic courts as State organs and as international decision-makers would also allow an active identification with and conscious promotion of common interests of the international community in the same manner as observed with the special interests of the forum State. In the area under observation in the instant study, that is, decisions of international institutions, such an identification with common international interests, if it exists at all, is only apparent to a much smaller degree.

A rare example for an explicit reliance of a domestic court on the interests of the international community is the judgment of the German Bundesgerichtshof of 22 June 1972, (BGHZ 59,83) as quoted above on p.26o. Although the pertinent international decisions had only limited authority and offered only a poor basis for formal arguments, the Court found it appropriate to decide in accordance with their policies. It specifically invoked the community interest of combatting the undesirable business practices in question.

A look at the attitude of domestic courts towards the different values demanded in litigation before them, as set out in chapter XIII.A., confirms the impression that international community interests play a subordinate role in their motives. Of course, the readiness of courts to protect and promote individual liberties also with the help of international decisions could be interpreted in the sense of an identification with internationalist humanitarian ideals. Situations calling for active cooperation in concerted community measures are, however, probably a better indicator of international identifications. In this field domestic courts have shown little readiness to make a positive contribution.

An appreciable change in the attitude of domestic courts, as well as of other internal decision makers, can only be expected in the wake of a fundamental shift of perspectives and a conscious reconsideration of their value preferences. Indications for such a shift can be observed to some extent in the sphere of the European Communities. One of the primary reasons for this development is probably the close institutional cooperation between the courts of Members and Commu-

nity organs, especially the Court of Justice of the European
Communities.

At the present stage of development the most promising solution for the general problem of the indifference of domestic
courts towards the interests of the international community
appears to lie in the establishment and extension of institutionalised international procedures of supervision. These
procedures of supervision could consist in the possibility
for a revision and repeal of final domestic decisions in
certain situations,(26) in the creation of appeals procedures to international decision-makers(27) or, more realistically, in a review without the power of cassation. The
effects of the activities of the supervisory organs acting
under the European Convention on Human Rights demonstrate
clearly that this system can lead to a gradual shift of perspectives of domestic courts. The most spectacular progress
towards more intensive international identifications by
domestic courts has, no doubt, been achieved with the help
of the system of preliminary rulings in the European Communities. At the present stage this method of influencing the
perspectives of domestic courts appears the most promising
way to achieve a more intensive identification with the
common interests of the international community.

(1) <u>Military Prosecutor v. Halil Muhamad Mahmud Halil Bakhis and Others</u>, Israel Military Court, Ramallah, 1o June 1968, 47 ILR 484, 1 Israel YBHR 462(1971).

(2) <u>Willis v. First Real Estate and Investment Co. et al.</u>, US Ct.of App. 5th Circ., 24 Jan.1934, 68 F.2 671, 11 AD 94(1919-42); see above p.258.

(3) See e.g. <u>National Iranian Oil Co. v. Sapphire Intl. Petroleums Ltd.</u>, District Court of Teheran, 1 Dec.1963, 9 ILM 1118(197o); <u>Excess Profits of Nationalized Copper Companies</u>, Special Copper Tribunal, Chile, 11 Aug.1972, 11 ILM 1o13(1972).

(4) See e.g. the cases in which defendants in trials for war crimes unsuccessfully sought to invoke the Human Rights Declaration: <u>In re Beck</u>, Netherlands, Special Court of Cassation, 11 Apr.1949, 16 AD 279(1949); <u>In re Rauter</u>, Netherlands, Special Court of Cassation, undated, 16 AD 546(1949); <u>In re Best and Others</u>, Supreme Court of Denmark, 17 March 195o, 17 ILR 434(195o).

(5) In <u>Roussety v. The Attorney General</u>, High Court of Mauritius, 3o March 1967, 44 ILR 1o8, a number of important statutes had been validated retroactively. An attempt to challenge this retroactive legislation with the help of the Universal Declaration, since some of the validated statutes also contained penal provisions, was unsuccessful.

(6) See e.g. <u>Occidental Petroleum Corp. v. Buttes Gas and Oil Co.</u>, US Dist.Ct. C.D.Calif., 17 March 1971, 331 F.Supp. 92; <u>Y. v. Public Prosecutor</u>, District Court of Breda (Netherlands), 11 Feb. a. 2o March 1957, 7 NTIR 282(196o).

(7) But see <u>Maghanbhai Ishwarbhai Patel and Others v. Union of India</u> Supreme Court of India, 1969, 9 IJIL 234(1969).

(8) <u>Diggs v. Shultz</u>, US Ct. of App.D.C. 31 Oct.1972, 47o F.2d 461; <u>Diggs v.Richardson</u>, Court of Appeals D.C., 17 Dec.1976, 555 F.2d 848; <u>Kangai v.Vance</u>, Court of Appeals D.C., 6 Oct. 1978, 73 AJIL 297(1979); <u>Bradley v.The Commonwealth of Australia and the Postmaster-General</u>, High Court of Australia, 1o Sept.1973, 1o1 Clunet 865(1974), 52 ILR 1(1979).

(9) See e.g. Mann, Judiciary and Executive in Foreign Affairs, 29 Transactions of the Grotius Society 143(1943);

McDougal, The Impact, p.83; Henkin, Vietnam in the
Courts of the United States: 'Political Questions', 63
AJIL 285(1969); *ibid.*, Foreign Affairs and the Constitution, p.2o5seq.; Treviranus, Außenpolitik im demokratischen Rechtsstaat, p.18seq.(1966).

(1o) See In re Jacqueline-Marie Bukowicz, Cour Civil de
Courtrai, 1o Oct.1952, UN Yearbook of Human Rights
21(1953) concerning the Universal Declaration of Human
Rights; Mbounya, Conseil d'Etat (Fr.), 3 Nov.1961, 8
AFDI 943(1962) concerning the Resolution terminating
the Trusteeship over Cameroon; Diggs v. Dent, US Dist.
Ct.D.C., 13 May 1975, 14 ILM 797(1975) concerning the
Resolution terminating the Mandate for South West
Africa. See also the reference in the last mentioned
case and in Diggs v. Shultz, US Ct.of App.D.C., 31
Oct.1972, 47o, F.2d 461 to the affirmative vote of the
United States to Security Council resolutions.

(11) Generally see Castaneda, Legal Effects of United Nations Resolutions, p.154. For a denial of effects of a
State's voting behavior on the authority of Security
Council Resolutions see the Advisory Opinion of the ICJ
on Namibia, ICJ Reports, 54(1971).

(12) Pinto, Juge interne français, p.88; see e.g. the Indian
case in which the Government had accepted the arbitral
award against it: Maghanbhai etc. above p.239.

(13) National Iranian Oil Co. v. Sapphire Intl. Petroleums
Ltd., above p.139.

(14) RGSt 63,395, above p.139.

(15) Ruiz Alicea v. U.S., above p.139.

(16) The Inge Toft, above p.139.

(17) Military Prosecutor v. Halil Muhamad Mahmud Halil Bakhis
and Others, Military Court Ramallah, 1o June 1968, 47
ILR 484. See above p.83.

(18) 36 ILR 5,74, cf. above p.84.

(19) U.S. v. Vargas, 29 Jan.1974, 37o F.Supp. 9o8, cf. above
p.84seq.

(2o) Cf. Israeli decisions on the status of Eastern Jerusalem and the West Bank of the river Jordan, which do not

mention pertinent United Nations Decisions: <u>Avalon Han-</u>
<u>zalis v. Greek Orthodox Patriarchate Religious Court</u>
<u>and Constandinos Nicola Papadopoulos</u>, Supreme Court, 1o
March 1969, 48 ILR 93; <u>Muhammad Abdullah Iwad and Zeev</u>
<u>Shimshon Maches v. Military Court, Hebron District and</u>
<u>Military Prosecutor for the West Bank Region, I.D.F.</u>,
Supreme Court, 13 Oct.197o, 48 ILR 63.

(21) <u>S. v. Tuhadeleni and Others</u>, Appellate Division, 22
Nov.1968, 18 ICLQ 789(1969), 52 ILR 29(1979).

(22) <u>Kangai v.Vance</u>, 6 Oct.1978, 73 AJIL 297(1979).

(23) <u>Madzimbamuto v. Lardner-Burke</u>, Appellate Division of
the High Court, 29 Jan.1968, 39 ILR 61; Cf. also <u>R.v.</u>
<u>Ndhlovu and others</u>, in the same court, 13 Sept.1968, 53
ILR 5o(1979). For an analysis of the conflicting loyal-
ties of Rhodesian judges see Palley, The Judicial
Process: U.D.I. and the Southern Rhodesian Judiciary,
3o Modern LRev. 263(1967).

(24) Per Beadle C.J., 39 ILR 2o9. Emphases original.

(25) Generally on the question of national prejudice of
domestic courts see Friedmann, The Changing Structure,
p.147seq.; *ibid.*, National Courts, p.447,453seq.;
Lauterpacht, Decisions of Municipal Courts, p.65;
Schwarzenberger, The Inductive Approach, p.25seq.;
Parry, The Sources, p.97; Falk, The Role of Domestic
Courts, p.19seq.; Lillich, The Proper Role, p.48;
Schermers, International Institutional Law, p.613seq.

(26) See e.g. the pertinent provisions in Art.3o2/2,3 and
3o5 of the Treaty of Versailles, and in Part 5, Art.7(2)
Convention on the Settlement of Matters Arising out of
the War and the Occupation between the Western Allied
Powers and Germany, 23 Oct.1954, 332 UNTS 219.

(27) See e.g. Art.37 Revised Rhine Navigation Act of 17
Oct.1868, Martens N.R.G., Vol.2o, p.335,365; Art.34/4
Moselle Treaty of 27 Oct.1956, BGBl 1956 II, p.1838,
1848; Part 1o, Art.2 and Part 3 Art.6 of the Convention
on the Settlement of Matters Arising out of the War and
the Occupation of 26 May 1952; Art.17 of Annex 4 and
Art.32 of the Agreement on German External Debts of 27
Feb.1953, 333 UNTS 3.

XIV. CONCURRENT JURISDICTION OF DOMESTIC COURTS AND INTERNATIONAL ORGANS

A. GENERAL POLICIES

In the preceding sections of the present study the considerations have always been based on the premise of the actual existence of an international decision which plays a rôle in domestic litigation. But international organs can already exercise an influence on the behavior of domestic courts before becoming active, or at any rate before reaching their decisions. The expectation of a possible or probable international decision by virtue of the jurisdiction of the international organ or actually pending proceedings raises the question of whether, and to what extent, domestic courts should take note of this coincidence of decision-making powers affecting cases before them.

The majority of cases in which future international decisions can affect the behavior of domestic courts involve the applying function, more specifically international judgments and awards.(1) Sometimes operative decisions of non-judicial international organs can also play a certain rôle. The possibility of future manifestations of the prescribing function of international organs plays no particular rôle in this context.

Any simple solution based on the intrinsic "priority" of either international or domestic proceedings is not likely to yield satisfactory results. International decision-makers have sometimes sought to derive such a principle of priority from an ostensible supremacy of international over national procedures. Thus, a French-Italian Conciliation Commission stated categorically that:

> The Conciliation Commission, an international tribunal set up by a treaty, has supremacy over municipal courts. If a municipal court is seized of this case, it is necessary, in order that the international tribunal may hear and decide the claim, that the claimants... should discontinue the proceedings in the municipal court.(2)

Domestic courts, on the other hand, have occasionally tried to base the opposite principle on the "exhaustion of local remedies rule". A court in Tangier(3) claimed that in the case of simultaneous proceedings before a national and an international tribunal the latter would have to adjourn its proceedings until the domestic court had given its decision. This, the Tangier court claimed, was a necessary consequence

of the principle of the exhaustion of remedies in municipal
law.

Neither assertion of priority is very convincing as a general
proposition. It is difficult to see why international procedures should necessarily take precedence over domestic litigation unless there are good reasons for the domestic court
to yield to the international tribunal in a particular case.
On the other hand, the principle of the exhaustion of local
remedies by no means takes account of all situations of concurrent jurisdiction. It is merely a bar to claims against a
State based on its liability for the wrongful decisions of
its organs, for as long as these decisions are not final. It
does not generally prevent an international decision-maker
from taking up a legal question just because this question
is pending before a domestic court.

A domestic court faced with an objection to its jurisdiction
based on the argument that there is an international procedure to settle a question pending before it has basically
three options. It can dismiss the objection altogether and
proceed to its own decision regardless of the likely outcome
of the international proceedings. Alternatively, it can adopt
the more cautious approach of suspending the proceedings in
order to await the outcome of the international claim. Finally, it can resign from its task altogether and refuse to decide on the claim before it.

Specific provisions on this problem of concurrent jurisdiction contained in the instrument setting up the international procedure, though often desirable, are the exception
rather than the rule. They regulate rather special situations
and give little guidance for a general solution to our
question.(4) In most cases it is, therefore, left to the
domestic courts to decide how to react to a possible collision between national and international proceedings.

The following basic considerations will be important for a
rational decision: A duplicity of proceedings on the national and international levels, with possibly conflicting
outcomes, is undesirable and should be avoided. A domestic
court which is prepared to render a rash decision on a
question likely to be decided by an international decision-
maker will not normally make a contribution towards an orderly settlement of the dispute. Moreover, it may see the solution reached in the international proceedings implemented by
appropriate government action regardless of its own decision.
On the other hand, an overcautious attitude towards international procedures can seriously affect the position of a

claimant. An exaggerated fear of a mere possibility of parallel proceedings may lead to a complete denial of legal remedies. Thus, it can, in effect, deprive a party seeking judicial protection of its day in court.

In striking a proper balance between these policies, a domestic court will have to examine a number of questions relating the national to the international proceedings: Is a possible international decision really relevant to the case pending before the domestic court? If so, how likely is it that the international decision will actually be made? Do the claimant or the court have any means to set the international proceedings in motion or to exercise any influence on their continuation?

B. THE RELEVANCE OF A POSSIBLE FUTURE INTERNATIONAL DECISION

The first question for a domestic court confronted with the jurisdiction of an international organ in a case pending before it is the possible relevance of such an international decision for the domestic proceedings. The future international decision can become relevant in one of several ways depending on the type of claim involved: The international proceedings can constitute a parallel attempt to pursue the claim also raised before the domestic court. The international proceedings can be directed at the clarification of a question which is a preliminary point in the domestic litigation. Finally, an identical or similar legal question can be pending in the international case which can be expected to provide a "precedent" for the domestic case.

1. Identity of Claims

The most obvious cases of concurrent jurisdiction arise in situations in which national and international proceedings are open to the same parties to pursue the same claim.(5) The traditional exclusion of non-State actors from international arenashas been subjected to a number of important exceptions and limitations in the course of this century.(6) The pursuit of individual claims of an international nature for which domestic courts were not regarded as satisfactory fora had previously been a prerogative of executive departments excercising diplomatic protection. These procedures were often costly and uneconomical. In certain specific situations direct access to international proceedings was, therefore, granted to individuals or corporations pursuing their own claims. These international procedures were set up by treaties like the Mixed Arbitral Tribunals established by the Peace Treaties after World War I, sometimes in the frame-

work of international organizations, like the Administrative
Tribunals of the UN and ILO. Alternatively procedures for the
settlement of disputes admitting also non-State actors were
established by agreement between the potential litigants
themselves, such as agreements of arbitration between States
or public enterprises and foreign investors.

In the absence of clear prescriptions delimiting the respective jurisdictions of national and international fora, parallel proceedings have often created insecurity and confusion
with domestic courts. This is best evidenced by attempts of
some courts to deny the relevance of parallel international
proceedings with the help of superficial formal arguments.

An obvious example is the system of Mixed Arbitral Tribunals
set up by the Peace Treaties after World War I. One of the
functions of these Tribunals was to decide on private law
claims between former enemy nationals. For this purpose
direct access to the Tribunals was granted to the claimants.
Prescriptions delimiting the respective competences between
the tribunals and domestic courts were absent, and it is not
surprising that local courts encountered considerable difficulties.

There are cases in which domestic courts, despite an obvious
material identity of proceedings, refused to take notice of
claims pending before Mixed Arbitral Tribunals. Thus, the
Supreme Administrative Court of Poland(7) dismissed a plea
of litispendence of the same claim before the German-Polish
Mixed Arbitral Tribunal "since the fields of the jurisdiction
of both Courts are different".

A similar decision by the Civil tribunal of Brussels is
hardly more convincing. In this case(8) the court countered
a plea of litispendence before the German-Belgian Mixed
Arbitral Tribunal by pointing out that the conditions for
the Arbitral Tribunal's jurisdiction had not been met in the
present case and, moreover, that litispendence could only be
recognized in relation to litigation before Belgian courts.
Neither of these arguments is persuasive. Quite apart from
the fact that it was hardly for the Belgian court to decide
on the International Tribunal's jurisdiction, a formalistic
conception of litispendence does not make much sense. In
particular where international organs have assumed functions
of domestic judicial organs, a focus restricted to identical
"fields of jurisdiction" or to the courts of the forum State
does not appear meaningful.

As pointed out, a traditional and in many areas still prevalent method of settling private claims involving foreign
governments and public bodies is through diplomatic protection involving the international representation of the
private claimant by his government. Where such a claim is
pursued by international litigation, the criteria for the
question of a concurrence of proceedings are somewhat more
complicated. Under these circumstances it would not be
satisfactory for a domestic court to take notice of the
international proceedings only if a test of formal identity
of the parties has been met.

Here too, courts have not always shown a proper awareness of
the potential implications of international proceedings. The
German Reichsgericht dismissed an objection of litispendence
of the same claim before the German-American Mixed Claims
Commission. It simply found that it could see no reason why
the jurisdiction of German courts should be ousted by a
registration of the claim with the Mixed Claims Commission.
(9)

French court practice shows examples of a more cautious
approach. The Tribunal Civil de la Seine(1o) refused to hear
a claim under similar circumstances. It substantiated its
refusal by pointing out that the treaty provisions setting
up an International Conciliation Commission had superseded
the domestic provisions on the competence of the ordinary
courts. This decision, although it is realistic in its
outcome, appears somewhat narrow in its reasoning. Criteria
concerning the validity of conflicting rules are not likely,
in all cases, to afford satisfactory solutions for choices
between procedures which may exist side by side.

An older French decision demonstrates that in the international pursuit of a claim pending before a domestic court not
only the claimant but also the defendant may change his
identity. In this case(11) the Conseil d'Etat rejected the
claim of a contractor directed against the French State for
payment of improvements carried out on territory subsequently ceded to Germany. It based its rejection on the fact that
proceedings between France and Germany to obtain compensation for exactly these improvements were pending before a
German-French Mixed Commission.

These examples are sufficient to demonstrate that the conditions of international intercourse frequently require different actors to appear in the international arena than in
domestic fora. As pointed out above, simultaneous proceedings for the settlement of materially identical claims

before domestic and international tribunals are liable to
lead to unsatisfactory results. A realistic attitude towards
the danger of concurrent proceedings will, therefore, not be
able to restrict an enquiry to the formal participants in
national and international proceedings. It will have to
pierce the veil of State-representation and look at the true
beneficiaries of a claim before determining whether there is
a substantial identity of proceedings.

This is not to say that such an international decision will
necessarily settle all the questions concerning the claim
which is pending before a domestic court. In particular,
certain questions of ownership and distribution may be left
open by an international tribunal. This lack of a complete
identity of claims in all its legal aspects should, however,
not induce the domestic court to turn a blind eye to the
international proceedings. A cautious court, which is prepared to await the outcome of international litigation and
to base its verdict on the decision reached there, may,
thus, turn a situation of competing jurisdictions into one
in which it is merely left with the task of implementing the
international judgment or award.

2. Future International Decisions on Preliminary Questions

A domestic court may also be referred to international
judicial proceedings which are not directed at resolving the
dispute which is pending before it but are merely concerned
with a legal question which is also relevant to the domestic
lawsuit. In such a situation, the outcome of the international litigation will by no means decide the claim before the
domestic court. It can, however, provide an answer to an
important preliminary question which is material to the
decision on the main issue.

A pertinent example is that of international judicial proceedings to settle a territorial dispute which is relevant
to the question of the domestic court's venue. In 1957 the
District Court of Breda(12) in the Netherlands had to decide
whether it was competent to hear a criminal case involving
an offence committed on a stretch of territory which was
subject to dispute between the Netherlands and Belgium. It
dismissed the application of the defendant to find that the
territory in question was Belgian and to terminate the
proceedings:

> The territory on which criminal offenses have allegedly
> been committed is the subject of a dispute between the
> Belgian and Netherlands Governments. This dispute will
> be submitted by both Governments to the International

Court of Justice at The Hague. So long as uncertainty
exists as to whether the territory is Belgian or Netherlands, it is undesirable that the courts of either of
the two countries will decide on this question.

Another typical situation in which an international judicial
organ's decision can be of relevance to a domestic case
arises where the municipal court has to apply a treaty which
provides for an international judicial procedure to settle
disputes concerning its interpretation. Even where this
international procedure is not designed to be exclusive, or
binding on the domestic court, its authority can make the
court reluctant to proceed with its own independent interpretation.(13)

In making a choice between awaiting the outcome of the
international case and proceeding to an independent decision,
a court has to examine carefully whether the expected international decision is really essential or material to the
domestic litigation. It will have to reject purely dilatory
claims of international "litispendence". If an international
legal question is sufficiently clarified, especially by
previous decisions of the international tribunal, a suspension of the domestic proceedings is dispensable. In other
cases, the connection between the legal issues pending
before the national and international judiciaries may be so
remote that the domestic court either cannot hope to obtain
any pertinent authority from the international decision or
the delay caused by a suspension of proceedings outweighs
the value of the expected international decision.

A decision of the Austrian Supreme Court(14) provides a good
example of such a situation. The case concerned divorce proceedings in which the trial court had based its decision on
the defendant's previous conviction for murder of her mother-
in-law. The defendant applied for a suspension of the proceedings since she had lodged a complaint against her conviction with the European Commission on Human Rights. In her
opinion the judgment was, therefore, not final. The Supreme
Court rejected the application holding that it could not see
a sufficiently close connection between the divorce proceedings and the case pending before the Human Rights Commission.

A domestic court which is aware of international proceedings
on related legal questions will, thus, have to strike a
careful balance between the benefits and disadvantages of
staying the proceedings in order to await the outcome of the
international case. Considerations of procedural expediency

will often militate in favor of a prompt and independent
decision. Considerations of international public policy and
of a uniform court practice may speak in favor of a more
reserved and cautious attitude.

An important factor in the domestic court's decision, whether
to suspend the proceedings pending before it or to proceed
to an autonomous decision on the merits, is, no doubt, the
question of time. The proliferation of activities of international institutions also increases the probability for
domestic courts that a legal question to be decided by it is
or will be under deliberation in some international organ.
The duration of contentious proceedings before judicial
international organs is usually predictable to a certain
extent. But the legal question which is important for the
domestic litigation can also be the subject of discussion in
some "political" international organ. The duration and
outcome of deliberations of this kind is often entirely
uncertain. An over-cautious policy of domestic courts,
trying to do justice to every possible development in international institutions by adopting a wait-and-see attitude,
would lead to unacceptable delays in domestic proceedings
and, therefore, cannot be recommended.

In addition to these policy considerations, a court can also
be moved by formal aspects in deciding whether to await a
future international decision. A domestic court which is not
prepared to give deference to international decisions,
because of doubts in their authority or lack of incorporation into the local law,(15) will not attribute much weight
to the prospects of a future international decision of this
kind.

3. Future International Decisions as Possible "Precedents".

A domestic court that is prepared to rely on international
decisions dealing with analogous cases may have knowledge of
pending international proceedings that deal with legal
questions identical or similar to those before it. A suspension of proceedings by the domestic court may, in due course,
furnish it with an important "precedent". Obviously, the
reservations outlined in the preceding section concerning
the relevance of the expected international decision must
also apply here. As set out in chapter III.E.3.b), the
authority of international decisions invoked as "precedents"
can vary considerably.

There is a case which demonstrates that domestic courts may
find a suspension of proceedings under these circumstances

worthwhile. The Tribunal de grande instance de Strasbourg(16) found another but similar case pending before the Court of Justice of the European Communities so important for the clarification of a question of Community Law in the case before it, that it stayed the proceedings until the European Court had decided the issue.

C. THE PROBABILITY OF A FUTURE INTERNATIONAL DECISION

These reflections have so far been based on the assumption that the international decision which may be of relevance to the case before the domestic court will in fact be forthcoming. This question itself can, however, be doubtful and is often decisive for the outcome of a domestic lawsuit. Where international proceedings are already pending, a domestic court is usually safe to assume that there will be an international decision eventually. This, however, is by no means certain in cases in which international procedures have been provided but where there is no firm indication that proceedings will in fact be instituted. Much will then depend on the circumstances of the individual case.

Under certain circumstances it is reasonably clear that no proceedings leading to an international decision will actually take place. Where, for instance, the international court or tribunal has already explicitly denied its jurisdiciton, a domestic court's refusal to proceed, based on the existence of an international procedure to settle the dispute, will inevitably lead to the denial of a judicial remedy. A case before the German Reichsgericht affords a pertinent example: In this case(17) the German-American Mixed Claims Commission had decided on only part of an American claim, since only one of the two debtors was a German. With respect to the remainder of the claim, it declared itself incompetent, but pointed out that this was without prejudice to the plaintiff's right to pursue this portion of the claim before another tribunal. When the plaintiff instituted proceedings before the ordinary German courts, the court of first instance declared itself without jurisdiction and held that the Mixed Claims Commission had erred in dismissing part of the original action and was exclusively competent for the entire claim. On appeal, the Reichsgericht set aside this decision. It found that the Mixed Claims Commission's finding on its competence had indeed been correct, and that, moreover, the international jurisdiction had not been exclusive anyway.

This case serves to demonstrate only too well that a negative conflict of competences caused by an exaggerated deference to international procedures may not only cause considerable difficulties to a claimant, but can also lead to a complete denial of justice and involve the corresponding danger of exposing the forum State to international responsibility.

Another situation in which there is no serious doubt that an international decision cannot reasonably be expected involves disputes for which international procedures have been envisaged, but the organs have either ceased to exist(18) or have never actually been set up.(19) Thus, in Manderlier v. U.N. and Belgium(2o) the plaintiff tried to pursue a claim for damages resulting from illegal acts of United Nations troops in the former Congo in the Belgian courts. He argued that in view of the failure of the United Nations to set up an appropriate mode of settlement for disputes of a private law character, as provided for in Section 29 of the Convention on the Privileges and Immunities of the United Nations(1 UNTS 16), the Belgian courts should hear his case. The Belgian court evidently appreciated the lack of an appropriate international procedure:

> The defendant /i.e. the UN7 considers quite wrongly that the previously mentioned Agreement, reached between the U.N. and Belgium on 2o February 1965, constitutes the appropriate method of settlement provided for by Section 29... The defendant has thus in reality been judge in its own cause. Such a procedure in no sense constitutes an appropriate method of settlement for deciding the dispute.

The Court, nevertheless, held that the Organization's immunity constituted a bar to the action:

> Be that as it may, it is for the United Nations, and for it alone, to set up the courts which would produce an appropriate method of settlement for the disputes which it may have with third parties. Immunity from jurisdiction has been conferred upon it, however inconvenient may be its results for litigants.

> ...in the absence of any appropriate court set up in pursuance of Section 29 of the Convention of 13 February 1946 ...one cannot see where the U.N. could be sued, nor how, nor on what legal basis (...), so long as it shelters behind its immunity from jurisdiction.(21)

Unlikely or uncertain future international decisions which are expected to resolve preliminary legal questions relevant to domestic proceedings can give rise to similar problems. An overcautious attitude towards the mere possibility of an international decision on a preliminary point, pertinent to the domestic case, can result in a breakdown of the lawsuit.

Thus, the mere existence of provisions on international
modes of dispute settlement has sometimes prompted courts to
withhold independent decisions,(22) or to refuse recognition
to foreign decisions,(23) without examining the question
whether an international decision on the particular point
was likely to be rendered. It is not difficult to perceive
that such an uncompromising policy of judicial restraint
will often lead to a "nondecision" in the sense described
in chapter II.A.3. The domestic court's blind submission to
the international procedure will then result in the failure
of the main claim.

D. ACCESS TO THE INTERNATIONAL FORUM

An essential consideration in choosing between an autonomous
decision or submission to a possible but uncertain international verdict is the question whether the international
forum is open or closed. In other words: Does the party who
seeks a decision, or the court itself, have access to the
international decision-maker? Can they exercise decisive
influence on the institution of proceedings? Where the
international forum is "closed" to claimant and court and
there are no indications that the parties who have access
will in fact start proceedings to settle the point in question, the domestic court will have to proceed with the
action on the merits if it does not want to jeopardize the
plaintiff's claim. Where the international decision-maker
presents an alternative forum to the plaintiff or can be
actively consulted on a preliminary point by an interested
participant - party or court - deference to the international proceedings will often be the better alternative.

1. Access to Pursue the Main Claim.

The traditional method of pursuing claims of individuals in
the international arena was the representation of the original claimant by the country of his nationality in the exercise of diplomatic protection. This method of pursuing
international claims is, however, subject to serious limitations. The country of the claimant's nationality may be
unable or unwilling to pursue the claim in the particular
case. Sometimes there is no State available to exercise
diplomatic protection.

Thus, in the German case, mentioned on p.335, the referral
of the claim back to the International Mixed Claims Commission by the court of first instance would have left the
plaintiff without any legal remedy since he had no access to
the Commission.

The situation was similar in a lawsuit instituted by the inhabitants of a territory under United States Trusteeship Administration in the United States federal courts against the Department of the Interior.(24) The District Court held that claims arising from the Trusteeship Agreement could only be pursued before the Security Council of the United Nations. The Court of Appeals reversed this decision. Its decision to admit the action was based not least on the procedural bars to the plaintiffs in the international arena:

> ...the alternative forum, the Security Council, would present to the plaintifffs obstacles so great as to make their rights virtually unenforceable.

The mere possibility of inter-State proceedings to recover a claim pending before a domestic court should, therefore, not necessarily induce a court to decline jurisdiction. Otherwise the plaintiff would often be deprived of any forum to pursue his claim.

The position is quite different where it is open to a claimant to pursue his claim independently before the international forum. In situations where an international procedure provides the plaintiff with a true alternative, the consequences of a domestic court's restrictive interpretation of its own jurisdiction are not usually fatal to the claim. No hardship will normally arise if the domestic court decides to refer the plaintiff to the international procedure. Nevertheless, the question of the international procedure's exclusive or optional nature is not totally without significance.

The mere setting up of an international procedure to settle disputes between parties who would otherwise have to litigate before domestic courts does not necessarily permit the conclusion that domestic proceedings are thereby precluded. In a particular case the domestic court has to decide whether the international procedure is exclusive or should merely provide an alternative forum for the claimant.

This question arose on several occasions in connection with claims which fell under the jurisdiction of the Mixed Arbitral Tribunals after World War I, but was never conclusively decided. Even the Mixed Arbitral Tribunals themselves were by no means agreed whether their jurisdiction was exclusive(25) or whether it merely constituted an alternative to proceedings before domestic courts.(26) The German Reichsgericht first seemed to think that German courts were debarred from hearing cases which fell under the Mixed Arbitral

Tribunals' jurisdiction.(27) It later changed its view and held that access to the Mixed Tribunals was merely a special right of Allied Powers' nationals which they could renounce by bringing a suit in the German courts.(28) Italian,(29) Roumanian,(3o) and French(31) courts expressed the opposite opinion.

The purpose of the system of Mixed Arbitral Tribunals would suggest that the opinion seeing them as an optional and not an exclusive forum is probably the better view. They provided the claimants with an additional and often more reliable and efficient forum to pursue their claims, but were probably not designed to prevent them from bringing their actions before the ordinary courts in the usual way. In situations like the one created by the establishment of the Mixed Arbitral Tribunals, there are no reasons why the plaintiff should not be left with a choice between international or municipal proceedings.(32) Once he has made this procedural choice he should, however, be bound by it.

Under certain circumstances, the creation of international modes of dispute settlement may, however, be specifically motivated by a desire to avoid the involvement of domestic courts. Similar problems which arise in connection with judicial procedures set up by international organizations to settle disputes arising from contracts of employment may, therefore, call for a different solution. Here too the individuals concerned are granted direct access to the Administrative Tribunals or similar bodies. Nevertheless, there have been repeated efforts to circumvent these procedures and to seize domestic courts of the claims. In most cases the international organization's immunity alone meant that these efforts had to fail. (See chapter XII.C.2. above). In fact, problems of immunity are so dominant in many of the pertinent decisions, that the question of the international organ's concurrent jurisdiction does not seem to have had any significant impact. In some of the judgments, however, the courts explicitly referred the international civil servants to the competent organs within the framework of the international organization.(33) Even where there was doubt as to whether these organs would provide the plaintiff with adequate judicial protection, domestic courts declined to intervene.(34)

International organizations display a strong endeavor to secure an independent exercise of their functions unimpaired by State-organs. The machinery of dispute-settlement, provided in the framework of the organization, thus, represents a certain procedural counterbalance to the organization's

immunity. In addition, the international organ specially set
up to deal with disputes arising within the organization
usually has a better knowledge of the material law to be
applied. Moreover, in disputes arising from employment with
the organization there are usually explicit contractual
submissions to the jurisdiction of the international organ.
All these arguments speak strongly in favor of an exclusive
jurisdiction for the international organs. Only a lack of
effective judicial protection of the individual in these
procedures could be a valid argument in favor of domestic
courts. Even then the organization's immunity from domestic
jurisdiciton will usually foil all attempts to enlist their
help.

Finally, there are cases in which the parties to a contract
specifically agreed to submit disputes to an international
judicial organ, usually an arbitral tribunal, at the exclusion of the ordinary courts. An agreement to submit disputes
to a *forum prorogatum* is usually based on sound practical
considerations such as doubts in the impartiality of domestic
courts or an easier enforcement of arbitral awards than of
foreign judgments. A party insisting on it is entitled to
its scrupulous observance. The available case material suggests that domestic courts were not inclined to support
plaintiffs' efforts to avoid agreed international procedures. The French Cour de cassation(35) dismissed actions of
this kind and referred the parties to the agreed arbitral
procedures. American courts went even a step further and
forced recalcitrant parties, usually foreign States, to
submit to the arbitration.(36) Here too, the main problem
was, however, not so much the demarcation of the respective
national and international jurisdictions as the question of
State immunity.(37)

2. Access to Clarify Preliminary Questions.

The existence of international procedures for the clarification of preliminary points pending in cases before domestic
courts has raised particular problems. Domestic courts
sometimes regarded international organs, which were usually
entrusted with the task of settling disputes concerning the
interpretation of treaties, as exclusively competent to
answer questions of this kind even in cases in which neither
the claimant nor the court had any influence on the institution of the international proceedings.(38) In the opinion of
these courts, the mere existence of an international jurisdiction to decide a question of international interest precluded them from making even an incidental decision on the
point. Where it was not open to an interested party or the

court itself to induce an international decision, this meant
that the court saw itself unable to proceed to the merits of
the case.(39)

This point is well illustrated by the divergent results
reached in the application of the NATO Status of Forces
Agreement of 1951 (199 UNTS 67) by domestic courts. Article
VIII para.5 provides for the settlement by the receiving
State of claims by a third person arising out of damage
caused by foreign forces in the performance of their official
duty. Para.8 of that Article provides for an arbitration between the sending State and the receiving State in case of a
dispute over the official nature of the act that inflicted
the damage. Domestic courts were faced with the problem of
how to deal with the question of the "official" or "private"
nature of tortious acts when applying Article VIII/5. The
receiving State as the defendant, understandably enough,
invariably claimed that the tort in question had been "private" and was not interested in an arbitration. The sending
State, which would have had to refund part of the damages,
was also not interested in having the official nature of the
tort established. The plaintiff had no means of influencing
the institution of the inter-State arbitration.

The French Cour de cassation held in several decisions(4o)
that the French courts had no jurisdiction to qualify independently the tortious act as "official" or "private", since
Article VIII/8 of the Agreement represented a "disposition
impérative de droit public international". Proceedings,
therefore, had to be suspended until an international award
had been rendered. A Canadian court, faced with the same
question, followed the French example.(41)

The decision of a United States federal court(42) was less
rigid in its attitude towards the necessity of an international decision under Article VIII/8. It found that it saw no
possibility to compel the United States to institute proceedings and would not accept a letter of the State Department
declaring that the illegal act had not taken place in the
course of official duties. The court found, however, that it
would accept an interpretation if the executive department
could prove that both the United States and Belgium, the
sending State, were agreed upon it. The American court,
thus, did not insist on the international proceedings, realizing that they would most probably never take place. Nevertheless, it permitted two interested parties to determine a
decisive preliminary point to the detriment of the plaintiff.

In a particularly instructive case before the Italian courts
the dispute arose from a collision between the plaintiff, an
Italian national, and a United States serviceman stationed
in Italy under the NATO Forces Agreement. When the plaintiff
sued the Italian Defense Ministry in accordance with the
Treaty provisions, the court of first instance(43) proceeded
to the merits of the claim denying the necessity or possibility of having recourse to arbitration. The representative
of the State appealed, contending that it was necessary to
institute an arbitral procedure. The Court of Appeal, after
setting aside the decision of the court below, suspended the
proceedings pending a decision of the arbitrator. The Italian government, however, informed the court that it saw no
reason to institute arbitral proceedings, seeing that the
Italian and United States Governments agreed that the act
causative of the accident was not in the exercise of official duties. Upon this, the Court of Appeal dismissed the
claim. On further appeal, the Court of cassation reversed
this decision.(44) It rejected the statement by the Government as conclusive of the rights to damages under the Convention, since such an interpretation would deprive the
injured person of his judicial protection under Article 24
of the Constitution. The qualification of the causative act,
therefore, remained for the Italian judge to decide.

Of the various solutions offered by the cases, only the one
adopted by the Italian Court of cassation can be considered
satisfactory. From the viewpoint of the protection of the
individual, the procedure provided by the NATO Status of
Forces Agreement must be regarded as infelicitous. Practice
has shown that disputes for which the international arbitral
procedure has been provided do not normally arise between
the potential parties to the arbitration but between an
individual and the receiving State. In such a situation, an
insistence on the international arbitration or a submission
to an understanding between the States concerned will more
likely than not lead to a "conspiracy"(45) of the two States
to the detriment of the aggrieved party. A faithful application of the provisions of the Treaty dealing with compensation, in situations as described above, can, therefore, only
be expected from the domestic courts themselves.

In the majority of similar cases, courts have adopted the
view that the mere possibility of an international decision
on a legal question pending before them was not to be regarded as a sufficient reason to withhold a decision on the
merits.(46) The German Reichsgericht,(47) when confronted
with the task of applying a decision of the Council of the
League of Nations, was quite unimpressed by the existence of

an inter-State procedure to have this decision interpreted.
Similarly, the Italian Court of cassation(48) held that
provisions in the Peace Treaty of 1949, concerning a Conciliation Commission to settle disputes arising from the application of certain parts of the Treaty, did not mean that the
ordinary domestic courts were unable to interpret the Treaty.
In an Austrian case the Administrative Court(49) adopted the
same solution under very similar circumstances.

In cases in which international procedures are "closed" to
the interested participants, and there is no firm indication
that proceedings will be instituted, it would, therefore,
not be appropriate to deny a jurisdiction to domestic courts
to decide on individual claims just because legal questions
relevant to such a claim fall under the jurisdiction of an
international decision-maker.

The situation is quite different where it is open to an
interested party or the court to initiate the international
proceedings. Where this possibility exists, much is to be
said in favor of a suspension of the proceedings and a
request for an international decision.

Sometimes domestic courts were able to obtain decisions on
important preliminary points without any institutionalised
procedure simply by making an informal inquiry with the international organization in question. (See chapter III.A.
above). In the majority of situations, however, a cooperation
of this kind between domestic courts and international
organs requires a well-organized procedure and cannot be
left simply to the initiative of the courts.

A system of preliminary rulings by international judicial
organs is particularly useful in situations in which it can
be expected that domestic courts will frequently have to
deal with questions of international concern in the course
of private litigation. In this situation neither a submission
of the entire case to an international decision-maker nor a
subsequent examination of the domestic decision's conformity
with the relevant international prescriptions affords an
entirely satisfactory solution. Often the most effective
method to achieve a uniform application of these prescrip-
itons is to single out the inclusive questions arising in
the course of the domestic proceedings and to separately
submit them for a preliminary ruling by the international
judicial body.

This technique was first employed in the German-Polish
Agreement on Upper Silesia of May 15, 1922. The Arbitral

Tribunal for which it provided was competent to determine questions concerning the interpretation of the Agreement which came up before domestic courts or administrative authorities.(5o) The domestic organ stayed the proceedings and submitted the question to the Arbitral Tribunal upon the application of one of the parties or the State-representative or upon the court's or authority's own initiative. The Tribunal's finding was binding for the case in which it was given. Where a domestic court or administrative authority wanted to depart from a previous ruling of the Tribunal, it had to make a reasoned submission. The Arbitral Tribunal's decision in such cases was again binding.

In the French-German Treaty of October 27, 1956,(51) returning the Saar-territory to Germany, the method of preliminary rulings was used to ensure the uniform application in French and Saar courts of French law remaining in force during the transition period.

The competence of the Court of Justice of the European Communities to give preliminary rulings on matters of Community Law is undoubtedly the principal example of this technique today and has received extensive scholarly attention. A detailed treatment would go far beyond the confines of the present study. Article 177 of the EEC Treaty(52) authorizes domestic courts to refer questions of Community Law, which have arisen in cases pending before them, to the Court for a conclusive opinion. Domestic courts of last instance are under an obligation to submit such questions. The European Court has found(53) that there is no need to resubmit a question where it had already given a ruling in a previous case that was materially identical. This does not, however, preclude the national judge from submitting a question of interpretation again, if he finds it appropriate to do so.

The German-Austrian Property Treaty of June 15, 1957(54) incorporated a similar procedure. An Arbitral Tribunal is competent to give binding rulings concerning the interpretation and application of the Treaty on questions submitted by the courts of either country.

Attempts to introduce this method of preliminary rulings to the European Court of Human Rights have met with no success. (55)

Finally, the Treaty establishing the Benelux Court,(56) whose task is the promotion of a uniform application of the common body of law in the three countries, provides for a procedure for the submission of preliminary questions by domestic courts, obviously inspired by Article 177 of the EEC Treaty.

Thus, if an answer to an important question before the
domestic court can be expected within a reasonable time
through international adjudication, much is to be said in
favor of consulting the international forum. The advantages
of its expert knowledge and of the unifying effect of its
practice will usually far outweigh the predictable but
limited delay caused to the domestic proceedings.

E. SUMMARY AND POLICY ALTERNATIVES

In determining whether there are parallel international
proceedings which would make it unwise for a domestic court
to proceed with a case, formalistic criteria like identical
territorial jurisdiction or an identity of parties should
not be given decisive importance. Only an ascertainment of
the ultimate beneficiaries is likely to reveal a material
identity of claims.

Deference should be given to international proceedings
concerned with preliminary questions pending before domestic
courts only after a careful examination of the international
decision's likely relevance. Where the benefits of the
international decision cannot be expected to outweigh the
disadvantages of the delay, a suspension of domestic proceedings does not appear justified.

In deciding whether to await the outcome of international
judicial proceedings, a domestic court will have to carefully
examine the probability that these proceedings will, in
fact, take place. Unless there are reasons to believe that a
pertinent international decision will actually be rendered
within a reasonable time, a domestic court should normally
proceed to an autonomous decision.

If the plaintiff has access to international proceedings as
an alternative way of satisfying his claim, a domestic court
will only be justified in dismissing the action if the
international procedure is clearly designed to represent a
substitute for domestic proceedings intended to exclude
resort to municipal courts.

The existence of an international procedure for the clarification of a preliminary legal question relevant in domestic
proceedings does not necessarily imply a lack of jurisdiction
on the part of domestic courts to decide these questions and
a resulting duty to await an international decision. If
neither an interested party nor the court itself has access

to the international decision-maker to initiate the proceedings, the only acceptable solution is an independent decision of the domestic court.

If it is open to a domestic court to consult an international judicial organ actively, a submission of unclear international legal questions has much to commend itself. Preliminary rulings are a particularly promising way of achieving
maximum uniformity and quality in domestic decision-making
on questions of inclusive concern.

(1) For an earlier study by this author see Concurrent Ju-
     risdiction of National and International Tribunals, 13
     Hous.L.Rev. 5o8(1976).

(2) S.A.I.M.I. Claim, 13 Nov.1951, 18 ILR 471(1951); see
     also the decision by the same Commission in the Guille-
     mot-Jacquemin Claim, 29 Aug.1949, 18 ILR 4o3(1951) and
     in the Ottoz Claim, 18 Sept.195o, 18 ILR 435(1951).
     Also the decision of the French-Mexican Mixed Claims
     Commission in the Jean-Baptiste Claire Case, 7 June
     1929, 5 AD 444(1929-3o), 5 RIAA p.516; and the decision
     of the British-Mexican Mixed Claims Commission of 3
     Aug.1931, 5 RIAA p.252.

(3) Public Prosecutor v. Aerts, 1o March 1939, 9 AD 52,
     58(1938-4o).

(4) For examples of exact prescriptions governing the
     interaction of national and international judicial
     organs, apart from European Community Law see especially
     the Convention on the Settlement of Matters Arising out
     of the War and the Occupation of 23 Oct.1954, 332 UNTS
     219 and the Agreement on German External Debts of 27
     Feb.1953, 333 UNTS 3. See esp. Erler, Die Beschränkung
     der rechtsprechenden Gewalt in der Bundesrepublik durch
     die Zuständigkeit internationaler Gerichte, in Göttin-
     ger Festschrift für das Oberlandesgericht Celle p.27
     (1961); Hallier, Völkerrechtliche Schiedsinstanzen,
     p.31seq.; cf. also the Conciliation Committee under the
     German-Austrian Property Treaty of 15 June 1957, Austri-
     an BGBl.119/1958. See esp. Seidl-Hohenveldern, The
     Austrian-German Arbitral Tribunal, p.27seq. See also
     the German-French Treaty of 27 Oct.1956 on the settle-
     ment of the Saar question, German BGBl.1956 II, p.1589,
     and Arts.1 and 2 of the Additional Protocol to the
     European Convention on State Immunity, ETS 74.

(5) On the analogous question of concurrent proceedings
     before internal and foreign courts see especially
     Szászy, International Civil Procedure, p.54oseq.;
     Schütze, Die Berücksichtigung der Rechtshängigkeit
     eines ausländischen Verfahrens, 31 RabelsZ 233(1967);
     Habscheid, Zur Berücksichtigung der Rechtshängigkeit
     eines ausländischen Verfahrens, 31 RabelsZ 254(1967);
     Vieira, La litispendencia en el derecho internacional
     privado, 25 Revista Esp.DI 395,413(1972).

(6) See especially Gormley, The Procedural Status of the
     Individual before International and Supranational

Tribunals (1966).

(7)   <u>Landwirtschaftlicher Zentralverband in Polen v. Liqui-
      dating Committee in Poznam</u>, 17 Nov.1927, 4 AD 476(1927-
      28).

(8)   <u>S.A.Belge H.A.V. v. Belgian State</u>, 14 July 193o, 5 AD
      447(1929-3o).

(9)   6 Jan.1925, RGZ 1o9,387,39o. It should be noted that
      the registration of the claim with the Mixed Claims
      Commission only took place after the action had been
      started in the German courts.

(1o) <u>Compagnie des Wagons-Réservoirs v. Ministry of Industry
      and Commerce and Italian Railways</u>, 7 Oct.195o, 18 ILR
      394(1951).

(11) <u>Ministre de la guerre c/ Hallet</u>, 28 Apr.1876, Sirey
      1878, 2,189.

(12) <u>Y. v. Public Prosecutor</u>, 11 Feb. and 2o March 1957, 7
      NTIR 282(196o).

(13) See e.g. <u>Danzig (Proceedings before the High Commissio-
      ner)</u>, Obergericht Danzig, 15 Feb.1934, 4 ZaöRV 954
      (1934), 7 AD 61(1933-34). In this case international
      proceedings were pending before the High Commissioner
      of the League of Nations to clarify a disputed inter-
      pretation.

(14) 29 Jan.1963, 18 ÖJZ 327(1963).

(15) See e.g. remarks by the Italian Corte di cassazione in
      <u>Goretti v. Ministero difesa</u>, 5 Feb.1971, 54 Rivista DI
      253,262(1971), to the effect that a possible future
      international arbitral award would not have consequen-
      ces for a litigation between private persons.

(16) <u>Etabl. Consten c/ Willy Leissner</u>, 3 June 1965, 12 AFDI
      89o(1966).

(17) 26 Sept.193o, 6o JW 15o(1931).

(18) In <u>Ditte c/ Joudro</u>, the French Court of cassation had
      to determine whether Joudro had refugee status. The
      necessary certificate by the representative of the
      League High Commissioner to this effect was unobtainable
      since the League of Nations had ceased to exist. The

Court found that the certificate by the international
organ was not an indispensible prerequisite for a
decision of French courts on this point. 19 Jan.1948,
37 RCDIP p.31o(1948).

(19) See also Italian cases in which the courts found that
the mere inclusion of arbitral clauses into the conditions of employment of international organizations
without an actual setting up of the competent decision
organs did not oust the jurisdiction of domestic courts:
Maida v. Administration for International Assistance,
Corte di cassazione, 27 May 1955, 39 Rivista DI 546
(1956), 23 ILR 51o(1956); Luggeri c. C.I.M.E., Tribunale Santa Maria Capua Vetere, 2o June 1966, 51 Rivista
DI 14o(1968) confirmed by the Court of cassation 11
Nov.1974, 2 Italian YBIL 347(1976); but see the earlier
case: Viecelli v. IRO, Trib. Trieste, 2o July 1951, 36
Rivista DI 47o(1953), 49 AJIL 1o2(1955).

(2o) Tribunal civil Brussels, 11 May 1966, 5 RBDI 374(1969),
45 ILR 446, confirmed by the Cour d'Appel of Brussels,
15 Sept.1969, 7 RBDI 743(1971), 98 Clunet 843(1971).

(21) 45 ILR 452, 455.

(22) Revici v. Conference of Jewish Material Claims against
Germany Inc., Supr.Ct.N.Y., 9 May 1958, 26 ILR 362(1958-
II). Cf. also the cases below XIV.D.2.

(23) Stê Energie Êletrique du Littoral Méditerranéen v. Com-
pagnia Imprese Elettriche Liguri, Corte di cassazione,
13 Feb.1939, 9 AD 12o(1938-4o).

(24) People of Saipan ex rel. Guerrero v. U.S.Dept. of the
Interior er al., Ct.of App. 9th Cir., 16 July 1974, 5o2
F.2d 9o, 69 AJIL 432(1975), cert. den. 42o U.S. 1oo3.

(25) To this effect: Rankin v. Turkish Government, English-
Turkish Mixed Arbitral Tribunal, 16 Dec.1929, 5 AD
444(1929-3o), IX Recueil 747(1929-3o); Héritiers Hector
de Backer c. Municipalitê de Philippopoli, Bulgarian-
Belgian Mixed Arbitral Tribunal, 27 Jan.1926, VI Recueil 144(1927).

(26) To this effect: Rafael Cappon and Son v. Vereinigte
Glühlampen und Elektrizitäts A.G., Hungarian-Romanian
Mixed Arbitral Tribunal, 17 July 1924, 5 AD 433(1929-
3o), IX Recueil 46o(1929-3o); Banque Meyer c. Gebr.
Weil, French-German Mixed Arbitral Tribunal, 19 July

1923, III Recueil 639(1924); <u>Nicaise c. Etat allemand</u>
<u>et Hoopmann</u>, German-Belgian Mixed Arbitral Tribunal, 21
Dec.1925, VI Recueil 93(1927); <u>Arfvidson ès qualités c.</u>
<u>Office allemand</u>, French-German Mixed Arbitral Tribunal,
17 July 1926, VI Recueil 846(1927); <u>Kairis c. Erckens</u>
<u>et Etat allemand</u>, German-Belgian Mixed Arbitral Tribu-
nal, 27 June 1928, VIII Recueil 183(1928-29).

(27) 11 Dec.1922, RGZ 1o6,56, 51 Clunet 483(1924).

(28) 16 Apr.1924, RGZ 1o8,5o; 31 May 1927, JW 2311(1927); 27
June 1928, RGZ 121, 337,341; 16 Jan. 1929, RGZ 123,13o,
132seq.

(29) <u>Soc. di Navigazione Adria v. Feher</u>, Corte di cassazione,
29 Jan.1936, 8 AD 429(1935-37); <u>The Gramophone Co. c.</u>
<u>Curatoli</u>, Court of Appeal Naples, 18 June 1924, 52
Clunet 487(1925).

(3o) <u>C. et G.Gaëtan C. Schlossfabrik A.G. Witte Schutte</u>,
Cour de Bucarest, 31 May 1923, 51 Clunet 1135(1924).

(31) <u>Bellens c/ Soc. Lanz</u>, Cour de Paris, 13 May 1922, 5o
Clunet 84o(1923).

(32) Cf. also explicit treaty provisions under which an
alternative between domestic courts and international
judicial organs is offered: Rhine Navigation Act (1868)
on the competences of the Central Commission, Martens
N.R.G. vol.2o, p.355 at 365. In this context see the
decision of the German Reichsgericht of 27 Oct.1915,
RGZ 87,251. See also the optional jurisdiction of
international organs under Chapter X, Art.12/1,2 of the
Convention on the Settlement of Matters Arising out of
the War and Occupation 332 UNTS, p.219 at 3o2 and under
Art.32/2, and Annex IV, Art.11/2 of the Agreement on
German external debts 333 UNTS, p.3 at 52,21o.

(33) <u>Marrê c/ UNIDROIT</u>, Tribunale di Roma, 12 June 1965, 5o
Rivista DI 149(1967), 95 Clunet 386(1968); <u>Dame Klars-</u>
<u>feld c/ Office franco-allemand pour la jeunesse</u>, Cour
d'appel de Paris, 18 June 1968, 15 AFDI 865(1969), see
also Larger in 14 AFDI 369(1968); Supr.Ct.Chile, 8
Nov.1969, UNJYB 237(1969).

(34) <u>Profili v. International Institute of Agriculture</u>, 26
Feb.1931, 23 Rivista DI 386(1931), 5 AD 413(1929-3o).

(35) Office National Interprofessionel des Céréales c/ Capi-
taine du S/S San Carlo, 14 Apr.1964, 92 Clunet 646(1965);
Société Transshipping v. Federation of Pakistan,
2 March 1966, 47 ILR 15o. In this case the decision
was, however, based on the defendant's immunity. See,
by contrast, the admission of an action in spite of an
arbitral agreement by the Supreme Court of India in
V/O Tractoroexport v. Tarapore, 1o IJIL 516(197o), 66
AJIL 637(1972). This decision is severely criticized by
Domke, New aspects of East-West trade arbitration, in
Commercial Arbitration, Essays in memoriam Eugenio
Minoli p.121,125(1974).

(36) Victory Transport Inc. v. Comisaria General de Abaste-
cimientos y Transportes, U.S.Ct. of App. 2d Cir., 9
Sept.1964, 336 F.2d 354, cert.den 381 U.S.934; Petrol
Shipping Co., U.S.Ct. of App. 2d Cir., 21 Apr.1966, 36o
F.2d 1o3, cert.den. 385 U.S.931; Cavac v. Board for
the Validation of German Bonds in the United States et
al., Dist.Ct. S.Dist.N.Y., 27 Oct. and 2 Nov.196o, 189
F.Supp.2o5, 31 ILR 4o1; Greenwich Marine Inc. v. S.S.
Alexandra and Ministry of Supply of the United Arab Re-
public, Ct.App. 2d Circ., 7 Jan.1965, 339 F.2d 9o1;
Pan American Tankers Corp. v. Republic of Viet-Nam, 25
Feb.1969, 296 F.Supp.361, 63 AJIL 826(1969). For fur-
ther references see Domke, The Enforcement of Maritime
Arbitration Agreements with Foreign Governments, in 2
Journal of Maritime Law and Commerce 617(1971); *ibid.*,
Arbitration, in Nationalism and the Multinational
Enterprise (Hahlo et al. Eds.) p.233,242(1973).

(37) See: Reisman, Nullity and Revision, p.8o6seq., Goldman
in 92 Clunet 647(1965), and Carabiber, L'immunité de
juridiction, p.23.

(38) Cf. also note 22 above.

(39) Cf. also Occidental Petroleum Corp. v. Buttes Gas & Oil
Co., U.S.Dist.Ct., C.D.Calif., 17 March 1971, 331
F.Supp.92. In a dispute between oil companies an international territorial question arose as a preliminary
point. The court declined to make a decision and found:
"Authoritative judicial resolution of international
boundary disputes is a function not of domestic courts,
but of international tribunals, acting upon the consent
of the contestant states". P.1o3. In the paricular case
there was no indication of international proceedings.
Contrast this decision with the one by the English
Court of Appeal between the same litigants, 5 Dec.1974,

The Times, 6 Dec.1974, 69 AJIL 435(1975).

(4o) Jallais v. Compagnie d'Assurances La Zurich, 1o July
1961, 42 ILR 136; Air Liquide and Another v. Coody and
Another, 1o July 1961, 42 ILR 135; Agent judiciaire du
Tresor c/ Dame veuve Gaulet et autres, 28 May 197o,
98 Clunet 3o8(1971).

(41) Gagnon v. R., 197o, 1o CanYIL 322(1972).

(42) Robertson v. U.S.,, Ct.of Appp., D.C., 11 July 1961,
294 F.2d 92o, 32 ILR 359(1969).

(43) Goretti v. Ministero difesa, 7 May 1966, 5o Rivista DI
171(1967).

(44) 5 Feb.1971, 54 Rivista DI 253(1971). To the same effect:
Ministero della Difesa v. Massimo Esposito, Corte di
cassazione, 5 July 1973, 2 Italian YBIL 358(1976).

(45) Cf. Ruziè in 98 Clunet 312(1971).

(46) Cf. also a statement by the Court of Justice of the
European Communities to this effect in Van Gend en Loos
v. Nederlandse Tariefcommissie, 5 Feb.1963, 2 CMLRep.
1o5 at 13o: "The fact that the Treaty in the aforemen-
tioned Articles/169 and 17o/, allows the Commission and
the member-States to bring before the Court a State
which has not carried out its obligations, does not
imply that individuals may not invoke these obligations,
in appropriate cases, before a national court"; to the
same effect see the decision of the German Bundesgerichtshof 14 Apr.1959, 2 CMLRep. 251(1963).

(47) RGZ 131,25o,255, 2 Feb.1931.

(48) Combes de Lestrade v. Ministry of Finance, 31 Oct.1955,
22 ILR 882(1955); Ministero del Tesoro v. Di Raffaele,
13 Nov.1974, 2 Italian YBIL 364(1976) with references
to further Italian cases on this point.

(49) Slg. 1834(F.), 23 May 1958, 89 Clunet 73o(1962).

(5o) RGBl. 1922 II, p.238. Arts.588,589,591. See especially
Kaeckenbeek, The International Experiment of Upper
Silesia, p.486seq.(1942); *ibid.*, The Character and Work
of the Arbitral Tribunal of Upper Silesia, 21 Transactions of the Grotius Society 27(1935).

(51) BGBl. 1956 II, p.1589; Art.42.

(52) Cf. also Art.15o of the Euratom Treaty and Art.41 of the Treaty establishing the Coal and Steel Community.

(53) Da Costa en Schaake N.V. et Al. c. Administration Fiscale Néerlandaise, 27 March 1963, 2 CMLRep. 224 at 237. See also (French) Cour de cassation, Deroche, Cornet et Soc. Promatex-France, 29 June 1966. Dalloz-Sirey, J.595 (1966).

(54) BGBl. 1958 II, p.13o. Generally see Seidl-Hohenveldern, The Austrian-German Arbitral Tribunal (1972).

(55) Cf. Robertson, Advisory Opinions of the Court of Human Rights, 1 René Cassin Amicorum Discipulorumque Liber 225 (1969); Schreuer, The Impact of International Institutions on the Protection of Human Rights in Domestic Courts, 4 Israel Yearbook on Human Rights 6o at 76 (1974).

(56) 31 March 1965, 13 European Yearbook 259(1965). In force 1 Jan.1974. See Ganshof van der Meersch, La juridiction internationale dans l'Union économique Benelux, 15 AFDI 245,258(1969); Schneider, The Benelux Court, 4 NYIL 193(1973). For a request for a ruling see Netherlands Supreme Court in Colgate-Palmolive v. Lucas Bols, 14 June 1974, 6 NYIL 372(1975).

XV. CONCLUSIONS

Domestic courts enjoy an unusual degree of discretion in deciding questions involving decisions of international institutions. Specific prescriptions regulating these questions are exceptional. The initiative in developing the law on this point is largely with the courts. For this reason, the policy considerations governing the conduct of the courts deserve particular attention. An attempt was made to focus on specific points of policy throughout the present study in the appropriate context. This concluding chapter shall summarize the most significant aspects of the practice of the courts and the most important policy alternatives in the light of the basic policy considerations as formulated and adopted at the outset in chapter I.E.

1. The behavior of courts only partly corresponds to the demand for the effectiveness of decisions of international institutions. In investigating the conditioning factors for the refusal of domestic courts to make decisions of international institutions controlling, we have to distinguish between formal arguments and the true motives underlying decisions. In a particular case, a formal argument put forward by a court may, of course, represent its true motive.

One possibility to frustrate the effectiveness of an international decision is its rejection because of its lack of authority. This argument, especially based on the "non-binding" character of international decisions, is employed only in relatively few cases. Only in connection with international "precedents" and recommendations of international organs is there a minority of cases in which deference to the international decision is refused for this reason. Even with international decisions whose legal force is disputed in theory, such as, decisions of the United Nations Security Council, the courts usually show no inclination to enter into the question of their legal relevance.

A review by domestic courts of international decisions in the light of alleged irregularities is also exceptional. The relatively few cases in which domestic courts found international decisions void raise the suspicion that "political" motives, especially identifications with the forum State's special interests, have played an important rôle.

We can, therefore, conclude that the professed goal of effectivenss for international decisions in domestic courts is not seriously threatened by arguments directed at their nullity or lack of authority.

An important but largely unsettled question for the effectiveness of international decisions is the behavior of courts in third States, that is to say, in States to which the international decision is not immediately addressed. These States and their organs are not under an obligation to comply with the international decisions but may be subject to a general obligation to cooperate in the implementation of international community measures. An active intervention of domestic courts also in favor of international decisions which have no immediate connecting link to the forum State could decisively enhance their effectiveness.

Dualist conceptions about the relationship of national and international law are a serious obstacle to the effectiveness of international decisions in many cases. A conspicuous phenomenon in this context is the diverse treatment accorded to different international decisions by the domestic courts. Thus, deference to operative decisions emanating from non-judicial international organs or to regulations almost invariably depends on domestic implementing legislation. On the other hand, courts usually find local implementing measures unnecessary where the international decision is invoked for the purpose of elucidating preliminary questions, of providing a "precedent", or where it is an official interpretation of a treaty.

In many situations implementing measures taken by individual States are necessary or useful to safeguard the observance of international decisions by domestic courts. An unqualified insistence on their "incorporation" into domestic law is, however, neither theoretically convincing nor practically feasible.

The question of the international decisions' internal promulgation is closely connected to the question of implementing measures. The attitude of courts towards the necessity of a local publication is not uniform. An optimum promulgation would appear desirable in the interest of the international decisions' effectiveness. An absolute insistence of domestic courts on a local publication as a precondition for application does not seem advisable.

Domestic prescriptions contradicting international decisions are only rarely an obstacle to their application. In most cases courts are able to avoid contradictions by a harmonizing interpretation. Courts are only rarely compelled to act openly contrary to an international decision because of a

conflicting internal prescription. There are also examples
of court decisions in favor of the international decision at
the cost of the domestic prescription. However, in these
cases courts do not speak of competing prescriptions but
simply apply the international decision as the materially
applicable law. Solutions of this kind accord with the goal
of effectiveness of international decisions without having
to fall back on constructions of a "primacy or priority of
norms".

In most cases the participation of the forum State in the
litigation does not show any adverse effects on the effectiveness of international decisions. Especially in cases
concerning wealth allocations, domestic courts are usually
neither prepared to accept demands for procedural privileges
in favor of the forum State nor influenced in reaching a
decision on the merits.

The immunity of foreign States is a general problem for the
effective implementation of international claims by domestic
courts. Contemporary court practice shows signs of an extension of the distinction between public and private claims
also to the implementation of decisions of international
institutions. A more judicious solution would consist in an
exclusion of sovereign immunity in all cases in which an
international decision-maker has made an authoritative
determination on the merits.

A policy of maximum effectiveness for the activities of
international institutions would call for an extensive right
to sue, but a limited liability to be sued for the institutions themselves. The practice of courts is largely in
accordance with these principles, usually on the basis of
specific prescriptions. Courts only rarely make attempts to
limit the procedural immunity of international organisations
in the interest of their opponents.

In contrast to these more formal arguments, there are a
number of aspects affecting decisions which cannot be phrased in traditional legal verbiage. The values at stake in
domestic litigation show a clear influence on the behavior
of courts concerning the effective implementation of or
deference to international decisions. The courts usually
adopt a neutral attitude towards cases involving wealth
allocations. Decisions of international organs dealing with
the protection of human rights are often treated in a way
which actively promotes their effectiveness. Problems of
State jurisdiction, like territorial questions, are avoided
unless the decision made by the international organ is

generally recognized or unless the forum State pursues a
strong independent line irrespective of the international
decision. Courts have been passive or disinterested towards
international community measures, such as, enforcement
action taken by the United Nations Security Council.

In cases in which the effectiveness of international decisions runs counter to important special interests of the
forum State, courts display a distinct tendency to identify
with the forum State's position. But in the vast majority of
cases under examination this problem is not acute and no
bias is discernible. Only in a very limited number of cases
does the forum State's interest in certain international
questions become so dominant that the aspect of compliance
with international decisions recedes into the background. A
conscious promotion of community interests in the effective
enforcement of international decisions is hardly discernible
in the practice of courts at the present stage.

Aspects of effectiveness for international decisions can
arise even before the international organ has made a decision. Where proceedings are pending before international
organs a court may decide to suspend the case before it in
order to await an international decision dealing with the
same claim or with a preliminary point.

2. The observance of human rights can play a rôle in several
contexts of domestic litigation dealing with decisions of
international institutions. The readiness of courts to give
deference to organized international endeavors for the
furtherance of individual liberties is relatively large.
This is borne out, in particular, by court practice dealing
with the Universal Declaration of Human Rights. Only rarely
do courts resort to formal arguments to defeat its application. Reliance by domestic courts on the practice of the
international supervisory organs of the European Convention
on Human Rights is not yet entirely satisfactory but there
is a clear trend towards improvement. Overall, however, we
may say that any obstacles lie not so much in an unwilling-
ness of the courts to give deference to the international
practice as in a dearth of information available to them.

Difficulties in the protection of human rights can also
arise with international institutions themselves and their
decisions or activities. The need for the effective protection of individual liberties has become more and more evident as a consequence of the extension of public functions
exercised by the State in more and more areas of human life.
As these public functions are increasingly taken over by

international institutions the need for the protection of
individual rights against these institutions will grow. So
far this problem has only attracted attention in the regional
context of European Community Law.

Part of the obstacles to the pursuit of individual claims
against international institutions themselves are created by
their procedural immunities. A limited reduction of these
immunities is sometimes desirable, but is only rarely within
the discretion of domestic courts.

Even without a participation of international institutions
in litigation, the protection of human rights against their
decisions or activities can be important. Much will depend
on the readiness of the courts to strike a reasonable balance
between the policies of, on the one hand, according effectiveness to international decisions and of, on the other
hand, reviewing them for their compliance with international
and national standards for the protection of human rights.
At present considerations of this kind are still only at a
rudimentary stage in the practice of the courts. They are
likely to grow in significance with the increase of activities of international institutions.

3. Respect for international decisions concerning wealth
allocations and their conversion into effective control over
the resources in question is only a special application of
the policy of making international decisions effective and
sometimes of the call for a protection of human rights. The
typical dangers in this area lie usually not so much in any
doubts in the international decisions' authority or in
dualist notions as in procedural privileges of the debtor or
procedural disadvantages of the claimant. Courts are usually
prepared to enforce claims to wealth against the forum
State. However, in spite of certain limitations, the immunity of foreign States and, to a lesser extent, of international organizations is still a serious obstacle to the pursuit
of claims to wealth even where they are based on authoritative decisions of international organs.

Another serious problem is the standing of individuals and
corporations in domestic proceedings for the pursuit of
claims based on international decisions in view of the fact
that they did not participate in the international proceedings leading to them. Already, court practice displays a
certain trend towards an improved protection of international claims to wealth. It is largely in the hands of the
courts to take the initiative for the closure of the remaining remedial gaps.

4. Finally, there is the general procedural policy of not
depriving a claimant of his day in court by blocking the
access to domestic proceedings for formal reasons. The
rejection of claims for formal reasons without an examination of their merits is a common way to deal with actions in
which decisions of international organs play a decisive
part. The narrow interpretation of the conditions for actions
may often have its cause in the courts' insecurity towards
the basis of the claim, namely, the decision of the international organ. The rejection of the claim *a limine* is often
substantiated by a lack of jurisdiction, the non-justiciabi-
lity of the claim - often under the slogan of "political
questions" - , the lack of a standing, and the immunity of
the defendant. In all these areas, the courts enjoy a considerable degree of independence and have already made use
of it in individual cases in favor of the plaintiffs. For
certain questions, like the immunity of foreign States or
international organizations, solutions through multilateral
treaties are also feasible.

In cases of competing jurisdictions of international organs
and domestic courts, the refusal to entertain a claim may be
caused by an exaggerated deference to a future international
decision. In situations of this kind it is incumbent upon
the courts to strike a sensible balance between the respect
for a possible decision of an international organ and an
adequate preservation of judicial remedies.

BIBLIOGRAPHY

AGO, R., Die internationalen Organisationen und ihre Funktionen im inneren Tätigkeitsgebiet der Staaten, in Rechtsfragen der Internationalen Organisation, Festschrift für Hans Wehberg (Frankfurt/M. 1956) p.2o.

AGO, R., La codification du droit international et les problèmes de sa réalisation, En hommage à Paul Guggenheim (Geneva, 1968) p.93.

AGRAWALA, S.K., Law of Nations as Interpreted and Applied by Indian Courts and Legislature, 2 IJIL 431 (1962).

AGRAWALA, S.K., International Law - Indian Courts and Legislature, New York (1965).

AKEHURST, M.B., The Law Governing Employment in International Organizations (Cambridge, 1967).

AKEHURST, M.B., Reprisals by Third States, 44 BYIL 1 (197o).

ADLER, C., Koordination und Integration als Rechtsprinzipien, Ein Beitrag zum Problem der derogatorischen Kraft des europäischen Gemeinschaftsrechts gegenüber einzelstaatlichem Recht (Brügge, 1969).

ALEXANDROWICZ, C.H., International Law in the Municipal Sphere according to Australian Decisions, 13 ICLQ 78 (1964).

ALEXANDROWICZ, C.H., The Convention on Facilitation of International Maritime Traffic and International Technical Regulations: (A Comparative Study), 5 ICLQ 621 (1966).

ALEXANDROWICZ, C.H., The Law-Making Functions of the Specialised Agencies of the United Nations (Sydney, 1973).

ALLEN, C.K., Law in the Making (Oxford, 1958).

ANDERSON, S.V., Supranational Delegation Clauses in Scandinavian Constitutions, 18 Western Political Quarterly 84o (1965).

ANZILOTTI, D., Il diritto internazionale nei giudizi interni (19o5).

ANZILOTTI, D., La responsabilité internationale des états, 13 RGDIP 5 (19o6).

ARANGIO-RUIZ, G., The Normative Role of the General Assembly of the United Nations and the Declaration of Principles of Friendly Relations, 137 RC 419 (1972, III)

ARNOLD, R., Das Rangverhältnis zwischen dem Recht der europäischen Gemeinschaften und dem innerdeutschen Recht (Würzburg, 1968).

ASAMOAH, O.Y., The Legal Significance of the Declarations of the General Assembly of the United Nations (The Hague, 1966).

AUFRICHT, H., Das Abkommen des Internationalen Währungsfonds und die Unerzwingbarkeit bestimmter Verträge, 6 ÖZöR

529 (1955).

AUFRICHT, H., The International Monetary Fund. Legal Bases, Structure, Functions (London, 1964).

AUFRICHT, H., The Fund Agreement: Living Law and Emerging Practice, (Princeton, 1969).

AUSTIN, J., Jurisprudence (1885)

BAILEY, K., Making International Law in the United Nations, 61 ASIL Proc 233 (1967)

BALLADORE PALLIERI, G., Le droit interne des organisations internationales, 127 RC 1 (1969, II).

BALLON, O., Einige Probleme der richterlichen Rechtsfortbildung, 94 JBl 598 (1972).

BARTIN, E., Principes de droit international privé, (Paris, 193o)

BASDEVANT, J., Règles générales du droit de la paix, 58 RC 471 (1936, IV).

BASDEVANT, J., Le rôle du juge national dans l'interprétation des traités diplomatiques, 38 RCDIP 413 (1949).

BATTIFFOL, H., Arbitration Clauses Concluded between French Government-Owned Enterprises and Foreign Private Parties, 7 Columbia Journal of Transnational Law 32 (1968).

BATTIFOL, H., Droit international privé (Paris, 197o).

BAUER, R., Die niederländische Verfassungsänderung von 1956 betreffend die auswärtige Gewalt, 18 ZaöRV 137 (1957).

BEBR, G., Judical Control of the European Communities (London, 1962).

BEBR, G., Directly Applicable Provisions of Community Law: The Development of a Community Concept, 19 ICLQ 257 (197o).

BEBR, G., Law of the European Communities and Municipal Law, 34 Modern LR 481 (1971).

BEBR, G., Community Regulations and National Law, 1o CMLRev. 87 (1973).

BEBR, G., How Supreme is Community Law in the National Courts?, 11 CMLRev.3 (1974).

BEBR, G., A Critical Review of Recent Case Law of National Courts, 11 CMLRev.4o8 (1974).

BEBR, G., Article 177 of the EEC Treaty in the Practice of National Courts, 26 ICLQ 241 (1977).

BEDDARD, R. The Status of the European Convention of Human Rights in Domestic Law, 16 ICLQ 2o6 (1967).

BEITZKE, G., Zivilrechtsfähigkeit von auf Staatsvertrag beruhenden internationalen Organisationen und juristischen Personen, 9 Berichte der Deutschen Gesellschaft für Völkerrecht 77 (1969).

BERBER, F., Die Rechtsquellen des internationalen Wassernutzungsrechts (München, 1955).

BERBER, F., Lehrbuch des Völkerrechts (München, 196o-1969).

BERGER, P., Bindung an Präjudizien im Völkerrecht?, 6 ÖZöR
    3o3 (1955).

BERNARD, P., Die Transformation der Normen der ICAO in die
    österreichische Rechtsordnung, 17 Zeitschrift für
    Verkeḣrsrecht 353 (1972).

BERNHARDT, R., Der Abschluß völkerrechtlicher Verträge im
    Bundesstaat (Köln, 1957).

BERNHARDT, R., Qualifikation und Anwendungsbereich des
    internen Rechts internationaler Organisationen, 12
    Berichte der Deutschen Gesellschaft für Völkerrecht 7
    (1971).

BERNHARDT, R., Homogenität, Kontinuität und Dissonanzen in
    der Rechtssprechung des Internationalen Gerichtshofs,
    33 ZaöRV 1 (1973).

BIANCHI, J.P., Security Council Resolutions in United States
    Courts, 5o Indiana Law Journal 83 (1974/75).

BINDSCHEDLER, R.L., Das Problem der Beteiligung der Schweiz
    an Sanktionen der Vereinigten Nationen, besonders im
    Falle Rhodesiens, 28 ZaöRV 1 (1968).

BINDSCHEDLER, R.L., Die Vollziehung völkerrechtlicher Verträ-
    ge in den EFTA-Staaten, Schweiz, 12 EFTA Bulletin No. 9
    p. 8 (1971).

BISSCHOP, W.R., Sources of International Law, 26 Transactions
    of the Grotius Society 235 (194o).

BLACKSTONE, W., Commentaries on the Laws of England, (1765).

BLASER, P.M., La nationalité et la protection juridique
    internationale de l'individu (1962).

BLECKMANN, A., Begriff und Kriterien der innerstaatlichen
    Anwendbarkeit völkerrechtlicher Verträge, (Berlin,
    197o).

BLECKMANN, A., Vorrang des Völkerrechts im Landesrechtsraum?
    Zum Urteil der belgischen Cour de cassation vom 27. Mai
    1971, 32 ZaöRV 516 (1972).

BLECKMANN, A., Sittenwidrigkeit wegen Verstoßes gegen den
    ordre public international. Anmerkung zum Urteil des
    BGH vom 22. Juni 1972, 34 ZaöRV 112 (1974).

BLECKMANN, A., Sekundäres Gemeinschaftsrecht und deutsche
    Grundrechte, Zum Beśchluß des Bundesverfassungsgerichts
    vom 29. Mai 1974, Zur Funktion des Art.24 Abs.1 Grund-
    gesetz, 35 ZaöRV 79 (1975).

BLEICHER, S.A., The Legal Significance of Re-Citation of
    General Assembly Resulutions, 63 AJIL 444 (1969).

BÖCKSTIEGL, K.H., Der Staat als Vertragspartner ausländischer
    Privatunternehmen (Frankfurt/M., 1971).

BOEHMER, G., Der völkerrechtliche Vertrag im deutschen Recht
    (Köln,1965).

BOLEWSKI, W.M., Zur Bindung deutscher Gerichte an Äußerungen
    und Maßnahmen ihrer Regierung auf völkerrechtlicher

Ebene (Marburg, 1971).

BOOYSEN, H. & STEPHAN,G.E.J., Decree No 1 of the United Nations Council for South West Africa, 1 South African Yearbook of International Law 63 (1975).

BORCHARD, E., The Diplomatic Protection of Citizens Abroad (New York, 1915).

BORCHARD, E., The Access of Individuals to International Courts, 24 AJIL 359 (193o).

BORCHARD, E., The Relation Between International Law and Municipal Law, 27 Virginia LRev. 137 (194o).

BRAND, R.A., Sucurity Council Resolutions: When do they give rise to Enforceable Legal Rights? The United Nations Charter, the Byrd Amendment and a Self-Executing Treaty Analysis, 9 Cornell International Law Journal 298(1976).

BRIDGE, J.W., The Legal Status of British Troops forming Part of the United Nations Force in Cyprus, 34 Modern Law Review 121 (1971).

BRIERLY, J.L., Règles générales du droit de la paix, 58 RC 1(1936, IV).

BRIGGS, H.W., The Law of Nations (New York, 1952).

BRINKHORST, L.J., Implementation of (non-self-executing) legislation of the European Economic Community, including directives, in: Legal problems of an enlarged European Community (1972) p. 69.

BROOKS, P.E.J., Security Council Decisions and Private Contracts in Conflict of Law Situations, 3 South African Yearbook of International Law 33(1977).

BUERGENTHAL, T., The Domestic Status of the European Convention on Human Rights, 13 Buffalo LRev. 354 (1964).

BUERGENTHAL, T., The United Nations and the Development of Rules Relating to Human Rights, 59 ASIL Proc 132 (1965).

BUERGENTHAL, T., The Effect of the European Convention on Human Rights on the Internal Law of Member States, in The European Convention on Human Rights ICLQ Suppl. 11 (London, 1965) p. 79.

BUERGENTHAL, T., Law-Making in the International Civil Aviation Organization (New York, 1969).

BUSTAMANTE Y SIRVEN, A.S. de, Droit International Public (Paris, 1934).

CAHIER, P., Étude des accords de siège conclus entre les organisations internationales et les états ou elles resident (Milano, 1959).

CAHIER, P., Le droit interne des Organisations Internationales, 67 RGDIP 563 (1963).

CARABIBER, C., Les jurisdictions internationales de droit privé (Neuchatel, 1947).

CARABIBER, C., L'Arbitrage international de droit privé

(Paris, 196o).

CARABIBER, C., L'immunité de juridiction et d'exécution des États collectivités et établissements publics au regard de l'obligation assumée par une clause compromissoire insérée dans les contrats internationaux de droit privé. International Arbitration Liber Amicorum for Martin Domke, p.23 (The Hague, 1967).

CARDOZO, B.N., The Nature of the Judicial Process (New Haven, 1974).

CASPER, G., Juristischer Realismus und politische Theorie im amerikanischen Rechtsdenken (Berlin, 1967).

CASSIN, R., La déclaration universelle et la mise ein oeuvre des Droits de l'homme, 79 RC 237 (1951, II).

CASTAÑEDA, J., Legal Effects of United Nations Resolutions (New York, 1969).

CASTAÑEDA, J., Valeur juridique des résolutions des Nations Unies, 129 RC 2o5 (197o, I).

CASTBERG, F., Histoire de l'interprétation d'une disposition constitutionelle, Mélanges Rolin (Paris, 1964) p.3o.

CASTLES, A.C., Legal status of U.N. resolutions, 3 Adelaide LRev. 68 (1967).

CAVARE, L., Le Droit International Public Positif (Paris, 1967).

CHAUVEAU, P., Droit aérien (Paris, 1951).

CHENG, B., United Nations Resolutions on Outer Space: 'Instant' International Customary Law?, 5 IJIL 23 (1965).

CLARK, C.E. & D.M. TRUBEK, The Creative Role of the Judge: Restraint and Freedom in the Common Law Tradition, 71 YaleLJ 255 (1961-62).

CLARK, J.R., Legal Aspects Regarding the Ownership and Distribution of Awards, 7 AJIL 382 (1913).

CODDING, G.A., Contributions of the World Health Organization and the International Civil Aviation Organization to the Development of International Law, 59 ASIL Proceedings 147 (1965).

COERPER, M.B., The Foreign Claims Settlement Commission and Judicial Review, 5o AJIL 868 (1956).

COLL, R.J., United States Enforcement of Arbitral Awards Against Sovereign States: Implications of the ICSID Convention, 17 HarvILJ 4o1 (1976).

CONDORELLI, L., La funzione del riconoscimento di sentenze straniere (Milano, 1967).

CONFORTI, B., La funzione dell' accordo nel sistema delle Nazioni Unite (Padua, 1968).

CONSTANTINESCO, L., Die unmittelbare Anwendbarkeit von Gemeinschaftsnormen und der Rechtsschutz von Einzelpersonen im Recht der EWG (Baden-Baden, 1969).

CROSS, Precedent in English Law (Oxford, 1979).

DAGTOGLU, P.D., The European Communities and Constitutional
    Law, 32 CambLJ 256 (1973).
DAHM, G., Die völkerrechtliche Verbindlichkeit von Empfehlun-
    gen internationaler Organisationen, 12 Die öffentliche
    Verwaltung 361 (1959).
D'AMATO, A., On Consensus, 8 CanYIL 1o4 (197o).
DEHAUSSY, J., Les conditions d'application des normes conven-
    tionelles sur le foi interne français, 87 Clunet 7o3
    (196o).
DE LOUTER, J., Le droit international public positif (Oxford,
    192o).
DENNING, Lord, From Precedent to Precedent (1959).
DETTER, I., Law Making by International Organizations (Stock-
    holm, 1965)
DICKINSON, E.D., International Political Questions in the
    National Courts, 19 AJIL 157 (1925).
DICKINSON, E.D., The Law of Nations as National Law: "Poli-
    tical Questions", 1o4 University of Pennsylvania LRev.
    451 (1956).
DIPLOCK, K., Courts as Legislators (1965).
DI QUAL, L., Les Effets des resolutions des Nations-Unies
    (Paris, 1967).
DOEHRING, K., Die Pflicht des Staates zur Gewährung diplo-
    matischen Schutzes (Köln, 1959).
DOMINICE, C., La nature juridique des actes des organisations
    et des juridictions internationales et leurs effets en
    droit interne, in Recueil de travaux suisses présentés,
    au VIIIe Congrès international de droit comparê (Basel,
    197o) p. 249.
DOMKE, M., (Ed.), International Trade Arbitration (1958).
DOMKE, M., International Aspects of Commercial Arbitration
    in the Americas, 8 Academia Interamericana de Derecho
    Comparado e Internacional, Cursos Monograficos 481(196o).
DOMKE, M., The Law and Practice of Commercial Arbitration
    (1968).
DOMKE, M., The Enforcement of Maritime Arbitration Agree-
    ments with Foreign Governments, 2 Journal of Maritime
    Law and Commerce 617 (1971).
DOMKE, M., Arbitration, in Nationalism and the Multinational
    Enterprise (Hahlo, Smith & Wright Eds.) (Leiden, 1973)
    p. 233.
DOMKE, M., New Aspects of East-West trade arbitration, in
    Commercial Arbitration, Essays in memoriam Egenio
    Minoli (1974) p. 121.
DRAPER, G.I.A.D., Civilians and the NATO Status of Forces
    Agreement (Leiden, 1966).
DRZEMCZEWSKI, A., European Human Rights Law in the United
    Kingdom: Some Observations, 9 Human Rights Journal 123
    (1976).

DRZEMCZEWSKI, A., The Authority of the Findings of the Organs
of the European Human Rights Convention in Domestic
Courts, Legal Issues of European Integration 1 (1973).
DUBOUIS, L., Le juge administratif français et les règles
du droit international, 17 AFDI 9 (1971).
DUGARD, C.J.R., The Legal Effect of United Nations Resolu-
tions on Apartheid, 83 The South African Law Journal 44
(1966).
DUGUIT, L., La fonction juridictionelle, 39 Revue de droit
public et de la science politique 165 (1922).
DUISBERG, C.-J., Das Völkergewohnheitsrecht nach der Recht-
sprechung der internationalen Gerichte (Frankfurt/M.,
1963).
DUNN, F.S., The Protection of Nationals (Baltimore, 1932).
DURANTE, F., L'ordinamento interno delle Nazioni Unite
(Mailand, 1964).

EAGLETON, C., Denial of Justice in International Law, 22
AJIL 538 (1928).
EAGLETON, C., International Organization and the Law of
Responsibility, 76 RC 319 (195o, I).
EASSON, A.J., The "Direct Effect" of EEC Directives, 28
ICLQ 319(1979).
ECONOMIDES, C.P., Nature juridique des actes des organisa-
tions internationales et leurs effets en droit interne,
23 Revue Hellénique de Droit International 225 (197o).
EHLERMANN, C.D., Primauté du droit communautaire mise en
danger par la Cour constitutionelle fédérale allemande,
18 Revue du Marché commun 1o (1975).
ELIAS, T.O., Modern Sources of International Law, in Trans-
national Law in a Changing Society, Essays in Honor of
P.C.Jessup (1972) p. 34.
ENGEL, S., Procedures for the *de facto* Revision of the
Charter, 59 ASIL Proceedings 1o8 (1965).
ENGEL, S., "Living" International Constitutions and the
World Court, 16 ICLQ 865 (1967).
ERADES, L., Is stare decisis an impediment to the enforce-
ment of international law by British courts?, 4 NYIL
1o5 (1973).
ERICHSEN, H.U., Zum Verhältnis von EWG-Recht und nationalem
öffentlichen Recht der Bundesrepublik Deutschland, 64
Verwaltungsarchiv 1o1 (1973).
ERLER, G., Das Grundgesetz und die öffentliche Gewalt inter-
nationaler Staatengemeinschaften, 18 Veröffentlichungen
der Vereinigung der Deutschen Staatsrechtslehrer 7
(196o).
ERLER, G., Die Beschränkung der rechtsprechenden Gewalt in
der Bundesrepublik durch die Zuständigkeit internatio-

naler Gerichte. Göttinger Festschrift für das Oberlandesgericht Celle, (1961) p. 27

ERLER, J., Rechtsfragen der ICAO: Die Internationale Zivilluftfahrtorganisation und ihre Mitgliedstaaten (Berlin, 1967).

ERMACORA, F., Verfassungsrecht durch Richterspruch (1961).

ERMACORA, F., Die Bedeutung von Entscheidungen der Menschenrechtskommission für die österreichische Rechtsordnung, 84 JBl 621 (1962).

ERMACORA, F., Das Problem der Rechtsetzung durch internationale Organisationen (insbesondere im Rahmen der UN), 1o Berichte der Deutschen Gesellschaft für Völkerrecht 51 (1971).

ESSER, J., Vorverständnis und Methodenwahl in der Rechtsfindung (Frankfurt/M., 197o).

ESSER, J., Grundsatz und Norm in der richterlichen Fortbildung des Privatrechts (Tübingen, 1964).

EUSTATHIADES, C.T., La responsabilité internationale de l'État pour des actes des organes judiciaires et le problème du déni de justice en droit international, (Paris, 1936).

EVERLING, U., Europäisches Gemeinschaftsrecht und nationales Recht in der praktischen Rechtsanwendung, 2o NJW 465 (1967).

FALK, R.A., The Role of Domestic Courts in the International Legal Order (New York, 1964).

FALK, R.A., On The Quasi-Legislative Competence of the General Assembly, 6o AJIL 782 (1966).

FALK, R.A., The Interplay of Westphalia and Charter Conceptions of International Legal Order, in R.A.Falk, C.E. Black (Ed.), The Future of the International Legal Order (Princeton, 1969) Vol.1 p. 32.

FALK, R.A., The Status of Law in International Society (Princeton, 197o).

FASCHING, H.W., Zur verfassungsrechtlichen Rechtfertigung der Bindung des Obersten Gerichtshofes an seine Grundsatzentscheidungen, in Festschrift für Hans Schima (Wien, 1969) p. 133.

FASCHING, H.W., Schiedsgericht und Schiedsverfahren im österreichischen und im internationalen Recht (Wien, 1973).

FAUCHILLE, P., Traité de droit international public (Paris, 1922).

FAWCETT, J.E.S., The British Commonwealth in International Law (London, 1963).

FELLER, A.H., The Mexican Claims Commission 1923-1934 (New York, 1935).

FENWICK, C.G., International Law (New York, 1965).
FEO, E.F., Self-execution of United Nations security council resolutions under United States law, 24 University of California Los Angeles Law Review 387 (1976).
FINCH, G.A., The Sources of Modern International Law (Washington, 1937).
FISCHER, P., Die schiedsgerichtliche Beilegung von privaten Investitionsstreitigkeiten im Lichte der Weltbankkonvention vom 18. März 1965, 1 VRÜ 262 (1968).
FISCHER, P., Die internationale Konzession (Wien, 1974).
FITZGERALD, G.F., The International Civil Aviation Organization - A Case Study in the Implementation of Decisions of a Functional International Organization, in The Effectiveness of International Decisions S.M. Schwebel (Ed.) (Leyden, 1971) p. 156.
FITZMAURICE, G., The General Principles of International Law, 92 RC 1 (1957, II).
FITZMAURICE, G., The Law and Procedure of the International Court of Justice 1951-1954, 34 BYIL 3 (1958).
FITZMAURICE, G., Some Problems Regarding the Formal Sources of International Law, in Symbolae Verzijl (The Hague, 1958) p. 153.
FITZMAURICE, G., Hersch Lauterpacht - the Scholar as Judge. Part II, 38 BYIL 1 (1962).
FITZMAURICE, G., Judicial Innovation - Its Uses and its Perils - As exemplified in some of the Work of the International Court of Justice during Lord McNair's Period of Office, in Cambridge Essays in International Law in honour of Lord McNair (London, 1965) p. 24.
FITZMAURICE, G., The Future of Public International Law and of the International Legal System in the Circumstances of Today, in Institut de Droit International, Livre du Centenaire 1873-1973 (Basel, 1973) p.196.
FOCSANEANU, L., Le droit interne de l'organisation des Nations Unies, 3 AFDI 315 (1957).
FOLZ, H.-E., Die Geltungskraft fremder Hoheitsäußerungen (Baden-Baden, 1975).
FORRESTER, I.S., Complement or Overlap? Jurisdiction of National and Community Bodies in Competition Matters after *SABAM*, 11 CMLRev. 171 (1974).
FOUCHARD, P., L'arbitrage commercial international (Paris, 1965).
FRANK, J., Law and the Modern Mind (1949).
FREYMOND, P., Les "décisions" de l'Organisation Européenne de Coopération Economique (O.E.C.E.), 11 SchwJIR 65 (1954).
FRIEDMANN, W., The Changing Structure of International Law (London, 1964).

FRIEDMANN, W., National Courts and the International Legal
    Order: Projections on the Implications of the Sabbatino
    Case, 34 George Washington LRev. 433 (1966).
FRIEDMANN, W., General Course in Public International Law,
    127 RC 39 (1969,II).

GANSHOF van der MEERSCH, W.J., La juridiction internationale
    dans l'Union économique Benelux, 15 AFDI 245 (1969).
GANSHOF van der MEERSCH, W.J., VANWELKENHUYZEN, A., La
    Constitution Belge in Corpus Constitutionell Vol.I
    (1968-72), p.569
GARNER, J.W., International Responsibility of States for
    Judgments of Courts and Verdicts of Juries amounting to
    Denial of Justice, 1o BYIL 181 (1929).
GAUDET, M., The European Communities, in The Effectiveness
    of International Decisions. S.M.Schwebel (Ed.)(Leyden,
    1971) p. 3o9.
GERMANN, O.A., Präjudizien als Rechtsquelle (Stockholm, 196o).
GIARDINA, A., The Implementation in Municipal Legal Systems
    of International Judgments and Decisions, to appear in
    Recueil des Cours 198o.
GILES, O.C., Uniform Commercial Law (Leyden, 197o).
GINTHER, K., Die völkerrechtliche Verantwortlichkeit inter-
    nationaler Organisationen gegenüber Drittstaaten (Wien,
    1969).
GLAESNER, H.J., Übertragung rechtsetzender Gewalt auf inter-
    nationale Organisationen in der völkerrechtlichen
    Praxis, 12 Die öffentliche Verwaltung 653 (1959).
GOLD, J., The Interpretation by the International Monetary
    Fund of its Articles of Agreement, 3 ICLQ 256 (1954).
GOLD, J., The Fund Agreement in the Courts (Washington,
    1962).
GOLD, J., LACHMANN, P.R., The Articles of Agreement of the
    International Monetary Fund and the exchange control
    regulations of Member States, 89 Clunet 666 (1962).
GOLD, J., Certain Aspects of the Law and Practice of the
    International Monetary Fund, in The Effectiveness of
    International Decisions, S.M.Schwebel (Ed.)(Leyden,
    1971), p. 71.
GOLD, J., Voting and Decisions in the International Monetary
    Fund (Washington, 1972).
GOLD, J., The Bretton Woods Agreement of July 22, 1944 in
    the Courts Part IV, 38 RabelsZ 863 (1974).
GOLD, J., Interpretation by the Fund, International Monetary
    Fund Pamphlet Series no.11.
GOLSONG, H., Das Problem der Rechtsetzung durch internatio-
    nale Organisationen (insbesondere im Rahmen der UN), 1o
    Berichte der Deutschen Gesellschaft für Völkerrecht 1
    (1971).

GORMLEY, W.P., The Procedural Status of the Individual before International and Supranational Tribunals (The Hague, 1966).

GORNY, G., Verbindlichkeit der Bundesgrundrechte bei der Anwendung von Gemeinschaftsrecht durch deutsche Staatsorgane (Berlin, 1969).

GRABITZ, E., Gemeinschaftsrecht bricht nationales Recht (Hamburg, 1966).

GRABITZ, E., Entscheidungen und Richtlinien als unmittelbar wirksames Gemeinschaftsrecht, 6 Europarecht 1 (1971).

GRASSI, M., Die Rechtsstellung des Individuums im Völkerrecht (1955).

GREEN, A.W., Political Integration by Jurisprudence (Leyden, 1969).

GROSS, L., The United Nations and the Role of Law, 19 International Organization 537 (1965).

GUGGENHEIM, P., La validité et la nullité des actes juridiques internationaux 74 RC 195 (1949, I).

GUGGENHEIM, P., Völkerrechtliche Schranken im Landesrecht (Karlsruhe, 1955).

GUGGENHEIM, P., Organisations économiques supranationales, indépendance et neutralité de la Suisse, 82 ZSR 221 (1963, II).

GURADZE, H., Die Europäische Menschenrechtskonvention (Berlin, 1968).

GURADZE, H., Zur Rechtsnatur normativer Entschließungen der Vollversammlung der Vereinten Nationen, 19 Zeitschrift f. Luftrecht u. Weltraumrechtsfragen 49 (197o).

GURADZE, H., Are Human Rights Resolutions of the U.N. General Assembly Law-Making? 4 Human Rights Journal 453 (1971).

GUYOMAR, G., L'arbitrage concernant les rapports entre États et particuliêrs, 5 AFDI 333 (1959).

HABSCHEID, Zur Berücksichtigung der Rechtshängigkeit eines ausländischen Verfahrens, 31 RabelsZ 254 (1967).

HAHN, H.J., Die Organisation für Wirtschaftliche Zusammenarbeit und Entwicklung (OECD). Entstehung und Rechtsordnung, 22 ZaöRV 49 (1962).

HAHN, H.J., Die Organisation für Wirtschaftliche Zusammenarbeit und Entwicklung (OECD), 12 Jahrbuch des öffentlichen Rechts 1 (1963).

HALE, M., History of the Common Law of England (182o).

HALLIER, H.-J., Völkerrechtliche Schiedsinstanzen für Einzelpersonen und ihr Verhältnis zur innerstaatlichen Gerichtsbarkeit (Cologne, 1962).

HAMBRO, E., The Sixth Committee in the Law Creating Function of the General Assembly, 21 Revista Esp.DI 387 (1968).

HAMBRO, E., The New Provision for International Collaboration in the Constitution of Norway, in Festschrift Guggenheim (Geneva, 1968) p. 557.

HAMBRO, E., Some Notes on the Development of the Sources of International Law,17 Scandinavian Studies in Law 77 (1973).

HANREICH, H. Die Beschlüsse internationaler Wirtschaftsorganisationen im österreichischen Rechtsquellensystem, 26 ÖZöR 173 (1975).

HARPIGNIES, R.H., Settlement of Disputes of a private Law Character to which the United Nations is a Party, 7 RBDI 451 (1971).

HAY, P., Federalism and Supranational Organizations (Urbana, 1966).

HAY, P., Supremacy of Community Law in National Courts, 16 AJCompL 524 (1968).

HEFFTER, A.W., Das europäische Völkerrecht der Gegenwart (Berlin, 1888).

HEILBORN, P., Grundbegriffe und Geschichte des Völkerrechts (Stuttgart, 1912).

HEISE, D., Internationale Rechtspflege und nationale Staatsgewalt (Göttingen, 1964).

HENKIN, L., Foreign Affairs and the Constitution (Mineola, N.Y., 1972).

HENKIN, L., Viet-Nam in the Courts of the United States: 'Political Questions', 63 AJIL 284 (1969).

HEXNER, E.P., Interpretation by Public International Organizations of their Basic Instruments, 53 AJIL 341 (1959).

HEXNER, E.P., Die Rechtsnatur der interpretativen Entscheidungen des Internationalen Währungsfonds, 2o ZaöRV 73 (1959/6o).

HEYDTE, F.A.v.d., Richterfunktion und "Richtergesetz", in Forschungen und Berichte aus dem öffentlichen Recht, Gedächtnisschrift für Walter Jellinek (Munich, 1955) p. 493.

HIGGINS, R., The Development of International Law through the Political Organs of the United Nations (Oxford, 1963).

HIGGINS, R., The Development of International Law by the Political Organs of the United Nations, 59 ASIL Proc 116 (1965).

HIGGINS, R., United Nations and Lawmaking: The Political Organs, 64 ASIL Proc 37 (197o).

HIGGINS, R., The Advisory Opinion on Namibia: Which UN Resolutions are Binding under Art. 25 of the Charter?, 21 ICLQ 27o (1972).

HILF, M., Sekundäres Gemeinschaftsrecht und deutsche Grundrechte, Zum Beschluß des Bundesverfassungsgerichts vom 29. Mai 1974, I. Auswirkungen auf die Gemeinschaftsrechtsordnung, 35 ZaöRV 51 (1975).

HOFFMANN, G., Das Verhältnis des Rechts der Europäischen

Gemeinschaften zum Recht der Mitgliedstaaten, 2o Die öffentliche Verwaltung 433 (1967).

HOLLOWAY, J., Are you Statisfied with Article 177?, in: Symposium Europa (Bruges, 1971) p. 229.

HOLMES, O.W., The Common Law (1881).

HORAK, F., Zur rechtstheoretischen Problematik der juristischen Begründung von Entscheidungen, in Die Entscheidungsbegründung in europäischen Verfahrensrechten und im Verfahren vor internationalen Gerichten, R. Sprung u. B. König (Ed.)(Vienna, 1974), p.1.

HOYT, E.C., The Unanimity Rule in the Revision of Treaties: A Re-Examination (The Hague, 1959).

HUBER, H., Die internationale Quasilegislative, 27 SchwJIR 9 (1971).

HUBER, M., Die Fortbildung des Völkerrechts auf dem Gebiete des Prozeß- und Landkriegsrechts durch die II. internationale Friedenskonferenz im Haag 19o7, 2 Jahrbuch des öffentlichen Rechtes 47o (19o8).

HUNNINGS, N.M., Constitutional Implications of Joining the Common Market, 6 CMLRev. 5o (1968-69).

HYDE, C.C., The Supreme Court of the United States as an Expositor of International Law, 18 BYIL 1 (1937).

IPSEN, H.P., The Relationship between the Law of the European Communities and National Law, 2 CMLRev. 379 (1964-65).

IPSEN, H.P., Europäisches Gemeinschaftsrecht (Tübingen, 1972).

JAFFE, L.L., English and American Judges as Lawmakers (Oxford, 1969).

JAKOBS, F., The European Convention on Human Rights in the English Courts, 2 EuGRZ 569 (1975).

JANSSEN-PEVTSCHIN, G., VELU, J., .VANWELKENHUYZEN, A., La Convention de sauvegarde des droits de l'homme et des libertés fondamentales et le fonctionnement des juridictions Belges, 15 Chronique de Politique Étrangère 199 (1962).

JENKS, C.W., The Impact of International Organizations on Public and Private International Law, 37 Transactions of the Grotius Society 23 (1951).

JENKS, C.W., International Immunities (London, 1961).

JENKS, C.W., The Proper Law of International Organizations (London, 1962).

JENKS, C.W., The Prospects of International Adjudication (London, 1964).

JENNINGS, R.Y., Recent Developments in the International Law Commission: Its Relation to the Sources of International Law, 13 ICLQ 385 (1964).

JENNINGS, R.Y., Nullity and Effectiveness in International
    Law, in Cambridge Essays in Honour of Lord McNair
    (London, 1965) p. 64.
JESSUP, P.C., The Doctrine of Erie Railroad v. Tompkins
    applied to International Law, 33 AJIL 74o (1939).
JIMÉNEZ de ARÉCHAGA, E., International Responsibility, in
    Manual of Public International Law, M. Sørensen (Ed.)
    (London, 1968) p. 531.
JOHNSON, D.H.N., The Effect of Resolutions of the General
    Assembly of the United Nations, 32 BYIL 97 (1955-56).
JULLIOT de la MORANDIÈRE, L., La sixième conférence de La
    Haye de Droit international privé, 55 Clunet 281 (1928).

KAECKENBEEK, G., The International Experiment of Upper
    Silesia (1942).
KAECKENBEEK, G., The Character and Work of the Arbitral
    Tribunal of Upper Silesia, 21 Transactions of the
    Grotius Society 27 (1935).
KAPLAN, M., KATZENBACH, N., The Political Foundations of
    International Law (New York, 1961).
KATZAROV, K., Hat der Bürger ein Recht auf diplomatischen
    Schutz?, 8 ÖZöR 434 (1957/58).
KAUFMANN, E., Règles générales du droit de la paix, 54 RC
    3o9 (1935, IV).
KAUFMANN, W., Die Rechtskraft des Internationalen Rechtes
    und das Verhältnis der Staatsgesetzgebungen und der
    Staatsorgane zu demselben (Stuttgart, 1899).
KELSEN, H., The Law of the United Nations (London, 1951).
KELSEN, H., Die Einheit von Völkerrecht und staatlichem
    Recht, 19 ZaöRV 234 (1958).
KELSEN, H., Principles of International Law (New York,
    1967).
KENT, J., Commentaries on American Law (1884).
KEWENIG, W.A., Die Problematik der Bindungswirkung von Ent-
    scheidungen des Sicherheitsrates, in Festschrift f. Ul-
    rich Scheuner (Berlin, 1973) p.259.
KHOL, A., Internationale Gesetzgebung und staatliche Rechts-
    anwendung, in Internationale Festschrift für Alfred Ver-
    droß (Munich, 1971) p. 167.
KIMMINICH, O., Das Völkerrecht in der Rechtsprechung des Bun-
    desverfassungsgerichts, 93 Archiv des öff.R. 485 (1968).
KISS, A.C., Nature juridique des actes des organisations et
    des juridictions internationales et leurs effets en
    droit interne, in Etudes de droit contemporain, 8. Con-
    grès international de droit comparé Pescara 197o Contri-
    butions françaises, p. 259.
KISS, A.C., La condition des étrangers en droit international
    et les droits de l'homme, in Miscellanea W.J. Ganshof
    v.d.Meersch Vol.I, (Brussels, 1972) p. 499.

KLECATSKY, H., Die Bundesverfassungsnovelle vom 4.März 1964
über die Staatsverträge, 86 JBl 349 (1964).
KLEIN, E., Sekundäres Gemeinschaftsrecht und deutsche Grund-
rechte, Zum Beschluß des Bundesverfassungsgerichts vom
29.Mai 1974, Stellungnahme aus der Sicht des deutschen
Verfassungsrechts, 35 ZaöRV 67 (1975).
KLEIN, K.H., Die Übertragung von Hoheitsrechten (1952).
KOLLER, A., Die unmittelbare Anwendbarkeit völkerrechtlicher
Verträge und des EWG-Vertrags im innerstaatlichen Be-
reich (Bern, 1971).
KOSTERS, J., Les fondements du droit des gens (1925).
KOVAR, R., L'applicabilité directe du Droit communautaire,
1oo Clunet 279 (1973).
KRAUS, H., Der deutsche Richter und das Völkerrecht, in Fest-
schrift f. Rudolf Laun (Hamburg, 1953) p. 223.
KRIELE, M., Theorie der Rechtsgewinnung (Berlin, 1967).
KRONECK, F., Die völkerrechtliche Immunität bundesstaatlicher
Gliedstaaten vor ausländischen Gerichten (Munich, 1958).
KRUSE, H.W., Das Richterrecht als Rechtsquelle des innerstaat-
lichen Rechts (Tübingen, 1971).
KUNZ, J.L., The United Nations Declaration of Human Rights,
43 AJIL 316 (1949).
KUTSCHER, H., Community Law and the National Judge, 89 LQR
487 (1973).

LACHMANN, P.R., The Articles of Agreement of the Internatio-
nal Monetary Fund and the unforceability of Certain Ex-
change Contracts, 2 NITR 148 (1955).
LACHS, M., Le rôle des organisations internationales dans la
formation du droit international. Mélanges offerts à
Henri Rolin (Paris, 1964) p. 157.
LAMBRINIDIS, J.S., The Structure, Function and Law of a Free
Trade Area (London, 1965).
LAMMASCH, H., Die Rechtskraft der internationalen Schieds-
sprüche (Olso, 1913).
LAMMASCH, H., Die Lehre von der Schiedsgerichtsbarkeit in
ihrem ganzen Umfange (Berlin, 1914).
LANDE, G.R., The Changing Effectiveness of General Assembly
Resolutions, 58 ASIL Proc 162 (1964).
LANGNER, G., WENGLER, W., Die Rechtsnatur der Bekanntmachung
über das Inkrafttreten völkerrechtlicher Verträge für
den Staatsbürger, 15 NJW 228 (1962).
LARENZ, K., Richterliche Rechtsfortbildung als methodisches
Problem, 18 NJW 1 (1965).
LARENZ, K., Über die Bindungswirkung von Präjudizien, in
Festschrift für Hans Schima (Vienna, 1969) p. 247.
LAURER, H.R., Der Beitritt Österreichs zu internationalen
Organisationen als Problem der innerstaatlichen Norm-
erzeugung, 2o ÖZöR 341 (197o).

LAUTERPACHT, E., The Legal Effect of Illegal Acts of Inter-
    national Organisations, in Cambridge Essays in Interna-
    tional Law in Honour of Lord McNair (London, 1965) p.88.
LAUTERPACHT, E., Implementation of Decisions of Internatio-
    nal Organizations through National Courts, in The
    Effectiveness of International Decisions S.M. Schwebel
    (Ed.) (Leyden, 1971) p. 57.
LAUTERPACHT, H., Decisions of Municipal Courts as a Source
    of International Law, 1o BYIL 65 (1929).
LAUTERPACHT, H., Règles générales du droit de la paix, 62 RC
    95 (1937, IV).
LAUTERPACHT, H., International Law and Human Rights (New
    York, 195o).
LAUTERPACHT, H., The Development of International Law by the
    International Court (London, 1958).
LEREBOURS-PIGEONNIÈRE, La Déclaration universelle des Droits
    de l'Homme et le droit international privé français,
    in Le Droit privé français au milieu du XXe sciècle.
    Etudes offertes à Georges Ripert (Paris, 195o) Vol.I,
    p. 255.
LE TALLEC, G., Le juge français devant le droit internatio-
    nal et le droit Communautaire, 18 Revue du Marché
    Commun 124 (1975).
L'HUILLIER, J., Eléments de droit international public
    (Paris, 195o).
LILLICH, R.B., International Claims: Their Adjudication by
    National Commissions (Syracuse, 1962).
LILLICH, R.B., The Proper Role of Domestic Courts in the
    International Legal Order, 11 VaJIL 9 (197o/71).
LILLICH, R.B., The Role of Domestic Courts in Promoting In-
    ternational Human Rights Norms, 24 New York Law School
    Law Review 153(1978).
LIMBURG, J., L'Autorité de chose jugée des décisions des
    juridictions internationales, 3o RC 523 (1929, V).
LIPSTEIN, K., The Doctrine of Precedent in Continental Law
    with Special Reference to French and German Law, 28
    J.of Comp.Legisl.and int. Law 34 (1946).
LLEWELLYN, K.N., The Common Law Tradition, Deciding Appeals
    (196o).
LORD, S., Individual Enforcement of Obligations arising under
    the United Nations Charter, 19 Santa Clara L.Rev. 195
    (1979).
LOUIS, J.-V., L'article 25bis de la Constitution belge, 13
    Revue du Marché Commun 41o (197o).

McDOUGAL, M.S., The Law School of the Future: From Legal
    Realism to Policy Science in the World Community, 56
    YaleLJ 1345 (1946/47).
McDOUGAL, M.S. and LASSWELL, H.D., The Identification and

Appraisal of Diverse Systems of Public Order, 53 AJIL
1 (1959).

McDOUGAL, M.S., The Impact of International Law on National
Law: A Policy-Oriented Perspective, 4 South Dakota Law
Review 25 (1959).

McDOUGAL, M.S., and FELICIANO, F.P., Law and Minimum World
Public Order (New Haven, 1961).

McDOUGAL , M.S., BEBR, G., Human Rights in the United Nations, 58 AJIL 6o3 (1964).

McDOUGAL, M.S. REISMAN, W.M., "The Changing Structure of
International Law", Unchanging Theory for Inquiry, 65
Columbia LRev. 81o (1965).

McDOUGAL, M.S., LASSWELL, H.D., and REISMAN, W.M., Theories
About International Law: Prologue to a Configurative
Jurisprudence, 8 VaJIL 188 (1967/68).

McRAE, D.M., Legal Obligations and International Organizations, 11 CanYIL 87 (1973).

McWHINNEY, E., International Law and World Revolution (1967).

MAESTRIPIERI, C., The Application of Community Law in Italy
in 1972, 1o CMLRev. 34o (1973).

MAILÄNDER, K.P., Zuständigkeit und Entscheidungsfreiheit nationaler Gerichte im EWG-Kartellrecht (Baden-Baden
1965).

MAINE, H.S., Ancient Law (193o).

MAKOWSKI, J., L'organisation actuelle de l'arbitrage international, 36 RC 263 (1931, II).

MALINTOPPI, A., Le racommandazioni internazionali (Milan,
1958).

MANGOLDT, H.v., Das Völkerrecht in den neuen Staatsverfassungen, 3 Jahrbuch f. internationales Recht 11 (195o/51).

MANGOLDT, H.v., KLEIN, F., Das Bonner Grundgesetz 2.Ed.
(1966, 1974).

MANGONE, G.J., A Short History of International Organization
(New York, 1954).

MANIN, A., L'Organisation de l'Aviation Civile Internationale (Paris, 197o).

MANIN, P., L'Organisation des Nations Unies et le maintien
de la paix (Paris, 1971).

MANN, F.A., Judiciary and Executive in Foreign Affairs, 29
Transactions of the Grotius Society 143 (1943).

MANN, F.A., Völkerrecht im Prozeß, 5 Süddeutsche Juristen
Zeitung 545 (195o).

MANN, F.A., The Private International Law of Exchange Control under the International Monetary Fund Agreement,
2 ICLQ 97 (1953).

MANN, F.A., Der Internationale Währungsfonds und das Internationale Privatrecht, JZ 442 (1953).

MANN, F.A., Bretton Woods Agreement in English Courts, 16
ICLQ 539 (1967).

MANN, F.A., The 'Interpretation' of the Constitutions of International Financial Organizations, 43 BYIL 1 (1968-69).

MARCUS, F., Die dänische Verfassung vom 5. Juni 1953 und das Thronfolgegesetz vom 27. März 1953, 15 ZaöRV 211 (1953/54).

MARKERT, K., Some Legal and Administrative Problems of the Co-Existence of Community and National Competition Law in the EEC, 11 CMLRev. 92 (1974).

MATSCHER, F., Zur Theorie der Anerkennung ausländischer Entscheidungen nach österreichischem Recht, in Festschrift für Hans Schima (Vienna, 1969)p. 265.

MATSCHER, F., Die Begründung der Entscheidungen internationaler Gerichte, in Die Entscheidungsbegründung in europäischen Verfahrensrechten und im Verfahren vor internationalen Gerichten, R. Sprung und B. König (Ed.) (Vienna, 1974) p. 429.

MATSCHER, F., Die Bedeutung von Verfahrensregelungen für die zwischenstaatlichen Beziehungen, Salzburger Universitätsreden, Vol 57 (1975).

MAUNZ, T., DÜRING, G., Kommentar zum Grundgesetz (1964).

MAX-PLANCK-INSTITUT für ausländisches öffentliches Recht und Völkerrecht, Gerichtsschutz gegen die Executive, 3. Rechtsvergleichung Völkerrecht (Köln, 1971).

MAYER-MALY, T., Rechtskenntnis und Gesetzesflut (Salzburg, 1969).

MEIER, G., Zur Geltung von Gemeinschaftsnormen im staatlichen Bereich, 14 AWB 2o5 (1968).

MEIER, G., Gemeinschaftsrecht und mitgliedstaatliches Gemeinrecht, 5 Europarecht 324 (197o).

MERKATZ, H.J. v., Les privilèges et immunités des organisations internationales et de leurs agents, 46 RDI 147 (1968).

MERLE, M., Le pouvoir réglementaire des institutions internationales, 4 AFDI 341 (1958).

MERTENS de WILMARS, J., Les enseignements communautaires des jurisprudences nationales, 6 Revue trimestrielle de droit européen 454 (197o).

MESTMÄCKER, E.-J., Europäisches Wettbewerbsrecht (München, 1974).

MEYER, B.S., Recognition of Exchange Controls after the International Monetary Fund Agreement, 62 YaleLJ 867 (1952/53).

MIAJA de la MUELA, A., Les principes directeurs des règles de compétence territoriale des tribunaux internes en matière de litiges comportant un élément international, 135 RC 1 (1972, I).

MIEHSLER, H., Qualifikation und Anwendungsbereich des internen Rechts internationaler Organisationen, 12 Berichte der Deutschen Gesellschaft für Völkerrecht 47 (1971).

MIEHSLER, H., Zur Autorität von Beschlüssen internationaler
    Institutionen, in Autorität und internationale Ordnung,
    Schreuer Ed., (Berlin, 1979).

MIELE, M., Les Organisations internationales et le domaine
    constitutionel des Etats, 131 RC 319 (197o, III).

MOORE, J.N., Prolegomenon to the Jurisprudence of Myres
    McDougal and Harold Lasswell, 54 Virginia Law Review
    662 (1968).

MORGENSTERN, F., Judicial Practice and the Supremacy of
    International Law, 27 BYIL 42 (195o).

MORI, R., Rechtssetzung und Vollzug in der Europäischen Frei-
    handelsassoziation(Winterthur, 1965).

MORRISSON, C.C., The Developing European Law of Human Rights
    (Leyden, 1967).

MOSLER, H., Internationale Organisation und Staatsverfassung,
    in Rechtsfragen der internationalen Organisation, Fest-
    schrift für Hans Wehberg (Frankfurt/M., 1956) p. 273.

MOSLER, H., L'application du droit international public par
    les tribunaux nationaux, 91 RC 619 (1957,I).

MOSLER, H., Repertorien der nationalen Praxis in Völker-
    rechtsfragen - Eine Quelle zur Erschließung des allge-
    meinen Völkerrechts?, En hommage à Paul Guggenheim
    (Geneva, 1968) p. 46o.

MOSLER, H., Nationale Gerichte als Garanten völkerrechtlicher
    Verpflichtungen, in Recht als Instrument van behoud en
    verandering (1972).

MÜLLER, J.P., Die Anwendung der Europäischen Menschenrechts-
    konvention in der Schweiz, 94 ZSR 373 (1975, I).

MÜLLER, K., Zum Begriff der "Anerkennung" von Urteilen in §
    328 ZPO, 79 Zeitschrift für Zivilprozeß 199 (1966).

MÜNCH, F., Internationale Organisationen mit Hoheitsrechten,
    in Rechtsfragen der internationalen Organisation,
    Festschrift für Hans Wehberg (Frankfurt, 1956) p. 3o1.

NADELMANN, K.H., Uniform Interpretation of "Uniform" Law: A
    Postscript, UNIDROIT Yearbook 1963, p. 63.

NANTWI, E.K., The Enforcement of International Judicial
    Decisions and Arbitral Awards in Public International
    Law (Leyden, 1967).

NATHANSON, N.L., The Constitution and World Government, 57
    Northwestern University LRev. 355 (1962).

NAWIASKY, H., Allgemeine Rechtslehre (Einsiedeln, 1948).

NERI, S., Rapports entre le droit communautaire et le droit
    interne selon la cour constitutionelle, 1o Rev.trim.dr.
    eur.154 (1974).

NGUYEN QUOC DINH, Les privilèges et immunités des organismes
    internationaux d'après les jurisprudences nationales
    depuis 1945, 3 AFDI 262 (1957).

NIPPOLD, O., Die zweite Haager Friedenskonferenz (Leipzig, 19o8).

NURICK, L., Certain Aspects of the Law and Practice of the International Bank for Reconstruction and Development, in The Effectiveness of International Decisions, S.M. Schwebel (Ed.)(Leyden, 1971) p. 1oo.

NUSSBAUM, A., Exchange Control and the International Monetary Fund, 59 YaleLJ 421 (1949/5o).

NYS, E., Le droit international (Brussels, 1912).

ÖHLINGER, T., Der völkerrechtliche Vertrag im staatlichen Recht (Wien, 1973).

OPHÜLS, C.F., Die Geltungsnormen des Europäischen Gemein-schaftsrechts, Festschrift für O. Riese (Karlsruhe, 1964) p. 1.

OPPENHEIM, L., The Science of International Law: It's Task and Method, 2 AJIL 313 (19o8).

OSIEKE, E., Unconstitutional Acts in International Organi-sations: The Law and Practice of the ICAO, 28 ICLQ 1 (1979).

PAHR, W., Verfassungsrechtliche Auswirkungen der Internatio-nalisierung der Menschenrechte, in Rene Cassin Amicorum Discipulorumque Liber, Vol.1 (Paris, 1969) p. 213.

PALLEY, C., The Judicial Process: U.D.I. and the Southern Rhodesian Judiciary, 3o Modern LR 263 (1967).

PANEBIANCO, M., Giurisdizione interna e immunità degli stati stranieri (Napoli, 1967).

PANHUYS, H.F. van, The Netherlands Constitution and Interna-tional Law, 47 AJIL 537 (1953).

PANHUYS, H.F. van, Relations and Interactions between Inter-national and National Scenes of Law, 112 RC 7 (1964,II).

PANHUYS, H.F. van, The Netherlands Constitution and Interna-tional Law, 58 AJIL 88 (1964).

PAPACOSTAS, Nature juridique des actes et des juridictions internationales et leurs effets en droit interne, 23 Revue Hellenique de Droit International 3o8 (197o).

PARRY, C., The Sources and Evidences of International Law (Manchester, 1965).

PARTSCH, K.J., Die Anwendung des Völkerrechts im innerstaat-lichen Recht, 6 Berichte der Deutschen Gesellschaft für Völkerrecht (Karlsruhe, 1964).

PATTERSON, E.W., Introduction to Jurisprudence (1951).

PESCATORE, P., Die unmittelbare Anwendung der europäischen Verträge durch die staatlichen Gerichte, 5 Europarecht 56 (197o).

PESCATORE, P., The Protection of Human Rights in the Euro-pean Communities, 9 CMLRev. 73 (1972).

PESCATORE, P., The Law of Integration (Leiden, 1974).

PINTO, R., Le juge interne francais devant les règles du
    droit international public, Revista Juridica de Buenos
    Aires 44 (1962).
PINTO, R., Consequences of the application of the Convention
    in municipal and international law, in Human Rights in
    National and International Law, A.H.Robertson (Ed.)
    (Manchester, 1968).
PIOTROWSKI, G., Les Résolutions de l'Assemblé générale des
    Nations Unies et la portée du droit conventionnel, 33
    RDI 111, 221 (1955).
PLOUVIER, L., Primauté du droit international et du droit
    communautaire en Belgique. Analyse de l'arrêt de la
    Cour de cassation du 27 mai 1971, 15 Revue du Marché
    Commun 171 (1972).
PRAAG, L. van, Juridiction et Droit international public
    (The Hague, 1915).
PRADIER-FODÉRÉ, P., Traité de droit international public
    (Paris, 1885).
PRASCH, G., Die unmittelbare Wirkung des EWG-Vertrages auf
    die Wirtschaftsunternehmen (Baden-Baden, 1967).
PRATAP, D., The Advisory Jurisdiction of the International
    Court (Oxford, 1972).
PRZETACZNIK, The Sovereign Immunity of Foreign States and
    International Commercial Arbitration, 57 Revue de Droit
    International 188, 291 (1979).

RALSTON, J., The Law and Procedure of International Tribu-
    nals (1962).
RANDELZHOFER, A., Das Recht der Europäischen Gemeinschaften
    und das nationale Recht, 135 Zs.f.d.ges.Handelsrecht
    u.Wirtschaftsrecht 237 (1971).
REISMAN, W.M., Nullity and Revision, The Review and Enforce-
    ment of International Judgments and Awards (New Haven,
    1971).
RENNER, R., Der Rechtsquellenwert innerstaatlicher Gerichts-
    urteile im Völkergewohnheitsrecht (Würzburg, 1957).
RESS, G., Die Wirkungen der Urteile des Europäischen Gerichts-
    hofes für Menschenrechte im innerstaatlichen Recht und
    vor innerstaatlichen Gerichten, Report to the 5th In-
    ternational Colloquy on the European Convention on Hu-
    man Rights, Frankfurt am Main 9-12 April 1980.
RIEGEL, R., Zum Verhältnis zwischen gemeinschaftsrechtlicher
    und innerstaatlicher Gerichtsbarkeit, 28 NJW 1049
    (1975).
RIESE, O., Luftrecht (Stuttgart, 1949).
RIESE, O., Einheitliche Gerichtsbarkeit für vereinheitlich-
    tes Recht? 26 RabelsZ 604 (1961).
RIEZLER, E., Internationales Zivilprozeßrecht und prozessua-
    les Fremdenrecht (Berlin, 1949).

RIGAUX, F., The Decree for the Protection of the Natural Re-
    sources of Namibia adopted on 27 September 1974 by the
    United Nations Council for Namibia, 9 Human Rights Jour-
    nal 451 (1976).
RIVIER, A., Lehrbuch des Völkerrechts (Stuttgart, 1889).
ROBERTSON, A.H., Advisory Opinions of the Court of Human
    Rights, René Cassin Amicorum Discipulorumque Liber Vol.1
    (Paris, 1969) p. 225.
ROBINSON, N., The Universal Declaration of Human Rights (New
    York, 1958).
ROLIN, H., Le contrôle international des juridictions natio-
    nales, 3 RBDI 1 (1967), 4 RBDI 16o (1968).
ROOT, E., The Relations between International Tribunals of
    Arbitration and the Jurisdiction of National Courts, 3
    AJIL 529 (19o9).
ROSENNE, S., The Law and Practice of the International Court
    (Leyden, 1965).
ROSENNE, S., Reflections on the Position of the Individual
    in Inter-State Litigation in the International Court of
    Justice, in International Arbitration Liber Amicorum
    for Martin Domke (The Hague, 1967) p. 24o.
ROSENNE, S., The Law of Treaties (Leyden, 197o).
ROSS, A., Theorie der Rechtsquellen (Leipzig, 1929).
ROSS, A., Lehrbuch des Völkerrechts (Stuttgart, 1951).
ROTHENBÜHLER, H.M., The Vietnam War and the American Judici-
    ary: An Appraisal of the Rôle of Domestic Courts in the
    Field of Foreign Affairs, 33 ZaöRV 312 (1973).
ROUSSEAU, C., Droit international public (Paris, 1971).
ROZAKIS, C.L., Treaties and Third States: a Study in the
    Reinforcement of the Consensual Standards in Interna-
    tional Law, 35 ZaöRV 1 (1975).
RUDOLF, W., Völkerrecht und deutsches Recht (Tübingen, 1967).
RUNDSTEIN, S., La justice internationale et la protection
    des interêts privés, 1o RDILC 431 (1929).
RUNGE, C., Die Zwangsvollstreckung aus Entscheidungen der
    europäischen Gemeinschaften, AWB 337 (1962).
RUPP, H.H., Zur bundesverfassungsgerichtlichen Kontrolle des
    Gemeinschaftsrechts am Maßstab der Grundrechte, 27 NJW
    2153 (1974).
RUZIÉ, M.D., Le juge français et les actes des organisations
    internationales, in L'application du droit international
    par le juge français, P. Reuter et al. (Ed.) (Paris,
    1972) p. 1o3.
RUZIÉ, D., Les procédés de mise en vigueur des engagements
    internationaux pris par la France, 1o1 Clunet 562
    (1974).

SABA, H., L'activité quasi-legislative des institutions
    spécialisées des Nations Unies, 111 RC 6o3 (1964,I).

SAGAY, I., The Right of the United Nations to Bring Actions
in Municipal Courts in Order to Claim Title to Namibian
(South West African) Products Exported Abroad, 66 AJIL
6oo (1972).

SCELLE, G., Précis de droit des gens (Paris, 1932, 1934).

SCELLE, G., Droit International Public (Paris, 1944).

SCELLE, G., Manuel de droit international public (Paris,
1948).

SCELLE, G., De la prétendue inconstitutionnalité interne des
traités, 58 Revue du droit public et de la science
politique 1o12 (1952).

SCELLE, G., Le phénomène juridique de dédoublement fonctionnel, in Rechtsfragen der Internationalen Organisation:
Festschrift für Hans Wehberg (Frankfurt/M, 1956) p.324.

SCHACHTER, O., The Development of International Law through
the Legal Opinions of the United Nations Secretariat,
25 BYIL 91 (1948).

SCHACHTER, O., The Enforcement of International Judicial and
Arbitral Decisions, 54 AJIL 1 (196o).

SCHACHTER, O., The Relation of Law, Politics and Action in
the United Nations, 1o9 RC 169 (1963, III).

SCHACHTER, O., The Quasi-Judicial Rôle of the Security
Council and the General Assembly, 58 AJIL 96o (1964).

SCHACHTER, O., Towards a Theory of International Obligation,
8 VaJIL 3oo (1967/68).

SCHACHTER, O., The Evolving International Law of Development, 15 Columbia Journal of Transnational Law 1 (1976).

SCHÄFFER, H., In welchem Ausmaß stellen Judikatur und Doktrin in der österreichischen Rechtsordnung Rechtsquellen dar?, Österreichische Landesreferate zum IX. Internationalen Kongreß für Rechtsvergleichung in Teheran
1974, p.9.

SCHARPF, F.W., Grenzen der richterlichen Verantwortung. Die
political-question-Doktrin in der Rechtsprechung des
amerikanischen Supreme Court (Karlsruhe, 1965).

SCHARPF, F.W., Judicial Review and the Political Question: A
Functional Analysis, 75 YaleLJ 517 (1965/66).

SCHÄTZEL, W., Rechtskraft und Anfechtung von Entscheidungen
internationaler Gerichte (Leipzig, 1928).

SCHÄTZEL, W., Die gemischten Schiedsgerichte der Friedensverträge, 18 Jahrbuch des öffentlichen Rechts 378 (193o).

SCHAUMANN, W., HABSCHEID, W.J., Die Immunität ausländischer
Staaten nach Völkerrecht und deutschem Zivilprozeßrecht,
8 Berichte der Deutschen Gesellschaft für Völkerrecht
(Karlsruhe, 1968).

SCHENCK, D.v., Das Problem der Beteiligung der Bundesrepublik Deutschland an Sanktionen der Vereinten Nationen,
besonders im Falle Rhodesiens, 29 ZaöRV 257 (1969).

SCHERMERS, H.G., International Institutional Law (Leiden,
1972, 1974).

SCHERMERS, H.G., The Namibia Decree in National Courts, 28
    ICLQ 81 (1977).
SCHEUNER, U., Die Rechtsetzungsbefugnis internationaler
    Organisationen, in Völkerrecht und rechtliches Weltbild,
    Festschrift für A. Verdroß (Wien, 1960) p. 229.
SCHEUNER, U., Comparison of the jurisprudence of national
    courts with that of organs of the Convention as regards
    other rights, in Human Rights in National and Interna-
    tional Law, A.H.Robertson (Ed.)(Manchester, 1968)
    P. 214.
SCHEUNER, U., An investigation of the influence of the
    European Convention on Human Rights and Fundamental
    Freedoms on national legislation and practice, in
    International Protection of Human Rights, A. Eide &
    A.Schou (Ed.) (Stockholm, 1968) p. 193.
SCHEUNER, U., Fundamental Rights in European Community Law
    and in National Constitutional Law, 12 CMLRev. 171
    (1975).
SCHINDLER, D., Supranationale Organisationen und schweizeri-
    sche Bundesverfassung, 57 Schweizerische Juristen-
    Zeitung 197 (1961).
SCHINDLER, D., Die innerstaatlichen Wirkungen der Entschei-
    dungen der europäischen Menschenrechtsorgane, Fest-
    schrift f. Max Guldener (Zurich, 1973)   p. 273.
SCHLOCHAUER, H.-J., Das Verhältnis des Rechts der Europäi-
    schen Wirtschaftsgemeinschaft zu den nationalen Rechts-
    ordnungen der Mitgliedstaaten, 11 Archiv des Völker-
    rechts 1 (1963/64).
SCHLOSSER, P., Das völkerrechtswidrige Urteil nach deutschem
    Prozeßrecht, 79 Zeitschrift für Zivilprozeß 164 (1966).
SCHLÜTER, B., Die innerstaatliche Rechtsstellung der inter-
    nationalen Organisationen (Cologne, 1972).
SCHLÜTER, B., The Domestic Status of the Human Rights Clau-
    ses of the United Nations Charter, 61 CalLR 110 (1973).
SCHMID, K., SCHMITZ, E., Der Paragraph 4 der Anlage zu
    Sektion IV des Teils X des Versailler Vertrags, 1 (Teil
    1) ZaöRV 251 (1929).
SCHNEIDER, J.W., The Benelux Court, 4 NYIL 193 (1973).
SCHORN, H., Die Europäische Konvention zum Schutze der
    Menschenrechte und Grundfreiheiten (1965).
SCHREUER, C.H., The Interpretation of Treaties by Domestic
    Courts, 45 BYIL 255 (1971).
SCHREUER, C.H., Unjustified Enrichment in International Law,
    22 AJCompL 281 (1974).
SCHREUER, C.H., The Authority of International Judicial
    Practice in Domestic Courts, 23 ICLQ 681 (1974).
SCHREUER, C.H., The Impact of International Institutions on
    the Protection of Human Rights in Domestic Courts, 4
    Israel Yearbook on Human Rights 60 (1974).

SCHREUER, C.H., The Implementation of International Judicial
    Decisions by Domestic Courts, 24 ICLQ 153 (1975).
SCHREUER, C.H., Beschlüsse internationaler Organe im öster-
    reichischen Staatsrecht, 37 ZaöRV 468 (1977).
SCHREUER, C.H., The Applicability of Stare Decisis to
    International Law in English Courts 15 NILR (1978).
SCHREUER, C.H., Recommendations and the Traditional Sources
    of International Law, 2o German Yearbook of Internatio-
    nal Law 1o3 (1977).
SCHREUER, C.H., The Relevance of United Nations Decisions in
    Domestic Litigation, 27 ICLQ 1 (1978).
SCHREUER, C.H., Some Recent Developments in the Law of State
    Immunity, 2 Comparative Law Yearbook 215 (1979).
SCHULZ, G., Entwicklungsformen internationaler Gesetzgebung
    (Göttingen, 196o).
SCHUMANN, E., Verfassungs- und Menschenrechtsbeschwerde
    gegen richterliche Entscheidungen (Berlin, 1963).
SCHUMANN, E., Menschenrechtskonvention und Wiederaufnahme
    des Verfahrens, 17 NJW 753 (1964).
SCHÜTZE, R.A., Die Nachprüfung von Entscheidungen des Rates,
    der Kommission und des Gerichtshofes nach Art. 187, 192
    EWG Vertrag, 16 NJW 22o4 (1963).
SCHÜTZE, R.A., Die Berücksichtigung der Rechtshängigkeit
    eines ausländischen Verfahrens, 31 RabelsZ 233 (1967).
SCHWAIGER, H., Zur normativen Grenze und innerstaatlichen
    Überprüfbarkeit sekundären Gemeinschaftsrechts, 21 RIW
    19o (1975).
SCHWARZENBERGER, G., The Inductive Approach to International
    Law (London, 1965).
SCHWEITZER, T.A., The United Nations as a Source of Domestic
    Law: Can Security Council Resolutions be Enforced in
    American Courts?, 4 Yale Studies in World Public Order
    162 (1978).
SCHWELB, E., The Influence of the Universal Declaration of
    Human Rights on International and National Law, 53 ASIL
    Proceedings 217 (1959).
SCHWELB, E., Neue Etappen der Fortentwicklung des Völker-
    rechts durch die Vereinten Nationen, 13 Archiv des
    Völkerrechts 1 (1966/67).
SCHWELB, E., Die Menschenrechtsbestimmungen der Charta der
    Vereinten Nationen und die Allgemeine Erklärung der
    Menschenrechte, 21 Vereinte Nationen 18o (1973).
SCHWELB, E., An Instance of Enforcing the Universal Declara-
    tion of Human Rights - Action by the Security Council,
    22 ICLQ 161 (1973).
SEIDL-HOHENVELDERN, I., Die Allgemeine Deklaration der Men-
    schenrechte als Rechtsquelle, 74 JBl 558 (1952).
SEIDL-HOHENVELDERN, I., Probleme der Anerkennung ausländi-
    scher Devisenbewirtschaftungsmaßnahmen, 8 ÖZöR 82
    (1957/58).

SEIDL-HOHENVELDERN, I., Commercial Arbitration and State
    Immunity, in Domke, International Trade Arbitration
    (1958).
SEIDL-HOHENVELDERN, I., Transformation or Adoption of Inter-
    national Law into Municipal Law, 12 ICLQ 88 (1963).
SEIDL-HOHENVELDERN, I., Internationale Präjudizentscheidun-
    gen zur Auslegung völkerrechtlicher Verträge, in Inter-
    nationale Festschrift für A. Verdroß (Munich, 1971)
    p.479.
SEIDL-HOHENVELDERN, I., The Austrian German Arbitral Tribu-
    nal (New York, 1972).
SEIDL-HOHENVELDERN, I., Britain's Entry into the Common
    Market, 25 Current Legal Problems 18 (1972).
SENELLE, R., Kommentar der belgischen Verfassung, Informa-
    tionsbericht, Sammlung "Ideen und Studien" Nr. 95
    (Brussels, 1974).
SEYERSTED, F., Settlement of Internal Disputes of Intergovern-
    mental Organizations by Internal and External Courts,
    24 ZaöRV 1 (1964).
SEYERSTED, F., Is the International Personality of Intergo-
    vernmental Organizations valid vis a vis Non-Members?,
    4 IJIL 233 (1964).
SEYERSTED, F., Jurisdiction over Organs and Officials of
    States, The Holy See and Intergovernmental Organiza-
    tions, 14 ICLQ 31, 493 (1965).
SEYMOUR, C., The Intimate Papers of Colonel House (Boston,
    1928).
SHAWCROSS and BEAUMONT, On Air Law (London, 1966-1974).
SHOCKEY, G.R., Enforcement in United States Courts of the
    United Nations Council for Namibia's Decree on Natural
    Resources, 2 Yale Studies in World Public Order 285
    (1976).
SIBERT, M., Traité de droit international public (Paris,
    1951).
SIMMA, B., Völkerrecht und Friedensforschung, 57 Die Frie-
    denswarte 65 (1974).
SIMMA, B., Methodik und Bedeutung der Arbeit der Vereinten
    Nationen für die Fortentwicklung des Völkerrechts, in
    Die Vereinten Nationen im Wandel, W.A. Kewenig (Ed.)
    (Berlin, 1975) p.79.
SIMMONDS, K.R., Van Duyn v. The Home Office: The Direct
    Effectiveness of Directives, 24 ICLQ 419 (1975).
SIMON, M., Enforcement by French Courts of European Communi-
    ty Law, 9o LQR 467 (1974).
SIMONS, W., Verhältnis der nationalen Gerichtsbarkeit zu der
    internationalen Schiedsgerichtsbarkeit und Gerichtsbar-
    keit, 9 Mitteilungen der deutschen Gesellschaft für
    Völkerrecht 35 (1929).

SINCLAIR, I.M., Nationality of Claims: British Practice, 27 BYIL 125 (195o).

SKUBISZEWSKI, K., The General Assembly of the United Nations and its Power to Influence National Action, 58 ASIL Proceedings 153 (1964).

SKUBISZEWSKI, K., Forms of Participation of International Organizations in the Lawmaking Process, 18 International Organization 79o (1964).

SKUBISZEWSKI, K., Enactment of Law by International Organizations, 41 BYIL 198 (1965-66).

SKUBISZEWSKI, K., A new Source of the Law of Nations: Resolutions of International Organizations, En hommage à Paul Guggenheim (Geneva, 1968) p. 5o8.

SKUBISZEWSKI, K., Resolutions of International Organizations and Municipal Law, 2 The Polish Yearbook of International Law 8o (1968/69).

SKUBISZEWSKI, K., Legal Nature and Domestic Effects of Acts of International Organizations, in Rapports polonais presenté au VIIIe Congrès international de droit comparé (Warsaw, 197o) p. 194.

SKUBISZEWSKI, K., Recommendations of the United Nations and Municipal Courts. 46 BYIL 353 (1972-73).

SLOAN, B.F., The Binding Force of a 'Recommendation' of the General Assembly of the United Nations, 25 BYIL 1 (1948).

SLOAN, B., Implementation and Enforcement of Decisions of International Organizations, 62 ASIL Proc 1 (1968).

SMITH, H.A., The Binding Force of League Resolutions, 16 BYIL 157 (1935).

SOHN, L.B., Protection of Human Rights through International Legislation, in Rene Cassin Amicorum Discipulorumque Liber, Vol.I (Paris, 1969) p. 325.

SOHN, L.B., Die allgemeine Erklärung der Menschenrechte, 8 Nr.2 Journal der Internationalen Juristen Kommission 21 (1967).

SØRENSEN, M., Les sources du droit international (Copenhagen, 1946).

SØRENSEN, M., Principes de Droit international public, 1o1 RC 1 (196o,III).

SPIROPOULOS, J., Traité théorique et pratique du droit international public (Paris, 1933).

SPOFFORD, C.M., Third Party Judgment and International Economic Transactions, 113 RC 117 (1964,III).

SPRUNG, R., KÖNIG,B., (Ed.) Die Entscheidungsbegründung in europäischen Verfahrensrechten und im Verfahren vor internationalen Gerichten (Vienna, 1974).

STAVROPOULOS, C.A., The United Nations and the Development of International Law 1945-197o, UN Monthly Chronicle 78 (197o,6).

STEIN, E., Application and Enforcement of International
    Organization Law by National Authorities and Courts, in
    The Effectiveness of International Decisions, S.M.
    Schwebel (Ed.) (Leyden, 1971) p. 66.
STOLL, J.A., L'application et l'interpretation du droit
    interne par les juridictions internationales (Brussels,
    1962).
STREBEL, H., Das Völkerrecht als Gegenstand von Verweisungen
    und Begriffsübernahmen, von Kollisionsregeln und Rezep-
    tion im nationalen Recht, 28 ZaöRV 5o3 (1968).
STRUPP, K., Grundzüge des positiven Völkerrechts (Bonn,
    1922).
STRUPP, K., Theorie und Praxis des Völkerrechts (Berlin,
    1925).
STRUPP, K., Les règles générales du droit de la paix, 47 RC
    257 (1934,I).
STUYT, A.M., Misconceptions about international (commercial)
    arbitration, 5 NYIL 35 (1974).
SUCHARITKUL, S., State Immunities and Trading Activities in
    International Law (London, 1959).
SUTHERLAND, P.F., The World Bank Convention on the Settle-
    ment of Investment Disputes, 28 ICLQ 367 (1979).
SUZUKI, E., The New Haven School of International Law: An
    Invitation to a Policy-Oriented Jurisprudence, 1 Yale
    Studies in World Public Order 1 (1974).
SWEENEY, J.M., The International Law of Sovereign Immunity.
    Policy Research Study, U.S.Dept.of State (1963).
SZÁSZY, I., International Civil Procedure, A Comparative
    Study (Leyden, 1967).

TAMMELO, I., Rechtslogik und materiale Gerechtigkeit (Frank-
    furt/M., 1971).
TAMMES, A.J.P., Decisions of International Organs as a
    Source of International Law, 94 RC 265 (1958, II).
TCHIRKOVITCH, S., La déclaration universelle des droits de
    l'homme et sa portée internationale, 53 RGDIP 359
    (1949).
TÉNÉKIDÈS, C.G., Rapports de droit interne et de droit
    international en matière de chose jugée, 15 RDILC 683
    (1934).
THIEME, W., Das Grundgesetz und die öffentliche Gewalt
    internationaler Staatengemeinschaften, 18 Veröffentli-
    chungen der Vereinigung der Deutschen Staatsrechts-
    lehrer 5o (196o).
THIRLWAY, H.W.A., International Customary Law and Codifi-
    cation (Leiden, 1972).
TREVES, T., Les décisions d'interprétation des Statuts du
    Fonds monétaire international, 79 RGDIP 5 (1975).

TREVIRANUS, H.D., Außenpolitik im demokratischen Rechtsstaat
    (Tübingen, 1966).
TRIEPEL, H., Völkerrecht und Landesrecht (Leipzig, 1899).
TUNKIN, G.I., Das Völkerrecht der Gegenwart (Berlin, 1963).
TUNKIN, G.I., Theory of International Law (Cambridge Mass.,
    1974).

UIBOPUU, H.J., Die sovjetische Doktrin der friedlichen
    Koexistenz als Völkerrechtsproblem (Vienna, 1971).
ULLMANN, E.v., Völkerrecht (Tübingen, 19o8).
ULLRICH, H., Das Recht der Wettbewerbsbeschränkungen des
    Gemeinsamen Marktes und die einzelstaatliche Zivilge-
    richtsbarkeit (Berlin, 1971).
UNITED NATIONS OFFICE of PUBLIC INFORMATION, The Universal
    Declaration of Human Rights: A Standard of Achievement
    (New York, 1963).
URBANEK, H., Das völkerrechtsverletzende nationale Urteil, 9
    ÖZöR 213 (1958/59).
URBANEK, H., Die Unrechtsfolgen bei einem völkerrechtsver-
    letzenden nationalen Urteil; seine Behandlung durch
    internationale Gerichte, 11 ÖZöR 7o (1961).

VALENTINE, D.G., The Court of Justice of the European Com-
    munities (London, 1965).
VALLAT, F.A., The Competence of the United Nations General
    Assembly, 97 RC 2o3 (1959, II).
VATTEL, E. de, Le droit des Gens (1758).
VERDROSS, A., Die Einheit des rechtlichen Weltbildes auf
    Grundlage der Völkerrechtsverfassung (Tübingen, 1923).
VERDROSS, A., Kann die Generalversammlung der Vereinten
    Nationen das Völkerrecht weiterbilden?, 26 ZaöRV 69o
    (1966).
VERDROSS, A., Völkerrecht und staatliches Recht, in: Die
    Wiener rechtstheoretische Schule, ausgewählte Schrif-
    ten von H. Kelsen, A.J. Merkl, u.A.Verdroß. Ed.: H.
    Klecatsky et al. (Vienna, 1968) p. 2o63.
VERDROSS, A., Die normative Verknüpfung von Völkerrecht und
    staatlichem Recht, in Festschrift für Adolf J. Merkl
    (Munich, 197o) p. 425.
VERZIJL, J.H.W., International Law in Historical Perspective
    (Leyden, 1968-1974).
VIEIRA, M.A., La litispendencia en el derecho internacional
    privado, 25 Revista Esp.DI 395 (1972).
VIGNES, C.H., Le règlement sanitaire international. Aspects
    juridiques, 11 AFDI 649 (1965).
VIRALLY, M., La valeur juridique des recommandations des
    organisations internationales, 2 AFDI 66 (1956).
VIRALLY, M., Droit international et décolonisation devant
    les Nations Unies, 9 AFDI 5o8 (1963).

VISSCHER, C. de,   Notes sur la responsabilité internationale
    des états, 8 RDILC 245 (1927).
VISSCHER, C. de, Le déni de justice en droit international,
    52 RC 366 (1935, II).
VISSCHER, P. de, Les tendances internationales des constitu-
    tions modernes, 8o RC 515 (1952, I).
VITANY, B., International Responsibility of States for their
    Administration of Justice, 22 NILR 131 (1975).
VOGLER, T., Die Spruchpraxis der Europäischen Kommission und
    des Europäischen Gerichtshofs für Menschenrechte und
    ihre Bedeutung für das deutsche Straf- und Verfahrens-
    recht, 82 Zeitschrift für die gesamte Strafrechtswissen-
    schaft 743 (197o).

WAELBROEK, M., The Application of EEC Law by National Courts,
    19 Stanford LR 1248 (1967).
WAELBROECK, M., Nature juridique des actes des organizations
    et des juridictions internationales et leurs effets en
    droit interne. Rapports belges au VIIIe Congrès inter-
    national de droit comparé Pescara (Brussels, 197o)
    p. 5o3.
WAGNER, H., Monismus und Dualismus: eine methodenkritische
    Betrachtung zum Theorienstreit. 89 Archiv des öffentli-
    chen Rechts 212 (1964).
WALDKIRCH, E.v., Das Völkerrecht in seinen Grundzügen darge-
    stellt (Basel, 1926).
WALZ, G.A., Völkerrecht und staatliches Recht (Stuttgart,
    1933).
WATSON, C.S., The European Convention on Human Rights and
    the British Courts, 12 Texas International Law Journal
    61 (1977).
WEHBERG, H., Kommentar zu dem Haager 'Abkommen betreffend
    die friedliche Erledigung internationaler Streitigkei-
    ten vom 18. Oktober 19o7', Archiv des öffentlichen
    Rechts, 1. Sonderheft 153 (1911).
WENGLER, W., Réflexions sur l'application du droit interna-
    tional public par les tribunaux internes, 72 RGDIP 921
    (1968).
WIDDOWS, K., Security Council Resolutions and Non-Members of
    the United Nations, 27 ICLQ 459 (1978).
WIEACKER, F., Privatrechtsgeschichte der Neuzeit (Göttingen,
    1967).
WIEBRINGHAUS, H., Das Gesetz der funktionellen Verdoppelung
    (Saarbrücken, 1955).
WILDHABER, L., Vorschläge zur Verfassungsrevision betreffend
    den Abschluß internationaler Verträge 65 Schweizerische
    Juristen Zeitung 117 (1969).
WILDHABER, L., Treaty-Making Power and Constitution (Basel,
    1971).

WILLIAMS, J.S., Extraterritorial Enforcement of Exchange
Control Regulations Under the International Monetary
Fund Agreement 15 VaJIL 319 (1975).
WINTER, J.A., Direct Applicability and Direct Effect. Two
Distinct and Different Concepts in Community Law, 9
CMLRev. 425 (1972).
WITENBERG, J.C., L'Organisation judiciaire, la procêdure et
la sentence internationales (1937).
WOLFF, E., Die internationalen Gerichte und die privaten
Interessen. Deutsche Landesreferate zum III. Interna-
tionalen Kongreß f. Rechtsvergleichung (London, 195o)
p. 974.

YEMIN, E., Legislative Powers in the United Nations and
Specialized Agencies (Leyden, 1969).

ZACKLIN, R., The Amendment of the Constitutive Instruments
of the United Nations and Specialized Agencies (Leyden,
1968).
ZACKLIN, R., The United Nations and Rhodesia. A Study in
International Law (New York, 1974).
ZEMANEK, K., Das Vertragsrecht der internationalen Organisa-
tionen (Vienna, 1957).
ZEMANEK, K., The United Nations and the Law of Outer Space,
19 Yearbook of World Affairs 199 (1965).
ZIEGER, G., Das Grundrechtsproblem in den Europäischen
Gemeinschaften (Tübingen, 197o).
ZIMMERMANN, E., Die Neuregelung der auswärtigen Gewalt in
der Verfassung der Niederlande, 15 ZaöRV 164 (1953/54).
ZORN, P., Das völkerrechtliche Werk der beiden Haager Konfe-
renzen, 2 Zeitschrift für Politik 321 (19o9).
ZULEEG, M., Das Recht der Europäischen Gemeinschaften im
innerstaatlichen Bereich (Cologne, 1969).
ZULEEG, M., Fundamental Rights and the Law of the European
Communities, 8 CMLRev. 446 (1971).
ZULEEG, M., Das Verhältnis des Gemeinschaftsrechts zum
nationalen Recht, Juristische Rundschau 441 (1973).
ZWEIGERT, K., Der Einfluß des europäischen Gemeinschafts-
rechts auf die Rechtsordnungen der Mitgliedstaaten 28
RabelsZ 6o1 (1964).

TABLE OF DOMESTIC CASES

SUBJECT INDEX

act of state: 136 seq.

administrative tribunals of international organizations: 135, 156, 28o-285, 33o, 339

advisory opinions: 1o, 68, 77seq., 8oseq., 9o, 92seq., 97, 129, 135seq., 151

arbitration: 24, 36, 46, 75-77, 92, 96, 98, 13o, 135, 137, 139, 146seq., 152, 193-199, 2o5, 227, 237, 261, 267, 272-278, 281, 285seq., 287, 289-291, 319, 327, 329seq. 34o-342, 349

Central Commission for the Navigation of the Rhine: 71

conflict of laws: 15, 33, 64, 146, 164, 166, 199, 257-263, 267, 317

Council of Europe: 12, 246, 253

dédoublement fonctionnel: 7, 143, 166, 321seq.

European Free Trade Association: 12, 25, 67, 19o, 216, 231

European Communities: 8, 25, 73, 94seq., 98, 1o4-1o6, 135, 142, 168seq., 189seq., 198, 21o, 227, 231, 242seq., 248, 281, 296, 322seq., 335, 344, 359

European Convention of Human Rights: 27, 1oo-1o4, 131, 25o-253, 323, 333, 358

European Danube Commission: 71

exequatur: 194-196, 21o, 274, 291

exhaustion of local remedies: 13, 327seq.

General Assembly resolutions: 1o, 12, 25, 43, 47, 5o-64, 78seq., 82seq., 122, 124, 139, 2o5, 222, 23o, 237, 245, 25o, 257-259, 28o, 318, 32o

human rights (see also Universal Declaration): 14, 16seq., 18, 24, 5o, 54seq., 241-243, 248, 312, 314seq., 322, 357-359

identifications: 138, 239, 241, 317-323, 355, 358

immunity of foreign states: 28, 34, 49, 92, 147, 195, 197, 265, 271-278, 291, 34o, 357, 359

immunity of international institutions and their staff: 26seq., 28, 49, 64, 74seq., 92, 94, 265, 269-271, 279-285, 336, 339seq., 357, 359

implied powers: 235

incorporation: 28, 7o, 73, 83, 1oo-1o2, 162-227, 231, 314seq., 316seq., 32o, 334, 356

International Bank for Reconstruction and Development: 68, 74, 28oseq.

International Center for the Settlement of Investment Disputes between States and Nationals of other States: 15o, 198seq., 278

International Civil Aviation Organization: 12, 25, 71seq., 123, 189-192

International Court of Justice (Permanent Court of International Justice): 26, 33seq., 43, 74seq., 78, 8o, 86,